Peacekeeping, Policing, and the Rule of Law after Civil War

The rule of law is indispensable for sustained peace, good governance, and economic growth, especially in countries recovering from civil war. Yet despite its importance, we know surprisingly little about how to restore the rule of law in the wake of conflict. In this book, Robert Blair proposes a new theory to explain how the international community can help establish the rule of law in the world's weakest and most war-torn states, focusing on the crucial but often underappreciated role of the United Nations. Blair tests the theory by drawing on original household surveys in Liberia; highly disaggregated data on UN personnel and activities across Africa; and hundreds of interviews with UN officials, local leaders, citizens, and government and civil society representatives. The book demonstrates that UN intervention can have a deeper, more lasting, and more positive effect on the rule of law than skeptics typically believe.

ROBERT A. BLAIR is Assistant Professor of Political Science and International and Public Affairs at Brown University, Rhode Island. His research focuses on post-conflict reconstruction and reform. He has published widely on these topics and has worked in various capacities for the UN Office of Rule of Law and Security Institutions, the Political Instability Task Force, and the US Agency for International Development.

Peacekeeping, Policing, and the Rule of Law after Civil War

ROBERT A. BLAIR
Brown University

CAMBRIDGE
UNIVERSITY PRESS

University Printing House, Cambridge CB2 8BS, United Kingdom

One Liberty Plaza, 20th Floor, New York, NY 10006, USA

477 Williamstown Road, Port Melbourne, VIC 3207, Australia

314–321, 3rd Floor, Plot 3, Splendor Forum, Jasola District Centre, New Delhi – 110025, India

79 Anson Road, #06-04/06, Singapore 079906

Cambridge University Press is part of the University of Cambridge.

It furthers the University's mission by disseminating knowledge in the pursuit of education, learning, and research at the highest international levels of excellence.

www.cambridge.org
Information on this title: www.cambridge.org/9781108835213
DOI: 10.1017/9781108891912

© Robert A. Blair 2021

This publication is in copyright. Subject to statutory exception and to the provisions of relevant collective licensing agreements, no reproduction of any part may take place without the written permission of Cambridge University Press.

First published 2021

A catalogue record for this publication is available from the British Library.

ISBN 978-1-108-83521-3 Hardback
ISBN 978-1-108-79981-2 Paperback

Cambridge University Press has no responsibility for the persistence or accuracy of URLs for external or third-party internet websites referred to in this publication and does not guarantee that any content on such websites is, or will remain, accurate or appropriate.

Contents

List of Figures	*page*	vii
List of Tables		ix
Acknowledgments		xi
List of Abbreviations		xv
1	Introduction	1
2	History of UN Intervention and the Rule of Law after Civil War	17
3	Conceptual Framework: Civil War through a Legal Lens	32
4	Theoretical Framework: Restoring the Rule of Law after Civil War	60
5	Cross-national Evidence: UN Intervention and the Rule of Law across Africa	90
6	Sub-national Evidence I: The Rule of Law and Its Discontents in Liberia	122
7	Sub-national Evidence II: Evaluating the UN from the Bottom-Up	155
8	Sub-national Evidence III: UN Intervention and the Rule of Law in Liberia	184
9	Implications for Africa and beyond	219
Bibliography		237
Index		261

Figures

1.1	Deployments of uniformed UN personnel by continent, 1990–2016	*page* 12
3.1	Necessary conditions and observable implications of the rule of law	34
3.2	Vicious cycle of threats to the rule of law	58
4.1	Mechanics of the theory	64
5.1	Deployments of UN uniformed personnel by country, 1990–2016	93
5.2	Deployments of UN civilian personnel by country, 1993–2016	94
5.3	Example of a UN Secretary-General budget request for the UN Operation in Côte d'Ivoire	96
5.4	Deployments of UN personnel assigned to rule-of-law-related activities by country, 2004–2016	97
6.1	Map of Liberia	124
6.2	UN-sponsored billboards in Liberia	145
7.1	Distribution of communities in Liberia survey sample	157
7.2	Distribution of UNMIL bases as of December 2004	173
8.1	Short-term effects of exposure to UNMIL on citizens' preferences using local leaders' reports of UNMIL presence	191
8.2	Short-term effects of exposure to UNMIL on citizens' preferences using citizens' reports of UNMIL presence	193
8.3	Short-term effects of exposure to UNMIL on local leaders' responses to list experiment	199
8.4	Medium-term effects of exposure to UNMIL on citizens' preferences using local leaders' reports of UNMIL presence	207
8.5	Medium-term effects of exposure to UNMIL on citizens' preferences using local leaders' reports of UNMIL presence, subsetting to communities exposed in 2010 only	208

Tables

4.1	Hypotheses	*page* 85
5.1	Trends in the rule of law across Africa, 1996–2016	102
5.2	Correlation between the rule of law and UN personnel and activities in Africa	108
5.3	Correlation between the rule of law and UN activities in Africa, disaggregating by type of activity	111
5.4	Correlation between the rule of law and UN activities in Africa, disaggregating by intensity of engagement	112
5.5	Correlation between executive constraints and UN personnel and activities in Africa	114
5.6	Correlation between judicial independence and UN personnel and activities in Africa	115
5.7	Placebo test correlation between the rule of law and UN arms embargoes	119
5.7	Placebo test correlation between the rule of law and UN arms embargoes	120
7.1	Exposure to UNMIL in Liberia survey sample	163
7.2	Community characteristics in Liberia survey sample	170
7.3	Citizen characteristics in Liberia survey sample	171
7.4	First stage relationship between exposure to UNMIL and proximity to the nearest UNMIL base	174
7.5	First stage relationship between exposure to UNMIL and proximity to Para	177
7.6	Correlation between birthplace and proximity to Para	178
7.7	Correlation between police presence and proximity to Para	178
7.8	Correlation between violence and proximity to Para	179

7.9	Correlation between individual- and community-level exposure to UNMIL	182
8.1	Citizens' preferences over potential security and justice providers in Liberia	186
8.2	Citizens' perceptions of potential security and justice providers in Liberia	188
8.3	Short-term effects of exposure to UNMIL on citizens' preferences using proximity to nearest UNMIL base as instrument	195
8.4	Short-term effects of exposure to UNMIL on citizens' preferences using proximity to Para as instrument	196
8.5	Local leaders' responses to list experiment in Liberia	197
8.6	Short-term effects of exposure to UNMIL on citizens' perceptions using local leaders' reports of UNMIL presence	203
8.7	Short-term effects of exposure to UNMIL on citizens' perceptions using citizens' reports of UNMIL presence	204
8.8	Medium-term effects of exposure to UNMIL on citizens' perceptions using local leaders' reports of UNMIL presence	210
8.9	Medium-term effects of exposure to UNMIL on citizens' perceptions using local leaders' reports of UNMIL presence, subsetting to communities exposed in 2010 only	211

Acknowledgments

I am grateful to the many people who helped make this book possible. The book began as part of my PhD dissertation at Yale University, where I received exceptional mentorship from my dissertation committee – Chris Blattman, Steven Wilkinson, and the chair of the committee, Nicholas Sambanis. I could not have asked for better advisors. I am especially grateful to Nicholas for the invaluable guidance he offered throughout my years in graduate school, and during the transition from writing a dissertation to publishing a book, and from being a graduate student to having advisees of my own. He has been an extraordinary mentor, advisor, collaborator, and friend. I am also extremely grateful to Chris, who taught me how to do fieldwork more or less from scratch. Much of what I know about research design I learned from him.

I am grateful to the many other current and former faculty members at Yale who generously commented on earlier iterations of this project, especially Kate Baldwin, Ana De La O Torres, Thad Dunning, Stathis Kalyvas, Jay Lyall, Mike McGovern, and Libby Wood. I also benefited from the thoughtful feedback I received from my peers at Yale and elsewhere, especially Ana Arjona, Cameron Ballard-Rosa, Abhit Bhandari, Graeme Blair, Grant Gordon, Pablo Kalmanovitz, Lucy Martin, Eoin McGuirk, Ben Morse, Tatiana Neumann, Will Nomikos, Steve Rosenzweig, Kevin Russell, and Andrés Vargas, among others.

I had the privilege of presenting excerpts of this book at a number of workshops and conferences. I received valuable feedback from participants at the 2013 and 2014 International Studies Association Annual Conventions; the 2013 and 2018 American Political Science Association Annual Meetings; the Order, Conflict, and Violence Seminar at Yale; the African Politics Working Group at Yale; the International Relations Seminar at Columbia University; the International Relations Seminar at Stanford University; the Center for International Security and Cooperation (CISAC) Research Seminar at Stanford; the Research Seminar at the University of California, Davis; the Development

Breakfast at Brown University; the Contemporary African Political Economy Research Seminar (CAPERS); and the Folke Bernadotte Academy working groups on peacekeeping operations and security sector reform, among others.

I was fortunate to work with a number of excellent research assistants over the course of this project, especially Omar Afzaal, Karina Bao, Paul Cumberland, Lucas Fried, Karla Ganley, Yuequan Guo, Evan Lehmann, Colombine Pezé-Heidsieck, Antonina Rytwinska, Yijie Zhu, and especially Kou Johnson, Matthew Siakor, and Prince Williams. I am also grateful to the students who assisted me and my collaborator Hannah Smidt in constructing the Peacekeeping Activities Dataset (PACT): Sam Berube, Victor Brechenmacher, Erin Brennan-Burke, Alexa Clark, Rachel Danner, Mara Dolan, Dylan Elliott-Hart, Ugochi Ihenatu, Ian Lefond, Julia Kirschenbaum, Divya Mehta, Ruth Miller, Remington Pontes, and Lucy Walke. This was a long, painstaking task, and their assistance was invaluable.

I am thankful to Kyle Beardsley, Lise Morjé Howard, and Aila Matanock for the insightful feedback they offered during my book workshop in fall 2018, and to my colleagues at Brown who attended the workshop to offer me guidance and support: Peter Andreas, Rose McDermott, Wendy Schiller, and Rebecca Weitz-Shapiro. I am especially grateful to Jeff Colgan, who was incredibly generous with his time and insights throughout this process. I revised and prepared the book for publication while on sabbatical as a CISAC Junior Faculty Fellow at Stanford, where I received helpful comments from Jim Fearon, Judy Goldstein, Ken Scheve, Ken Schultz, Harold Trinkunas, and especially Jeremy Weinstein, my senior faculty mentor. I also thank Naaz Barma, Desha Girod, David Lake, and the anonymous reviewers who provided valuable feedback on an earlier version of this manuscript.

Most of the data for the sub-national analyses in this book was collected in collaboration with Chris Blattman and Alex Hartman; much of the data for the cross-national analyses was collected in collaboration with Hannah Smidt. I am grateful to Chris, Alex, and Hannah for all their help throughout this process. Some of the findings in this book were previously published in my 2019 *International Organization* article "International Intervention and the Rule of Law after Civil War: Evidence from Liberia." Figures from that article are reprinted with permission from the IO Foundation. I also received generous funding for this project from the Folke Bernadotte Academy, Humanity United, the MacMillan Center for International Affairs at Yale, the National Science Foundation, and a Vanguard Charitable Trust. I am grateful for their support.

I am extraordinarily thankful to the many UN officials and Liberian citizens, civil society representatives, and government officials who shared their insights with me in surveys and interviews conducted over 15 months of fieldwork in the country. They were exceptionally generous with their time, and they brought to life the dynamics of international intervention in Liberia in ways that informed every aspect of this book. I have done my best to represent their views faithfully. I am especially grateful to Chris Agoha, Cara Chester, Kate

Acknowledgments

Cummings, Ibrahim Gborie, Bob Kett, and Josh Riggins. Liberia is a beautiful, perplexing, infuriating, and exhilarating place. It will always have a special place in my heart.

I am of course beyond grateful to my family and friends, for this and for everything. Thank you to Billie, my most constant companion during the last year and a half of research and writing. Finally, a very special thank you to Caitlin Sanford. You have told me repeatedly how excited you are to read this book. I will never believe you, but I will always be grateful for your encouragement and enthusiasm.

Abbreviations

ACABQ	Advisory Committee on Administrative and Budgetary Questions
AFL	Armed Forces of Liberia
BINUB	United Nations Integrated Office in Burundi
BINUCA	United Nations Integrated Peacebuilding Office in the Central African Republic
CAR	Central African Republic
CLJAS	Criminal Law and Judicial Advisory Service
DDR	Disarmament, Demobilization, and Reintegration
DPKO	Department of Peacekeeping Operations
DRC	Democratic Republic of the Congo
ECOMOG	Economic Community of West African States Monitoring Group
ECOWAS	Economic Community of West African States
FPU	Formed Police Unit
GPP	Government-Provided Personnel
HIPPO	Independent High-level Panel on Peace Operations
IGNU	Interim Government of National Unity
JCSC	Justice and Corrections Standing Capacity
LNP	Liberian National Police
LURD	Liberians United for Reconciliation and Democracy
MINURCAT	United Nations Mission in the Central African Republic and Chad
MINUSCA	United Nations Multidimensional Integrated Stabilization Mission in the Central African Republic
MINUSMA	United Nations Multidimensional Integrated Stabilization Mission in Mali
MINUSTAH	United Nations Stabilisation Mission in Haiti

MONUC	United Nations Mission in the Democratic Republic of Congo
MODEL	Movement for Democracy in Liberia
MONUSCO	United Nations Organization Stabilization Mission in the Democratic Republic of the Congo
NGO	Non-governmental Organization
NPFL	National Patriotic Front of Liberia
OCHA	United Nations Office for the Coordination of Humanitarian Affairs
ONUB	United Nations Operation in Burundi
ONUMOZ	United Nations Operation in Mozambique
ONUSAL	United Nations Observer Mission in El Salvador
OROLSI	United Nations Office of Rule of Law and Security Institutions
P4P	Providing for Peacekeeping
PACT	Peacekeeping Activities Dataset
PKOLED	Peacekeeping Location Event Data
SPC	Standing Police Capacity
SWAPOL	South West African Police
ULIMO	United Liberation Movement of Liberia for Democracy
UNAMA	United Nations Assistance Mission in Afghanistan
UNAMID	United Nations–African Union Mission in Darfur
UNAMIR	United Nations Assistance Mission for Rwanda
UNIFIL	United Nations Interim Force in Lebanon
UNITA	National Union for the Total Independence of Angola
UNIPSIL	United Nations Integrated Peacebuilding Office in Sierra Leone
UNMIBH	United Nations Mission in Bosnia and Herzegovina
UNMIK	United Nations Mission in Kosovo
UNMIL	United Nations Mission in Liberia
UNMIS	United Nations Mission in Sudan
UNMISS	United Nations Mission in South Sudan
UNMIT	United Nations Integrated Mission in Timor-Leste
UNOCI	United Nations Operation in Côte d'Ivoire
UNOL	United Nations Peace-building Support Office in Liberia
UNOMIL	United Nations Observer Mission in Liberia
UNOSOM I	United Nations Operation in Somalia I
UNOSOM II	United Nations Operation in Somalia II
UNPOL	United Nations Police
UNTAC	United Nations Transitional Authority in Cambodia
UNTAES	United Nations Transitional Administration for Eastern Slavonia, Baranja and Western Sirmium
UNTAET	United Nations Transitional Administration in East Timor
UNV	United Nations Volunteer

1

Introduction

The first time the police visited Zowienta, a small rural village in the war-ravaged West African nation of Liberia, the devil came out to expel them. A team of Liberian National Police (LNP) officers was visiting Zowienta as part of the "Confidence Patrols" program, an initiative aimed at repairing the LNP's deeply damaged relationship with Liberian citizens. During a series of civil wars that wracked the country from 1989 to 2003, the police served as instruments of repression and terror. After the fighting stopped, the LNP was overhauled under the auspices of the United Nations Mission in Liberia (UNMIL), a large, multidimensional peacekeeping operation. While many challenges remained, by most accounts UNMIL's efforts were largely a success, and the officers patrolling Zowienta bore little resemblance to the LNP of the past.

But this was early in the Confidence Patrols initiative, and residents were understandably wary. In Liberia, the "devil" – typically a man in a mask and ceremonial garb – is a traditional religious figure associated with the country's powerful secret societies (Ellis 1995, 188; Little 1965). As in many African countries, secret societies and other customary institutions resolve disputes, adjudicate crimes, and perform myriad related functions of local governance in rural Liberian communities. Often they coexist and compete with the police and courts for citizens' trust, loyalty, and cooperation. When the two collide, conflict is frequently the result.

Zowienta was a case in point. The officers' arrival had provoked unrest in the village, and the devil demanded that they retreat to their guesthouse while calm was restored. While the officers were inside, a group of young men began circling the guesthouse, shouting and scraping machetes along the outer walls. They let the air out of the tires on the officers' truck, effectively marooning the team in the village. The message the young men intended to deliver was unambiguous. Zowienta had suffered at the hands of the LNP in the past. The police were not welcome anymore.

The incident in Zowienta illustrates a broader predicament afflicting many of the world's weakest and most war-torn states. The rule of law is essential for sustained peace, good governance, and economic growth. Where it is strong, the rule of law provides a credible, unified framework for resolving disputes, allowing citizens to seek redress for grievances through transparent, publicly promulgated laws enforced by effective, legitimate security and justice institutions – police forces, courts, prisons – rather than vigilantism or violence.[1] These laws and institutions preserve order, mitigate uncertainty, and facilitate collective action. Their effectiveness and legitimacy are often intimately intertwined with the effectiveness and legitimacy of the state as a whole (Brzoska and Law 2013; World Bank Group and United Nations 2018, 166). They are "essential for society to function – much more so than many other components of governance" (Arjona, 2016, 69).

Establishing the rule of law is also an integral part of peacekeeping, state-building, and post-conflict reconstruction more generally. A rule of law imperative has been inscribed in numerous United Nations (UN) resolutions and reports, and in the mandates of every multidimensional UN peacekeeping operation deployed since 1999. It is ingrained in US foreign policy as well, from the long, costly campaigns to erect stable states in Iraq and Afghanistan, to ambitious US-funded security and justice sector reform programs in Africa, Asia, Eastern Europe, Latin America, and the Middle East (McLeod, 2010). As Thomas Carothers wryly observed some twenty years ago, "one cannot get through a foreign policy debate these days without someone proposing the rule of law as a solution to the world's troubles" (Carothers, 1998, 95). Carothers's observation has become only more apt in the two decades since, as initiatives dedicated to rule-of-law promotion have continued to multiply with "ever-increasing interest" among policymakers and practitioners (Carothers, 2009, 50–1).

In countries recovering from civil war, however, restoring the rule of law often proves a "Sisyphean task" (Haggard and Tiede, 2013, 465). Obstacles abound at three distinct but interrelated levels. At the national (macro) level, many government officials flout legal limits on their power, encroach on the independence of the judiciary, and exploit the police to intimidate real and perceived opponents of the regime. As a result, at the local (micro) level, many citizens reject the state's role as a purveyor of security and justice, opting to rely on informal (non-state) authorities instead – chiefs, elders, vigilante groups, gangs, warlords. These informal authorities occupy an amorphous "meso level" between citizens and the state. Some informal authorities are more popular, efficient, and accessible than their formal counterparts (Isser, 2011). But some also subvert the rule of law, contesting the state's jurisdiction over even the most serious incidents of crime and violence, and resolving disputes in ways that violate basic due process protections – for example, through mob

---

[1] I provide a more formal definition of the rule of law in Chapter 3.

justice or trial by ordeal. In the worst cases, tensions between formal and informal authorities may escalate into renewed paroxysms of violence (Sisk and Risley, 2005).

International institutions are increasingly tasked with overcoming these obstacles. But whether they are likely to succeed remains an open question. This book asks whether, how, and under what conditions international intervention can help (re)establish the rule of law in countries recovering from civil strife, focusing in particular on the role of the UN. The rule of law hinges not just on the integrity of state officials and the quality of state laws and institutions at the macro level, but also on the attitudes and behaviors of citizens and non-state authorities at the micro and meso levels, respectively. Can international organizations like the UN establish the necessary conditions for the rule of law at each of these levels? At the macro level, can international intervention shield the judiciary from political interference and reinforce constitutional constraints on executive power, even in settings where oversight is poor and corruption is rampant? At the micro level, can it enhance citizens' cooperation with state officials and institutions and increase their compliance with state laws, even when those laws conflict with local norms, rules, and customs? And at the meso level, can international interveners induce non-state authorities to respect state laws and renounce the use of extrajudicial punishment, even in places where jurisdictional boundaries are blurred?

Given the challenges, it is tempting to assume that international efforts to establish the rule of law in the wake of civil war are doomed to fail. Many analysts subscribe to precisely this view. While academics have long argued that UN missions are effective at protecting civilians and preventing civil wars from reigniting, they are generally much more skeptical of the UN's ability to rebuild states and repair damaged state/society relationships. Scholars have criticized international organizations for taking a "breathtakingly mechanistic approach" to rule-of-law promotion (Carothers, 2006, 21), and for pursuing "cookie-cutter" reforms with an almost "template-like quality" (Clunan and Trinkunas, 2010, 288). Many believe the UN should abandon these efforts altogether, either because international intervention is an ineffective mechanism for rehabilitating weak and war-torn states (Luttwak, 1999; Weinstein, 2005), or because states themselves are ineffective mechanisms for sustaining order in the developing world (Anderson, 2004; Brooks, 2005; Herbst, 1996).

THE ARGUMENT

This book argues that such pessimistic perspectives are misguided. Skeptics underestimate how successful the UN can at rehabilitating state institutions and closing the gap between state laws and "lived values" that tends to characterize communities long accustomed to state absence or predation (Fukuyama, 2010, 37). The book provides a new theory to explain how UN intervention can promote the rule of law, anecdotal examples to illustrate the theory in action, and systematic empirical evidence to demonstrate its validity. I do not dispute critics' claims that UN efforts at rule-of-law reform generally follow a more or less standardized template, though always with some adjustments for context. These claims are correct. But the fact that UN missions follow a template is not in itself an indictment of their approach. This book offers theory and evidence to show that the template works.

The book makes four contributions to the study and practice of international intervention – one conceptual, one theoretical, one empirical, and one practical. Conceptually, the book offers a framework for understanding the necessary conditions for the rule of law in post-conflict countries. The rule of law is widely viewed as a "panacea for all the problems that afflict many non-Western countries, particularly in post-conflict settings" (Rajagopal, 2008, 1348). Some have gone so far as to describe it as the "foundation of a civilized society" (Bingham, 2011, 171). Perhaps unsurprisingly, the concept is associated with a variety of lofty but disparate goals, from equality to human rights to peace itself. Definitions are equally myriad and conflicting – a "complex admixture of positive assumptions, inchoate political and legal theory, and occasionally wishful thinking" (Rodriguez, McCubbins, and Weingast, 2009, 1455). This book proposes a more coherent definition that preserves the essential elements of existing accounts while adapting them to the realities of law and daily life in the developing world.

Legal scholars typically conceptualize the rule of law in terms of the quality of state laws, the behavior of state officials, and the performance of state institutions. These are important concerns, but they do not address what Simon Chesterman rightly describes as the "heart of the problem," which is "to whom people turn for solutions to problems that would normally be considered legal" (Chesterman, 2007, 19). In the rich, industrialized nations of the West, state institutions are typically the only venues for adjudicating all but the pettiest disputes, and even when non-state alternatives exist, they are usually subject to the ultimate jurisdiction of the state. Not so in countries recovering from civil war. In these settings, security and justice are provided not by a unitary sovereign state, but by a multitude of formal and informal institutions whose jurisdictions shift and evolve over time. In many conflict and post-conflict environments, informal institutions are at least as prominent and powerful as formal ones, and often more so (World Bank Group and United Nations 2018, 167; see also Isser 2011). The relationship between formal and informal security and justice providers is sometimes symbiotic but often adversarial, with each actor angling to transform its own rules, whether state law or "some other implicit code," into the "routine basis upon which people act" (Migdal and Schlichte, 2005, 15).

What does the rule of law even mean under these challenging and ambiguous circumstances? Drawing on the positivist tradition in legal theory and the empirical literature on civil war, this book posits three necessary conditions for the rule of law in post-conflict countries, which I develop in detail in Chapter 3. First, state authorities must abide by constitutional constraints on their power, and must defer to an independent, legally designated arbiter (e.g. a Supreme Court) when jurisdictional conflicts arise. Second, citizens must rely on state rather than non-state authorities to adjudicate crimes that fall unambiguously under state jurisdiction (e.g. murder). Third, non-state authorities must comply with legal limits on their power and renounce mechanisms of dispute resolution that violate state law in and of themselves (e.g. mob justice or trial by ordeal). These are the macro-, micro-, and meso-level conditions for the rule of law, respectively. They are interrelated and mutually reinforcing, each helping to sustain the others.

Theoretically, the book proposes a solution to three puzzles that follow immediately from this conceptual framework. In countries recovering from civil war, why do some state authorities abide by constitutional constraints while others ignore them? Why do some citizens rely on state authorities to intervene when crimes are committed or violence occurs, while others seek redress for even the most serious grievances through non-state alternatives? Why do some of these non-state alternatives defer to the ultimate jurisdiction of the state, while others defy it? These questions apply to the macro, micro, and meso levels, respectively. I argue that the answers lie in part in the actions (or inactions) of international interveners, and that UN missions, in particular, can play an indispensable role in establishing the necessary conditions for the rule of law at all three levels simultaneously.

The book's core theoretical claim is that UN missions promote the rule of law by acting as catalysts for state reform at the macro level, surrogates for reformed states at the micro and meso levels, and liaisons between state authorities, non-state authorities, and citizens across the three levels of my analysis. States recovering from civil war typically remain feeble long after the fighting stops, incapable of enforcing their rule beyond a handful of relatively isolated enclaves, or of restoring the confidence of citizens long estranged from, or persecuted by, state institutions. With sufficient time and resources,[2] UN missions can serve as "temporary stand-ins" for these states (Hampson, 1997, 708), restructuring and reforming them from within while reviving respect for them from without. The former process – reconstruction of state capacity – has been relatively well documented, though seldom empirically evaluated.[3] The latter process, restoration of state authority, remains understudied and poorly understood.

At the macro level, UN missions catalyze state reform by drafting laws and lobbying for their passage, as UNMIK did in Kosovo, UNIPSIL did in Sierra Leone, and BINUCA did in the Central African Republic (CAR) (Tansey, 2009; UN Criminal Law and Judicial Advisory Service, 2013); by coordinating or promoting the separation of powers between state institutions with overlapping jurisdictions, as ONUSAL did in El Salvador (Howard, 2008); by recruiting,

---

[2] Of course, not all UN missions, and not all international interveners, are equally equipped to promote the rule of law. I address the question of generalizability in detail in Chapter 9.
[3] I discuss exceptions in Chapter 2.

vetting, and training judges, police officers, and prison wardens, as UNTAET did in East Timor (Chesterman, 2001), and as many other UN missions have done in Asia, Africa, and beyond (UN Criminal Law and Judicial Advisory Service, 2013); by monitoring arbitrary arrests, indefinite detentions, and other excesses of state power, as MINURCAT did in CAR and MONUSCO did in the Democratic Republic of Congo (DRC) (UN Secretary-General 2009, 2012b); and, when monitoring fails, by mediating or forcibly resolving disputes between elites with competing claims to executive power, as UNOCI did in Côte d'Ivoire (Smith, 2011).

UN missions complement these macro-level activities with micro- and meso-level efforts to induce adherence to state laws and encourage cooperation with state officials and institutions. This involves two interconnected roles. First, UN missions serve as substitutes for the state in the eyes of local populations – proxies for centralized power in the absence of a powerful center. UN missions are "institutions of local governance"; while their mandates derive from the international community, they are increasingly expected to "act as domestic authorities" and thus assume responsibilities "traditionally understood to reside with the sovereign state" (Whalan, 2014, 19, 24). By modeling the state in the eyes of citizens, UN missions demonstrate, by example, the relative merits of formal over informal security and justice provision; sensitize civilians to an increased third-party presence in and around their communities; create opportunities for government officials to claim credit for the UN's own achievements; and instill habits, norms, and beliefs that empower the state as a legitimate purveyor of order at the local level. UN missions thus help to create an "ideological backdrop" that elevates the role that newly reformed security and justice institutions will eventually play in post-conflict societies (Kaspersen, Eide, and Hansen, 2004, 18).

In this sense, UN intervention "amounts to nothing more nor less than intervening in a social contract, in the relationship between society, the individuals that compose it, and the state" (Pouligny, 2006, xvii). This is not merely a theoretical point. Civilians often perceive UN missions as proxies for the state, for better or worse, as in El Salvador, where locals believed the UN "acted as the state," or Haiti, where UN personnel were "described in terms very similar to those used to describe the state" (Pouligny, 2006, 101, 103), or Kosovo, where UNMIK created a system of authority so state-like that it was known as "UNMIKistan" (Higate and Henry, 2009, 47). I have heard this idea echoed in my research on UNMIL in Liberia, where I spent more than fifteen months conducting fieldwork for this book between 2009 and 2015. As one rural resident succinctly put it to me, "UNMIL and government, that's the same thing."[4]

---

[4] Gbarnga, October 22, 2010. Of course, these comparisons are not always flattering. But as I discuss in Chapter 4, accounts claiming that host populations resent UN presence are typically anecdotal (e.g. Pouligny 2006) or focused on "least-likely" cases (e.g. Autesserre 2010; Veit 2011), and are belied by systematic survey evidence from multiple host countries (Blair, Blattman, and Hartman 2011; Krasno 2005, 2006; Mvukiyehe and Samii 2008, 2010).

By acting as surrogates for reformed states at the local level, UN missions transmit internationally sanctioned standards of governance to the countries in which they intervene – a process that Roland Paris aptly describes as a "globalization of the very idea of what a state should look like and how it should act" (Paris, 2002, 638). In Paris's account, this process occurs cross-nationally, through the diffusion of norms and institutional models from the Global North to the Global South, and from more developed to less developed countries. I argue that a similar process occurs sub-nationally as well, through interactions between citizens and UN personnel on a face-to-face, day-to-day basis. UN missions transmit norms by intervening "at the heart of the state–society relationship" (Whalan, 2014, 218). This is a crucial but often overlooked role for the UN to play. Establishing the rule of law is not just about preparing states to govern citizens. It is also about preparing citizens to be governed by states.

Second and equally important, UN missions serve as liaisons between citizens and states at the micro level, and between state and non-state authorities at the meso level. At the micro level, UN missions disseminate information to help citizens better understand their legal rights and obligations, as BINUB did in Burundi and UNAMA did in Afghanistan (UN Department of Peacekeeping Operations 2010a, 2011b); establish mobile courts and legal aid offices in rural areas, as UNMISS did in South Sudan and UNAMID did in Darfur (UN Criminal Law and Judicial Advisory Service 2013, 2016); organize town hall meetings to promote citizen cooperation with the police, as UNMIL did in Liberia (Friedman and MacAulay, 2014); and facilitate sustained, mutually respectful contact between civilians and state security and justice personnel, as UN missions do through joint patrols and co-location with government counterparts around the world.

At the meso level as well, UN missions train non-state authorities in state-approved conflict resolution techniques, as UNMISS did in South Sudan (UN Secretary-General, 2015b); intervene to ensure that criminal offenses are adjudicated in accordance with state laws, as MONUSCO did in DRC (UN Criminal Law and Judicial Advisory Service, 2013); and investigate and denounce abuses committed by informal authorities, as UNOCI did in Côte d'Ivoire (Diène, 2014; Palus, 2013). These efforts can help align non-state authorities' actions with both national and international standards for the rule of law.

By addressing the macro, micro, and meso dimensions of international intervention simultaneously, my theory provides a corrective to accounts that focus exclusively on state reconstruction and reform in the capital city. Most research addresses these macro-level processes alone, ignoring the subtler but equally important mechanisms through which state authority is projected nationwide. In promoting the rule of law, rehabilitating state institutions is often just the "tip of the iceberg" (Manning, 2003, 36). As the incident in Zowienta illustrates, the rule of law is more than just a set of institutions. It is also a "normative system that resides in the minds of ... citizens" (Carothers,

2006, 20), and that cannot be manufactured by the "simple expedient of creating formal structures and rewriting constitutions and statutes" (Brooks, 2003, 2285). Establishing the rule of law thus requires a "transformation in mentality as much as it does in politics" (Chesterman, 2005, 181). The UN's success in achieving this transformation depends on the beliefs and behaviors not just of political and military elites but also of the population writ large. Theories focused on macro-level dynamics shed little light on the mechanisms through which these micro- and meso-level changes might occur.

Both thematically and methodologically, this book sits squarely at the intersection of international relations and comparative politics. International relations scholars will recognize elements of both constructivist and realist (or rationalist) perspectives in my theory. Realists typically emphasize the role that incentives, sanctions, rules, and institutions play in shaping actors' behavior. Constructivists acknowledge the importance of these factors but tend to focus on norms and beliefs instead. Realists argue that coercion (broadly defined, and not necessarily involving the use of physical force) is the most prominent mechanism through which behavior change occurs. Constructivists assert the importance of persuasion, socialization, and inducement instead – what Michael Barnett and Martha Finnemore describe as "normative resources" (Barnett and Finnemore, 2005). My argument draws on both of these schools of thought, illustrating the ways that UN missions combine material and normative resources to compel change among citizens and state and non-state authorities alike.

But my theory also extends beyond existing accounts – realist, constructivist, and otherwise – by integrating national- and local-level peacekeeping into a single unified framework. I argue that the UN acts as a catalyst, surrogate, and liaison *simultaneously*, and that this simultaneity is key to understanding the UN's efficacy. The "traditional" model of international intervention assumed that "local-level action could be deferred for years while national state structures were being recreated" (Sisk and Risley, 2005, i) – a sort of "if you build it they will come" approach to rule-of-law promotion. I argue that this approach is misguided. Efforts to restructure state institutions must be accompanied from the outset by the "practical establishment of state authority throughout the national territory" (Manning, 2003, 26). By acting as catalysts, surrogates, and liaisons, UN missions advance both of these goals simultaneously. This book thus complements the recent "local turn" in peacekeeping research (Leonardsson and Rudd, 2015), while also illuminating the ways that national and local peacekeeping practices interact with and, in the best cases, reinforce one another.

TESTING THE ARGUMENT

Empirically, the book provides the first systematic analysis of the impact of UN intervention on the rule of law after civil war, using uniquely rich data from both within and across countries. As Stephen Haggard and Lydia Tiede note, despite the "exploding practical interest" in rule-of-law promotion in post-conflict settings, empirical research remains "surprisingly limited" (Haggard and Tiede, 2013, 406). This is true even within the UN system, which typically relies on retrospective anecdotal studies of particular missions or projects, and which lacks a coherent and coordinated approach to measuring the impact of rule-of-law-related activities (Geneva Centre for the Democratic Control of Armed Forces, 2012, 5). As a result, there is a risk that "assumptions, isolated observations, and anecdotal accounts are elevated to the status of facts" about how UN rule-of-law promotion works and what it has achieved (Sannerholm et al., 2012, 11). Research has lagged behind practice, obscuring the UN's prior successes and limiting its ability to learn from past mistakes (Kavanagh and Jones, 2011, 26).

To evaluate the UN's impact on the rule of law, this book blends macro-level evidence from thirty-three post-conflict African countries with micro- and meso-level evidence from Liberia, one of the world's poorest, most aid-dependent, and most war-ravaged states. Cross-nationally, I combine existing data on the number of uniformed UN personnel deployed to each peacekeeping operation in Africa since the end of the Cold War with new datasets capturing the number of civilian personnel deployed to each mission, the number of personnel assigned specifically to rule-of-law-related tasks, and the frequency of rule-of-law-related activities undertaken in the field. I built the latter dataset with my collaborator Hannah Smidt using the UN Secretary-General's own publicly available progress reports, which include detailed discussions of the UN's strategies for promoting legal, security sector, justice sector, and prison reform. The dataset also captures the intensity of UN involvement in each of these activities – monitoring, training, provision of technical and material assistance, etc. While other scholars have coded similar activities using UN mandates (Lloyd, 2017), UN Secretary-General progress reports are unique in capturing not just what peacekeepers are *mandated* to do, but also what they *actually* do on the ground.

After testing the macro-level implications of my argument across Africa, I then focus on Liberia to establish the theory's micro- and meso-level foundations. Liberia is both a hard and a crucial case for evaluating my theory. It is one of the least developed countries in the world, where more than a decade of civil war precipitated state collapse and the disintegration of an already tenuous rule of law. Formal and informal security and justice providers coexist within a constitutionally hybrid legal system, but the boundaries between them are ambiguous and jurisdictional conflicts are rife. Anecdotally at least, UNMIL was effective and legitimate enough to plausibly overcome these obstacles, and the UN has long viewed the mission as success. But Liberia is not so unique as to preclude external validity. Indeed, many of the problems afflicting Liberia are typical of post-conflict countries more generally, especially in Africa, and UNMIL shared many similarities with other missions in the region – including resource constraints and accusations of misconduct.

To test UNMIL's impact on the rule of law, I leverage an original panel survey covering 243 rural Liberian towns and villages over a period of four years. My focus on rural areas is intentional: despite rapid urbanization, some 60–70 per cent of all African citizens continue to live outside of cities (Boone, 2014), and many civil wars begin in regions within the state's *de jure* borders but beyond its *de facto* control. The survey yields a wealth of data on Liberians' attitudes towards state institutions, including their perceptions of state corruption and bias, and their willingness to defer to state jurisdiction in the most severe cases of crime and violence. The survey also includes a list experiment designed to measure the prevalence of trial by ordeal, an illegal but still widely practiced mode of adjudication in rural regions.[5] My ability to combine rigorous, systematic data at multiple levels of analysis is itself an important empirical contribution to the literature on peacekeeping and the rule of law, much of which remains impressionistic and anecdotal.

I use this survey of 243 Liberian communities to estimate the effects of UNMIL's presence on Liberians' perceptions of, and reliance on, formal over informal authorities, and on informal authorities' reliance on legal over illegal mechanisms of dispute resolution. My results are robust to multiple identification strategies, including one that leverages an attack on peacekeepers in neighboring Côte d'Ivoire to generate as-if random variation in the intensity of exposure to UNMIL on the Liberian side of the border. I further contextualize my quantitative results with qualitative insights gleaned from in-depth, semi-structured interviews conducted with dozens of civilians and government and UN personnel during fifteen months of fieldwork on the ground. By combining quantitative and qualitative data at cross-national and sub-national levels of analysis, the book triangulates between multiple measurement, identification, and estimation strategies, providing the most comprehensive assessment to date of the UN's sometimes complex effects on the rule of law both within and across countries.

Lastly, from a practical perspective, the book generates a number of lessons for UN missions in the field. I show that UN presence has strong, persistent, and overall positive effects on the rule of law after civil war; that these effects manifest both within and across countries, at the macro, micro, and meso levels; and that they are transmitted at least in part through relatively mundane, interpersonal interactions. Unlike much research on UN intervention, this book focuses primarily on the activities that peacekeepers actually pursue during their deployments, from legal and constitutional reforms at the national level to patrols and interventions to resolve disputes at the local level. UN missions have much more discretion over these specific operational decisions than over the broad contents of their mandates, meaning that the former

---

[5] List experiments help overcome the problems of social desirability bias and non-random refusal to respond that are common in surveys, especially when respondents are asked sensitive questions. I discuss the benefits of list experiments in further detail in Chapter 7.

Scope of the Argument

are particularly relevant for practical purposes. I show that UN missions are especially effective at promoting the rule of law when they are proactive not just in rehabilitating state institutions at the macro level, but also in reviving the authority of those institutions at the micro and meso levels, and when they invest not just in troops and Military Observers, but also in the civilian and police personnel who typically assume responsibility for propelling rule-of-law reform.

SCOPE OF THE ARGUMENT

While the theory and evidence presented in this book are potentially generalizable to many types of international intervention in many settings, I focus in particular on UN intervention in Africa since the end of the Cold War. I focus on the UN because no other institution has engaged in rule-of-law promotion in such a deep or sustained way, especially in countries recovering from conflict. Rule-of-law reform is now perceived as a "core peacekeeping task" (Carlson, 2006, 2) and an "integral part of the UN's approach to peace and security" (Sannerholm et al., 2012, 14). While foreign donors and non-governmental organizations (NGOs) participate in rule-of-law-related activities as well, most play narrow advisory roles and limit their efforts to countries with intact (if defective) security and justice institutions (Trenkov-Wermuth, 2010, 10).

Regional peacekeeping operations like ECOMOG in West Africa typically have more "traditional" mandates, which do not involve rule-of-law promotion at all (Heldt and Wallensteen 2011; Ruggeri, Gizelis, and Dorussen 2012, 9). While these operations may be quicker to deploy than other multilateral missions, and may have a greater interest and better understanding of the contexts in which they operate, they are often poorly funded and equipped, and tend to prioritize military intervention above other forms of engagement (World Bank Group and United Nations, 2018, 92, 238). The UN takes a much more comprehensive approach, and operates in many more settings. Over the past twenty years, UN deployments have increased by more than 600 per cent. The number of police and military personnel deployed to UN peacekeeping operations nearly tripled from the turn of the millennium to the late 2010s alone (World Bank Group and United Nations, 2018, 35). Today, the UN manages thirteen peacekeeping operations worldwide, staffed by tens of thousands of personnel. Many of these missions operate in the hardest cases, where the rule of law is all but non-existent. Indeed, only the UN has been mandated to establish new legal systems "virtually from the ground up" (Trenkov-Wermuth, 2010, 10).

Of course, not all UN missions are equally equipped to pursue rule-of-law reform. My theory applies directly to transitional administrations, such as UNTAET in East Timor, where UN missions assume responsibility for *all* functions of the state. The theory applies equally directly to missions that are not officially designated as transitional administrations, but that are nonetheless given sweeping mandates for legal, political, and institutional reform – UNMIL in Liberia or MINUSMA in Mali, for example. Missions of this sort are increasingly common, particularly in Africa, where the expansion of UN mandates in recent years has been especially dramatic, and where UN missions are often more state-like than host states themselves. But as we will see, the UN's role as a catalyst, surrogate, and liaison runs deeper than even these examples would suggest, and the theory is applicable to most UN missions on the ground today.

I nonetheless opt to focus on Africa because it is the locus of UN intervention worldwide. Since the early 2000s, the share of UN personnel deployed to African countries has grown dramatically relative to other parts of the world. Figure 1.1 plots the number of UN peacekeepers, police officers, and Military

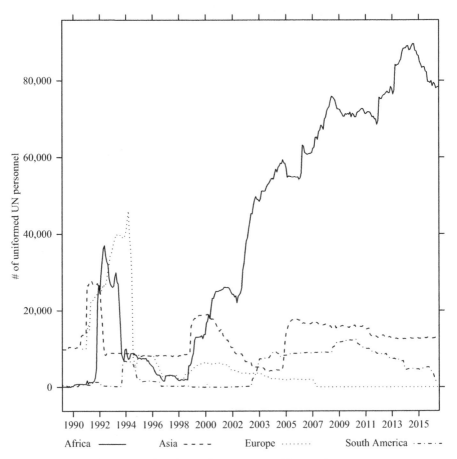

FIGURE 1.1 Deployments of uniformed UN personnel by continent, 1990–2016
Source: Providing for Peacekeeping project.

Observers in Africa, Asia, Europe, and South America since the end of the Cold War, using data from the *Providing for Peacekeeping* (P4P) project.[6] Over the course of the 1990s, the UN's focus shifted from Asia to Africa to Europe, then back to Asia. With the turn of the millennium, however, the UN began directing its efforts much more specifically towards Africa. By 2016, the number of uniformed personnel deployed to African countries was almost five times the number deployed to all other regions of the world combined. These missions tend to have especially extensive mandates, in which the rule of law features prominently. They also tend to operate in some of the most challenging environments, where prospects for the rule of law are especially dim.[7] Africa thus constitutes the most important test case for the efficacy of UN rule-of-law promotion around the world.

I focus on the years since the end of the Cold War in order to capture changes in the dynamics of UN intervention while also ensuring consistency in peacekeeping priorities over time. Some of the UN's most conspicuous failures of the early 1990s occurred in Africa – notably the disastrous UNOSOM I mission in Somalia and the tragically inadequate UNAMIR mission in Rwanda. Ignoring these missions would paint too rosy a picture of UN intervention, and would likely overestimate the UN's effectiveness in promoting the rule of law. But I exclude missions completed before the end of the Cold War because these predated the era of multidimensional peacekeeping (or "peacebuilding"), in which missions are mandated not just to separate belligerents and monitor ceasefires, but also to transform the social, political, and economic fabric of host states. The rule of law lies at the heart of this transformation. While it is possible that earlier missions inadvertently promoted the rule of law, they were not mandated or expected to do so, and including them would likely yield too bleak an account of the UN's record.

Finally, a word on terminology. Throughout this book, I use the term "peacekeeping" broadly to refer to UN missions and the civilian and military personnel of which they are composed. These include not just "blue helmets," but also UN police officers, advisers, lawyers, human rights officials, and other civilian staff. While many of the activities I describe in this book might be more appropriately characterized as "peacebuilding" (Call, 2007a), I use the term peacekeeping in order to distinguish the actions of UN missions from those of the myriad bilateral, multinational, governmental, and non-governmental organizations that participate in the wider peacebuilding process.

---

[6] See www.providingforpeacekeeping.org/.
[7] According to data collected by Richard Sannerholm and co-authors, of the 36 peacekeeping operations deployed to Africa between 1989 and 2012, 28 were deployed to countries with "intense" civil wars that caused at least 1,000 battle-related deaths in at least one calendar year (Sannerholm et al., 2012, 23).

PLAN OF THE BOOK

Chapter 2 traces the history of UN rule-of-law reform and summarizes the limited empirical record on its efficacy (or lack thereof). Chapters 3 and 4 develop the conceptual and theoretical framework that undergirds the rest of the book. Chapter 3 begins by canvassing existing definitions of the rule of law, many of which are problematic in their tendency to conflate the rule of law with an assortment of empirically related but conceptually distinct phenomena. The most influential definitions also tend to underestimate or altogether ignore the insidious challenges to the rule of law that often plague countries recovering from civil strife. These are the settings in which the rule of law is arguably most urgently needed, but also where it is most sorely misunderstood. Chapter 3 posits a three-dimensional conceptualization of the rule of law that better reflects the lived realities of these countries.

Chapter 4 then develops a theory to explain how UN intervention can help establish the rule of law along all three dimensions proposed in Chapter 3. UN missions serve simultaneously as catalysts for state reform, surrogates for reformed states, and liaisons between state authorities, non-state authorities, and citizens themselves. Peacekeepers are thus responsible not just for rehabilitating formal institutions at the macro level, but also for restoring the authority of those institutions at the micro level, and for rationalizing their relationship with informal institutions at the meso level. Chapter 4 documents the repertoire of strategies that UN missions have developed to pursue these goals, providing illustrative examples from around the world. After describing these strategies, the chapter proposes a set of theoretical hypotheses for my empirical analysis to test. The chapter concludes by considering several rival theories, each of which generates more pessimistic predictions than my own.

Chapter 5 tests the macro-level implications of my theory across all UN missions in Africa since the end of the Cold War. The chapter begins by showing that increases in the number of UN personnel are associated with stronger executive constraints, greater judicial independence, and improved rule of law more generally. The nature and magnitude of this relationship vary over time in largely intuitive ways. While UN presence is only weakly and inconsistently associated with the rule of law during periods of ongoing conflict, a more pronounced positive correlation materializes immediately after the fighting stops. The correlation holds for both uniformed and civilian personnel, and for four different types of engagement in rule-of-law-related activities: police reform, justice sector reform, prison reform, and legal reform. The relationship is strongest during the "golden moment" for reform that begins shortly after civil war termination (UN Department of Peacekeeping Operations, 2013, 6), and is most robust when the UN monitors, pressures, or assists host governments, rather than bypassing them entirely.

Chapters 6–8 then examine the impact of UN intervention on micro- and meso-level indicators for the rule of law in Liberia. Chapter 6 introduces the case by describing historical and contemporary obstacles to the rule of law in Liberia, focusing in particular on the dynamics of contestation between formal and informal security and justice providers. In Liberia, as in other African settings, many citizens perceive the police and courts as corrupt, ineffective, and inaccessible, and so opt to rely on informal authorities to adjudicate crimes and resolve disputes, even in cases over which the state claims both original and ultimate jurisdiction. Informal authorities dispense quick and inexpensive justice, but they are also beset by inefficiencies and biases of their own, and often rely on mechanisms of adjudication that violate state law and undermine the rights of the accused. UNMIL was intimately involved in efforts to resolve these problems.

As Chapters 7 and 8 show, these efforts yielded some important successes. Chapter 7 summarizes my approach to testing UNMIL's impact on Liberia; Chapter 8 presents my results. I find that exposure to UNMIL increased citizens' reliance on formal over informal authorities in the most serious criminal cases, and increased informal authorities' reliance on legal over illegal mechanisms of dispute resolution. Perhaps surprisingly, Chapter 8 also shows that UNMIL's presence did not mitigate Liberians' perceptions of state bias, and actually *exacerbated* their perceptions of state corruption – at least in the short term. The chapter attributes these apparently conflicting effects to the messages UNMIL delivered to Liberian citizens, urging them to obey state laws and trust state institutions, while simultaneously encouraging them to recognize and report acts of state malfeasance. Importantly, however, I find that these adverse effects diminished over time, while UNMIL's more beneficial effects were still detectable even two years later, and even in communities that reported no further exposure to UNMIL personnel. While I cannot say for certain whether these results will persist after UNMIL's withdrawal in 2018, taken together, they suggest the possibility of a durable and overall positive change in citizens' attitudes towards state authority in Liberia.

The book concludes in Chapter 9 by considering the generalizability of my findings and their implications for the study and practice of UN intervention in the future. From an academic perspective, my results suggest that UN missions have a more profound impact on the rule of law than is typically assumed, and that their effects are transmitted not just through state reconstruction and reform at the national level, but also through face-to-face, day-to-day interactions with host populations at the local level. The salience of these interactions has long been recognized in research on police/community relations (Tyler 2004, 2006; Tyler and Fagan 2008; Tyler and Huo 2002) and state/society relations more generally (Joseph and Nugent, 1994), but has only recently begun to emerge in the study of international intervention. I argue that more attention should be paid to these micro- and meso-level dynamics, which are vital to the UN's success (Autesserre, 2014a; Kathman et al., 2017).

From a more practical perspective, I argue that UN missions must be sensitive to the role they play as state surrogates, especially in the eyes of local populations. My theory implies that the UN's actions affect civilians' perceptions not just of the mission, but of the host state itself. If UN personnel engage in acts of negligence or abuse, the consequences may reverberate long after their mandate is complete, damaging state/society relations in lasting ways. Anticipating and avoiding this outcome should be a priority for peacekeeping operations in Africa and beyond.

2

History of UN Intervention and the Rule of Law after Civil War

As UN missions have grown in scope and complexity, restoring the rule of law has become increasingly central to their mandates and exit strategies, which hinge on the transfer of legal and political power to legitimate, effective security and justice institutions (UN Peacekeeping Best Practices Section, 2008, 87–88). UN missions have assumed responsibility for drafting laws and lobbying for their passage; revising constitutions; training judges, prosecutors, and police officers; building courthouses, police stations, and prisons; monitoring extrajudicial punishments, arbitrary arrests, and indefinite detentions; assisting with criminal investigations and prosecutions; improving coordination both between and among state and non-state authorities; and more generally elevating the role of the state as a purveyor of security and justice. All of these activities are designed in part to foster the rule of law.

But the notion that UN missions should even attempt to pursue rule-of-law reform in post-conflict settings is a relatively recent innovation. From the inception of peacekeeping in the middle of the twentieth century until the 1990s, most UN missions adhered to a "traditional" template: lightly armed UN troops or unarmed Military Observers deployed to monitor ceasefires and separate belligerents with the consent of the parties to the conflict. UN police officers served as a "haphazard supplement" to troops and Military Observers (Kaspersen, Eide, and Hansen, 2004, 7). The use of force was prohibited except in self-defense, and peacekeepers were enjoined not to interfere in the host state's economy, politics, or culture. Impartiality was paramount, insulating peacekeepers from great power politics and shielding them from charges of favoritism by the belligerents themselves.

This changed with the shift from traditional peacekeeping to multidimensional "peacebuilding" in the late 1980s and early 1990s – a term that entered the UN's lexicon with the publication of Secretary-General Boutros Boutros-Ghali's *Agenda for Peace* in 1992. UN missions were still mandated to monitor ceasefires and enforce peace agreements in the short term, but were now expected to "identify and support structures which will tend to consolidate peace" in the long run as well (UN Secretary-General, 1992, para. 55). This agenda culminated in three transitional administrations – UNTAES in Eastern Slavonia (launched in 1996), UNMIK in Kosovo (1999), and UNTAET in East Timor (1999) – in which the UN assumed responsibility for all of the executive, legislative, and judicial functions usually reserved for host states. But even in missions not officially designated as transitional administrations, the range of goals that peacekeepers were mandated to achieve became more diverse and ambitious after the Cold War. Today, UN advisory groups continue to warn against the "narrow focus on cessation of hostilities" that characterized earlier missions, urging peacekeepers to pursue ever-more transformative objectives in the countries where they intervene (UN Secretary-General's Advisory Group of Experts, 2015, 8).

Few of these objectives are as important as the rule of law, a concept that now lies "at the very heart" of the UN's institutional identity (UN Secretary-General, 2004c, 4). The UN views rule-of-law promotion as vital to peacekeeping success (Carlson, 2006, 2). In 1996, the UN Security Council passed its first resolution that explicitly mentioned the rule of law as a goal to which post-conflict countries should aspire (UN Security Council, 1996). Four years later, the *Report of the Panel on United Nations Peace Operations* (2000), known as the "Brahimi Report," advocated a "doctrinal shift" towards the integration of rule-of-law personnel – including most obviously UN police officers, but also legal, judicial, and corrections officials – into all multidimensional peacekeeping operations (UN Security Council, 2000, 7). Following the Brahimi Report's recommendations, the UN Security Council has incorporated the rule of law in one way or another into the mandates of all new multidimensional missions since 1999. For some of these missions, the rule of law became the "main objective" (Kaspersen, Eide, and Hansen, 2004, 7).

UN rule-of-law promotion typically targets four links in the "justice chain": laws, police forces, courts, and prisons (Sannerholm et al., 2012). Police reform was the first of these objectives to enter the UN's repertoire, and became a "central and often successful" component of many UN mandates in the post–Cold War years (Trenkov-Wermuth, 2010, 3). While the idea of establishing a UN police force emerged as early as 1948, and while UN Police (UNPOL) officers contributed to peacekeeping in the Congo beginning in 1960, it was not until 1989, with the deployment of UNTAG in Namibia, that police reform rose to its current status among the UN's priorities. UNTAG was not directly responsible for maintaining law and order in Namibia, nor was it officially mandated to train the Namibian police. Nonetheless, UNTAG police officers attempted to impart principles of "even-handed," "non-discriminatory," and "democratic" policing, and conducted joint patrols and co-deployments with their Namibian counterparts in order to monitor their adherence to these principles (Howard, 2019, 69). UNTAG's police contingent also tracked the progress of politically sensitive cases through the criminal justice system, and assisted the mission's civil affairs officers in defusing conflicts that arose during preparations for national elections in 1989.

Other missions followed UNTAG's lead. In 1991, ONUSAL was mandated to rebuild the police and reform the judiciary in El Salvador (though the latter goal was secondary to the former); UNTAC in Cambodia (established in 1992) and UNMIBH in Bosnia and Herzegovina (1995) were both mandated to restore law and order, independently and in coordination with the host state's police forces. In El Salvador, despite receiving far fewer police officers than it was allotted in its mandate, ONUSAL succeeded in preventing the new National Civilian Police from acting in an "openly politicized and abusive manner" during the peace process, and helped identify and de-escalate potential sources of unrest before they spiraled out of control (Stanley and Loosle, 1998, 16). The mission also successfully dissuaded the government from populating the new police force with members of the repressive National Police and Treasury Guard, and successfully secured funding for a police training academy despite government stonewalling (Howard, 2008, 112–13). These experiences suggested that UN missions could play a productive role in rehabilitating post-conflict police forces, even in inauspicious political environments. Optimistic accounts from within the policy community suggested that police reform might even obviate the need for subsequent military engagement (Carnegie Corporation of New York, 1997, xxvi, 64–5).

Host states varied in their receptivity towards UN-sponsored police reform, in some cases welcoming UN involvement only after their own resource and capacity constraints became too severe to ignore. In Mozambique, for example, the government was initially adamantly opposed to the establishment of a UN police force; the General Peace Agreement of 1992 made no mention of UN policing, or of international involvement of any kind with the Mozambican police. Faced with the specter of rising crime and mounting civil strife, however, the government changed course, requesting the deployment of a UN police contingent to train the National Police Affairs Commission and the Rapid Intervention Police and monitor preparations for the elections of 1994. While the Mozambican police resisted oversight, and while ONUMOZ had no authority to reprimand officers who were caught engaging in misconduct, the mission nonetheless opened rebel-controlled territories to domestic police presence; curbed human rights abuses in more remote regions of the country; and contributed to the "calm atmosphere" surrounding voter registration, campaigning, and voting during the 1994 elections (Howard, 2008, 206–8).

These early efforts at police reform were not, however, accompanied by equally ambitious attempts to rehabilitate the rest of the civil and criminal justice system. Compared to the UN's auspicious early experiences with police reform, legal, correctional, and (especially) judicial reform proved considerably more challenging. In some cases the UN's efforts to reform these sectors encountered vociferous opposition from host governments; in others, they were simply too narrow, tepid, and disjointed to succeed. In Cambodia, for example, UNTAC was mandated to help the Supreme National Authority implement justice sector reforms in anticipation of national elections to be held in 1993. UNTAC did manage to draft a new penal code, and to issue new rules in specific areas of Cambodian law (Howard, 2008, 150). Cambodia's civil war had eviscerated the judiciary, however, and UNTAC devoted insufficient attention and resources to the problem, with results that were "disappointing" and "inconsequential" (Trenkov-Wermuth, 2010, 3).

A similar pattern played out in other post-conflict settings, even in missions that were otherwise generally successful. For example, in addition to its work reforming the police, UNTAG in Namibia spearheaded a "moderately successful" campaign to abolish or amend fifty-six discriminatory laws dating back to the colonial and apartheid periods. But even these reforms were dampened by the mission's inability to overrule Namibia's administrators-general, who rejected efforts to repeal a highly controversial system of ethnic administration enshrined in the country's "AG-8" law (Trenkov-Wermuth, 2010, 16). Similarly, in Mozambique, a debilitated judiciary ensured there would be few, if any, repercussions for the human rights violations that ONUMOZ documented (Howard 2008, 207).

The limitations of rule-of-law reform in missions more generally regarded as failures are even starker. In Rwanda, the UN did little more to promote the rule of law than draft occasional reports – this, despite overt discrimination in the courts, where ethnic Tutsis continued to enjoy preferential treatment over the Hutu majority. In Somalia, the mandate of UNOSOM II reflected "conflicting priorities," and appears to have been drafted with "almost no plan for how to interpret or implement" the mission's goals (Howard, 2008, 27). Meanwhile, miscommunication with then Under-Secretary-General for Peacekeeping Operations Kofi Annan stymied attempts at justice sector reform before they even began. Mission leadership believed that restructuring the judiciary would be UNOSOM's "ticket out of Somalia." But as Martin Ganzglass wryly puts it, the ticket was "never even purchased" (Ganzglass, 1997, 33).

These failures were problematic precisely because of the close connections between the components of the state security and justice apparatus – the police, courts, and prisons, as well as the law itself. As a 2006 report laments, "UN investment in police reform has often been undermined by a lack of corresponding and coherent support to the judicial system" (Carlson, 2006, 2). The UN learned this lesson the hard way in Haiti, where abuses and inefficiencies in the judiciary undermined the performance of the newly reformed police. Chastened by this experience, the UN began to view the various dimensions of rule-of-law promotion as integral to one another, and to acknowledge that failure along one dimension could stymie success along the others (Mani 2002, 56; Trenkov-Wermuth 2010, 4).

As a 2009 report explains,

When the number of police officers working in peacekeeping operations is enhanced, the numbers of criminal cases leading to arrests inevitably multiply. As a result, the number of persons arrested, detained, and imprisoned also increases. Without a readily available presence of rule of law actors such as prosecutors, judges, lawyers, and correctional staff to deal with these detainees, prisons often become overcrowded, with pre-trial detainees forming the bulk of the number of prison inmates. Deteriorating prison conditions in turn lead to escapes, riots, and other disturbances having an impact not only on the prisons, but also on the larger security situation in the post-conflict country. (UN Department of Peacekeeping Operations, 2009, 4)

The 2015 report of the High-Level Independent Panel on United Nations Peace Operations (HIPPO) similarly warns that "progress at one end of the justice chain is often undermined by failures or delays at another" (High-Level Independent Panel on United Nations Peace Operations, 2015, xi, 40). These interdependencies make coordination especially essential for rule-of-law promotion. Police reform on its own does not suffice. Establishing the rule of law requires a more "balanced and holistic" approach (Carlson 2006, 2; see also Carnegie Corporation of New York 1997, xxvii, 65; Kaspersen, Eide, and Hansen 2004, 8).

The UN has made progress towards operationalizing this approach in the years since the Brahimi Report was released, though police reform remains the most common rule of law-related activity across UN missions worldwide (Sannerholm et al., 2012). In 2003, a Criminal Law and Judicial Advisory Service (CLJAS) was established at UN headquarters in New York, consisting of Justice, Corrections, and Policy teams. A Rule of Law Coordination and Resource Group was created in 2006, and the following year the UN Secretary-General established the Inter-Agency Security Sector Reform Task Force charged with developing an "integrated, holistic, and coherent" approach to security sector reform (UN Department of Peacekeeping Operations, 2012b, 19). Also in 2007, the Office of Rule of Law and Security Institutions (OROLSI) was established within the Department of Peacekeeping Operations (DPKO), and a Standing Police Capacity (SPC) was created to provide "start-up" policing capabilities for UN missions (UN Department of Peacekeeping Operations, 2013, 6). The UN also devised Formed Police Units (FPUs) to expand the capacity of UNPOL, and to perform crowd control and other functions where the host state's police forces are "unprepared, unwilling, or overwhelmed" (Carlson, 2006, 7). A Justice and Corrections Standing Capacity (JCSC) became operational in 2011 to complement the SPC.

This multiplicity of actors distinguishes the UN from many other international organizations engaged in rule-of-law reform, for better and for worse. UN missions are unusual in that they encompass many separate but interconnected agencies operating under the same banner within the same country at the same time. This can create coordination problems, as I discuss later in the chapter. But it can also serve as a sort of "force multiplier" as each unit magnifies the impact of the others. Networks are most effective when they are "dense, with many actors, strong connections among groups in the network, and reliable information flows" (Keck and Sikkink, 1998, 28). The UN is aware of this, and has worked to facilitate coordination and communication between offices (e.g. through the "integrated" mission model, introduced in 2008, and the "Delivering as One" philosophy, first articulated by former UN Secretary-General Kofi Annan in 2005). The rule of law is a multidimensional problem, to which the UN increasingly aspires to offer multidimensional solutions.

As UN missions began more actively integrating the various appendages of the host state's justice system into the process of macro-level reform, they also began more directly engaging civilians and non-state actors at the micro and meso levels, respectively. The 2000 Brahimi Report was already explicit in its recommendation that peacekeepers spend more time learning about local norms and cultures both before and during their deployments (UN Security Council, 2000). The 2015 HIPPO report further urges UN missions to "move beyond merely consulting the local population to actively include it in their work"; the perspectives of citizens and non-state actors "should be streamlined into the consideration of political strategy," and should be used as a metric for evaluating success (High-Level Independent Panel on United Nations Peace Operations, 2015, 78).

Efforts to elicit local perspectives take many forms, both formal (e.g. seminars, workshops, and public information campaigns) and informal (e.g. casual conversations while on patrol) (Howard, 2019; Sannerholm et al., 2012). Often framed as "community empowerment" or "participatory peacekeeping," communication and information sharing are believed to foster confidence between peacekeepers and the populations whose welfare they are mandated to serve (World Bank Group and United Nations, 2018, 59–60). Often the UN incorporates representatives of the host state into these activities as well. As the 2012 *Civil Affairs Handbook* rightly notes, "in order to restore the state's authority it is necessary to restore its legitimacy and this can only be achieved when the government and the society are engaged in an open and responsive dialogue" (UN Department of Peacekeeping Operations Policy and Best Practices Service, 2012, 191).

The UN has reaffirmed its commitment to a rule-of-law agenda in multiple resolutions and reports issued over the past two decades. A 2004 UN Secretary-General report on *The Rule of Law and Transitional Justice in Conflict and Post-Conflict Societies*, for example, describes the rule of law as a necessary condition for peacebuilding more generally: "the consolidation of peace in the immediate post-conflict period cannot be achieved unless the population is confident that redress for grievances can be obtained through legitimate structures for the peaceful settlement of disputes and the fair administration of justice" (UN Secretary-General, 2004c, 3). In a 2011 report, the DPKO similarly asserts that "strengthening the rule of law is necessary not only as a pillar of efforts to mitigate against a lapse into conflict, but also for creating an environment which permits other peacebuilding processes to succeed" (UN Department of Peacekeeping Operations, 2011b, 23). A 2015 Special Committee on Peacekeeping Operations report describes the rule of law as a priority of "critical importance ... in countries in conflict and emerging from conflict in order to help stabilize the situation, extend state authority, end impunity, tackle the underlying causes of conflict, and build lasting peace" (UN Special Committee on Peacekeeping Operations, 2015, 37). These are just three examples among many.

The rule of law has become equally integral to the mandates of UN missions in the field. Again, examples are myriad. Prior to the 2010–11 civil war in Côte d'Ivoire, UNOCI was mandated to help the government restore the "authority of the judiciary and the rule of law," and to re-establish the "authority of the State" more generally (UN Security Council, 2007a, 3–4). After the civil war, UNOCI's mandate was expanded to "develop the police, judiciary, prisons, and access to justice" throughout the country (UN Security Council, 2011b, 6). In DRC, MONUC was responsible for "building effective rule of law capacity, including justice and corrections" (UN Security Council, 2009, 8). Similarly, in Chad and CAR, MINURCAT was tasked with "the promotion of the rule of law, including through support for an independent judiciary and a strengthened legal system" (UN Security Council, 2007b, 3). And in South Sudan, UNMISS was mandated to "support the Government ... in developing its capacity to provide security, to establish rule of law, and to strengthen the security and justice sectors" (UN Security Council, 2011a, 4).

The legal and normative foundation for these operations has also become more explicit in recent years, beginning with the UN Secretary-General's 2004 report on *The Rule of Law and Transitional Justice in Conflict and Post-Conflict Societies* and continuing with his 2008 "Guidance Note" on *UN Approach to Rule of Law Assistance*, which first articulated the UN's framework for rule-of-law reform. These reports drew on standards developed over the past several decades, including the *Basic Principles on the Independence of the Judiciary* (issued in 1985), the *Standard Minimum Rules for the Administration of Juvenile Justice* (1985), and the *Guidelines on the Role of Prosecutors* (1990). Together, the UN believes these documents offer "universally applicable standards" that "must therefore serve as the normative basis for all United Nations activities in support of justice and the rule of law" (UN Secretary-General, 2004c, 5). Complementing these standards is a variety of technical manuals and guidelines, including the *Primer for Justice Components in Multidimensional Peace Operations*; the *Guidelines on the Methodology for Review of Justice and Corrections Components in UN Peace Operations*; the *Policy Directive on Prison Support in UN Peacekeeping Operations*; and the *UN Police Handbook*, among others.

This proliferation of policies notwithstanding, some aspects of UN rule-of-law promotion (especially legal and constitutional reform) continue to lack "standard-setting documents," and it is not clear whether or to what extent existing standards actually guide the actions of UN missions in the field (Sannerholm et al., 2012, 15, 18). Moreover, despite its increasing centrality to the mandates of UN missions around the world, rule-of-law reform remains underfunded and understaffed, especially outside of the security sector. As the Brahimi Report lamented, "the United Nations has faced situations in the past decade where the Security Council has authorized the deployment of several thousand police in a peacekeeping operation but has resisted the notion of providing the same operation with even 20 or 30 criminal justice experts" (UN Security Council, 2000, 7). While this situation has improved in the years since the Brahimi Report was published, legal, judicial, and correctional reform, continue to consume only a very small portion of the UN's peacekeeping budget.[1]

Meanwhile, responsibility for rule-of-law reform has shifted repeatedly, creating coordination problems within the UN system. Perhaps unsurprisingly for a large international organization, the UN's rule-of-law regime has tended towards bloat over time. At one point more than 40 different departments or agencies claimed partial ownership over the UN's rule-of-law agenda (Sannerholm et al., 2012, 21), creating "competition and discord" and resulting in the implementation of multiple overlapping programs in the same countries at the same time (Carlson 2006, 14; see also Trenkov-Wermuth 2010, 11). This problem diminished with the creation of the Rule of Law Coordination and Resource Group in 2007, which has fostered greater harmony among the various entities now involved in rule-of-law reform. But with so many UN bodies operating in the same arena simultaneously, some confusion, miscommunication, and duplication of effort is inevitable (Sannerholm et al., 2012, 9). Whether the UN is capable of promoting the rule of law despite these challenges remains an open question – one to which we have surprisingly few empirical answers.

What We Know about Rule-of-Law Promotion

The empirical record on UN rule-of-law promotion is thin and contradictory. Theoretically, most studies of UN intervention focus on the role that UN missions play in mitigating commitment problems and information asymmetries between armed actors. This is especially true of cross-country research (Doyle and Sambanis 2000, 2006; Hultman, Kathman, and Shannon 2016; Walter 1997), but similar perspectives can be found in within-country studies (Mvukiyehe, 2018) and cross-country studies focused on within-country

---

[1] Of the approximately $7.1 billion devoted to peacekeeping operations in 2014, for example, just 0.4 per cent was spent on justice sector personnel, and another 0.4 per cent on corrections personnel. These constituted 0.28 per cent and 0.35 per cent, respectively, of the approximately 120,000 personnel deployed to UN missions worldwide (UN Department of Peacekeeping Operations, 2014a).

dynamics (Ruggeri, Dorussen, and Gizelis, 2017). As important as these roles are, they are more salient to the short-term goal of preventing violence than the longer-term task of rehabilitating state institutions, restoring state authority, and reestablishing the rule of law.

Empirically, most studies of peacekeeping focus on a narrow range of outcomes, most of them related to violence of one sort or another: violence against civilians (Hultman, 2010; Hultman, Kathman, and Shannon, 2013; Kreps and Wallace, 2009), mass killings (Melander, 2009), battles between governments and rebel groups (Ruggeri, Dorussen, and Gizelis, 2017), battle-related deaths more generally (Hultman, Kathman, and Shannon, 2014), conflict contagion – whereby violence in one location spills over into neighboring regions or countries (Beardsley, 2011; Beardsley and Gleditsch, 2015) – and the recurrence of civil and international war (Doyle and Sambanis 2000, 2006; Fortna 2003, 2004, 2008a; Gilligan and Sergenti 2008; Hultman, Kathman, and Shannon 2013; Sambanis 2008).[2] These are natural outcomes to analyze – we are talking about *peace*keeping, after all – but they capture only one of the myriad dimensions of UN intervention around the world.

Most research also continues to operationalize peacekeeping in coarse ways, distinguishing different types of missions with different types of mandates (e.g. traditional vs. multidimensional) and different troop compositions, but neglecting much or all of the variation in what UN personnel actually do on the ground, especially at the micro level. Micro-level activities are often key to peacekeeping success, and understanding them is essential to understanding peacekeepers' impact on host countries, especially outside the capital city (Autesserre 2010, 2014b, Kathman et al. 2017). In peacekeeping, as in warmaking, "a good deal is played out in daily contacts, often at a highly individual level" (Pouligny, 2006, 141). Yet most scholars ignore these dynamics (Higate and Henry, 2009, 156).

Relatedly, most studies of UN intervention are either entirely cross-national or entirely sub-national. Cross-national studies can yield generalizable lessons, but rely on coarse proxies for UN intervention, and often require strong, untestable assumptions about the comparability of wildly disparate settings. Sub-national studies use more granular data and minimize contextual differences between units of analysis, but may lack external validity, as results from one country may not generalize to others. Few scholars have attempted to integrate cross-national and sub-national perspectives on peacekeeping into a single empirical or theoretical framework.

The UN has conducted ad hoc evaluations of its rule-of-law-related initiatives, but these tend to be impressionistic. They typically rely on descriptive statistics and anecdotal evidence alone, and generally ignore the challenges of attributing causality to particular UN-sponsored programs. After the 2010 earthquake in Haiti ravaged the justice sector, for example, the UN

---

[2] I discuss exceptions to this trend in Chapter 4.

optimistically concluded that "the speed with which the judiciary was able to begin functioning again was a clear sign that the progress made with the support of MINUSTAH's Justice Section was not lost" (UN Department of Peacekeeping Operations, 2010b, 14). But there is no way to know how quickly the judiciary would have begun functioning again in the absence of MINUSTAH's intervention. In Darfur, the months following a UNAMID-led training program for tribal elders and rural court judges witnessed an increase in the number of criminal cases transferred from the customary to the statutory justice sector, in accordance with Sudanese law (UN Criminal Law and Judicial Advisory Service, 2016). But again, it is impossible to know how many cases would have been transferred from rural to state courts if UNAMID had never intervened.

To my knowledge there has been only one other study to date that systematically tests the relationship between peacekeeping and the rule of law across countries. In an analysis of all civil wars that ended between 1970 and 1999, Stephen Haggard and Lydia Tiede find that the presence of a UN mission is correlated with stronger executive constraints, which they speculate may be a result of "explicit constitutional engineering on the part of outside parties" (Haggard and Tiede, 2013, 414). But they also find that UN presence is *not* correlated with other potential proxies for the rule of law, including Freedom House indices of political rights and civil liberties. As Haggard and Tiede note, however, their results are "preliminary." Estimating the impact of international intervention on the rule of law requires resolving "complex issues of endogeneity especially in regard to the influence of UN intervention" – issues that Haggard and Tiede by their own account do not attempt to address (Haggard and Tiede, 2013, 414).

Moreover, since their analysis ends in 1999, it necessarily excludes some of the most important multidimensional missions in Africa to date, including UNAMSIL in Sierra Leone (deployed in 1999), UNMIL in Liberia (2003), ONUB in Burundi (2004), UNOCI in Côte d'Ivoire (2004), UNMIS in Sudan (2005), MONUC (1999) and MONUSCO (2010) in DRC, UNMISS in South Sudan (2011), MINUSMA in Mali (2013), and MINUSCA in CAR (2014). Indeed, as discussed earlier, it was not until the mid-1990s that the UN began conceptualizing the rule of law as integral to the process of post-conflict reconstruction and reform (UN Security Council, 1996), and it was not until 1998 that the first mission to include the phrase "rule of law" in its mandate – MINURCA in CAR – was deployed.[3] Omitting these later missions risks underestimating the UN's effectiveness in promoting the rule of law.

---

[3] This observation is based on data from Gabriella Lloyd's *Tasks Assigned to Missions in their Mandates* project (Lloyd, 2017). Before MINURCA, UNTAG in Namibia was mandated to ensure that "law and order [is] impartially maintained"; see https://peacekeeping.un.org/mission/past/untagM.htm.

Other scholars have assessed the UN's impact on outcomes that are empirically connected to the rule of law but conceptually different from it. These analyses have yielded mixed results. Michael Doyle and Nicholas Sambanis, for example, find that multidimensional peacekeeping operations not only reduce the risk that civil war will recur, but also promote "participatory" peace, characterized by a "minimum level of political openness." They speculate that this effect is due to the "institutional development that UN missions foster in the immediate postwar period," though they do not test this hypothesis in a direct way (Doyle and Sambanis, 2006, 73, 131–2). Studies by Birger Heldt and Jasina Steinert and Sonja Grimm reach similar conclusions (Heldt, 2012; Steinert and Grimm, 2015). More broadly, Lise Morjé Howard argues that UN missions can, under certain conditions, build state institutions strong and legitimate enough to endure even after peacekeepers withdraw (Howard 2008, 2019).

But other studies yield much more pessimistic conclusions. Page Fortna finds that peacekeepers do not increase the likelihood of democratization after civil war, regardless of the type of mission deployed (traditional, observer, multidimensional, or enforcement), the proxy for democratization used (Polity scores or Freedom House rankings), or the time frame considered (one, two, or five years after civil war termination). She concludes that peacekeeping has neither a clear positive nor a clear negative impact on democratization, and that positive and negative effects appear to "cancel each other out" (Fortna, 2008b, 39). Roland Paris goes further, arguing that the UN's efforts to engineer liberal democracy tend only to provoke instability. This, he argues, is the result of an inherent tension between Western ideals and the social, cultural, and economic realities of post-conflict states (Paris, 1997). Kimberley Marten takes this line of reasoning to its logical extreme, arguing that democratization under UN tutelage has been a "failed experiment," and that "the notion of imposing liberal democracies abroad is a pipedream" (Marten, 2004, 14, 155).

These studies help illuminate the complex and potentially contradictory relationship between international intervention and democratization after civil war. But they too are limited in important ways. Most obviously for my purposes, they do not address the rule of law. Democracy and the rule of law may be related – indeed, the latter is arguably a prerequisite for the former (Barro, 2000) – but they are not the same thing. UN missions may succeed in promoting democracy but not the rule of law, or vice versa, and we cannot infer one relationship from the other. Like Haggard and Tiede, these studies also typically focus on the period before rule-of-law promotion became a key component of UN mandates. Doyle and Sambanis, for example, limit their analysis to civil wars that ended by 1997. Fortna focuses on those that ended by 1999. Heldt considers only those that ended by 2005. If we want to know whether UN missions promote the rule of law, we should focus on the years when they were trying to do so.

Furthermore, most studies assess the impact of peacekeeper presence on democracy and other outcomes by comparing countries with UN missions to those without. But as I discuss in Chapter 5, this approach requires strong and often implausible assumptions about the comparability of heterogeneous units of analysis. Some scholars have justified this approach by arguing that peacekeepers tend to deploy to the "hard cases," where the risk of conflict recurrence is most severe; if this is true, then confounding should presumably bias estimates of the UN's efficacy towards the null of no effect (Doyle and Sambanis 2000, 2006; Fortna 2004, 2008a; Gilligan and Stedman 2003). But this is an assumption-laden claim in and of itself, one belied by studies documenting subtler and potentially more problematic biases in UN deployment patterns. Scholars have shown, for example, that peacekeepers are more likely to deploy to European conflict zones than African ones (Gilligan and Stedman, 2003); that the UN Security Council is less likely to impose time limits on missions deployed to countries whose governments share policy preferences with the "P5+1"[4] (Allen and Yuen, 2014); and that peacekeepers are more likely to deploy when the UN has already expressed a clear, public preference for one party to the conflict – especially when that party has already sustained casualties (Benson and Kathman, 2014).

These dynamics may bias assessments of the UN's efficacy in unknown and probably unknowable ways. Biases of this sort are likely to be especially severe when comparing across countries, and when distinguishing between only the broadest of mission characteristics – e.g. whether they have traditional, multidimensional, or enforcement mandates (Doyle and Sambanis 2000, 2006), or whether they were authorized under Chapter VI or Chapter VII of the UN charter (Fortna 2003, 2004, 2008a). These distinctions may be informative, but may also be misleading, as even missions with similar mandates may differ dramatically in their operational capabilities, and in the activities they pursue on the ground. Within-country studies mitigate some of the potential biases associated with cross-country studies, but most of these focus on "least-likely" cases, such as DRC, where international interveners have most obviously struggled (Autesserre, 2010; Veit, 2011).

Beyond the Prevailing Pessimism

Rigorous empirical studies of the relationship between intervention intervention and the rule of law are few and far between. Some of the most trenchant critiques of international intervention as a mechanism for rule-of-law promotion are based on intuitions, anecdotes, and selective case studies, rather than systematic empirical evidence. These accounts are narrow and impressionistic; many are case studies published as book chapters in edited volumes, typically with "little or no overlap" between them (Bellamy, Williams, and Griffin, 2004, 12). Case studies are valuable in that they provide rich, detailed narratives

---

[4] The acronym "P5" refers to the five permanent members of the UN Security Council: China, France, Russia, Britain, and the USA. Germany is often included as the "+1."

of post-conflict processes, often informed by first-hand experience. But most are unsystematic in specifying their dependent variable; few articulate explicit, falsifiable hypotheses to test; and even fewer grapple with the challenges of causal inference in the presence of potentially confounding variables.

The theory motivating this book, described briefly in Chapter 1 and developed more thoroughly in Chapter 4, generates optimistic predictions that stand in stark contrast to the pessimism that pervades many academic accounts. At the macro level, the theory predicts that UN missions should increase state authorities' compliance with legal limits on their power, safeguard the independence of the judiciary, and improve the quality of state security and justice provision. At the micro level, UN missions should increase citizens' reliance on the police and courts when crimes are committed or violence occurs. And at the meso level, UN missions should increase non-state authorities' adherence to jurisdictional boundaries and reduce their reliance on illegal mechanisms of dispute resolution. While not all UN missions will succeed in achieving these goals – indeed, some will fail repeatedly and spectacularly – on average, I expect UN intervention to have positive and potentially lasting effects on all three dimensions of the rule of law.

But of course, while UN missions *can* promote the rule of law, it is by no means a foregone conclusion that they *will*, or that their effects will be benign. Tensions can arise not just in the logistics but in the *logics* of rule-of-law promotion under UN tutelage – contradictions that may "lurk beneath the more visible, day-to-day challenges," and that may not be resolvable through "best practices" alone (Paris and Sisk, 2009a, 3). For example, while my theory assumes that international interveners are generally benevolent, the UN is no stranger to scandal, and there have been many highly publicized cases of UN personnel engaging in unprofessional or even illegal behavior. If UN missions act as *predatory* state surrogates, then their presence may have the pernicious effect of alienating citizens and inadvertently reinforcing loyalty to informal over formal institutions. Conversely, UN missions may prove so effective and legitimate that they "crowd out" the state, inducing dependence and becoming a crutch that host governments find progressively more difficult to lay down. Time and resource constraints may force peacekeepers to coordinate with informal authorities, who may exploit this dynamic to consolidate control over the territories they govern, potentially undermining efforts to empower the state. Alternatively, attempts to assert the primacy of state law may provoke resistance from communities long accustomed to autonomy.

Some analysts recognize these tensions but nonetheless endorse international intervention as a mechanism for resurrecting war-wracked states (Call 2008b, 365; Fukuyama 2004, 120–1; Zartman 1995b, 267–8). Some propose relaxing the standards of success to accommodate lower but more reasonable expectations – thus, for example, calls to eschew "good governance" in favor of "good enough governance" (Grindle, 2002). Others urge international interveners to focus less on building states and more on supporting the constellation of civil society organizations that sustain order in places where the state cannot (Autesserre, 2010; Pouligny, 2006). Still others advocate delegation of state authority to some supranational entity through "shared sovereignty," "neotrusteeship," or, more provocatively, "post-modern imperialism" (Fearon and Laitin, 2011; Krasner, 2004; Pfaff, 1995). Some – a minority – believe the international community should abandon intervention altogether, either because "aided recovery" is a failed model for reviving state laws and institutions,[5] or, more polemically, because the state itself is a failed model of social and political organization.[6]

Empirical evidence remains scant on all sides of this debate, especially as it pertains to the rule of law. Anecdotes can be informative, intuitions can be insightful, and some may be correct. But we cannot know until we test them. Too much of what we think we know about international intervention and the rule of law is derived from least-likely cases, theory without evidence, evidence without theory, and stories that may not generalize beyond the experiences of the storyteller. A more measured assessment is likely to reveal successes obscured by a literature "overwhelmingly focused on failure" (Autesserre, 2014a, 496). Meanwhile, UN missions continue to deploy with ever-larger numbers of personnel and ever-more ambitious mandates. The current pillars of international humanitarian law (notably the Responsibility to Protect) favor increasingly intrusive third-party encroachment into the domestic affairs of predatory or incompetent states. While the legacies of Iraq and Afghanistan may limit American adventurism abroad for the time being (though even this is uncertain), the trend, overall, appears to be towards more rather than less international intervention.

The aim of this book is not to diminish the very serious problems of negligence and abuse that have plagued too many UN missions in the field. Nor is the goal to suggest that the constraints imposed by tight budgets and fickle contributions from UN member states can be easily overcome. But there are a

---

[5] Inspired by Charles Tilly's maxim that "war made the state and the state made war" (Tilly, 1975, 41), these critics typically argue that civil strife is a catalyst for state consolidation and reform, and should be allowed to run its course until one side or the other achieves victory. International intervention stunts the process of "internal, institutional change" that civil war reflects; "autonomous recovery," in contrast, elevates leaders strong enough to defeat their rivals and implement "far-reaching policy reforms" (Weinstein, 2005, 5). From this perspective, international intervention is as much the problem as the solution (Englebert and Tull, 2008, 125). Rather than investing in ever-more costly attempts to build peace, the international community should learn to "give war a chance" (Luttwak, 1999).

[6] The state, these critics argue, has had a short and unhappy history (Brooks, 2005, 1169), one characterized by "cruelty and coercion" (Anderson, 2004, 4), and by "slavery, conscription, taxes, corvée labor, epidemics, and warfare" (Scott, 2010, ix). If this is true in Europe and North America, then it is especially true in the developing world, where many "failed" states were never functional to begin with (Anderson, 2004; Brooks, 2005; Herbst, 1996), and where the very notion of statehood was often imposed from abroad through conquest and colonial rule (Davidson, 1993).

variety of channels through which international intervention might help establish the rule of law, scandals and scarce resources notwithstanding. As Séverine Autesserre rightly notes, "the obstacles to peacekeeping and peacebuilding are such that the most puzzling question is not why international efforts fail but rather why they sometimes succeed" (Autesserre 2014a, 496; see also Fortna 2008a, 2–4; Howard 2008, 2–3). The effects of international intervention on the rule of law should be treated as an empirical question – one to which we have no clear empirical answers.

3

Conceptual Framework

Civil War through a Legal Lens

In recent decades, scholars and practitioners have converged on the shared hope that establishing the rule of law might prove a panacea for an almost bewildering variety of social, political, and economic ills, especially in the developing world (Rajagopal, 2008, 1348). The rule of law is believed to be indispensable for protecting human rights,[1] stimulating economic growth,[2] safeguarding liberal democracy,[3] consolidating state authority,[4] and preventing civil strife.[5] The rule of law is arguably *sui generis* in the unanimity it seems

---

[1] The Universal Declaration of Human Rights and other instruments of international humanitarian law explicitly connect the rule of law to human rights protection, as does the European Court of Human Rights, whose Convention "draws its inspiration" from rule-of-law principles (Bingham, 2011, 66).

[2] As Jelle Janssens notes, "virtually all development organizations" have incorporated rule-of-law promotion into their programming. This includes the World Bank and the International Monetary Fund, as well as a variety of bilateral donors and private foundations (Janssens, 2015, 14). Alan Greenspan, former chairman of the US Federal Reserve, has gone so far as to describe the rule of law as the single most important contributor to economic growth worldwide (Bingham, 2011, 38). Establishing the rule of law and ensuring access to justice are key to the UN's own Sustainable Development Goals (SDGs), especially SDG 16, promoting "peaceful and inclusive societies." See https://sustainabledevelopment.un.org/sdg16.

[3] The European Commission's strategy for combating illiberalism among the continent's newer democracies, unveiled in 2014, is officially known as the "rule of law mechanism," and is grounded in the assumption that democracy and the rule of law are inextricably intertwined (Müller, 2016, 58).

[4] Anja Kaspersen and co-authors argue, for example, that "consolidating the rule of law is an intrinsic part of a state-building process" (Kaspersen, Eide, and Hansen, 2004, 11).

[5] A 2006 UN report describes rule-of-law reform as "inextricably linked" to implementing peace agreements and "supporting a safe and secure environment" (Carlson, 2006, 2). The Carnegie Corporation's 1997 report on *Preventing Deadly Conflict* identifies rule-of-law promotion as one of the most important "preventive actions" to reduce the risk of civil war (Carnegie Corporation of New York, 1997, xviii). As the joint UN and World Bank *Pathways for Peace* report argues, "a breakdown of justice systems and the rule of law generally can inflame the grievances that may be mobilized for conflict and create incentives for violent behavior" (World Bank Group and United Nations, 2018, 166–7).

to inspire. From democracy promotion to humanitarian relief to peacekeeping itself, virtually every other dimension of the "Western donor consensus" is hotly contested (Carothers, 2009, 51). Not so the rule of law, one of those "few but fortunate concepts that has universal support" (Sitaraman, 2012, 183). Legal theorist Tom Bingham puts the point eloquently: "in a world divided by differences of nationality, race, color, religion, and wealth, [the rule of law] is one of the greatest unifying factors, perhaps the greatest, the nearest we are likely to approach to a universal secular religion" (Bingham, 2011, 174).[6]

Yet for all its perceived importance as a policy goal, the rule of law as a concept remains elastic and widely misunderstood. The conflation of the rule of law with so many empirically related but conceptually distinct phenomena has encouraged rhetorical and ideological overuse, uncritical thinking, and unrealistic expectations among those dedicated to promoting it (Carothers 2009, 51; Jensen 2008, 119). The rule of law remains an "exceedingly elusive notion," plagued by "rampant divergence of understandings" (Tamanaha, 2004, 5). By some accounts, conflict over the meaning of the rule of law is intrinsic to the concept itself;[7] to others, intractable ambiguities have rendered the concept unusable and unworthy of further debate (Shklar, 1998). Meanwhile, rule-of-law promotion programs continue to proliferate at ever-increasing cost and with ever-expanding scope.

In Chapter 2, I traced the history of the UN's attempts to promote the rule of law in weak and war-torn states, and summarized the existing evidence, such as it is, that might help us assess the efficacy of the UN's efforts. In this chapter I develop a conceptual framework to illuminate the necessary conditions for the rule of law in the wake of conflict. I begin by reviewing the most prominent definitions of the rule of law from both policy and scholarly circles, focusing in particular on the "positivist" and "pluralist" traditions within legal theory and legal anthropology, respectively. While valuable, I argue that these definitions are all similarly limited in their inappropriateness for the developing world, and for post-conflict countries in particular. My definition preserves the attractive features of existing accounts while introducing additional dimensions that better capture the nuances of legality in countries recovering from civil war.

My point of departure is H. L. A. Hart's simple but powerful conceptualization of legal systems as the confluence of "primary" and "secondary" rules. I rely on Hart's account not just because it has been immensely influential in the field of legal theory (Hadfield and Weingast, 2014, 28), but also because it is uniquely applicable to countries recovering from conflict. I propose a three-dimensional theory of the rule of law that draws on Hart's intuitions, but adapts them to situations in which formal (state) and informal (non-state) security

---

[6] Legal scholar Brian Tamanaha makes a similar point in a 2008 interview with *The Economist* magazine, arguing that "no other single political ideal has ever achieved global endorsement" (The Economist, 2008).

[7] Jeremy Waldron, for example, describes the rule of law as an "essentially contested concept," meaning that definitional debates are inherent to it (Waldron, 2002).

> **At the macro level,**
> state authorities adhere to legal limits on their power, respect the independence of the judiciary, and abstain from extrajudicial punishment. This also implies that:
>   1. laws are clear, coherent, and publicly promulgated
>   2. police, courts, and prisons are integrated and capable of coordination
>
> **At the micro level,**
> citizens rely on state authorities to adjudicate cases that fall unambiguously under state jurisdiction. This also implies that:
>   3. citizens know and understand the law
>   4. citizens have relatively easy access to the police and courts
>   5. citizens view state authorities as legitimate
>
> **And at the meso level,**
> non-state authorities defer to state authorities in cases that fall unambiguously under state jurisdiction, and abstain from extrajudicial punishment in cases that fall under non-state jurisdiction. This also implies that:
>   6. non-state authorities know and understand jurisdictional boundaries
>   7. non-state authorities are trained in legal mechanisms of dispute resolution
>   8. non-state authorities are integrated and capable of coordination with state authorities

FIGURE 3.1 Necessary conditions and observable implications of the rule of law

and justice providers coexist and compete within the boundaries of a single sovereign state.

I posit three necessary conditions for the rule of law in these settings. First, state authorities must abide by legally imposed restrictions on their power, must respect the independence of the judiciary, and must refrain from the use of extrajudicial punishments, arbitrary arrests, and indefinite detentions. Second, citizens must defer to state authorities to adjudicate incidents of crime and violence over which the state claims ultimate jurisdiction (e.g. murder). Finally non-state security and justice providers must not usurp the state's authority, and must renounce mechanisms of dispute resolution that violate state law. I define these as the macro, micro, and meso dimensions of the rule of law, respectively; Figure 3.1 summarizes them and their observable implications, which I develop in more detail in the rest of the chapter. The chapter concludes by describing how these three dimensions of the rule of law constitute a chicken-and-egg problem that weak and war-torn states inevitably struggle to resolve on their own.

A POSITIVIST PERSPECTIVE ON THE RULE OF LAW

What is the rule of law, and how would we know it if we saw it? As typically used in casual conversation and policy debate, the rule of law seems to encompass a laundry list of social, political, and economic desiderata (Hadfield and Weingast, 2014, 26). The International Commission of Jurists, for example, describes the rule of law as a mechanism to "create and maintain the conditions which will uphold the dignity of man as an individual," and promote the "establishment of the social, economic, educational, and cultural conditions which are essential to the full development of his personality" (Committee I of the International Congress of Jurists at New Delhi 1959, clause 1, cited in Raz 1979, 210–11). Some scholars have adopted similarly maximalist positions. Tom Bingham, for example, proposes a "thick" conceptualization of the rule of law that encompasses the right to life, liberty, security, education, and fair trial; respect for private and family life; freedom of thought, expression, conscience, religion, assembly, and association; prohibitions on torture, slavery, and other forms of forced labor; and a variety of other ancillary goals.[8]

Maximalist definitions have a certain appeal, incorporating a variety of policy priorities that most would agree are, at the very least, important correlates (if not components) of the rule of law. With so many dimensions, however, maximalist definitions also risk embracing "just about every political ideal which has found support in any part of the globe during the post-war years," thereby stretching the concept beyond analytical or practical tractability (Raz, 1979, 211). Some of these ideals are clearly requisites for the rule of law – the right to a fair trial, for example. But others, I argue, are clearly not (e.g. the right to education, or freedom of religion). By invoking so many disparate goals, maximalist definitions fail to distinguish the core from the peripheral dimensions of the rule of law, and the necessary conditions from the merely incidental ones. If the rule of law means "everything good that people desire from government," then ultimately it means nothing at all (Tamanaha, 2004, 113).

Maximalist definitions also justify equally maximalist policy agendas, raising the standards of success beyond the capacity of most policymakers to meet them while simultaneously draining the rule of law of its divisive political implications. Maximalist definitions re-imagine broad disputes over social, political, and economic values as narrower conflicts over the rule of law. But disparate policy goals demand disparate policy agendas, and collapsing them in this way only obfuscates the trade-offs necessary to achieve them. Establishing the rule of law is not a technical or apolitical exercise, though some of its policy appeal derives precisely from this mischaracterization. Any attempt to reform state laws and institutions and restore their authority nationwide will inevitably generate significant distributional consequences, with winners who benefit from the implementation of particular policies and losers who do not. Maximalist definitions ignore this reality, turning the rule of law into a "proxy battleground" and precluding more thoughtful analysis of competing values on their own terms, and of the steps needed to advance them (Tamanaha 2004, 113; see also Rajagopal 2008).

---

[8] Bingham derives these requirements from Britain's 1998 Human Rights Act, which he describes as a "convenient framework" for incorporating human rights into a thick definition of the rule of law (Bingham, 2011, 68).

The trouble with maximalist definitions becomes especially obvious when they are subjected to empirical examination. Conceptual stretching is common among empirical studies of the rule of law, with unfortunate consequences for analysis. Stephan Haggard and Lydia Tiede, for example, argue that the many dimensions of the rule of law necessitate as "wide-ranging an evaluation as possible." Accordingly, they operationalize the rule of law using a variety of proxies as diverse as political rights, civil liberties, judicial independence, corruption, and protection of private property (Haggard and Tiede, 2013, 407–8). With so many proxies to consider, it is hardly surprising that their study yields valuable but contradictory results.

This book adopts a more minimalist perspective drawn from the positivist tradition in legal theory. Positivist accounts of the rule of law focus on the "formal, structural, institutional, and procedural" characteristics of legal systems (Waldron, 2008, 40).[9] They are united by the idea that laws become binding as a result not of their content (e.g. the extent to which they protect human rights), but of their "pedigree," or the manner in which they were enacted (e.g. according to some constitutionally prescribed procedure) (Dworkin, 1967, 17–18). While the necessary conditions for the rule of law vary across positivist accounts, the ideal legal systems they describe are similar in that they allow all actors, both public and private, to go about their lives without fearing that the rules regulating their behavior will be unknowable, unenforceable, or subject to the whims of those who created them (Hayek 2006, 75–6; Raz 1979, 211; Waldron 2008, 7, 40).

These are "positive" requirements in that they do not include representation, equality, or any of the other normative goals to which a government might aspire, or the normative standards to which it might be held. Yet while positivist criteria are not moral per se, neither are they "without moral significance" (Waldron, 2008, 40). As Lon Fuller argues, while the rule of law need not advance a particular substantive end – liberty, for example, or respect for human rights – governance by rules rather than arbitrary power is nonetheless necessary for respecting "man's dignity as a responsible agent," and for preventing the most egregious affronts to "responsible agency" (Fuller 1969, 162; see also Raz 1979, 221).[10] Positivist definitions thus preserve some of the moral foundations of

---

[9] Even among positivists, a distinction is sometimes drawn between accounts that emphasize "structure" (laws and legal institutions) and those focused on "procedure" (the process through which legal institutions make and enforce laws). In my view, structural and procedural perspectives reinforce one another, and can be easily integrated. See, for example, Raz (1979), a "structural" account of the rule of law that nonetheless includes several procedural criteria. The similarities are more important than the differences, and the line between them is often blurred.

[10] While most "substantive" accounts are broader and more exacting than positivist ones, they similarly characterize legal systems as comprising rules that can, in principle, be fully enumerated and faithfully enforced. Other substantive accounts go further by denying this core ontological claim. Perhaps most famously, Ronald Dworkin argues that legal systems must be conceptualized not just as systems of rules, but also as systems of principles. Principles do not arise from any particular decision of the courts or legislature, and they can only be validated through a "sense of appropriateness developed in the profession and the public" (Dworkin, 1967, 41).

maximalist accounts while avoiding conceptual slippage and practical over-ambitiousness. As Joseph Raz puts it, adherence to positivist requirements is "a necessary condition for the law to be serving any good purpose at all" (Raz, 1979, 225). Flouting these requirements is not merely immoral; it results in a legal system that is "simply not engaged in the basic activity of law" (Shapiro, 2013, 394), that is "not properly called a legal system at all" (Fuller, 1969, 39).[11]

Perhaps the most influential positivist account of the rule of law, and the one from which most others (including my own) are derived, is H. L. A. Hart's famous characterization of legal systems as the confluence of "primary" and "secondary" rules. Primary rules specify the rights and duties of individuals: laws prohibiting burglary, for example, are primary rules, as are laws defining the scope of property rights for landowners. Secondary rules specify how primary rules are created, adjudicated, altered, or eliminated. The appellate process in the USA, for example, is regulated by secondary rules.[12] While primary rules can exist on their own, secondary rules only make sense in relation to other rules. They are not just rules, but "rules about rules" (Colvin, 1978, 200).

Secondary rules distinguish laws from norms (etiquette, for example), and legal systems from other systems of rules. Hart goes so far as to characterize the introduction of secondary rules as "a step forward as important to society as the invention of the wheel" (Hart, 2012, 41). In a "pre-law" society, rules become binding only insofar as they are accepted and practiced by most members

---

Dworkin is clearly correct that rules must be supplemented by principles. This is most obvious when positive laws contain moral qualifiers – words like "cruel" or "unreasonable," for example. To determine what these qualifiers imply, judges must use principles that originate outside the law, and decide cases accordingly (Dworkin, 1986). Still, in countries with dysfunctional security and justice sectors, focusing on moral principles at the expense of empirical rules is a guarantee of further dysfunction. The existence of rules to guide behavior is a *sine qua non* of legal systems, whatever other principles those systems may also entail (Radin 1989, 785; Raz 1979, 218).

[11] The normative undertones of positivist accounts are obvious even in the way they characterize law itself. Fuller writes of an "inner morality" of law (Fuller, 1969, 41). Scott Shapiro characterizes legal systems as "enterprises for solving moral problems" (Shapiro, 2013, 358). And Jeremy Waldron argues that positive criteria "go to the heart of what we value about law," and make it "something worth treasuring as well as something worth studying" (Waldron, 2008, 40–1).

[12] Hart distinguishes primary from secondary rules as follows:

Under rules of the one type, which may be considered the basic or primary type, human beings are required to do or abstain from certain actions, whether they wish to or not. Rules of the other type are in a sense parasitic upon or secondary to the first; for they provide that human beings may by doing or saying certain things introduce new rules of the primary type, extinguish or modify old ones, or in various ways determine their incidence or control their operations. Rules of the first type impose duties; rules of the second type confer powers, public or private. Rules of the first type concern actions involving physical movement or changes; rules of the second type provide for operations which lead not merely to physical movement or change, but to the creation or variation of duties or obligations. (Hart, 2012, 81)

of that society. Such a system is static and inefficient, however, and foments uncertainty as society expands. Legal systems overcome these limitations by introducing secondary rules of change, adjudication, and recognition. The rule of change prevents stasis by conferring the power to make, modify, or abolish laws on particular individuals or institutions. The rule of adjudication reduces inefficiency by specifying which individuals or institutions are responsible for applying the rules and determining when they have been violated. And the rule of recognition resolves uncertainty by identifying an ultimate arbiter of disputes to which all other rule-making and -enforcing bodies are subject.

Of these three secondary rules, the rule of recognition is the most important, and the only one whose validity depends on general acceptance and adherence, rather than on another specific rule. For example, for the state to serve as the ultimate arbiter of disputes, actors within the legal system must respect its claim to ultimate authority, which then becomes a "social fact." Hart describes the rule of recognition as the "foundation of a legal system," since it protects against the ambiguity that otherwise prevails when multiple authorities claim jurisdiction over the same territories or the same classes of disputes. Without a rule of recognition, "if doubts arise as to what the [primary] rules are or as to the precise scope of some given rule, there will be no procedure for settling this doubt." Where the rule of recognition is strong, the rule of law is strong as well. Where it is contested, or is met with "general disregard," no legal system exists at all (Hart, 2012, 42, 92, 100, 103).

Hart's account of the rule of law was derived from, and designed to apply to, the established, stable legal systems of the UK and other Western countries. But it offers valuable insights into the challenges faced by weak and wartorn states as well – insights that neither legal theorists nor empirical scholars of civil war have yet appreciated. According to Stathis Kalyvas's influential definition, civil war involves "armed combat within the boundaries of a recognized sovereign entity between parties subject to a common authority at the outset of the hostilities." While conflict of this sort may serve any number of purposes, it becomes civil war only when it "challenges existing authority, even when also serving additional goals." Civil war is thus a political problem, involving "armed contestation of sovereignty" around "mutually exclusive claims to authority that produce a situation of divided or dual sovereignty." This definition encompasses revolutions, insurrections, insurgencies, anti-colonial uprisings, and resistance against foreign occupation. It excludes riots, crime, and "low-level banditry" – categories of violence that are distinct from civil war in that they "leave sovereignty pretty much intact" (Kalyvas, 2006, 17–19).

My conceptualization of the rule of law begins from the observation that civil war itself can be fruitfully reframed in Hartian terms. Civil war is, in essence, a situation in which the secondary rules of change, adjudication, and (especially) recognition become fundamentally and violently contested. Civil war occurs

From Positivist Theory to Pluralist Reality 39

when one or more organized non-state actors mobilize to reject the state's claim to determine which rules are and are not binding (the rule of recognition); to make, modify, or abandon those rules as the state sees fit (the rule of change); and to punish those who violate the state's rules (the rule of adjudication), through the application of force if necessary. In Barrington Moore's famous formulation, over the course of rebellion, "a new crime becomes the basis of a new legality," such that "huge sections of the population become part of a new social order" – one organized around new secondary rules (Moore, 1966, 100).

Seen in this way, civil war is not just a political but also a *legal* problem. Indeed, in an important sense, civil war is the conceptual inverse of the rule of law. Secondary rules are what make the state sovereign within its own borders – independent from, and exercising some degree of control over, all other mechanisms for rule-making and enforcement. During civil war, a significant portion of the population violently repudiates the state's claim to sovereign authority. The secondary rules of the system become contested, and competing elites use organized violence to determine whose rules are binding, and how those rules will be enacted and enforced. The result is a devolution of legal and political authority from the center to the periphery, from the capital to the hinterlands, and from state to non-state actors. As I. William Zartman memorably explains, in periods of civil strife, "power devolves to the peripheries when (because) the center fights among itself. Those in central power are too busy defending themselves against attacks from their colleagues to hold onto the reins of power over the countryside. Local authority is up for grabs and local power-grabbers grab it" (Zartman, 1995a, 10).

FROM POSITIVIST THEORY TO PLURALIST REALITY

Hart's theory offers a powerful framework for understanding the relationship between civil war and the rule of law. But for my purposes, his and other positivist accounts suffer from a tendency to focus exclusively on state laws, institutions, and officials, all but ignoring citizens and other forms of authority – the "local power-grabbers" in Zartman's formulation.[13] Hart, for example, while recognizing the "Janus-faced" nature of legal systems (Hart, 2012, 117), nonetheless conceptualizes the rule of recognition as applying largely if not wholly to government officials.[14] In Hart's account, to the extent that the rule of

---

[13] The same is generally true of substantive accounts. See, for example, Bingham (2011) and Dworkin (1967).
[14] Though to *which* government officials is not entirely clear. On this point, see Raz (1979); Shapiro (2009). As both Raz and Shapiro note, Hart at times seems to suggest that the rule of recognition applies to all government officials (Hart, 2012, 116–17), while at others he focuses exclusively on judges (Hart, 2012, 105, 108).

law demands anything of citizens at all, it requires only that they obey primary rules, not secondary ones.[15] And compliance with primary rules is, according to Hart, a "relatively passive matter," requiring only that citizens "acquiesce" to whatever laws are imposed on them (Hart, 2012, 117).

This view is not unique to Hart. Many other legal theorists have adopted similar positions. Fuller's criteria for the rule of law require nothing of citizens (Fuller, 1969), nor do Bingham's (Bingham, 2011). Waldron emphasizes that citizens have rights (e.g. within the court system), but ultimately demands nothing of them either (Waldron, 2008). Raz requires that "people should be ruled by the law and obey it," but goes on to clarify that the rule of law depends only on the extent to which "people will *be able to be* guided" by the law (Raz, 1979, 213, my emphasis). Raz is referring here to the characteristics of laws themselves, not to the actions of the citizens whose behavior is being "guided." These perspectives ignore the complex and often deeply contested nature of legality in much of the developing world, and the critical role that both citizens and non-state authorities play in strengthening or subverting the rule of law in these contexts.

In many developing countries, and in post-conflict settings in particular, the state is just one of many institutions that claim the right to create and enforce rules that structure social, political, and economic life. Examples abound: clans and "secret houses" in East Timor (Bowles and Chopra, 2008; Brown and Gusmao, 2009), chiefs in Zambia (Baldwin, 2015), warlords in Afghanistan (Blair and Kalmanovitz, 2016; Mukhopadhyay, 2014), *dozos* in Côte d'Ivoire (Hellweg, 2011), *kamajors* in Sierra Leone (Ero, 2003), paramilitaries in Colombia (Duncan, 2006), and rebel groups in Peru, Nepal, and elsewhere (Arjona, 2016). These entities are politically amphibious – neither states nor citizens nor civil society organizations per se. Rather, they occupy what Paul Staniland aptly calls the "pivotal 'meso-level' analytical space between the local and the national" (Staniland, 2012, 246). While a variety of entities operate in this space, I focus in particular on meso-level security and justice providers – non-state groups and individuals who make rules that do not originate in state law, and who enforce those rules using mechanisms

---

[15] Though Hart is somewhat ambiguous on this point as well. At times he broadens the rule of recognition to encompass "the practice of the courts, legislatures, officials, *or private citizens*" (Hart, 2012, 104, my emphasis). But as Raz observes, for most of Hart's theory, citizens' behavior is irrelevant to the rule of recognition, whose existence depends solely on the actions of law-creating and -enforcing officials (Raz, 1979, 92). Elsewhere Hart argues that while secondary rules cannot impose duties on citizens, they *can* confer powers. These powers are conferred indirectly, through the mechanism of duties imposed on government officials (on this point see Colvin 1978). But even if this is Hart's position, it only adds to the constraints imposed on government officials, conferring powers on citizens but imposing no duties on them.

that operate independently of (though sometimes in coordination with) state institutions.[16]

Meso-level security and justice providers are especially pervasive in post-conflict settings, where they are often at least as powerful as the police and courts, and sometimes more so (Isser, 2011). In Hart's terminology, these settings are characterized by multiple rules of recognition that coexist within the same territory – one rule of recognition that emanates from the state at the macro level, the other(s) from the various meso-level actors and institutions operating in areas within the state's *de jure* borders but beyond its *de facto* control. In Kosovo, for example, the police and courts coexist in an uneasy equilibrium with a multitude of private security companies, gangs, and customary mechanisms of dispute resolution grounded in traditional Albanian law, known as the *Kanun* (Janssens, 2015). In Guatemala, a resurgence of Mayan Law after the end of the civil war culminated in an agreement that divided the previously monist legal system into statutory and customary components (Sieder, 2001). Operating between and alongside these two components is a vast network of vigilante groups, many of them relics of the civil war itself (Bateson, 2013).

The relationships that emerge within this meso-level space are complex and highly context-dependent – sometimes cooperative, sometimes conflictive, often overlapping. In Sierra Leone, for example,

> ... the extended family may protect the home, but it may be the youth that sorts out the fight at the village bar, the customary chief that settles the inheritance dispute, the community peace monitors that address war looting, the vendors' committee that mediates a settlement over debt repayment by another market trader, the taxi drivers' association attendant that handles the taxi park disturbance, the commercial security guard that secures the entrance to the city bank, the mine monitors that check the legality of the diamond dealers' trading and the [Sierra Leone Police] that respond to the traffic fatality. (Baker, 2005, 371)

This situation is typical of many developing countries, where security and justice are provided not by a unitary "sector," but rather by a "shifting terrain of security coalitions, which are assembled and reassembled as crises occur, or reforms take place" (Cawthra and Luckham, 2003, 17).

These arrangements become even more complicated during periods of conflict when rebel groups and informal institutions compete with one another, and with the state, to win civilians' loyalties. In many cases, rebel groups have no choice but to defer to the authority of existing non-state purveyors of security and justice, or to at least share power with them. In Mozambique,

---

[16] I refer to these actors interchangeably as "non-state" and "informal." I sometimes also describe them as "customary" or "traditional," though I reserve this designation for actors such as chiefs and elders, whose claim to authority derives from their connection to tradition and custom. This designation would not apply, for example, to rebel groups that provide security and justice within the territories they control.

for example, the Mozambican National Resistance delegated responsibility for dispute resolution to *régulos*, traditional chiefs who are believed to serve as intermediaries between the living and the ancestral spirits. Similarly, the Free Aceh Movement in Indonesia relied on religious leaders known as *Ulamas* to adjudicate most conflicts in the territories it controlled. In Sudan, the Sudan People's Liberation Movement established a "tense agreement" under which chiefs ensured some degree of civilian cooperation with the rebels, who, in return, ensured some degree of safety for chiefs, and recognized their authority to maintain order and resolve disputes (Arjona 2016, 33; Mampilly 2011).

Informal security and justice providers play a pivotal role in these settings, mediating and often obstructing the relationship between citizens and the state, and between national laws and local norms, rules, and customs. Yet despite its importance, the meso-level space in which these actors operate remains arguably the most neglected level of political analysis (Mudde, 2007, 217). Establishing the rule of law is much more complex in countries where multiple rules of recognition compete with one another, but because these complexities rarely arise in the Global North, they have received scant attention from legal theorists. Fuller, for example, devotes just two pages to the issue, and his solution is incomplete and contradictory.[17] Hart[18] and Raz[19] offer similarly brief and inconclusive accounts.

---

[17] Fuller allows for the existence of "more than one legal system governing the population," but seems to view this situation as mostly unproblematic. While he concedes that the coexistence of rival legal systems can "give rise to difficulties for both theory and for practice," he believes these can be easily resolved through something akin to an appellate system. He concludes optimistically that "historically dual and triple systems have functioned without serious friction, and when conflict has arisen it has often been solved by some kind of voluntary accommodation" (Fuller, 1969, 123–4). This perspective is far too sanguine to apply to weak and war-wracked states, where jurisdictional conflicts are rife and "voluntary accommodations" are rare (Leander, 2002; Migdal, 1994; Sisk and Risley, 2005).

[18] In the original formulation of his theory, Hart asserts but does not explain why multiple rules of recognition cannot coexist within a single legal system (Hart, 2012). In subsequent writing, he clarifies that recognition remains unitary even in these situations, as long as competing rules are organized hierarchically (Hart, 1965). In formulating this solution, Hart cites the example of English law, which consists of both precedent and statute, where the former is subordinate to the latter. But precedent and statute are two relatively easily reconcilable sources of law within a single state-sanctioned legal system. The situation becomes much more complex when one source of law operates in opposition to that system, or outside of it altogether. Scott Shapiro rightly criticizes Hart's answer as simplistic and incomplete: at the very least, it lacks a viable "conflict resolution provision" when competing sources of law clash with one another (Shapiro, 2009, 12).

Hart also raises the possibility of a "revolutionary break" after which some (but not all) laws from a prior regime are imported into a new one whose very existence violates the rule of recognition undergirding the first. Hart seems to believe this situation will resolve itself when "things settle down" (Hart, 1965, 1295). But this answer is unsatisfying as well, and it underestimates the upheaval that *actual* revolutionary breaks typically cause, especially when the old rule of recognition was tenuous to begin with.

[19] Raz sees "no reason to suppose that every legal system has just one rule of recognition. It may have more." He notes, however, that every legal system must include "means of resolving conflicts between laws of the various sources" (Raz, 1979, 96). This is true but unspecific, and fails to address the problems that arise when one source of law rejects the jurisdiction of another altogether, and therefore also rejects the "means of resolving conflicts" between them.

This tendency to ignore jurisdictional conflicts between formal and informal institutions is symptomatic of a more general problem afflicting positivist perspectives, most of which are grounded in the legal systems of the rich, industrialized West. As Gillian Hadfield and Barry Weingast rightly observe, the "great majority of academic and policy work" tends to equate the rule of law with "the institutions and practices in those (relatively few) parts of the world where [it] has been largely achieved" (Hadfield and Weingast, 2014, 22). While these accounts may help illuminate what the rule of law *is*, they ignore the question of how and under what conditions it emerges in the first place. Where an unstable and ineffective state is just one of many potential purveyors of security and justice, its actions in isolation leave the rule of law underdetermined. Efforts to promote the rule of law "need local compliance with regulations and standards, but also deeper support for the values underpinning them and the change they represent" (Whalan, 2014, 4). Many states produce laws that in principle *can* guide behavior, but in practice do not. And many citizens reject the notion that formal institutions should guide behavior at all – a rejection far more profound than the mundane forms of non-compliance that Hart and others contemplate.

A potential corrective to this blind spot in the positivist tradition is the concept of "legal pluralism," which refers to situations in which two or more legal or quasi-legal systems coexist within the same society. These situations are not exceptional; indeed, according to legal pluralists, they exist to a greater or lesser extent in most societies, with "continuous variation" between systems that are more and less plural (Merry, 1988, 879). Proponents of legal pluralism as an alternative paradigm for rule-of-law promotion criticize the "top-down, state-centered approach" typically associated with the UN and other international institutions (Golub, 2003, 3), which often prove reluctant to engage with traditional, customary, and other "non-Western" sources of law (Clunan and Trinkunas, 2010, 288). Advocates of legal pluralism deride this as a form of "legal centralism," which, by their account, rests on the assumption that "law is and should be the law of the state, uniform for all persons, exclusive of all other law and administered by a single set of state institutions." From the perspective of legal pluralism, this assumption is "a myth, an ideal, a claim, an illusion" (Griffiths 1986, 20; see also Janse 2013, 186).

But if legal positivism places too much emphasis on the state and its laws, legal pluralism suffers from the opposite problem. Many legal pluralists interpret all rules as "laws," and all entities that make and enforce rules – families, corporations, factories, sports leagues, whatever – as law-making and -enforcing institutions. Indeed, if we follow some legal pluralists in broadening the definition of "legal system" to include any "semi-autonomous social field" (Moore, 1973) – meaning any social field with the capacity to make and enforce rules – then virtually all legal systems are plural, both historically and today (Merry, 1988, 871), and virtually all forms of social control are "*more* or *less* legal" (Griffiths, 1986, 39, emphasis in the original).

This perspective obscures more than it clarifies, fomenting "deep conceptual confusion" about what law is and is not, and driving legal pluralism into a conceptual cul-de-sac (Tamanaha 2008, 390; see also Merry 1988, 878). If legal positivists are misguided in failing to appreciate the role that non-state institutions play in making and enforcing rules, legal pluralists are misguided in failing to acknowledge the features of states that make them different from all other rule-making and -enforcing institutions. The state may not be ideal in any normative sense, but it is plainly distinct in the breadth of rights it claims to protect and the variety of duties it seeks to impose (Tamanaha, 2008, 411). State law is "a body of authoritative standards" designed to regulate the behavior of all other rule-making and -enforcing entities, and states provide machinery for the "authoritative settlement of disputes," without which the inefficiencies that Hart identified in "pre-legal" societies are all but inevitable (Raz, 1979, 33, 111).

Legal pluralists also tend to underestimate the problems that arise when formal and informal security and justice providers compete with each other. As Santos Boaventura de Sousa rightly argues, "there is nothing inherently good, progressive, or emancipatory about legal pluralism" (Boaventura de Sousa, 2002, 114–15). Yet many legal pluralists glorify informal institutions and demonize their formal counterparts, especially in post-conflict settings. The literature is awash in romantic references to the "adaptive capacities" (Boege, Brown, and Clements, 2009, 14) and "creative responses" to conflict (Debiel et al., 2009, 39) that characterize non-state institutions, and to "wholesome and ingenious entrepreneurship" at the local level as the "foundations for a new order" in countries wracked by civil strife (Sawyer, 2005a, 57). These perspectives are not entirely wrongheaded: the coexistence of formal and informal institutions *can* sometimes prove mutually advantageous, and the restoration of state authority can sometimes be a consensual process (Baldwin, 2015; Migdal, 1994; Mukhopadhyay, 2014). Both formal and informal institutions can, in principle, contribute to peace, and the UN and other organizations are increasingly involved in efforts to strengthen both simultaneously (Blattman, Hartman, and Blair, 2014).

But in many cases, the coexistence of formal and informal institutions foments administrative ambiguities and jurisdictional disputes, some of which may escalate into renewed violence. As Timothy Sisk and Paul Risley observe, "frictions between traditional authorities and modern state authorities also drive local-level conflicts, particularly in settings that have witnessed persistence of longstanding forms of community self-rule ... that run counter to the authority of the state and its laws and institutions" (Sisk and Risley, 2005, 8). Moreover, while some informal institutions are quicker, less expensive, more accessible, and more effective than their formal counterparts (Isser, 2011), others are corrupt, biased, exclusionary, or even authoritarian, as recent evidence from Indonesia (Olken, 2010), Afghanistan (Murtazashvili, 2016), India (Véron et al., 2006), and numerous other countries attests (Autesserre, 2014a, 495).

In the worst cases, rule by informal authorities can degenerate into a sort of "decentralized despotism" (Mamdani, 1996, 37). In Côte d'Ivoire, for example, traditional hunters known as *dozos* leveraged their training and weapons to become "unofficial police" during a crime wave in the 1990s, patrolling communities, arresting criminals, and restituting victims of theft. But they gradually transformed from an alternative source of law enforcement into a source of alternative laws, independent of the state and backed by the *dozos'* rapidly expanding coercive capacity. They also became a political force to be reckoned with, supporting the opposition in the contested presidential election of 1995, siding with a cadre of ex-soldiers in a failed coup d'état in 2002, and aligning with President Alassane Ouattara in the civil war of 2010–11. Summarizing these transitions, Joseph Hellweg explains that "within a decade, *dozos* had transformed themselves from hunters to auxiliary police to enemies of the state," eventually coming to occupy a "third space somewhere in between and beyond the dichotomies of state and civil society" (Hellweg, 2011, 1–5, 16, 18) – that "pivotal meso-level analytical space" that Staniland describes (Staniland, 2012, 246).

Tensions between formal and informal institutions often prove an impediment to the rule of law. In East Timor, for example, "significant gulfs" between statutory and customary law eventually devolved into an equilibrium characterized by "the worst of both systems" (Brown and Gusmao 2009, 61–2; see also Hohe 2003, 336). In Haiti, inconsistencies between state laws and local customs opened a "divide between legality and daily life" that proved difficult to close. By some accounts, this divide rendered legal doctrines and texts "at best useless, and at worst in the service of the strongest, of injustice" (Pouligny, 2006, 102). In Iraq, while customary law is not officially recognized, "vague provisions" allow for its use in court rulings, creating an ungainly legal patchwork in which some judges incorporate customary principles, while others "vehemently insist that Iraq should have only one modern legal system" (Asfura-Heim, 2011, 270). Even where state law delineates a division of labor between formal and informal institutions, uncertainty often prevails. In Mozambique, the 2004 Constitution nominally institutionalizes legal pluralism, but in a way that is unclear and subject to "widely divergent interpretations and on-the-ground implementation" – a situation that all but precludes the authoritative settlement of disputes (Lubkemann, Kyed, and Garvey, 2011, 41).

All of which raises both practical and conceptual problems for the rule of law, and for the many international institutions committed to promoting it – especially the UN. How, for example, to establish the UN's principle of "supremacy of law" in places where jurisdictional boundaries are blurred? How to ensure "avoidance of arbitrariness" and "procedural and legal transparency" across amorphous and ever-evolving constellations of security and justice providers (UN Secretary-General, 2004c, 4)? How to determine whether the rule of law even exists in places where the state is just one of many potential venues for adjudicating crimes and resolving disputes?

A THREE-DIMENSIONAL CONCEPTUALIZATION OF THE RULE OF LAW

In answering these questions, I combine theoretical intuitions from the positivist and pluralist traditions in legal theory and legal anthropology with empirical insights from recent research on civil war. I propose a three-dimensional conceptualization of the rule of law that preserves Hart's secondary rules as its centerpiece while also accounting for the realities of fragmented legal and political power in countries torn by civil strife. While composed of multiple dimensions, my argument is simple: the rule of law requires that state authorities, non-state authorities, and citizens all abide by the same secondary rules of recognition, adjudication, and change. This, in turn, requires that laws themselves are reasonably clear and coherent, and that state security and justice institutions are reasonably accessible, independent, and effective.

Importantly, these necessary conditions do not specify the scope or structure of secondary rules, and are in principle compatible with a variety of different legal systems, from those in which state institutions adjudicate all but the pettiest of crimes, to those in which non-state authorities resolve most disputes for most of the population. My definition is also compatible with both civil and common law systems, and while it demands that all actors within a given legal system abide by a single rule of recognition, it does not require eliminating non-state institutions altogether, nor does it require subjugating them to a tyrannical state. (I discuss the normative implications of my argument later in the chapter.) Nor are my requirements absolute – the rule of law is not a binary variable, and there can be more or less of it in a given country at a given time. The more fully these interlocking requirements are met, the more robust the rule of law will be.

My theory has distinct but interrelated implications for the three sets of actors involved – states, citizens, and non-state authorities. I call these the macro, micro, and meso dimensions of the rule of law, respectively. I address them in turn.

MACRO-LEVEL RULE OF LAW: At the macro level, the rule of law requires that state authorities act within their legally-circumscribed jurisdictions. State authorities must learn to "think inside the box" (Shapiro, 2013, 398)[20] – to

---

[20] This requirement is related to the concept of judicial discretion, but is broader and has more profound implications for the rule of law. Judicial discretion involves the application of non-legal criteria (e.g. principles) to legal questions, many of which are relatively quotidian. Dworkin, for example, cites the example of *Henningsen v. Bloomfield Motors, Inc.*, in which an American court ruled that car manufacturers can be held liable for making defective parts, even if they possess a contract expressly limiting their liability. While Dworkin describes this as an "important question," he does not seem to view the case itself as especially significant, and suggests that "almost any case in a law school casebook would provide examples that would serve as well" (Dworkin, 1967, 23–4). In these cases, judicial discretion merely fills the inevitable gaps between a legal system's primary rules (Raz, 1979, 96). When government officials transgress secondary rules, in contrast, they implicitly call into question the validity of the system itself.

abide by the secondary rules specifying the scope of their powers to enact, enforce, modify, and adjudicate infractions of primary rules. When jurisdictional disputes arise, they must be adjudicated by some independent, legally recognized arbiter – e.g. a Supreme Court, or a commission erected specifically for the purpose of resolving the dispute – and that arbiter's decisions must be accepted as binding.

A coup d'état is perhaps the most obvious violation of this requirement, but lesser violations regularly occur throughout the developing (and, indeed, developed) world. When executives exceed their constitutionally specified term limits; usurp or undermine the legally guaranteed powers of another branch of government; or defy injunctions issued by a body that wields review powers over them (e.g. a Supreme Court), they violate the system's secondary rules, and thus the first requirement for the rule of law. Violations by actors other than the executive are common as well, including by the judiciary itself – for example, when a lower court ignores a higher court ruling, or when a higher court renders constitutionally indefensible decisions to curry favor with, or advance the electoral agenda of, a political ally. Violations also occur when the police indulge in extrajudicial punishments or arbitrary arrests, or when prisons allow indefinite detentions, as these actions involve the use of force beyond the state's constitutionally circumscribed authority, rupturing the mutuality of constraint that binds citizens to state institutions and exacerbating the asymmetry of power between them (Fuller, 1969).

This macro-level requirement for the rule of law thus hinges on the behavior of state officials, the quality of state laws, and the efficacy and professionalism of state security and justice institutions, especially the police, courts, and prisons. Violations can be intentional or inadvertent: state authorities may flout restrictions on their power because they do not understand the nature of those restrictions, do not have the skills necessary to abide by them, or do not wish to obey them in the first place. Violations along one link in the justice chain also exacerbate violations along the others. Ambiguous or contradictory laws are less likely to constrain the actions of overzealous executives. Weak, ineffective judiciaries are more likely to be susceptible to political interference. Untrained, unskilled police officers are more likely to detain civilians outside the bounds of the law, while dysfunctional prisons are more likely to allow these detentions to drag on indefinitely.

Conversely, the more efficiently these institutions can coordinate with one another, and the clearer the boundaries between them, the less likely each of them is to breach the others' jurisdictions or to cause one of the others to exceed the legal limits of its authority. For example, police officers should be less likely to exact extrajudicial punishments if they can easily transfer criminal cases to the courts, and if they know those cases will be swiftly adjudicated. The rule of law at the macro level also depends on monitoring and supervision: the more robust the oversight mechanisms in place both within and between the state security and justice sectors, the less likely either of them is to engage in abuses of power. As we will see in the next chapter, these are precisely the sorts of reforms that UN missions increasingly pursue in post-conflict settings.

MICRO-LEVEL RULE OF LAW: For many legal positivists (including Hart), the mutuality of constraint between citizens and states is "mutual" only in a thin sense, demanding little of citizens beyond their compliance with the state's primary rules. This may be appropriate in places where the state is strong and the rule of law is consolidated; in these settings, the fact that some citizens subvert state authority does not threaten its viability. But as the civil war literature illustrates, in war-wracked societies, citizens can impede the penetration of state laws and institutions in a variety of ways, often with adverse consequences for the rule of law.

Some citizens undermine the state inadvertently, because they do not have sufficient access or information to do otherwise. For example, citizens may contravene the state's jurisdictional claims because they do not know what is and is not illegal under state law, or because they cannot easily report crimes to the police or register cases with the courts. Others undercut the state intentionally. Indeed, while some citizens may welcome the reintroduction of state rule, many will not, and there is no *a priori* reason to assume they will simply accept and comply with newly reconstituted state institutions, just because those institutions exist. Citizens' local loyalties often supersede their trust in national institutions, and where formal law conflicts with informal norms, rules, and customs, citizens may privilege the latter over the former.

Even when state authorities succeed in establishing a physical presence nationwide, citizens can still subvert them by relying on non-state alternatives to adjudicate criminal cases, or by opportunistically playing competing institutions against one another (i.e. "forum shopping"), often with "serious social and political ramifications" (Tamanaha, 2008, 410). Citizens typically know when they are subject to multiple authorities with overlapping jurisdictions, and respond strategically to that knowledge (Wickham-Crowley, 1987, 482). They are rarely passive, generally have strong preferences over potential security and justice providers, and often manipulate the "tenor" of competing legal regimes through direct demands and indirect forms of resistance and insubordination (Mampilly, 2011, 67). These problems are likely to be especially severe in countries where the state is an "exotic import" (Mayall, 2005, 48); where state institutions have never been viewed as "natural" providers of public goods (Call, 2008b, 14); where citizens have long been accustomed to state predation; or where peripheral communities have long enjoyed autonomy from the center. These situations are common in the world's weakest and most war-torn states, and are anathema to the rule of law.

At the micro level, the rule of law thus requires that citizens respect the division of labor between formal and informal mechanisms of dispute resolution, as defined by the secondary rules of recognition, adjudication, and change. In particular, the rule of law requires that citizens defer to formal institutions in cases that fall unambiguously under formal jurisdiction. As legal theorist Eric

Colvin explains, "the existence of legal officials presupposes secondary rules which are constitutive of their status." To assert that a government official has the authority to make or enforce rules is also to assert that "other people, citizens as well as other officials, are expected to respect his attempts to do so" (Colvin, 1978, 200). While some non-state authority could, in principle, be recognized as the ultimate arbiter of disputes, in the post-Westphalian system of states, the rule of recognition almost always resides in the state itself. And while informal institutions may be authorized to adjudicate some classes of disputes – non-violent conflicts over land use or boundaries, for example – almost all states claim both original and ultimate jurisdiction over the most serious incidents of crime and violence (e.g. murder). The rule of recognition requires that citizens respect that claim.

In this sense, establishing the rule of law requires a transformation more profound than can be achieved through legal or institutional reforms alone. Such reforms are important: in the wake of civil war, laws must be amended, constitutions revised and ratified, judges trained, police officers recruited and deployed, and courthouses and police stations built or repaired. Because these processes lend themselves to relatively easy quantification, they are often used as yardsticks for measuring progress towards the rule of law after conflict (UN Department of Peacekeeping Operations and UN High Commissioner for Human Rights, 2011).

But establishing the rule of law also requires more basic changes in "how citizens relate to state authority" (Carothers, 2009, 59–60) – a "cultural transformation" through which citizens long estranged from state institutions learn to respect their authority and rely on them to intervene when crimes are committed or violence occurs (Hadfield and Weingast 2014, 27; see also Cao 2007; Stromseth, Wippman, and Brooks 2006). As Simon Chesterman asks, "what would a woman do if her property were stolen – go to the police? Or what would a man do if his brother were murdered" (Chesterman, 2007, 19)? The rule of law hinges crucially on the answers to these questions.[21]

Micro-level rule of law thus depends on a combination of information, access, personal beliefs, and social norms. Citizens cannot defer to state authorities if they cannot or do not know how to access the police and courts, if they do not know which types of cases the police and courts do and do not adjudicate, or if they do not understand what is and is not illegal in the first place (as is common in cases of domestic violence, for example). Under these circumstances, even citizens who might otherwise prefer to respect the rule of law may inadvertently fail to do so. More challenging are the cases in

---

[21] My distinction between the macro- and micro-level dimensions of the rule of law echoes Chesterman's distinction between rule of law's "political" and "sociological" dimensions. The former refers to the behavior of government officials (especially the executive), the latter to the actions of citizens. I expand Chesterman's typology by arguing that in hybrid legal systems, some of the most insidious threats to the rule of law arise at neither the macro (political) nor the micro (sociological) level, but at the "meso" level between them.

which citizens intentionally undermine the rule of law, either because they do not view the state as a legitimate purveyor of security and justice, or because they know that *others* do not view the state as legitimate, and therefore fear social sanctions for engaging with it. Again, as we will see in the next chapter, UN missions are increasingly involved in efforts to resolve these problems.

MESO-LEVEL RULE OF LAW: These macro- and micro-level challenges are compounded when state and non-state authorities make competing jurisdictional claims, impose contradictory rules, rely on incompatible norms of dispute resolution, or follow disparate "styles and orientations" in the way they respond to civil or criminal complaints. While these differences can sometimes be reconciled or ignored, often they cannot, creating uncertainty for disputants who "cannot be sure in advance which legal regime will be applied to their situation" (Tamanaha, 2008, 375, 400).

There may be cases where the state is so weak, and non-state authorities so strong, that delegating power from the center to the periphery is the only viable option, normatively and empirically (Blair and Kalmanovitz, 2016) – a possibility that I discuss in further detail later in the chapter. In most cases, however, the rule of law at the meso level requires that non-state authorities defer to the ultimate jurisdiction of the state, at least in cases that fall unambiguously within the state's purview. Moreover, even in cases they *are* authorized to adjudicate, non-state authorities must refrain from using mechanisms of dispute resolution that violate state law – lynchings, for example, or trial by ordeal. No matter how effective these mechanisms may be, the rule of law requires that they be supplanted by legally sanctioned alternatives.

In the wake of civil war, challenges to this requirement can arise for multiple reasons and from multiple sources simultaneously. Rebel groups often erect institutions for maintaining order in the territories they control. These institutions can prove remarkably resilient over time, even after a peace agreement is signed and the rebel group itself has (ostensibly) demobilized (Arjona, 2014, 24). In some cases, rebel institutions survive the conflict more or less intact; in others, the remnants of partially demobilized rebel factions erect new institutions to seize control of recently pacified territories. Similar dynamics may arise between states and informal institutions developed to *resist* rebel rule. In Guatemala, for example, Regina Bateson traces the post-conflict prevalence of lynchings, torture, and other acts of "collective vigilantism" to the presence of civil patrols: self-defense groups that emerged in communities devastated by the Guatemalan civil war, and that endured long after the conflict was officially over. Civil patrols facilitated collective action and endowed citizens with a new set of incentives and capabilities to engage in extralegal violence – actions that directly subverted the rule of law in the post-conflict period (Bateson, 2013, 18–19).

In other cases the same informal authorities that contested state jurisdiction before and during the civil war continue to do so after the transition to peace. The *dozos* in Côte d'Ivoire (described earlier) are a case in point. The *kamajors* in Sierra Leone are another. Like the *dozos*, *kamajors* are traditional hunters that defended their communities from both rebel- and government-inflicted violence during the Sierra Leonean civil war. As they became more powerful, however, they began erecting "parallel security structures" grounded in their own independent penal codes. While the government attempted to contain them – one *kamajor* commander was indicted for war crimes by the Special Court for Sierra Leone, along with two of his lieutenants – they nonetheless continued to enjoy near autonomy. By the time the civil war ended, they had become a "law unto themselves" (Ero 2003, 239–41; see also Zack-Williams 2002, 150).

Similar dynamics arise in many post-conflict settings, especially in Africa, where chiefs, elders, secret societies, and other traditional leaders remain highly influential at the local level, often subverting efforts to extend the reach of state law. In some districts of Mozambique, for example, Stephen Lubkemann and colleagues estimate that over 20 per cent of all crimes are resolved by customary authorities in contravention of Mozambican law, which forbids the customary sector from adjudicating criminal cases. This dynamic is not necessarily a result of ignorance of the law among Mozambican citizens, nor of their dissatisfaction with formal institutions (though that is common too), but is rather a "strategic" choice intended to enhance the power of non-state authorities (Lubkemann, Kyed, and Garvey, 2011, 55). The rule of law requires rationalizing these relationships and (re-)establishing the supremacy of the state, even if non-state authorities retain responsibility for some judicial and security functions. Civil wars create opportunities for "local power-grabbers" to grab power from the state (Zartman, 1995a, 10). In order to establish the rule of law, the state must grab at least some of that power back.

Violations of the meso-level requirements for the rule of law are not always so blatant or deliberate. Like their formal counterparts, some informal security and justice providers may not understand the legal limits on their authority, may lack the knowledge and skills to implement legally sanctioned procedures of adjudication, and may not be familiar with the available mechanisms for referring cases to the formal sector when they are legally required to do so. Other informal authorities may overstep legal limits on their power because they have no incentive to refrain from doing so, either because they know they will not be punished for their transgressions, or because they do not believe the state will learn about those transgressions in the first place. As with the macro and micro levels, and as we will see in the next chapter, overcoming these meso-level obstacles to the rule of law is increasingly important to the UN's operations in post-conflict settings.

ADVANTAGES OF MY APPROACH

My three-dimensional conceptualization of the rule of law has a number of advantages over alternative approaches. By combining legal positivism, legal pluralism, and empirical research on civil war, my theory preserves key intuitions from all three literatures while also leveraging each to identify and correct oversights in the others. Refracting legal positivism through civil war scholarship helps clarify aspects of the rule of law that legal theorists typically ignore – in particular, the pivotal role that citizens and non-state authorities play in consolidating or eroding secondary rules. Legal positivists tend to focus on the "supply side" of the rule of law, i.e. the behavior of government officials and the performance of government institutions. In many countries, however, and in post-conflict settings in particular, the demand side is equally important. Where do citizens' loyalties lie, and how malleable are they? Do non-state authorities accept or contest state jurisdiction? Do they attempt to impede the penetration of state law? Legal positivists generally ignore these questions, but they are essential to the rule of law in much of the developing world.

Conversely, legal positivism provides a powerful analytical framework for understanding the implications of civil war for the rule of law, and for illuminating threats to the rule of law that persist even after the fighting stops – threats that have gone underappreciated in civil war scholarship. Legal systems are often profoundly transformed by conflict processes, and these transformations shape "the very possibility of durable peace" (Arjona, 2016, 310). But how? Studies of civil war are surprisingly silent on this question. Legal positivism provides a framework for answering it. In particular, legal positivism helps us see that while non-state institutions (rebel-devised or otherwise) are unlikely ever to be entirely consonant with their state counterparts, reconciling them is made more difficult when each is grounded in its own secondary rules of recognition, adjudication, and change.

In these cases, "divided" or "dual sovereignty" at the local level is likely to persist long after national peace agreements are signed. As Carrie Manning explains, "informal authority structures and armed civilian security forces empowered during the war often continue to create disturbances long after the parties that created them have consummated a formal peace agreement in the capital" (Manning, 2003, 38). The more these structures are embedded in and validated by secondary rules, the more of a challenge they are likely to pose.

While my definition of the rule of law derives primarily from Hart, it encompasses several other influential positivist accounts, and some prominent substantive accounts as well. If state authorities are to abide by secondary rules of recognition, adjudication, and change, then they must respect the independence of the judiciary, and must apply the law "in good faith, fairly, for the purpose for which the powers were conferred, without exceeding the limits of such powers and not unreasonably" (Bingham, 2011, 60). If citizens and informal authorities are to respect secondary rules as well, then the law itself must be stable, predictable, clear, comprehensible, and publicly promulgated, and must not impose duties beyond individuals' capacities to fulfill them (Bingham, 2011; Fuller, 1969; Raz, 1979). Citizens must also have relatively easy access to the police and courts, which must provide reasonably fair and equal treatment, without imposing prohibitive costs or inordinate delays (Raz, 1979). In this sense, the three dimensions of the rule of law are tightly interwoven, such that violations along one dimension precipitate further violations along the others as well.

In embracing legal positivism, however, my definition also avoids the conceptual ambiguities that afflict many maximalist accounts. This book subscribes to Raz's dictum that the rule of law is "just one of the virtues which a legal system may possess and by which it is to be judged" (Raz, 1979, 211). My definition does not impose unrealistic criteria on weak and war-torn states – states that struggle to meet even the most charitable conditions for democracy and human rights (Blair and Kalmanovitz, 2016; Doyle and Sambanis, 2006) – and it allows for the possibility that the relationship between the rule of law and other apparently related outcomes may be far more complex and contingent than is typically assumed. Maximalist accounts are remarkably "conflict-free," and tend to posit a "harmonious and mutually reinforcing relationship" between the rule of law, development, security, human rights, and other policy goals (Rajagopal, 2008, 1375). In some cases, however, advancing one of these goals may require delaying or even reversing progress towards one or more of the others. My theory can accommodate this reality.

Finally, my definition is advantageous in that it echoes some of the UN's own language on the rule of law. The UN Secretary-General's "Guidance Note" of 2008 defines the rule of law as a "principle of governance in which all people, institutions and entities, public and private, including the state itself, are accountable to laws that are publicly promulgated, equally enforced and independently adjudicated, and which are consistent with international human rights norms and standards." Establishing the rule of law thus requires adopting measures to "ensure adherence to the principle of supremacy of law, equality before the law, accountability to the law, fairness in the application of the law, separation of powers, participation in decision-making, legal certainty, avoidance of arbitrariness, and procedural and legal transparency" (UN Secretary-General, 2008b, 1). This understanding of the rule of law also echoes some of the legal and scholarly accounts described above (Sannerholm et al., 2012, 14).

While my definition is perhaps less ambitious than the UN's, the two definitions nonetheless mirror each other in important ways. The UN's emphasis on the supremacy of law, accountability to the law, legal certainty, independent adjudication, and avoidance of arbitrariness resonates with the Hartian requirement of respect for secondary rules of recognition, adjudication, and change – rules that are designed to foster consistency and transparency in the way laws are enacted and enforced. Moreover, while my definition does not encompass *all* human rights, it does imply many of the rights enumerated in instruments such as the International Covenant on Civil and Political Rights, which includes, for example, prohibitions on arbitrary arrest, indefinite detention, and punishment for acts that are not crimes under the law.

Perhaps most notably, like my conceptualization, the UN's definition imposes requirements not just on state institutions, but on "*all* people, institutions and entities, *public and private*, including the state itself." This is a key point of convergence between my definition and the UN's. It is also a key point of *divergence* between my (and the UN's) definition on the one hand and definitions proposed by many legal positivists (including Hart) on the other.

NORMATIVE IMPLICATIONS OF A POSITIVIST PERSPECTIVE

Like positivist accounts more generally, my theory is not devoid of moral content, and the empirical conditions for the rule of law that I propose arguably encompass important substantive ends as well – ends that are especially urgent in countries recovering from conflict. Civil wars are typically characterized by capricious or purely predatory uses of state power; legal systems that meet positivist criteria protect against this arbitrariness. Civil wars also foment uncertainty and unpredictability for citizens, businesses, and civil society organizations, especially when conflict is accompanied by a proliferation of rule-making and -enforcing institutions. Legal systems that meet positivist criteria provide "stable, secure frameworks" to facilitate planning and order social and economic life (Raz, 1979, 219–20, 225).

But my positivist definition of the rule of law is also susceptible to at least three important normative objections. First, legal pluralists have long argued that positivists focus too much on the state, and that establishing positivist conditions for the rule of law requires subjugating or eliminating non-state mechanisms for making and enforcing rules. I am sensitive to this concern; indeed, I have argued elsewhere that there are some conditions under which states should be compelled to devolve legal and political power to non-state actors operating within their borders (Blair and Kalmanovitz, 2016). But these are exceptional cases. Devolution of power makes sense only when the state has failed or collapsed, and when non-state authorities have proven themselves capable of establishing territorial control, protecting basic rights, and generating significant popular support among the civilians over whom they claim the right to rule. These situations are rare. In most cases, the rule of law is only possible when all actors within a territory submit to the sovereign authority of the state.

Importantly, my theory does *not* require that informal security and justice providers be eradicated. I allow for both state and non-state authorities to play a role in adjudicating crimes and resolving disputes, and I am mostly agnostic as to the appropriate division of labor between them – though as a practical matter, in the majority of countries the state claims both original and ultimate jurisdiction over the most serious criminal complaints. Whatever the division of labor, my definition demands that it be understood and respected by all actors within the system. Moreover, when jurisdictional conflicts arise, my definition requires that all actors defer to the authority of some ultimate arbiter. While, in most countries, that ultimate arbiter is the state, the rule of law does not require neutralizing or marginalizing non-state authorities altogether. It requires integrating them more directly into the legal system and ensuring that they do not overstep boundaries prescribed by the system's secondary rules of recognition, adjudication, and change.

Nor does my theory require imposing a particular legal regime on countries that might not welcome such an imposition. My theory is compatible with civil law, common law, religious (e.g. Islamic) law, and various combinations thereof. Legal systems do not need to be imported wholesale into post-conflict settings in order to conform to my minimalist conditions for the rule of law. Indeed, UN missions typically do not foist legal systems onto the countries in which they intervene, and usually adhere instead to a principle of "continuity of the legal system," which preserves existing legal codes and doctrines but modifies them in order to make them more coherent with one another, and to bring them into closer compliance with international standards. These reforms are not normatively neutral, but nor are they overly intrusive, requiring that entire legal traditions be abandoned or replaced.

Second and related, proponents of maximalist definitions of the rule of law criticize legal positivism on the grounds that it is compatible with totalitarianism and other forms of state predation and exclusion. Some legal positivists unabashedly embrace this critique. Raz, for example, argues that

... a non-democratic legal system, based on the denial of human rights, on extensive poverty, on racial segregation, sexual inequalities, and religious persecution may, in principle, conform to the requirements of the rule of law better than any of the legal systems of the more enlightened Western democracies. (Raz, 1979, 211)

Elsewhere Raz goes so far as to claim that slavery may be consistent with positivist rule-of-law principles, as long as it is instituted through laws that are prospective, stable, clear, general, and not subject to the whims of those who made them (Raz, 1979, 221).

While I agree with Raz that the rule of law is just one of many potentially desirable characteristics for a legal system to have, and that the rule of law must be separated from the other virtues to which a government might aspire, I do not see how even minimalist definitions of the rule of law can possibly be consistent with abuses of this magnitude, at least as they are practiced in real life. A (perhaps *the*) defining feature of most totalitarian regimes is the absence of constraints on the power of the executive. This is fundamentally anathema to the rule of law – even a minimalist conception of it. Similarly, a defining feature of most cruel, exclusionary governments is the ability of those who wield executive power to arbitrarily or retroactively change the rules of the system, or apply the rules selectively, or ignore them altogether. This, too, is irreconcilable with the rule of law.

In other words, while it is true that the rule of law does not require democratic representation, it does not permit most forms of authoritarianism as it is actually practiced. And while it is true that the rule of law does not guarantee human rights broadly defined, it does protect against many of the worst transgressions. Nor should we underestimate just how profound a transformation the rule of law implies for countries recovering from civil war. The normative implications of positivist accounts are especially salient in these settings. Societies that are ruled by law are arguably *morally* superior to those that are ruled by force, even if they are not also liberal democracies. And the rule of law is arguably a necessary condition for values like liberalism and democracy to take root (Barro, 2000).

This latter point helps address a third normative objection. If the rule of law is always a virtue, then it would seem that civil war – which I define as rule of law's conceptual opposite – can never be justified. Scholarship on the normative basis of rebellion is vast, spanning centuries; engaging with it in any serious way is beyond the scope of this book. Suffice it to say that while the rule of law can protect against many of the most serious offenses that governments commit, it cannot defend against all of them. In this respect it is like any other principle of governance, all of which are imperfect in this way. Civil war may sometimes be justified even in societies where the rule of law is strong. But this alone does not diminish the rule of law's value, especially in countries already wracked by conflict.

THE RULE OF LAW AS A CHICKEN-AND-EGG PROBLEM

While I view the macro, micro, and meso dimensions of the rule of law as inextricably intertwined, I do not assume that any one of them is logically or empirically prior to the others. Here I depart from studies of statebuilding after civil war, most of which assume that reconstituting state institutions must be the "first step in any statebuilding process" (Lake, 2010, 2–3). Statebuilding scholars typically focus on "the creation of new government institutions and the strengthening of existing ones" (Fukuyama, 2004, ix); the design of policies to "establish, reform, or strengthen the institutions of the state" (Call, 2008b, 4); and the rehabilitation of "the machinery of the state, from courts and legislatures to laws and bureaucrats" (Paris and Sisk, 2009a, 14–15). Some have gone so far as to characterize deference to state institutions as an inevitable or even mechanical consequence of state reconstruction, arguing that post-conflict governments can count on "strong grassroots demand for better state-provided security" that "cannot and will not be satisfied by non-state providers" (Goldsmith, 2002, 9).

I argue, in contrast, that the micro and meso dimensions of the rule of law may be as much prerequisites for the macro dimension as the latter is for the former. This creates a chicken-and-egg problem that countries recovering from civil war inevitably struggle to resolve on their own.[22] While the rule of law could, in theory, be strong along one dimension but weak along the others, in general the three dimensions strengthen or weaken in tandem. Many citizens will refuse to cooperate with state security and justice institutions unless they believe those institutions are capable of effectively enforcing the law, preventing crime, and resolving disputes. But effective law enforcement, crime prevention, and dispute resolution typically require citizen cooperation (Tyler and Huo, 2002).

Likewise, the disintegration of state institutions may empower and embolden non-state actors, just as non-state actors' attempts to circumvent state authority may hasten the disintegration of state institutions. This vicious cycle is depicted in Figure 3.2. The longer the cycle persists, the more difficult it is to disrupt. In Somalia, for example, the "very success of local adaptation" to state collapse all but eliminated incentives to support a "revived state" (Menkhaus, 2008, 189). State consolidation in these cases tends to be characterized not by the "mutual empowerment" of state and non-state actors, but rather by "mutually exclusive goals" that cannot be easily reconciled (Migdal, 1994, 24).

Following the preceding discussion, I distinguish between two classes of obstacles to the rule of law in post-conflict settings. The first arises because actors want to respect the rule of law, but cannot. At the macro level, state authorities may transgress legal limits on their power because they do not know where those limits lie; because the laws establishing those limits are vague or contradictory; or because the jurisdictions of ostensibly independent agencies are so unclear that transgressions are inevitable. Case files and criminal records are often lost during periods of conflict, and legal codes themselves are often incoherent and outdated, or products of dictatorship or colonialism – vestiges of the same political systems that ignited civil war in the first place. Under these circumstances, even the most conscientious state authorities may find themselves inadvertently but repeatedly on the wrong side of the law.

Similar ambiguities may beset informal institutions at the meso level. Non-state authorities may violate jurisdictional boundaries because they do not know where those boundaries begin and end, and may rely on illegal mechanisms of dispute resolution because they do not know those mechanisms are illegal in the first place, or because they are not trained in the use of legal alternatives (e.g. mediation). Similarly, at the micro level, citizens may unintentionally undermine state authority because they do not know what is

---

[22] My argument here is analogous to claims about the catch-22 between state capacity and legitimacy. As Pierre Englebert writes, "creating legitimacy out of efficiency is a catch-22 in the context of low legitimacy states. Indeed legitimacy results in time $t + 1$ from the efficiency displayed in time t. But successful implementation of developmental policies in time t requires a certain preexisting level of state legitimacy" (Englebert, 2000, 100). Bruce Gilley similarly argues that the "frequently offered policy advice to 'build effective institutions' may be unworkable: institution building depends on generating the revenues and compliance that only legitimacy itself can ensure. But the lack of legitimacy itself is the problem" (Gilley, 2009, 89).

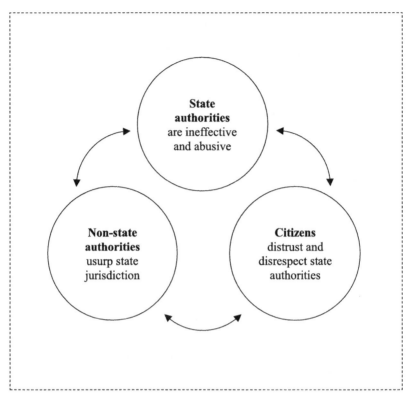

FIGURE 3.2 Vicious cycle of threats to the rule of law

and is not illegal under state law; because they do not know how to contact the police and courts; or because the nearest courthouse or police station is simply too far away. During civil war, security and justice sector infrastructure is often looted, damaged, or destroyed, and many judges and police officers flee or are killed. In the most extreme cases of state failure or collapse, the state security and justice apparatus may disintegrate altogether. This all but ensures violations of the rule of law at the micro level.

The second class of challenges arises because individuals and officials do not *want* to respect the rule of law. At the micro level, citizens may intentionally disregard jurisdictional boundaries if they believe non-state authorities are more effective and legitimate providers of security and justice, or if they fear social sanctions for cooperating with the state. Citizens and authorities at all levels may also benefit from the lack of clear, enforceable restrictions on their actions. In the absence of such restrictions, state officials can indulge in corruption, and can insulate themselves from external oversight and internal competition; non-state authorities can preserve autonomy within the communities they claim the right to govern; and citizens can seek redress for grievances with whichever authority they believe will be most sympathetic, regardless of whether or not that authority is legally authorized to adjudicate their claim.

These problems are further compounded by incomplete information at the micro level and institutional dysfunction at the macro level. In many cases, authorities do not believe they will be punished for wrongdoing, either because they do not think citizens will find out (or even care), or because they know the institutions responsible for exacting those punishments are too feeble to enforce them. In this sense, obstacles to the rule of law at each level of my analysis – macro, micro, and meso – exacerbate those at the other levels as well.

Minimal though they may be, my three conditions for the rule of law thus pose a daunting challenge for states recovering from civil war. The causal arrows point in all directions, each dimension being a necessary condition for the others. Citizen non-compliance may cause institutional collapse (Dorff, 1999, 67), may be caused *by* institutional collapse (Zartman, 1995a, 5), or may be "a process parallel to, but not a by-product of, institutional collapse" (Lemay-Hébert, 2009, 28). Non-state authorities may refuse to cede political power to a weak and illegitimate state, but strengthening and legitimizing the state may require that non-state authorities first cede some political power to it. How to solve this chicken-and-egg problem? The rest of this book will attempt to answer this question, focusing on the crucial role that international intermediaries play in promoting the rule of law along all three dimensions simultaneously.

4

Theoretical Framework

Restoring the Rule of Law after Civil War

Why do some countries successfully transition from civil war to the rule of law while others do not? At the macro level, why do some governments adhere more closely to constitutional constraints while others ignore them? Why do some police forces become more capable and professional while others remain mired in patterns of incompetence and misconduct? Why do some judiciaries reassert their independence while others wither under incessant political meddling? At the micro and meso levels, why do some citizens rely on the police and courts when crimes are committed or violence occurs, while others seek redress for even the most serious grievances through non-state security and justice providers? Among these non-state actors, why do some respect legal limits on their jurisdictions while others defy them?

This book argues that the presence or absence of international intervention helps account for this variation both across countries and over time. In Chapter 3, I developed a conceptual framework for defining the rule of law in post-conflict settings. I described the rule of law as a chicken-and-egg problem that manifests along three distinct but interrelated dimensions: the macro, micro, and meso levels. In this chapter, I offer a theory to explain how the UN and other international intermediaries can promote the rule of law along all three of these dimensions simultaneously. Throughout the chapter I provide illustrations of the theory at work, gleaned from the secondary literature and the UN's own primary accounts of the successes and shortcomings of peacekeeping operations around the world. I begin by reviewing the necessary conditions for the rule of law at the macro, micro, and meso levels. I then present a broad overview of my theory, followed by a detailed discussion of the mechanisms undergirding it. I conclude by considering three alternatives to my theory, which I test in the chapters that follow.

MAKING THE RULE OF LAW A POSSIBILITY

The strength of the rule of law depends on the beliefs and behaviors of three sets of actors: state authorities at the macro level, citizens at the micro level, and non-state authorities at the meso level. At the macro level, state authorities must act within their legally defined jurisdictions; must defer to an independent, constitutionally designated arbiter when jurisdictional conflicts arise; and must abstain from arbitrary arrests, indefinite detentions, and other transgressions. In order for state authorities to abide by these restrictions, the laws establishing them must be clear, comprehensible, and publicly promulgated.

At the micro level, citizens must rely on formal rather than informal authorities to adjudicate crimes over which the state claims both original and ultimate jurisdiction – murder, for example. This, in turn, requires that citizens enjoy relatively easy access to the police and courts. At the meso level, informal authorities must act within their jurisdictions as well, and must refrain from resolving disputes in ways that violate state law. Together, these requirements imply that all actors at all levels abide by shared secondary rules of recognition, adjudication, and change, such that the rule of law becomes a social fact – a reality that all individuals and institutions within the system can count on and plan around.

Obstacles to the rule of law manifest in myriad forms and at all three levels of my analysis: ambiguous or incoherent laws; incomplete information about what those laws actually say; coordination problems between state security and justice providers, and between the state and its non-state counterparts; insufficient access to the police and courts; incompetence and malfeasance among both formal and informal authorities; a lack of oversight and accountability; and personal beliefs and social norms that militate against deference to state laws and institutions. Some of these obstacles prevent actors within the legal system from respecting the rule of law, even if they might prefer to. Others arise because actors do not want to respect the rule of law in the first place. Some manifest at all three levels of my analysis – the absence of information, for example. Some, like social norms, are more prominent at the micro level; others, such as unprofessionalism, are more obvious at the macro and meso levels. But in most cases they are intertwined, each exacerbating the others.

UN missions have developed a repertoire of strategies to shape the beliefs and behaviors of actors at all three of these levels.[1] My core theoretical claim is that UN missions promote the rule of law by acting simultaneously as catalysts for state reform at the macro level, surrogates for reformed states at the micro and meso levels, and liaisons between state authorities, non-state authorities, and

---

[1] My description of UN rule-of-law promotion as a three-dimensional process echoes Anja Kaspersen and co-authors' recommendation that UN missions should engage multiple levels of society simultaneously. They describe these as the "grass-roots level," the "mid-level," and the state or "top" level (Kaspersen, Eide, and Hansen, 2004, 20). These correspond roughly to the micro, meso, and macro levels of my analysis.

citizens across the three levels. As catalysts for state reform, UN missions alter the legal, institutional, and physical architecture of the state – revising laws, redesigning institutions, repairing infrastructure, and recruiting and retraining state security and justice personnel. UN missions catalyze reform along all four links in the justice chain – the police, courts, and prisons, as well as the law itself – using a combination of monitoring, advocacy, and material and technical assistance to host governments. Depending on the scope of their mandates, UN missions may also implement reforms on their own, with little to no host government involvement. These activities typically fall under the purview of UN police officers and civilian personnel, rather than troops or Military Observers. Peace processes create (potentially narrow) windows of opportunity for reform, but states recovering from civil war are typically too fragile to exploit them. UN missions catalyze reform in places where states themselves cannot.

But state reform alone is not enough. To the extent that international interveners are expected to transform weak and war-torn states into stable, liberal democracies at the national level, the foundations of that transformation must emerge at least in part at the local level, in the "political attitudes and behaviors of ordinary citizens" (Mvukiyehe and Samii 2017, 255; see also Stedman, Rothchild, and Cousens 2002, 20). There is no reason to expect that citizens will readily cooperate with state security and justice providers in the wake of conflict, or that their cooperation will simply "trickle down" from efforts to improve state capacity and performance at the macro level. Citizen cooperation must be fostered proactively. The UN does this by acting as a surrogate for reformed states, and as a liaison between state authorities, non-state authorities, and citizens themselves. As surrogates, UN missions temporarily assume responsibility for functions typically associated with states, then perform those functions until the host government is capable of doing so on its own. By substituting for the state on a temporary basis, UN missions demonstrate, by example, the relative merits of formal over informal dispute resolution; sensitize citizens to increased third-party presence in and around their communities; and create opportunities for state officials to claim credit for public goods they did not actually provide.

From a practical perspective, the dynamics of substitution are often mundane, involving routine patrols, public works projects, and interventions to resolve impending or ongoing disputes. These are functions usually associated with states; by performing them on the state's behalf, UN missions instill respect for the "*idea* of the state," even as the reality remains absent or dysfunctional (Chesterman, 2007, 3, emphasis in the original). Through their interactions with citizens on a face-to-face, day-to-day basis, peacekeepers impart new norms that legitimize the state as a purveyor of security and justice, and, over time, reorient citizens' understanding of what order even *is*: centralized as well as localized, mediated by both formal and informal institutions, each with their own legally delineated jurisdictions.

As the process of state reform progresses, UN missions also serve as liaisons between citizens and the state, disseminating information, creating opportunities for sustained, mutually respectful contact, and depolarizing previously hostile relations between them. UN missions also serve as liaisons between state and non-state authorities, clarifying and coordinating their respective roles and instructing non-state authorities in the use of state-sanctioned mechanisms of dispute resolution. By strengthening ties between the formal and informal sectors, UN missions can gradually "pull" each towards greater respect for the rule of law (The World Bank, 2011, 156). In this way, UN missions rehabilitate the state from the top down while inducing deference to it from the bottom up.

But a change of this sort is inevitably slow and uncertain. Especially early in the process, UN missions must incentivize compliance with new legal and institutional frameworks, providing reasons for actors at all three levels to believe compliance is in their own best interest. Peacekeepers must also monitor and sanction non-compliance, using whatever mechanisms are at their disposal – from naming and shaming to physical force – to punish those who subvert the new secondary rules of recognition, adjudication, and change. Over time, however, compliance becomes habitual as actors at all levels learn to navigate the new legal and institutional landscape. Once these habits become self-sustaining, the rule of law becomes a social fact. Figure 4.1 depicts the mechanics of the theory in brief.

My theory departs from previous accounts that conceptualize peacekeeping more narrowly as a mechanism for separating belligerents and resolving commitment problems; that focus more on UN troops and Military Observers than on UN police or civilian personnel; and that emphasize coercion over other mechanisms of attitudinal and behavioral change (Doyle and Sambanis, 2006; Hultman, Kathman, and Shannon, 2013; Ruggeri, Dorussen, and Gizelis, 2017; Walter, 1997). Few scholars have addressed peacekeepers' equally if not more important role as catalysts for state reform,[2] and fewer still have considered the UN's role as state surrogate and liaison.[3] My theory helps fill this gap in our understanding of the way peacekeeping works.

If my theory is correct, then we should expect UN presence to enhance the quality of state security and justice provision, reinforce the independence

---

[2] Howard's work is one of only a few exceptions (Howard 2008, 2019). Doyle and Sambanis argue that the UN's effects on "participatory peace" are transmitted in part through institutional reform, but they provide only anecdotal evidence to support this interpretation (Doyle and Sambanis, 2006, 131–2).

[3] Though this is beginning to change. See, for example, Mvukiyehe (2018); Whalan (2014). Fen Osler Hampson describes UN missions as "temporary stand-ins for local authorities who are unable or unwilling to perform ... needed administrative tasks themselves." But Hampson's account focuses on the UN's contributions to "administration and governance" at the macro level, ignoring its effects on state/society relations at the micro and meso levels (Hampson, 1997, 707–8).

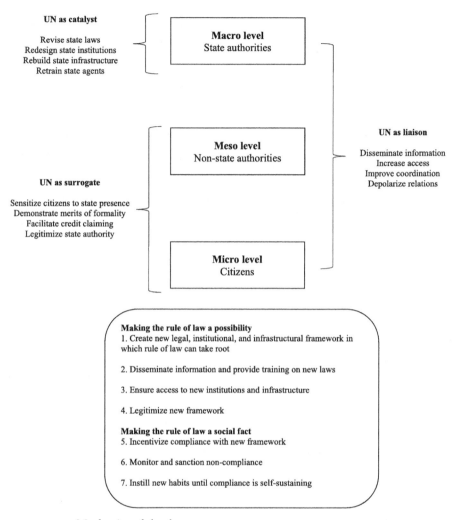

FIGURE 4.1 Mechanics of the theory

of the judiciary, and increase adherence to legal limits on state power at the macro level. UN presence should also increase citizens' reliance on state security and justice providers at the micro level, especially in cases that fall unambiguously under state jurisdiction. Finally, UN presence should inculcate respect for state laws and institutions among non-state authorities at the meso level, thus sharpening jurisdictional boundaries and curtailing the use of illegal mechanisms of dispute resolution. The remainder of this chapter describes the theoretical intuitions underlying these empirical propositions in further detail, providing examples along the way to illustrate the theory at work.

UN MISSIONS AS CATALYSTS

As catalysts for state reform at the macro level, UN missions revise state laws, redesign state institutions, rebuild state infrastructure, and reshape the beliefs and behaviors of state security and justice personnel. UN missions have sought to revise post-conflict laws and constitutions since at least the late 1990s (Fortna, 2008b, 45). While writing laws and lobbying for their passage does not guarantee they will be obeyed, just as amending constitutions does not ensure they will be respected, codification helps create a shared understanding of what the rules of the legal system are, and how and by whom they will be enforced.

Before and during civil war, laws and constitutions are often treated as palimpsests, written and rewritten to suit the whims of successive regimes. The result is a thicket of internally incoherent rules grafted onto one another without regard for consistency or interpretability, incapable of preventing abuses of power – or, indeed, designed to enable them. While UN missions seldom attempt to reengineer legal systems from scratch,[4] reform can nonetheless help reorient these systems towards internationally sanctioned standards of equity and due process. As Martha Finnemore observes, "codifying a new social purpose into a treaty, into a new organization, or into new resolutions by existing organizations are powerful ways to reshape social structures and social purpose." Once created, these rules can "turn the vision of a few into social reality for many" (Finnemore, 2004, 148).

Post-conflict countries are often uniquely susceptible to reforms of this sort. Peacekeeping operations typically deploy at moments of convulsive political change and institutional upheaval. The "extraordinary circumstances of war and its termination both compel and provide windows of opportunity" to

---

[4] To the contrary, UN missions typically abide by the principle of "continuity of the legal system," itself derived from the laws of belligerent occupation. The UN Secretary-General has flirted at times with the possibility of developing "model" legal codes that could be imported more or less wholesale into all of the countries in which the UN intervenes. The 2000 Brahimi Report, for example, urged the Secretary-General to "evaluate the feasibility and utility of developing an interim criminal code, including any regional adaptations potentially required, for use by such operations pending the re-establishment of local rule of law and local law enforcement capacity" (UN Security Council, 2000, 14). But a panel of experts concluded that model codes would be neither practical nor desirable (Trenkov-Wermuth, 2010, 23).

The principle of continuity of the legal system requires that new laws be based on existing ones. From the UN's perspective, this approach ensures that post-conflict legal systems are "rooted in local legal and cultural customs" and "potentially familiar to some of the local population." But the principle has sometimes put the UN in the rather awkward position of resurrecting legal standards and protocols previously abandoned by the host country, as it did in Somalia with the Italian penal code, East Timor with the Indonesian legal code, Afghanistan with the constitution of 1964, and Kosovo with the laws of the Federal Republic of Yugoslavia (which UNMIK abandoned in favor of Kosovo's own 1989 legal code following protests by Kosovar jurists). Moreover, a principle designed to apply to belligerent occupation may be inappropriate for UN missions that are mandated not only to restore justice locally, but also to rehabilitate the local justice system – and that, in any event, may want to avoid being perceived as occupying powers (Trenkov-Wermuth, 2010, 5, 23).

overhaul the state apparatus and revitalize its relationship with citizens (Call, 2008b, 9), and the UN itself has identified the early months of a peace process as the most "opportune moment to work for change" (Carlson, 2006, 2). New elites are elevated to positions of authority; old ones are purged or flee. New institutions are introduced, and old ones are abandoned or revamped. Citizens return from displacement *en masse*, disrupting whatever local balance of political power may have emerged in their absence. The tumult inherent in these transitions can plunge countries back into conflict, but can also prove conducive to reform, creating a proliferation of potential allies for UN missions to recruit, and a variety of potential pressure points for them to exploit.

In Haiti, for example, MINUSTAH advised the government on the adoption of three "fundamental" laws designed to strengthen the judiciary and reinforce its independence from the executive branch (UN Criminal Law and Judicial Advisory Service, 2013). These laws created a Superior Council for the Judiciary tasked with overseeing the work of Haitian judges and prosecutors, and a School for Magistrates responsible for providing academic, professional, and deontological training for justice sector personnel (UN Department of Peacekeeping Operations, 2010b, 13). MINUSTAH then sought "progressive buy-in" for a three-year Justice Reform Plan that included implementation of the newly adopted laws; oversaw the nomination, election, and vetting of future members of the Superior Council; and pressured the government to "modernize" these and other elements of the civil and criminal justice system (UN Department of Peacekeeping Operations, 2010b, 13–14). UN missions have pursued similar reforms in Liberia, CAR, Chad, Côte d'Ivoire, DRC, Sierra Leone, Afghanistan, Kosovo, Libya, East Timor, South Sudan, and elsewhere.

Some critics have accused the UN of favoring "grand legal and judicial reform plans" over smaller, more pragmatic reforms (The World Bank, 2011, 154). While there is some validity to this critique, legal and constitutional reforms can serve as a guide to help post-conflict countries navigate hazardous transitional terrain. In Namibia, for example, UN Security Council Resolution 435 of 1978 called for elections to form a constituent assembly, which, in turn, would draft and ratify a constitution for the newly independent state. UNTAG would oversee the process. The parties agreed to a set of "constitutional principles" in 1982, but these were only interpreted as binding after the Security Council adopted them on the eve of UNTAG's deployment. When the parties to the assembly submitted draft constitutions for consideration, several referred explicitly to the 1982 principles. The assembly eventually unanimously agreed to adopt the principles as the "framework to draw up a constitution." UNTAG monitored the drafting process and alerted the assembly when particular provisions ran afoul of the 1982 principles. Once ratified, the constitution helped unify the parties under a single set of secondary rules, the first of which proclaimed the new constitution to be the country's "Supreme Law" (Szasz, 1994, 349, 353).

UN missions also help restructure the institutions responsible for enforcing the law and dispensing security and justice in post-conflict societies. This can involve creating new institutions, clarifying the division of labor between existing institutions, or integrating previously isolated institutions in the hope of alleviating coordination problems and preventing jurisdictional disputes. In El Salvador, for example, ONUSAL pressured the government to delegate responsibility for public security away from the military and towards the newly reformed police. Under ONUSAL's guidance, the size of the army was reduced by more than half, 100 officers from the top brass were purged for human rights abuses, and a new system of civilian oversight was put in place. These are generally regarded as some of the mission's more significant accomplishments, important not just for assuaging the parties to the peace, but also for reducing jurisdictional ambiguities and increasing consistency between the law as enacted and the law as enforced (Howard, 2008, 114).

The need to preserve the independence of the judiciary while simultaneously linking it as closely as possible to the other branches of the justice system makes post-conflict institutional reform especially delicate but also especially vital for the rule of law. No matter how effective each of these branches may be in isolation, the weakness of one can easily offset the strength of the others. Avoiding these problems requires more than mere capacity building. It also requires coordination among the various institutions whose capacity is being built. In Afghanistan, for example, UNAMA devised a Provincial Justice Coordination Mechanism for police officers, prosecutors, and judges, which served as a forum for addressing deficiencies afflicting the justice system as a whole – the inability of police officers to serve summonses, for example, or of criminal defense attorneys to access detention centers (UN Department of Peacekeeping Operations 2010b, 2011b). Similarly, in Mali, MINUSMA's Justice and Corrections Section established "coordination forums" for court clerks, police officers, prosecutors, prison wardens, and investigating and presiding judges (UN Department of Peacekeeping Operations, 2015a).

UN missions also construct or repair the infrastructure to which state security and justice personnel are ultimately assigned – courthouses, police stations, prisons – while also building roads and bridges to connect rural areas to urban centers. These projects are generally not intended to serve as "humanitarian or long-term development support"; rather, they are designed to demonstrate "early peace dividends" and to expand the state's infrastructural and administrative capacity beyond the relatively narrow enclaves to which it may otherwise be confined (UN Department of Peacekeeping Operations Policy and Best Practices Service, 2012, 224–5). The inability to establish a physical presence nationwide is a perennial problem for many of the world's weakest and most war-torn states (Herbst, 2000). Construction of infrastructure can help these states "broadcast" political power throughout their territories.

In Mali, for example, the 2012 coup d'état resulted in the destruction of much of the state's justice and corrections infrastructure in the north of the country. MINUSMA was tasked with rebuilding in order to extend state authority nationwide. By the end of 2015, MINUSMA had reopened seven of twelve northern tribunals and seven of sixteen prisons, using air assets to redeploy government personnel to these newly refurbished structures (UN Criminal Law and Judicial Advisory Service, 2016). Similarly, in Côte d'Ivoire, UNOCI reopened all thirty-six Courts of First Instance and three Appeals Courts in the aftermath of the 2010–11 post-electoral crisis, and established six legal clinics staffed by 1,800 UNOCI-trained lawyers and clerks (UN Criminal Law and Judicial Advisory Service, 2016). And in DRC, MONUSCO's Rule of Law Section helped over 300 magistrates deploy to their posts in "deep-field" locations throughout the country – places where the presence of the Congolese state was either limited or non-existent (UN Department of Peacekeeping Operations, 2012a, 17).

Finally, UN missions can reshape the beliefs and behaviors of formal authorities themselves, typically through training administered both in the classroom and in the field. Training is part of the mandate of every multidimensional peacekeeping operation on the ground today, and can be conceptualized as a form of "persuasive power" through which international interveners educate, inform, and socialize state security and justice personnel into new modes of operating and new ways of engaging with civilian populations (Howard, 2019, 42). Like many other international organizations, UN missions attempt to transform the actions and attitudes of state officials by "establishing, articulating, and transmitting norms that define what constitutes acceptable and legitimate state behavior" (Barnett and Finnemore, 1999, 713). Training is the mechanism through which UN missions promote this change.

UN training typically blends "hard" tactical skills with "softer," more normative ones. This is an important feature of the UN's approach, as the former may help increase buy-in for the latter. For example, police officers may be more receptive to training in human rights protections if it is accompanied by lessons in forensics and interrogation techniques; prison guards may be more amenable to training in juvenile justice if it is coupled with instruction in crowd control. Moreover, even tactical training may be conducive to the rule of law if it reduces misconduct, and even curricula focused on tactical skills may have normative implications – for example, if police officers learn to be more attentive to the gendered dimensions of crimes when conducting investigations.

Examples of UN-sponsored training programs are myriad. In South Sudan, UNMISS's Judicial Affairs Section held weekly advisory sessions for police officers and prosecutors on legal detention periods and the evidence required to prove common criminal offenses in court (UN Department of Peacekeeping Operations, 2012a). In Sudan, UNAMID trained prosecutors, judges, and lawyers on international fair trial standards, the legal rights of juveniles, and the appropriate application of Sudanese law (UN Secretary-General, 2011b). In Chad, MINURCAT instructed prison wardens on international human rights standards and best practices in prison management – lessons that were reinforced by UN corrections officers co-located at prisons around the country (UN Department of Peacekeeping Operations, 2010a, 12). And in CAR, BINUCA hosted seminars on the newly promulgated Criminal and Criminal Procedure Codes for judges, lawyers, law school professors, court clerks, prison personnel, police officers, and gendarmes (UN Department of Peacekeeping Operations, 2011b). BINUCA complemented these seminars with the nationwide distribution of some 3,500 hard copies of the new Codes (UN Criminal Law and Judicial Advisory Service, 2013).

While most of these initiatives target the macro level, UN missions increasingly use training to reshape the beliefs and behaviors of informal authorities at the meso level as well. In Darfur, for example, rural courts administered by tribal elders known as *ajaweed* historically resolved most disputes outside of urban centers, including conflicts over land and cattle that often proved especially prone to escalation. By 2008, however, armed conflict had forced the closure of every rural court in the region. UNAMID oversaw the reopening of 114 rural courts and trained some 150 tribal elders and rural court judges in state-approved mediation techniques and the legal division of labor between the formal and informal sectors in Sudan. Similarly, in Côte d'Ivoire, UNOCI organized "reconciliation" forums for chiefs in areas prone to inter-ethnic tensions (UN Secretary-General, 2007c), convened seminars on state-sanctioned methods of alternative dispute resolution (UN Secretary-General, 2014a), and held "working sessions" on human rights for traditional and customary leaders (UN Secretary-General, 2008a).

UN MISSIONS AS SURROGATES

As catalysts for state reform, UN missions enhance the state's ability to provide security and justice. As surrogates for reformed states, they instill personal beliefs and social norms that elevate the state's role as a security and justice provider. The rule of law requires that citizens and non-state authorities respect the state's claim to original and ultimate jurisdiction over the most serious incidents of crime and violence – murder, for example. It also requires that informal authorities renounce illegal mechanisms of dispute resolution – for example, mob justice or trial by ordeal. In stable societies, most people obey state laws and cooperate with state security and justice institutions not (primarily) because they fear coercion, but because of their "cultural internalization of the existing legal order." Where internalization has not occurred, new "cultures of law and order" must be created (Kaspersen, Eide, and Hansen, 2004, 9).

But new legal cultures do not enter into a normative vacuum. To the contrary, they emerge in a "highly contested normative space" where they must compete with other norms, beliefs, and incentives, some of which militate against respect for the rule of law (Finnemore and Sikkink, 1998, 897). Host states foment some of this contestation, but so do citizens and informal authorities. Indeed, "sometimes the primary roadblock to norm change is the people within the state rather than the state itself" (Cloward, 2015, 380).

UN missions overcome this roadblock by acting as "temporary stand-ins" for weak and war-torn states (Hampson, 1997, 708) – proxies for centralized power in the absence of a powerful center. Peacekeepers assume roles "normally associated with the sovereign duties of a state," thus blurring the line between international intervention and local governance (Whalan, 2014, 23). By substituting for the state, UN missions reaffirm the "power and importance of the state as a political unit" while simultaneously transmitting a set of "internationally approved norms of domestic governance into the internal affairs of war-shattered states" (Paris, 2002, 650, 655). This process of norm diffusion occurs not just across countries but within them as well, through peacekeepers' interactions with civilians on a face-to-face, day-to-day basis.

Most of these interactions occur in the context of patrols, public works projects, and interventions to resolve impending or ongoing disputes. These activities are important not just because they promote stability, but also because they mimic the state's role as a purveyor of security, justice, and other public goods. By assuming responsibilities that usually reside with the state, UN missions "make an authority claim based on a hierarchical relationship similar in function, if not in origin, to that between the state and its citizens" (Whalan, 2014, 24, 52). While "seemingly routine," these face-to-face, day-to-day interactions can nonetheless have a "profound effect" on citizens' perceptions of the mission, the state, and the peace process itself (Higate and Henry, 2009, 83). In isolated rural communities in particular, where foreign donors and international NGOs generally do not operate and where the very idea of centralized power may seem alien, the arrival of uniformed peacekeeping personnel is a significant event in and of itself – a fact that is often overlooked in studies focused exclusively on macro-level reform (Kathman et al., 2017).

Patrols are the modal peacekeeping activity (Howard, 2019, 141). They are the mechanism through which UN missions provide security and establish a physical presence throughout the host country, even where roads are rough and infrastructure dilapidated. More subtly but more profoundly, patrols are also a mechanism for consolidating and legitimizing host state authority. This is explicit in the UN's own policies, which suggest that "by instilling a sense of security, [patrols] can contribute to creating an environment for the host state to begin reasserting its sovereign authority and re-establishing ties to local communities" (UN Department of Peacekeeping Operations and UN Department of Field Support, 2014, 7).

While on patrol, UN personnel perform functions typically associated with state security forces, and, equally important, typically *not* associated with non-state actors. Like their host government counterparts, UN soldiers and police officers usually carry weapons, wear uniforms, and travel in vehicles distinguished by official institutional insignia. While they exercise some discretion in the way they interact with citizens, they nonetheless follow rules, routines, and standard operating procedures that are typical of formal authority and atypical of informal alternatives. By mimicking state security forces, UN missions sensitize citizens to third-party presence in their communities and offer "social proof" that relying on third parties to provide security is acceptable, appropriate, and advantageous (Cialdini, 2008).

Beyond patrolling, UN missions routinely intervene to prevent the escalation of small-scale conflicts into large-scale crises. In the aftermath of civil war, "skirmishes, low-level incidents, and accidents" are inevitable, and much of peacekeeping involves "on-the-spot, low-level mediation and arbitration" (Fortna, 2008a, 97). UN missions are, in this sense, "constabulary interventions" (Last, 1997, 30). In some countries, this constabulary role is quite literal. In Cambodia, Kosovo, and East Timor, for example, the UN Security Council endowed peacekeepers with "executive policing" mandates that involved "substituting UN police for deeply dysfunctional or non-existent domestic police forces" (Howard, 2019, 145). Peacekeepers could effect arrests, detain suspects, and more generally perform all public security and domestic law enforcement functions while simultaneously recruiting and retraining the local police officers to whom these functions would eventually be transferred.

Given the near impossibility of establishing a fully functioning justice system *within* a peacekeeping operation, subsequent UN missions have not held executive policing powers, though in many cases their authority has approached that of their predecessors in Cambodia, Kosovo, and East Timor. In CAR, for example, MINUSCA was authorized to use "Urgent Temporary Measures" (UTMs) to maintain law and order in areas where the police and courts were absent or ineffectual. A MINUSCA task force was created to arrest suspects and transfer them to the national police, and to oversee the progression of cases through the rest of the criminal justice apparatus (UN Department of Peacekeeping Operations, 2015b). By the middle of 2018, MINUSCA had made 550 arrests under the UTMs, resulting in the prosecution of 167 offenders (UN Department of Peacekeeping Operations, 2018). At the same time, MINUSCA staff trained police, prosecutors, and investigating magistrates to process the cases of suspects detained under the UTMs (UN Criminal Law and Judicial Advisory Service, 2016).

Like patrols, interventions to resolve disputes are important not just because they help stabilize unstable situations, but also because they allow peacekeepers to illustrate, by example, the relative advantages of formal over informal conflict resolution. This is akin to a "demonstration effect." In economics, demonstration effects describe situations in which exposure to new goods, institutions, or ways of life foments dissatisfaction with a previously acceptable status quo. Demonstration effects have been used to explain the economic impact of contact between foreigners and locals in the context of international trade (Kattel, Kregel, and Reinert, 2011, 141), but they may also explain the *political* and *legal* impact of contact between peacekeepers and civilians in the context of international intervention. This too is explicit in UN policies, especially as they relate to UN policing. Through their "independence, impartiality, commitment to UN values, and compliance with international human rights," UN police officers are believed to "create strong positive expectations of host state police, foster popular confidence in the police, and engender legitimacy in the eyes of local populations" (UN Department of Peacekeeping Operations and UN Department of Field Support, 2014, 6–7). In other words, UN policing is designed in part to generate demonstration effects.

Public works projects can legitimize state authorities as well. Paving roads, building bridges, and repairing courthouses and police stations – these activities are intended not just to project state power, but also to build the "legitimacy and capacity of local authorities" (UN Department of Peacekeeping Operations Policy and Best Practices Service, 2012, 224–5). Public works projects can facilitate dialogue between civilians, the state, and peacekeeping personnel. They can also create opportunities for government officials to claim credit for the UN's own accomplishments. Citizens often struggle to accurately attribute credit and blame even in information-rich environments (Johns, 2011), and government officials are adept at claiming credit for achievements over which they have little or no control (Grimmer, Messing and Westwood, 2012). In information-poor environments (like most post-conflict settings), credit claiming is likely to have even starker effects.

Citizens who mistakenly attribute UN-funded projects to the state, or who credit the state for attracting international largesse, may be more likely to view state authorities as legitimate purveyors of security, justice, and other public goods (Cruz and Schneider, 2017; Guiteras and Mobarak, 2015). Even if citizens know that third parties are responsible for providing services, they may reward government officials anyway.[5] Credit claiming may be especially likely in the context of UN missions, which, unlike NGOs and foreign donors, are expected – indeed, *mandated* – to improve citizens' relationships with host states.

---

[5] Recent studies suggest that credit claiming does not necessarily depend on misinformation or confusion. For example, in his evaluation of the National Solidarity Programme (NSP) in Afghanistan, Sultan Barakat finds that even when Afghans are aware of the international origins of NSP funds, they nonetheless credit domestic institutions for the benefits they receive (Barakat, 2009). Andrew Beath and colleagues similarly show that the NSP enhances civilians' perceptions not just of coalition forces, but of the Afghan government itself (Beath, Christia, and Enikolopov, 2013). Jason Lyall and co-authors find that a US-funded cash transfer and job training program in Afghanistan has similar effects (Lyall, Zhou, and Imai, 2020). And Simone Dietrich and co-authors show that information about foreign funding of health clinics in Bangladesh enhances rather than erodes citizens' perceptions of government (Dietrich, Mahmud, and Winters, 2017).

At worst, knowledge of third-party public goods provision seems to have no effect on citizens' perceptions of government. In a survey experiment in India, Dietrich and Matthew Winters find that respondents view government no less favorably after learning that a popular HIV/AIDS program was foreign-funded (Dietrich and Winters, 2015). On the relationship between foreign aid and state legitimacy more broadly, see Blair and Roessler (2018).

Peacekeepers may be especially open to acting in ways that invite credit capture. In Lebanon, for example, UNIFIL officials are explicit that "our goal is to allow the [Lebanese security forces] to assume control of southern Lebanon .... The more credible they are, the more credible we are" (Howard, 2019, 123). Subsequent studies have suggested that UNIFIL's approach indeed helped "build the credibility" of Lebanon's state security personnel in the eyes of civilians (Newby, 2018, 132–3). Credit claiming was a recurring theme in my qualitative interviews with UN officials in Liberia as well. As a UN police officer explained to me, "all of our contributions are to be totally attributed to the [local police]. Everything we do for them, they are supposed to get the credit."[6]

UN MISSIONS AS LIAISONS

Finally, as liaisons between state authorities, non-state authorities, and citizens, UN missions disseminate information about formal laws and facilitate access to formal institutions while aligning informal mechanisms of dispute resolution with their formal counterparts. UN missions' role as liaisons is arguably simpler than their role as catalysts or surrogates, but it is no less important. Citizens cannot report crimes to the police if they do not know how, or if they do not know what is and is not a crime. Non-state authorities cannot adjudicate conflicts within the limits of the law if they do not know where those limits lie. In many post-conflict settings, confusion about these apparently basic logistical and jurisdictional questions abounds.

As liaisons, UN missions clarify and correct misunderstandings about the mechanics of the newly rehabilitated justice system. They do this through a combination of structured workshops, seminars, and public information campaigns, as well as through more casual interactions in the context of patrols, public works projects, and interventions to resolve disputes, which create opportunities for contact and communication between the mission and the population it is mandated to serve – contact that is vital to peacekeeping success, but that generally receives scant attention in the peacekeeping literature (Whalan, 2014, 75, 210).

While seemingly mundane, information can alert citizens and non-state authorities at the micro and meso levels to ongoing state reforms at the macro level, increasing engagement with the reform process and generating demand for more effective state security and justice provision. Information can also reduce the search and financial costs involved in reporting a crime to the police, registering a case with the courts, or cooperating in a criminal investigation (Blair, Karim, and Morse, 2019), thus creating "exit options" for citizens who would prefer to seek redress for grievances through state authorities, but opt

---

[6] JR, Monrovia, October 5, 2013.

not to because they do not know how, or because they do not understand the division of labor between state and non-state security and justice providers (Aldashev et al., 2012). Informal institutions may seek to prevent some of this information from reaching their communities, lest it undermine their power locally (Mvukiyehe and Samii, 2017, 257). UN missions can insure that information penetrates, despite this resistance. Indeed, in many post-conflict settings, UN missions are the only actor capable of disseminating information nationwide.

All contemporary peacekeeping operations serve as vehicles for diffusing information of this sort (Howard, 2019). During Liberia's constitutional review process of 2013, for example, UNMIL printed and distributed more than 21,000 copies of the Liberian constitution, alongside civic education materials designed to educate Liberians about the process and their role in it (UN Department of Peacekeeping Operations, 2014a). UNMIL also disseminated information about ongoing legal, judicial, and security sector reforms via UN radio, pamphlets, workshops, and other mechanisms (UN Secretary-General, 2004a).

In Namibia, UNTAG dispatched staff across forty-two district and regional offices and encouraged them to interact with civilians as often as possible. Many of these interactions were ad hoc. Namibia is approximately 90 per cent Christian; to maximize opportunities for contact, UNTAG personnel often lingered after church services to discuss their operations with citizens. The mission complemented these efforts with daily press briefings for local and international media; skits and plays illustrating "how citizens should expect to be treated by a legitimate police force" and "how to register complaints," among other themes; and the distribution of some 600,000 T-shirts, pins, posters, and other articles communicating the mission's messages (Howard, 2019, 66–7).

More profoundly, information can alter the way crimes are adjudicated and change citizens' understanding of what is and is not a crime in the first place. In East Timor, more than one-third of all criminal cases involve incidents of gender-based violence, typically domestic abuse. But this likely represents only a fraction of the true prevalence of these crimes, most of which either are never reported due to social stigma, or are resolved informally through the intervention of local leaders or family members. In addition to drafting and advocating for the passage of a Law Against Domestic Violence, which for the first time criminalized domestic violence and thereby obligated police officers to investigate and prosecutors to litigate, UNMIT's Administration of Justice Support Unit conducted trainings, workshops, seminars, and briefings throughout the country to publicize the law's existence and encourage its use. The mission cast a wide net, targeting local leaders, health care providers, lawyers, reporters, police officers, NGOs, and, perhaps most important, victims and witnesses of domestic abuse (UN Department of Peacekeeping Operations, 2011b).

As catalysts for state reform at the macro level, UN missions improve coordination between previously isolated state actors and agencies. As liaisons at the micro and meso levels, UN missions similarly facilitate communication and cooperation between citizens and the state, and between state and non-state authorities. For example, in addition to disseminating information, rebuilding state infrastructure, and redeploying state agents to their areas of responsibility, peacekeepers can help connect citizens to the state by conducting joint patrols with local police officers and establishing mobile courts staffed by local and international justice sector personnel.

Joint patrols are a staple of every multidimensional peacekeeping operation on the ground today, designed to foster contact between civilians and state security forces and "[extend] the geographical reach of host state police services" (UN Department of Peacekeeping Operations and UN Department of Field Support, 2014, 7). Mobile courts provide legal advice and adjudicate crimes in places where victims and witnesses would otherwise have to travel prohibitively long distances to register their cases. Mobile courts also serve as venues for citizens to engage with formal authorities. Like joint patrols, mobile courts are now a fixture of UN intervention, having been deployed to rural regions of Chad, Côte d'Ivoire, Kosovo, Liberia, DRC, South Sudan, and elsewhere (UN Criminal Law and Judicial Advisory Service, 2013).

In South Sudan, for example, six UNMISS-supported mobile courts rendered 438 judgments in the span of a year (UN Department of Peacekeeping Operations, 2014a), and processed a backlog of cases in the capital city of Juba over the course of three months in 2016 (UN Criminal Law and Judicial Advisory Service, 2016). In DRC, mobile court proceedings are jointly managed by MONUSCO's Prosecution Support Cells and Congolese military justice officers. In the country's vast hinterlands, these proceedings often constitute citizens' first contact with a government institution. Between December 2011 and September 2013, MONUSCO supported twenty-two mobile court hearings that resulted in 183 judgments and 161 convictions. These hearings aimed not only to reduce impunity, but also and more ambitiously to "instill an emerging sense of trust in the justice system" among the Congolese population (UN Department of Peacekeeping Operations, 2014a, 30).

By building trust in this way, mobile courts, joint patrols, and other relatively mundane activities may help depolarize strained relations between civilians and the state. Criminologists have found that citizens' attitudes towards the police are influenced by their interactions with individual officers (Tyler and Huo, 2002), and that mutually respectful interpersonal contact can repair even deeply damaged police/community relations (Diamond and Lobitz, 1973; Rusinko, Johnson, and Hornung, 1978). Recent research suggests that even a single interaction may be sufficient to produce this effect,[7] and that citizens' trust and cooperation may depend more on the nature of these interactions than on police officers' effectiveness in actually deterring or investigating crimes (Tyler, 2004). Mobile courts and joint patrols create opportunities for contact in structured, monitored settings, potentially assuaging civilians' fears and mitigating their resistance to institutions long perceived as predatory.

UN missions can help depolarize relations and improve coordination between state and non-state authorities as well. In post-conflict settings, the formal and informal sectors often operate in isolation from, and in competition with, one another. Peacekeepers can help rationalize these relationships and neutralize the tensions that often arise in places where the boundaries between state and non-state authorities are vague or contested. In Chad, for example, MINURCAT's Judicial Advisory Unit organized joint workshops for representatives of the statutory and customary sectors in order to foster "rapprochement and greater understanding of the different legal systems." The unit also helped establish an "inter-agency rule of law coordination mechanism" to harmonize the formal and informal sectors (UN Department of Peacekeeping Operations, 2010b, 9).

Similarly, in South Sudan, UNMISS hosted workshops for police officers, prosecutors, judges, and customary court authorities in order to improve their understanding of one another's roles within the civil and criminal justice systems. In Liberia, UNMIL organized a "consultative forum on traditional justice" that brought non-state authorities into direct dialogue with the Liberian National Bar Association, the Ministry of Justice, the Liberian Law School, other members of the judiciary, and the UNMIL Human Rights and Protection Section. The forum addressed "constitutional ambiguity" and the "jurisdictional delineation" of the statutory and customary sectors, while providing chiefs and other non-state authorities an opportunity to voice concerns about the "erosion of their culture and traditional practices" and the "imposition of human rights standards" that conflicted with customary rules and norms (UN Department of Peacekeeping Operations, 2010b, 17).

MAKING THE RULE OF LAW A SOCIAL FACT

INCENTIVIZING COMPLIANCE: A perennial challenge for UN missions is to ensure that the reforms they seek to inculcate will persist after the last peacekeeper withdraws. UN missions do this by incentivizing and monitoring compliance and sanctioning non-compliance.

---

[7] This point is contested. Lorraine Mazerolle and co-authors argue that "a little bit of nice goes a long way" in police/citizen interactions (Mazerolle et al., 2013, 55). But Nusret Sahin and colleagues counter that "a 'quick fix' is not possible when it comes to the issue of people's broader views about the police" (Sahin et al., 2017, 164). Wesley Skogan similarly argues that positive encounters with individual officers have no effect on general confidence in the police (Skogan, 2006). See also Blair, Karim, and Morse (2019) and Nagin and Telep (2017).

Many of the activities that UN missions pursue are in the interest of both citizens and host states: paving roads, for example, or building courthouses and police stations, or training judges, police officers, and other government personnel. Host states benefit from increased infrastructural and logistical capacity, while citizens benefit from higher quality services and better connectedness and mobility. Many citizens also value the information that UN missions provide, which is often perceived as more accurate and trustworthy than domestic alternatives. Non-state actors may come to value this information as well, as in Cambodia, where the neutrality and transparency of Radio UNTAC "contrasted sharply with the factional propaganda that had dominated the twelve-year civil war" (Whalan, 2014, 124). The more benefits peacekeepers deliver, the more receptive host governments and populations are likely to be towards the other, potentially more controversial reforms they are mandated to pursue.

To further align international goals with local incentives, UN missions often implement training or public works projects in response to solicitations from citizens and host states. In Lebanon, for example, after civilians requested additional training for local police officers, UNIFIL's contingent of Italian Carabinieri instructed their domestic counterparts in search and seizure techniques and other basic tactical skills (Howard, 2019, 123). Similarly, in West Darfur, UNAMID partnered with the UN Development Programme to retrain judges and rehabilitate courts in response to a request from the region's Chief Judge. UNAMID also worked with the Language Department of the University of Zalingei to develop a forty-day English language proficiency course for judges.[8] This began as a technical exercise focused on legal terminology related to wills and estate planning, bankruptcy, insurance, and tax and intellectual property law. But at the request of the participants, it was expanded to cover international human rights and juvenile justice standards, and the relationship between these standards and applicable Sudanese law (UN Department of Peacekeeping Operations, 2012a).

UN missions also incentivize compliance by serving as conduits for funding from both the UN itself and the international community writ large. In Côte d'Ivoire, for example, in the first year following the 2010–11 civil war, UNOCI raised $2 million to rehabilitate infrastructure in the justice and corrections sectors, attracting donations from the European Union and the German and US governments, among other donors (UN Department of Peacekeeping Operations, 2012a). UNOCI also secured an 18 million Euro "global justice reform package" from the European Commission to support amendments to the country's criminal laws and procedures, the establishment of an office within the Ministry of Justice to vet and monitor judges, and the

---

[8] The Sudanese legal system combines common and Sharia law; the former is conducted primarily in English, the latter in Arabic. Sharia law covers only a limited number of crimes, however, and only common law incorporates jurisprudence, which is available primarily in English.

creation of a *Maison des Avocats*, among other initiatives (UN Department of Peacekeeping Operations, 2010b, 10).

Similarly, in Sierra Leone, UNIPSIL collaborated with the Ministry of Justice on a 2007 report documenting shortcomings in the prison system, which resulted in the delivery of a $1.5 million grant from the UN Peacebuilding Fund to support the implementation of the report's recommendations (UN Department of Peacekeeping Operations, 2011a). Not all of these reforms will be palatable to host states; some may be outright objectionable. But the UN's ability to harness funds from a wide range of sources, and for an equally wide range of purposes, can provide a powerful incentive for compliance, even where political will is otherwise weak.

More amorphously but no less importantly, UN missions incentivize compliance by acting as "custodians of the seals of international approval and disapproval" (Claude 1966, cited in Finnemore and Sikkink 1998, 903). The UN purports to embody the "collective will of the international community" (UN Criminal Law and Judicial Advisory Service, 2016, 3). This is what peacekeeping scholars sometimes refer to as the UN's "source legitimacy" (Whalan, 2014, 65). While UN missions inevitably face resistance from state authorities that benefit from the status quo, in many cases they are able to establish alliances with actors that are eager for the approval of the international community, and willing to take costly and potentially controversial actions to secure it. For practical purposes, international approval can help states secure diplomatic recognition and foreign aid and investment. It can also serve to bolster domestic support, as international legitimacy often becomes an "essential contributor to perceptions of domestic legitimacy held by a state's own citizens" (Finnemore and Sikkink, 1998, 903).

A similar line of reasoning applies to non-state authorities. Some informal security and justice providers reject the state altogether, but many of them benefit from the elevated legal and political status that UN missions confer, both informally (by engaging with them as interlocutors) and formally (by endorsing laws that recognize their position within a hybrid legal system, as UNAMSIL did in Sierra Leone). In DRC, for example, Autesserre describes how "a local leader with whom diplomats and UN staff negotiated became an important actor in the eyes of the population and other warring parties, because he was seen as worthy of international attention" (Autesserre, 2010, 191). This strategy can backfire, for example by further entrenching informal authorities that reject the state's jurisdictional claims (Barnett, Fang, and Zürcher, 2014; Veit, 2011). But if used selectively and targeted carefully, the promise of recognition can help incentivize non-state actors to comply with rule-of-law-related reforms.

The efficacy of incentives is thus reinforced by the legitimacy that UN missions often (though not always) enjoy. This legitimacy is derived in part from peace agreements and UN mandates; in part from the "legitimacy pull" of the UN Security Council, which has been shown to induce compliance from otherwise recalcitrant parties (Hurd, 1999, 402); in part from the "good offices" of Special Representatives to the Secretary-General in each host state, which UN missions leverage in order to "build and sustain support on rule of law issues, and to maintain pressure on national stakeholders to exercise good governance and implement institutional reforms" (UN Criminal Law and Judicial Advisory Service, 2016, 3); and in part from the competence and professionalism that most UN personnel exhibit in the field (Whalan, 2014). (I discuss the consequences of abuses committed by UN personnel later in the chapter.)

One of the intuitions at the heart of my theory is that the UN's legitimacy is "fungible and transferable", and thus can be "exported by association from the holder to other actors" (Hurd, 2002, 38–9). UN missions, like other international organizations, exercise a form of "delegated authority": they play a prominent role in post-conflict reconstruction and recovery only because UN member states mandate them to do so (Barnett and Finnemore, 2005, 171–2). But I argue that the converse of this relationship is equally important. UN missions delegate authority back to the states they are tasked with rebuilding. This dynamic is most obvious in transitional administrations, but it arises in virtually all multidimensional peacekeeping operations. The UN revises state laws, rehabilitates state institutions, and recruits, retrains, and redeploys state security and justice sector personnel. At the same time, it "acts out" the state in the eyes of local authorities and populations. Through this process, UN missions lend legitimacy first to the idea of the state, then, as reforms progress, to the reality as well.

MONITORING COMPLIANCE: UN missions also monitor the actions of both state and non-state authorities to ensure their adherence to new legal standards and institutional arrangements. Monitoring is central to the concept of peacekeeping (Howard, 2019), which was originally conceived as a mechanism for documenting the actions of belligerents, communicating that information to all parties to the conflict (as well as to the UN Security Council itself), and thereby increasing the likelihood of compliance with the terms of ceasefires and peace agreements. Monitoring in contemporary peacekeeping operations serves a similar purpose, except that it has now been adapted to apply more broadly to state (and non-state) authorities undergoing processes of rehabilitation and reform.

Monitoring is especially important when peacekeepers attempt to induct state security and justice sector personnel into entirely new modes of engaging with civilian populations. In Namibia, for example, UNTAG introduced the British model of "policing by consent," which emphasizes minimal use of force and a more "bureaucratic" approach to law enforcement. To ensure compliance with these new standards, UNTAG police officers accompanied their local counterparts on foot and vehicle patrols and observed their behavior through co-deployment at police stations (Howard, 2008, 75–6). UNTAG also monitored the politicized and deeply distrusted South West African Police (SWAPOL) to promote more "even-handed," "non-discriminatory," and "democratic" tactics (unpublished UN Report, cited in Howard 2019, 69), and established specialized units responsible for tracking the progress of sensitive criminal cases. UNTAG civilian police officers reported misconduct they observed to their SWAPOL counterparts' superiors, and, when necessary, to officials in South Africa, who remained responsible for overseeing SWAPOL's operations. In one instance, the Special Representative even had a SWAPOL commander fired (though this was rare).

In prisons, UN missions monitor the prevalence of arbitrary arrests and prolonged pre-trial detentions – two of the most common abuses of state power in post-conflict settings. In Burundi, BINUB conducted inspections alongside members of the General Prosecutor's office to verify the legality of pre-trial detentions, resulting in the provisional release of 240 prisoners after the first two rounds of inspections (UN Department of Peacekeeping Operations, 2011b). In South Sudan, UNMISS helped register undocumented detainees, renew expired remand warrants, and identify potentially bailable cases. The mission also established liaison officers within prisons and mobile courts, and facilitated visits by judges and prosecutors to prisons throughout the country. The goal was to "increase the level of awareness and change the mindset of judges, prosecutors, and prison officials regarding prolonged and arbitrary detention." Whether or not any "mindsets" were changed, the South Sudanese government did manage to redress over 7,500 cases of prolonged and arbitrary detention within a period of two years (UN Department of Peacekeeping Operations, 2014b, 6).

UN missions also monitor non-state authorities' adherence to legal restrictions on the types of cases they are and are not authorized to adjudicate, and the types of methods they are and are not authorized to use to adjudicate them. In South Sudan, customary courts are allowed to resolve certain classes of disputes, especially non-violent ones, but are forbidden from effecting arrests (UN Department of Peacekeeping Operations, 2014b). Customary authorities routinely ignore this restriction, however, and many South Sudanese detainees have never been charged with a crime that is recognized under South Sudanese law. Customary courts also sometimes apply punishments that are proscribed by law, such as "blood compensation," whereby female relatives of convicted murderers are forcibly given in marriage to the families of victims (UN Department of Peacekeeping Operations, 2011b). UNMISS has been active in identifying these cases, referring them to the relevant statutory authorities, and applying pressure to ensure their resolution (UN Criminal Law and Judicial Advisory Service, 2016).

Similarly, in Liberia, the Tribal Governor Court system exercises jurisdiction over tribal conflicts, with governors presiding over hearings in a variety of cases, including marriage, divorce, child custody and support, and property rights. Tribal governors have no legal training, however, and while they typically mediate rather than adjudicate, some decisions are rendered in contravention of both Liberian and international law. Cases that should be referred to state courts are often routed through tribal courts instead, resulting in a "diversion of a significant workload from the criminal justice system" (UN Department of Peacekeeping Operations, 2011b, 13). After conducting an audit of the Tribal Governor Court system, UNMIL's Legal and Judicial System Support Division helped develop mechanisms to regulate the tribal courts and trained tribal governors and clerks in due process protections and other rule-of-law principles. To complement these efforts, UNMIL audited the progression of cases through both the formal and informal sectors, and collaborated with the Carter Center, an NGO, to train ninety-three Tribal Governors on the basics of Liberian law (UN Department of Peacekeeping Operations, 2012a).

SANCTIONING NON-COMPLIANCE: UN missions complement incentives with the strategic use of sanctions. This is the aspect of peacekeeping that most directly evokes realist conceptions of power. While all international interventions operate under resource constraints, they "do have material means to shape the behavior of many states on many occasions", and, potentially, the behavior of citizens and non-state authorities as well (Barnett and Finnemore, 2005, 176). Most obviously, when authorized under a Chapter VII mandate, UN missions can use physical force to coerce both state and non-state authorities into respecting the rule of law – though, given the UN's doctrinal commitment to impartiality and consent, this typically only occurs after monitoring and mediation have failed.

In Côte d'Ivoire, for example, the UN helped force incumbent President Laurent Gbagbo to concede the violently contested presidential election of 2010 to opposition candidate Alassane Ouattara. The crisis began when the Ivorian Constitutional Court overturned the Independent Electoral Commission's previous decision certifying Ouattara's victory. The president of the Court was a prominent Gbagbo loyalist, having previously served as Minister of the Interior under his administration, and had long been active in Gbagbo's party, the Ivorian Popular Front.

The Court's decision flew in the face of observations from multiple international election observers, according to whom Ouattara was the "almost universally acknowledged" victor (Smith, 2010).[9] UNOCI certified the results of the November runoff and attempted to mediate the resulting crisis, in collaboration with the African Union and the Economic Community of West African States (ECOWAS). When these efforts failed, UNOCI coordinated with French forces to provide military and logistical support to Ouattara's *Forces Nouvelles*, firing on pro-Gbagbo militias and destroying heavy weapons

---

[9] The Court usurped the Independent Electoral Commission's authority by claiming it had missed its deadline to release provisional results. This was technically true but highly misleading, given that a Gbagbo loyalist had physically prevented the chairman from reading the results, thus causing the delay. In overturning the Commission's decision, the Court nullified results of the election in seven of Côte d'Ivoire's thirty-one regions, all of them Ouattara strongholds, effectively invalidating hundreds of thousands of votes with little evidence of voter fraud or intimidation (Human Rights Watch, 2010; Lewis and Cocks, 2010).

depots around Gbagbo's home. Gbagbo surrendered one week after these attacks began, and the Constitutional Court, under pressure from the UN and other domestic and international actors, finally certified Ouattara's victory (Smith, 2011). UNOCI subsequently helped erect a Special Investigation Cell to investigate and prosecute war crimes perpetrated during the crisis. When the Ivorian government threatened to dramatically reduce the scope of these investigations, UNOCI successfully lobbied for the new agency's mandate to be extended and protected (UN Criminal Law and Judicial Advisory Service, 2016).

While the use of sanctions does not necessarily require engaging in armed conflict, it does inevitably involve some form of coercion, military or otherwise. In some cases, sanctions are literal and direct – for example, when UN member states impose economic sanctions on governments accused of violating the terms of a peace agreement. In other cases they are more indirect, as when UN missions facilitate the prosecution of individuals implicated in abuses of power. In DRC, for example, MONUSCO's Prosecution Support Cells (PSC) provide technical advice and logistical support to a cadre of investigators and prosecutors operating in the country's restive eastern provinces, where courts are either incapacitated or non-existent. The PSC program originated in 2010; by the middle of 2018, PSCs had processed some 800 case files involving over 1,000 individuals and resulting in hundreds of convictions, including in several landmark cases – perhaps most notably, the 2017 conviction of Congolese Colonel Jules Becker for war crimes (UN Department of Peacekeeping Operations, 2018). The UN views PSCs as a complement to the Congo's defective military justice system, which is ill-equipped to adjudicate the sheer number of crimes committed by individuals acting in official military or police capacities (UN Department of Peacekeeping Operations, 2012a). PSCs are also perceived as a vehicle for restoring citizens' trust in the state security and justice sectors more generally, "contributing to the gradual building of public confidence in the ability and willingness of national authorities to address impunity" (UN Criminal Law and Judicial Advisory Service, 2016, 7).

Finally, UN missions can "name and shame" those who violate rule-of-law principles, damaging reputations and inviting scrutiny from both domestic and international audiences. Constructivist scholars have long recognized the role that naming and shaming can play in international diplomacy (Barnett and Finnemore, 2005; Finnemore and Sikkink, 1998; Keck and Sikkink, 1998). But naming and shaming is arguably more powerful when deployed in settings where a peacekeeping operation is already on the ground. UN missions have used this mechanism to target state and non-state authorities alike: naming and shaming was equally integral to UNTAG's efforts to curb SWAPOL abuses in Namibia as it was to UNOCI's attempts to constrain the *dozos* in Côte d'Ivoire. The *dozos* devised "laws of their own that did not depend on the state," assuming an "exceptional status within the state" and positioning themselves as alternatives to the state itself (Hellweg, 2011,

18, 221–2). UNOCI investigated and publicly denounced these transgressions (Palus, 2013), and held "sensitization campaigns" to pressure *dozos* to respect state laws in the country's volatile western regions (UNOCI News, 2013). The UN is often criticized for merely condemning actions that it believes violate domestic or international laws. In some cases words alone do not suffice. But especially when backed by the promise of incentives and the threat of sanctions, naming and shaming can shape behavior even when physical force is not an option.

INSTILLING HABITS: UN missions alter beliefs and behaviors through both active, intentional mechanisms (e.g. training) and more passive or unintentional ones (e.g. demonstration effects, which can occur without UN personnel ever explicitly encouraging reliance on state laws and institutions). Over time, these changes become entrenched through a process of repetition and habit formation. For example, while most UN missions do not have an executive policing mandate, international interveners regularly assume responsibility for a variety of domestic policing tasks: investigating incidents of crime and violence, apprehending suspects and transferring them to the host state's custody, ensuring that criminal cases are resolved in accordance with state law, and otherwise compensating for the severe capacity constraints under which post-conflict police forces typically operate (Kathman et al., 2017, 34). This, in turn, can create an expectation among local populations that criminal cases will not simply be ignored, instilling a habit of reporting to, and cooperating with, third–party security and justice providers. Over time, relying on the police may come to seem natural and normal, even when it constitutes a radical departure from the status quo.

Iteration can be a powerful mechanism for internalizing new norms and behaviors (Finnemore and Sikkink, 1998, 906). By inducing actors to behave in ways that conform to new normative frameworks, UN missions can help make compliance habitual, such that non-compliance begins to require "special consideration and psychic costs" (Hurd, 1999, 388). This mechanism is equally relevant at the macro, micro, and meso levels. As Finnemore and Sikkink observe,

> ... many norms, including some of the most powerful ones, have been so internalized that we no long think seriously about alternative behaviors. In this view, actors no longer think seriously about whether "the state" is the best or most efficient form of political organization (it almost certainly is not). They just set up more and more states to the exclusion of other political forms. They no longer think seriously about whether international institutions are the best way to solve international problems (again, a mixed bag). They just set up more and more international institutions. (Finnemore and Sikkink, 1998, 913)

Finnemore and Sikkink are describing internalization of norms at the macro level. But the same process occurs at the micro level, for example when citizens stop at red lights in the middle of the night, or pay taxes when the risk of being audited is low, or – most relevant for my purposes – call the police when their home is burglarized. For many individuals, these decisions are not really "decisions" at all; they are habits. Once a habit has been repeated enough times, the need to reduce cognitive dissonance may force beliefs to follow. In this sense, the new beliefs that UN missions seek to inculcate may develop *after* habituation to new behaviors, and as a consequence of it. As Finnemore rightly notes, "habits create beliefs as much as beliefs create habits" (Finnemore, 2004, 158–9).

Habit formation also connects the macro, micro, and meso dimensions of rule-of-law reform. UN missions' macro-level efforts reinforce, and are reinforced by, complementary initiatives at the micro and meso levels. Legal reform at the macro level, for example, can be a potent catalyst for behavioral and attitudinal change at the micro level: "whole populations do not suddenly believe in human equality or decolonization or liberalism or communism the moment laws are passed. But living within a system of law that enforces behavior in accord with these purposes gradually changes people's views and acceptance of these new purposes" (Finnemore, 2004, 159). As citizens assimilate views that are more consistent with rule-of-law principles, they may become more likely to demand that state and non-state authorities abide by those principles as well, and more likely to take potentially costly actions that advance those principles on the ground – reporting crimes to formal rather than informal authorities, for example, or disavowing the use of mob justice.

EMPIRICAL PREDICTIONS AND RIVAL HYPOTHESES

My theory of UN missions as catalysts, surrogates, and liaisons generates three sets of empirical predictions for me to test, summarized in the first column of Table 4.1. If UN missions succeed in catalyzing macro-level state reform, then their presence should reinforce the independence of the judiciary, improve the quality of state security and justice provision, and increase adherence to constitutional constraints on state power. These effects should be transmitted primarily through the presence of UN police officers and civilian personnel, who are typically responsible for security sector reform and other rule-of-law-related initiatives, rather than through the presence of UN troops or Military Observers, and should be strongest in countries where peacekeepers actually engage in rule-of-law-related reforms (rather than merely being mandated to do so).

These effects should be a function of some combination of legal, security sector, justice sector, and prison reform, and should be strongest when the UN engages the host state through monitoring, advocacy, and assistance (in the form of training and material and logistical support), rather than bypassing the host state altogether. Intuitively, these effects should be strongest early in the peace process, once UN missions are able to shift focus from preventing

TABLE 4.1 *Hypotheses*

	My theory UN is catalyst, surrogate, and liaison	Rival theory #1 UN is negligent and predatory	Rival theory #2 UN crowds out state and non-state authorities	Rival theory #3 UN is time- and resource-constrained
Macro level	↑ adherence to legal limits on state power ↑ independence of judiciary ↓ extrajudicial punishment	↓ adherence to legal limits on state power ↓ independence of judiciary ↑ extrajudicial punishment	≈ or ↓ adherence to legal limits on state power ≈ or ↑ independence of judiciary ≈ or ↑ extrajudicial punishment	≈ or ↓ adherence to legal limits on state power ≈ or ↓ independence of judiciary ≈ or ↑ extrajudicial punishment
Micro level	↑ reliance on state authorities ↓ reliance on non-state authorities ≈ reliance on UN	↓ reliance on state authorities ↑ reliance on non-state authorities ↓ reliance on UN	↓ reliance on state authorities ↓ reliance on non-state authorities ↑ reliance on UN	≈ reliance on state authorities ↑ reliance on non-state authorities ≈ reliance on UN
Meso level	↑ deference to state authorities ≈ deference to UN ↓ extrajudicial punishment	↓ deference to state authorities ↓ deference to UN ↑ extrajudicial punishment	↓ deference to state authorities ≈ or ↑ deference to UN ≈ or ↓ extrajudicial punishment	↓ deference to state authorities ↑ or ≈ deference to UN ↑ or ≈ extrajudicial punishment

violence to reforming state institutions, and when the "window of opportunity" for reform is especially wide (Call 2007b, 11, 2008b, 9).

If UN missions similarly succeed in their role as surrogates and liaisons, then their presence should increase citizens' willingness to rely on the state over non-state authorities to resolve incidents of crime and violence that fall unambiguously under state jurisdiction. Importantly, the UN's presence should increase reliance on the state *without* inducing dependence on peacekeepers themselves. These effects may be a result of information provision, demonstration, credit claiming, depolarization, or some combination of the above. More important for my purposes, these effects should be transmitted at least in part through relatively mundane, routine interactions – in particular, patrols, public works projects, and interventions to resolve disputes, which together create myriad opportunities for UN personnel to engage with civilians at the micro level. At the meso level as well, UN missions should increase non-state authorities' deference to the state – again, without inducing dependence on the UN itself – and reduce their reliance on extrajudicial mechanisms of conflict resolution. These effects should similarly be transmitted at least in part through day-to-day, face-to-face interactions.

These are optimistic predictions, and they run counter to the pessimism that characterizes most recent research on the effects of international intervention on outcomes other than violence. Skeptics have raised at least three sets of concerns. First, while my theory (implicitly) assumes that UN missions are benevolent, peacekeepers have been implicated in numerous scandals involving negligence towards civilian populations in need of protection (UN Office of Internal Oversight Services, 2014), or, worse, sexual exploitation and abuse of local women and girls (Beber et al., 2017). In these cases, the UN's role as a catalyst for state reform and surrogate for reformed states may work at cross purposes, validating citizens' fears of predation at the hands of centralized authorities.

Exposure to predatory peacekeepers at the micro level may diminish citizens' willingness to rely on both the mission and the state. Exposure may also reinforce citizens' loyalty to informal authorities over both formal and international alternatives. At the meso level as well, non-state authorities may exploit misconduct by peacekeeping personnel to justify greater autonomy from the state, ignoring jurisdictional boundaries and flouting legal limits on their power. And at the macro level, state authorities may interpret peacekeepers' malfeasance as a license to engage in ever more blatant transgressions of their own.

Second and conversely, peacekeepers may prove so effective and legitimate that they "crowd out" host states, inducing dependence and impeding the transfer of authority from international to national institutions. While reforms are being implemented, international interveners inevitably assume many of the state's core functions, from protection of civilians to construction of roads and other infrastructure. Indeed, the logic of state surrogacy hinges on international interveners playing these roles. But doing so may also suppress the incentives of would-be domestic reformers at the macro level, on whose initiative the rule of law partially depends. At the most extreme, international interveners risk reducing governments to mere "implementing bureaucracies," and states themselves to "superficially sovereign phantoms" (Veit, 2011, 44). In East Timor, for example, UNTAET aimed to create a self-sufficient state while simultaneously concentrating all executive and legislative power within the mission itself. This "central contradiction" was not lost on the Timorese Cabinet, whose members complained that they were "caricatures of ministers in a government of a banana republic." They had "no power, no duties, no resources to function adequately." They had, in other words, been crowded out (Chesterman, 2001).

Crowding out at the macro level should either erode the rule of law or leave it unchanged. It should have similar or more pernicious effects at the micro and meso levels. Citizens' perceptions are crucial to the success of international interventions (Giffen, 2013), and UN missions must justify their own presence at the same time that they legitimize the newly reconstituted state – goals that may sometimes prove impossible to reconcile. As David Lake argues, effective, legitimate third-party intervention risks inducing dependence on interveners themselves: "earning legitimacy for the international trustee is in tension with the need to rebuild the legitimacy of the nascent state itself .... To the extent that the public attaches legitimacy to the international trustee, the state may have more difficulty in earning the support and loyalty of those same individuals" (Lake, 2010, 3).[10] Berit Bliesemann de Guevara similarly warns of the "severe difficulty" of generating legitimacy for the state and the mission simultaneously (Bliesemann de Guevara, 2008, 363).

At the meso level as well, skeptics have criticized UN missions for their tendency to "neglect" informal institutions (Englebert and Tull, 2008, 119), "duplicate" or "circumvent" the efforts of "locally popular substate groups" (Reno, 2008, 114), and more generally "reject the appeal of forms of authority organized at levels other than the state" (Call, 2008c, 1499). In attempting to win citizens' support, UN missions may inadvertently induce dependence on their own personnel at the expense of both the state and its non-state competitors. In the best cases, non-state security and justice providers may defer to peacekeepers over the state, abstaining from the use of illegal or extrajudicial punishments, but relying on the UN rather than the state to adjudicate incidents that fall under state jurisdiction. In the worst cases, crowding out may provoke

---

[10] This problem is not unique to the UN. Concerns about crowding out hindered the expansion of the NATO-led International Security Assistance Force (ISAF) in Afghanistan, which was reluctant to deploy beyond its original sphere of operations in and around Kabul, lest it contaminate citizens' perceptions of the state. In this case it was the USA that opposed ISAF's expansion, which the UN viewed as essential to the viability of the still-nascent Transitional Administration (Chesterman, 2002, 38).

a backlash among both formal and informal authorities, who respond by breaching legal limits on their respective powers.

Finally, UN missions often face pressure from troop-contributing countries to cut costs and expedite withdrawal. Peacekeepers rely on contributions from UN member states, which are notoriously "stingy," "fickle," and "biased" (Bertram, 1995, 389). At the macro level, the exigencies of keeping the peace during delicate transitional moments may force UN missions to prioritize stability over reform, and may require delaying important but potentially contentious decisions about the distribution of political power – decisions that are necessary for establishing the rule of law, but that may risk a return to armed conflict if they privilege some parties to the peace over others (Call and Cousens, 2008, 3). As Bruce Jones and Feryal Cherif bluntly put it, "the UN is ill-equipped in personnel systems and other terms to deploy adequate levels of civilian staff to occupy the space left by the collapse of national government systems" (Jones and Cherif, 2004, 22). In these cases, peacekeepers may simply reproduce the macro-level status quo.

At the meso level as well, time- and resource-constrained UN personnel may come to rely on non-state authorities to provide intelligence, facilitate freedom of movement, and lower the social and cultural barriers to entry into rural communities. Non-state authorities may then leverage their role as international interlocutors to bolster citizens' loyalty and justify increased administrative autonomy from the state. In the Congo, for example, Alex Veit argues that the UN's presence tended to "strengthen, reconstruct, or modify rather than transcend patterns of indirect rule by local strategic groups" – patterns that the mission itself regarded as "inherently illiberal" (Veit, 2011, 17).[11] The more powerful citizens perceive informal authorities to be, the more

---

[11] Michael Barnett and co-authors model this dynamic as a zero-sum game between state and non-state actors, each competing to capture the "rents" that peacekeepers provide. Peacekeepers prefer stability and liberalization (in that order); to get either, however, they must elicit the cooperation of both state ("primary") and non-state ("secondary") elites. These elites prefer to avoid reforms that might erode their autonomy (e.g. democratic liberalization), but also prefer to monopolize the resources that peacekeepers offer, whether material or symbolic (e.g. the legitimacy that secondary elites may derive from being included as signatories to UN-brokered peace agreements). Barnett et al.'s model yields the rather pessimistic result that, as long as governments have longer time horizons than peacekeepers – a very likely scenario – then the equilibrium outcome is a form of "compromised peacebuilding" that merely reproduces the status quo, illiberal as that may be (Barnett, Fang, and Zürcher, 2014).

Again, this problem is not unique to the UN. In Afghanistan, for example, the US military allied with non-state warlords, mercenaries, and militias, all of whom contributed to counterinsurgency operations against the Taliban. By paying these non-state actors for manpower and intelligence, the USA may have inadvertently emboldened "actual or potential opponents of a stronger central state," impeded extension of the central government into peripheral territories, and even "ostracized a majority of the population" (Suhrke, 2009, 239). Perhaps unsurprisingly, even before US troops began to withdraw, some commentators had already concluded that "delimited warlord rule" was the "outer bound of the achievable" in Afghanistan (Biddle, 2011).

likely they are to rely on those authorities to resolve disputes. Time and resource constraints may also prevent peacekeepers from affecting citizens' attitudes towards the state at all. As Michael Pugh categorically states, international actors simply "cannot transpose ideal forms of politics and governance or repress the local customs and devices of everyday life" (Pugh, 2011, 314–15).

In other words, while there are theoretical reasons to believe international interveners *can* strengthen the rule of law, whether they actually *do* remains an open empirical question. The risk of null or even adverse effects looms large. Ultimately, however, most criticisms of international intervention as a mechanism for restoring the rule of law remain speculative, and the empirical record is limited. Given that UN missions only rarely exercise their mandate to use force it may actually be more realistic to expect peacekeepers to promote the rule of law than to protect civilians or rout rebel groups – goals that often require putting UN personnel in harm's way. *A priori*, there are reasons for both optimism and pessimism. The remainder of this book provides evidence to adjudicate between these competing perspectives.

5

Cross-national Evidence

UN Intervention and the Rule of Law across Africa

Chapters 3 and 4 introduced my conceptual and theoretical framework for understanding the relationship between international intervention and the rule of law after civil war. Chapter 3 characterized the rule of law in post-conflict settings as a chicken-and-egg problem with macro-, micro-, and meso-level dimensions. Chapter 4 then proposed a theory to explain how UN missions and other international interveners can help resolve this problem by promoting the rule of law along all three dimensions simultaneously. The chapter also introduced three rival theories, summarized in Table 4.1. In the remainder of the book, I test the observable implications of these competing theories both within and across countries, using a combination of quantitative and qualitative data.

In this chapter, I estimate the relationship between UN intervention and macro-level proxies for the rule of law across all post-conflict African countries since the end of the Cold War. As discussed in Chapter 2, my analysis improves on previous research by focusing specifically on the rule of law, rather than violence or democratization, the two most commonly studied outcomes in the peacekeeping literature; by measuring UN presence with greater nuance than was previously possible, drawing on data sources that have never been used for purposes of research; by operationalizing the rule of law in multiple ways, using proxies that correspond as closely as possible to the conceptual framework developed in Chapter 3; and by extending the time frame of previous studies to include more recent UN missions with explicit rule-of-law-related mandates, including some of the most ambitious multidimensional peacekeeping operations in Africa (or anywhere, for that matter) to date.

The chapter begins by introducing three new datasets designed to capture the extent and nature of UN peacekeeping in Africa. These three datasets record (1) the number of civilian personnel deployed to each UN mission in Africa using annual budget performance reports prepared by the UN's Advisory Committee on Administrative and Budgetary Questions (ACABQ); (2) the number of civilian and police personnel assigned specifically to rule-of-law-related tasks using annual budget requests submitted to the UN General Assembly; and (3) the extent to which each UN mission actually engages in rule-of-law-related activities using the UN Secretary-General's occasional progress reports. Of these three sources of data only the last has been used for purposes of research, and only in limited ways, as I discuss later in the chapter. The three datasets constitute an important empirical contribution in and of themselves, given that most studies of peacekeeping and the rule of law rely on selective case studies and anecdotal evidence alone (Geneva Centre for the Democratic Control of Armed Forces 2012, 5; Sannerholm et al. 2012, 11). I further complement these datasets with information on the number of uniformed personnel deployed to each UN mission in Africa gleaned from the *Providing for Peacekeeping* (P4P) project.[1]

My theory predicts that UN presence should improve the quality of state security and justice provision, strengthen the independence of the judiciary, curb misconduct by government officials, and more generally increase adherence to legal limits on state power. The UN's impact should be more pronounced during periods of peace than during ongoing civil war; should be driven more by the presence of UN police officers and civilian personnel than by UN troops or Military Observers; should be transmitted through a combination of legal, police, justice sector, and prison reform; and should be strongest when peacekeepers engage host states in the process of reform, rather than bypassing them altogether.

Consistent with the predictions of my theory, in this chapter I show that increases in both uniformed and civilian peacekeeping personnel are strongly positively correlated with the rule of law after civil war. The magnitude of the correlation varies in ways that confirm my theoretical intuitions. While conflict is ongoing, peacekeeper presence is weakly or even negatively associated with the rule of law. This makes sense, as periods of civil strife generally force UN missions to prioritize the short-term exigencies of keeping the peace over the longer-term challenges of establishing the rule of law. Once the fighting stops, however, the correlation becomes more pronounced, and more positive. While the association holds for both uniformed and civilian personnel, it is stronger for the latter, and is stronger still for personnel that are assigned specifically to rule-of-law-related tasks. Police reform, justice sector reform, prison reform, and legal reform tend to be implemented in tandem, and are all positively correlated with the rule of law. The correlations are most robust in the one to two years after civil war termination – a period that the UN itself has identified as the "golden moment" for reform (UN Department of Peacekeeping Operations, 2013, 6) – and in settings where the UN monitors, pressures, or assists host state institutions, rather than bypassing them altogether.

---

[1] See http://www.providingforpeacekeeping.org/.

While these are correlations, not relationships of cause and effect, I minimize potential biases by estimating the association between peacekeeping and the rule of law within rather than between countries, thereby eliminating all time-invariant confounders. I also control for some of the most problematic time-varying confounders, including economic growth, foreign aid, regime type, and the incidence of violence in the post-conflict period. By operationalizing both peacekeeping and the rule of law in multiple ways, and by testing the relationship between them at multiple points in time, I further mitigate the risk that my results are an artifact of particular models or coding decisions. I also address potential confounding due to secular improvements in the rule of law after civil war termination, or to the UN's tendency to implement rule-of-law promotion alongside a variety of ancillary peacebuilding tasks. Taken together, my results suggest that UN missions can indeed serve as catalysts for macro-level rule-of-law reform in Africa, the site of some of the most brutal and intractable conflicts since the end of the Cold War.

MEASURING PEACEKEEPING

Measuring peacekeeping is deceptively simple. Most studies operationalize peacekeeper presence in rather coarse ways, distinguishing between different types of missions (e.g. "robust" vs. "non-robust") with different types of mandates (e.g. traditional vs. multidimensional) while ignoring much of the variation in what UN personnel actually do in the field (Beardsley 2011; Doyle and Sambanis 2000, 2006; Fortna 2004, 2008a; Gilligan and Sergenti 2008; Kreps and Wallace 2009; Melander 2009). I improve on these studies by operationalizing peacekeeping using four different sources of data. To begin, I code the number of uniformed personnel deployed to each peacekeeping operation in Africa since the end of the Cold War using data from the International Peace Institute's *P4P* project. The *P4P* dataset is based on the UN's archival records, and covers all past and ongoing UN missions since 1990. Figure 5.1 plots the *P4P* data across all countries in my sample.

While *P4P* distinguishes between UN troops, police officers, and Military Observers, I combine these three categories of uniformed personnel into a single count. I do this because different categories of UN personnel tend to be very highly correlated with each other over time, expanding and contracting more or less in tandem.[2] Simultaneity makes it difficult to estimate the marginal contribution of each category, since including multiple highly correlated independent variables in a single statistical analysis can produce misleading results. Aggregation avoids this problem, albeit while sacrificing some conceptual precision. While knowing the number of uniformed personnel

---

[2] Among the African missions in my sample, the correlation between the number of UN troops and UN police officers is 0.81; the correlation between troops and Military Observers is 0.85; and the correlation between police officers and Military Observers is 0.68.

Measuring Peacekeeping 93

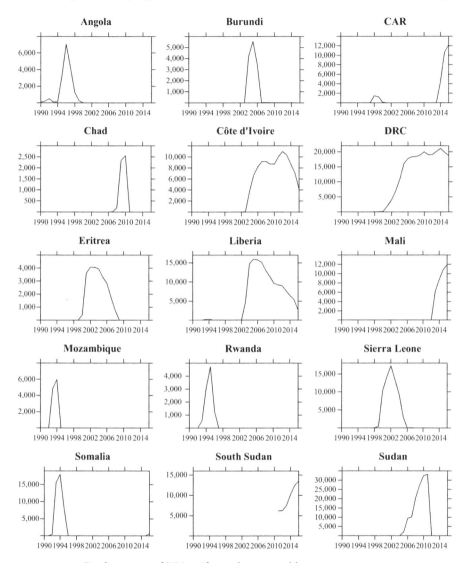

FIGURE 5.1 Deployments of UN uniformed personnel by country, 1990–2016
Source: *Providing for Peacekeeping* project. The y-axis is scaled differently for each country for purposes of legibility.

deployed to a given mission does not tell us whether or to what extent that mission engages in rule-of-law-related activities, it does provide a signal of the mission's capacity to do so. Since larger missions typically enjoy more abundant resources and more expansive mandates, intuitively, all else equal, they should be better positioned to catalyze state reform and thereby promote the rule of law.

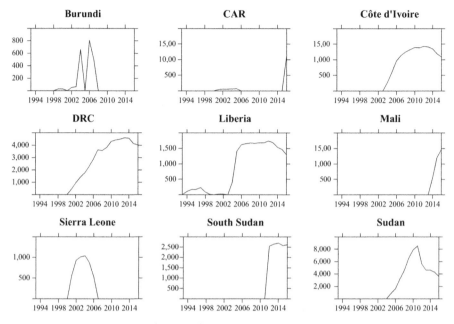

FIGURE 5.2 Deployments of UN civilian personnel by country, 1993–2016
Source: Advisory Committee on Administrative and Budgetary Questions (ACABQ) annual budget performance reports. The y-axis is scaled differently for each country for purposes of legibility.

P4P captures uniformed personnel only. Often, however, it is the UN's civilian staff that is most intimately involved in efforts to promote the rule of law – revising laws and constitutions, retraining judges and lawyers, monitoring prisons, etc. Yet, despite the importance of civilian personnel to the increasingly multidimensional goals that UN missions pursue, there is no publicly available dataset that records their numbers in a systematic way. I therefore draw on ACABQ annual budget performance reports to build what is, to my knowledge, the first dataset of civilian contributions to peacekeeping operations. ACABQ reports are available beginning in 1993, and are unique in distinguishing between eight different categories of UN personnel: troops, police officers, formed police units (FPUs), Military Observers, international staff, national staff, government-provided personnel (GPP), and UN Volunteers (UNVs).[3] For simplicity and to avoid multicollinearity, I collapse the four categories of civilian staff (international staff, national staff, GPPs, and UNVs) into a single count. Figure 5.2 plots the distribution of civilian

---

[3] Some reports further disaggregate between temporary and permanent staff, or between different categories of national staff (e.g. "national officers" vs. "national general service staff"). I do not draw these distinctions in my analysis.

Measuring Peacekeeping 95

personnel across the nine African countries for which budget performance reports are available.[4]

Of course, civilian personnel engage in many activities other than rule-of-law reform. As a more direct measure, I use the UN Secretary-General's annual budget requests to code the number of UN personnel assigned specifically to rule-of-law-related tasks, including police reform, justice sector reform, prison reform, and legal reform. Budget requests are unique in specifying personnel numbers for each component of a mission's mandate, as the example in Figure 5.3 illustrates. Unfortunately, budget requests are only available beginning in 2004, and only capture the number of personnel approved by the General Assembly, rather than the number deployed in the field. But these limitations are not as restrictive as they may seem. While there is always a gap between what the General Assembly approves and what the mission actually receives, in general, the correlation between approved and actual numbers is very close to 1, suggesting that the former is a useful proxy for the latter.[5] Figure 5.4 plots the number of personnel assigned specifically to rule-of-law-related tasks across the nine countries for which budget requests are available.[6]

To code the number of personnel assigned specifically to rule-of-law-related tasks, I search each budget request for any mention of police reform, justice sector reform, prison reform, legal reform, or other phrases that indicate engagement with the rule of law, including the phrase "rule of law" itself. For example, in the UNOCI budget request pictured in Figure 5.3, the third component, "peace consolidation," includes a sub-component related to police reform, and the fourth component, "law and order," includes sub-components related to police, justice sector, and prison reform.

Following a recommendation from researchers at the Folke Bernadotte Academy (Sannerholm et al., 2012), I exclude personnel assigned to DDR, monitoring of ceasefires, or investigations of human rights abuses, unless the investigations specifically target state security or justice sector personnel, or non-state security and justice providers. I include only UN police officers, FPUs,

---

[4] Budget performance reports always refer to the UN's fiscal year, which runs from July 1 of one year to June 30 of the next. All of the other variables in my analysis refer to the calendar year. To avoid reverse causality, I code all personnel numbers as corresponding to the first half of the fiscal year, then lag those numbers by an additional year.

[5] I can use ACABQ budget performance reports to estimate the correlation between approved and actual numbers, at least in the aggregate. Among the nine countries for which budget performance reports are available, the correlation between approved and actual UN troops is 0.97; the correlation between approved and actual UN police officers is 0.96; the correlation between approved and actual UN Military Observers is 0.96; and the correlation between approved and actual civilian personnel is 0.97. This does not imply that UN missions receive as many personnel as they request. In general, they do not. It simply implies that the gap between approved and actual numbers tends to be more or less constant over time.

[6] Like the ACABQ's budget performance reports, budget requests always refer to the UN's fiscal year. Again, to avoid reverse causality, I code all personnel numbers as corresponding to the first half of the fiscal year, then lag those numbers by an additional year.

A/66/753

Human resources[a]	Military observers	Military contingents	United Nations police	Formed police units	International staff	National staff[b]	Temporary position[c]	United Nations Volunteers	Government-provided personnel	Civilian electoral observers	Total
Executive direction and management											
Approved 2011/12	—	—	—	—	25	16	—	1	—	—	42
Proposed 2012/13	—	—	—	—	27	16	—	1	—	—	44
Components											
Safe and secure environment											
Approved 2011/12	192	9 535	—	—	26	9	—	21	—	—	9 783
Proposed 2012/13	192	9 395	—	—	26	9	—	21	—	—	9 643
Humanitarian and human rights											
Approved 2011/12	—	—	—	—	32	73	—	34	8	—	147
Proposed 2012/13	—	—	—	—	32	73	—	34	8	—	147
Peace consolidation											
Approved 2011/12	—	—	—	—	26	108	25	169	—	—	328
Proposed 2012/13	—	—	—	—	26	108	—	14	—	—	148
Law and order											
Approved 2011/12	—	—	595	820	25	25	—	5	34	—	1 504
Proposed 2012/13	—	—	555	1 000	25	25	—	5	34	—	1 644
Support											
Approved 2011/12	—	—	—	—	310	577	44	123	—	—	1 054
Proposed 2012/13	—	—	—	—	309	577	20	114	—	—	1 020
Total											
Approved 2011/12	192	9 535	595	820	444	808	69	353	42	—	12 858
Proposed 2012/13	192	9 395	555	1 000	445	808	20	189	42	—	12 646
Net change	—	(140)	(40)	180	1	—	(49)	(164)	—	—	(212)

[a] Represents highest level of authorized/proposed strength.
[b] Includes National Officers and national General Service staff.
[c] Funded under general temporary assistance.

The actions to be taken by the General Assembly are set out in section IV of the present report.

FIGURE 5.3 Example of a UN Secretary-General budget request for the UN Operation in Côte d'Ivoire

Source: UN General Assembly. "Budget for the United Nations Operation in Côte d'Ivoire for the period from 1 July 2012 to 30 June 2013." ©United Nations 2012. Reprinted with the permission of the United Nations.

and civilian personnel in my tally; while troops and Military Observers are sometimes listed under rule-of-law-related components, they seldom engage in rule-of-law-related tasks, and including them artificially inflates my numbers, especially in missions with more ambiguous mandates. If a particular mandate component includes the rule of law in one year, I code it as including the rule

Measuring Peacekeeping 97

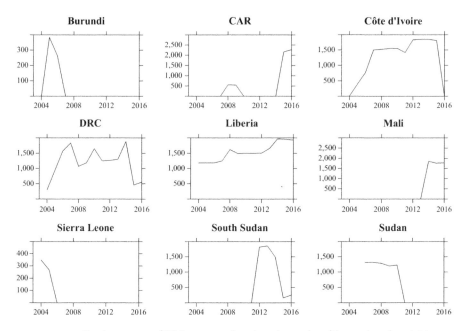

FIGURE 5.4 Deployments of UN personnel assigned to rule-of-law-related activities by country, 2004–2016

Source: UN Secretary-General annual budget requests. The *y*-axis is scaled differently for each country for purposes of legibility.

of law in the next year as well, unless there is clear evidence of a shift in priorities. Figure 5.4 plots these numbers across the nine countries for which budget requests are available.[5]

Finally, even personnel who are specifically assigned to rule-of-law-related tasks may fail to fulfill those tasks if competing priorities arise during deployment. I therefore use the UN Secretary-General's progress reports to construct an even more direct measure of engagement in rule-of-law-related activities. Progress reports are typically published four to seven times per year, and are more informative than personnel numbers, since peacekeeping operations with similar compositions may nonetheless adopt different operational repertoires in the field (Smidt, 2016). Progress reports are more informative than mandates as well, since missions may pursue apparently similar mandates in radically different ways (Holt and Taylor, 2009; Kathman et al., 2017). Unlike mandates, and unlike personnel numbers and configurations, progress reports capture not just what peacekeepers are expected to do, but also and more importantly what they *actually* do on the ground. Unforeseen changes in circumstances may force UN missions to deviate from, or delay progress on, particular aspects of their mandates. Progress reports capture these subtleties in ways that other data sources cannot.

Mine is not the first attempt to harness progress reports for this purpose. My approach builds on research by Han Dorussen, Theodora-Ismene Gizelis, and Andrea Ruggeri, who use progress reports to construct the PKOLED dataset, which captures 104 categories of peacekeeping-related events in all African countries from 1989 through 2005 (Dorussen and Gizelis 2013; Ruggeri, Gizelis, and Dorussen 2011, 2012). PKOLED event categories vary widely, from "establishment of headquarters" to "letter writing" to "election preparation and monitoring." Capturing this diversity of activities is an important improvement on prior research. But while PKOLED offers uniquely disaggregated data on peacekeeping activities, it is also limited in two crucial ways. First and most obviously, because it stops in 2005, it misses what proved to be one of the most important decades for multidimensional peacekeeping in Africa. Second and more significant, because PKOLED is an event dataset, it omits many important peacekeeping activities that simply cannot be coded in event data format.[7] The result is an incomplete and potentially inaccurate account of the activities peacekeepers actually pursue on the ground.

In collaboration with University of Zürich political scientist Hannah Smidt, I used UN Secretary-General progress reports to construct the Peacekeeping Activities Dataset (PACT), which records UN missions' engagement in thirty-seven different activities from 1989 through 2016, ranging from control of small arms and light weapons to voter education to humanitarian relief. We believe these thirty-seven categories encompass virtually the entire universe of activities that peacekeepers pursued during these years. Our dataset distinguishes activities undertaken by peacekeepers from those undertaken by other UN agencies (e.g. the UN Development Programme or the UN High Commissioner for Refugees), other multinational institutions (e.g. the World Bank), international NGOs (e.g. Doctors Without Borders), and bilateral donors (e.g. the Government of Japan, or the US Agency for International Development). We do not code activities undertaken by domestic governments or NGOs. The dataset also distinguishes between different levels of engagement in each activity: monitoring; conducting outreach (i.e. providing information or "raising awareness" among host populations); attending meetings; advocating; assisting (e.g. training host government personnel); providing material or logistical support; sanctioning; or implementing (i.e. engaging in an activity without the host government's involvement).

For each paragraph in each progress report, a team of coders determined whether the mission or some other international actor engaged in any of our thirty-seven activity categories, as well as the level of engagement in that

---

[7] For example, in Liberia, PKOLED records no events involving technical assistance to the Liberian military between 1997 and 2005; only two events involving UN "military or policing operations"; and only two involving assistance with voter or political party registration. A review of the UN Secretary-General's progress reports from these years reveals that UNMIL was in fact much more actively engaged in all three of these activities than PKOLED suggests, but that the activities are described in ways not easily captured in event data format.

activity.[8] While the format of the progress reports varies somewhat across missions, they are always structurally similar, facilitating cross-country and over-time comparisons.[9] To maximize data quality, roughly 40 per cent of all progress reports were double- or triple-coded. Overuse of the passive voice and technical, bureaucratic language often leaves room for interpretation as to the nature of the activity being pursued, the identity of the actor(s) pursuing it, and/or the intensity of the activity itself. Often there is no "right" answer.

Rather than attempt to adjudicate between competing coding decisions on a paragraph-by-paragraph basis, we created two versions of the dataset, one that features all activities recorded by any coder, and another that features only activities recorded by multiple coders.[10] Fortunately, the degree of inter-coder reliability is generally quite high – 78 per cent or above for the activities included in my analysis here – and many of the remaining discrepancies disappear when I aggregate from the report level to the country-year level. The two versions of the dataset provide upper and lower bounds on the activities that each mission pursued, and while my analysis focuses on the first version, the results I report are robust to the second as well.

We believe PACT is the most detailed and comprehensive dataset available on peacekeeping activities in Africa. But it is not without limitations. Beyond the issue of inter-coder reliability, progress reports may be selective and biased, and may focus on activities that each mission deems most important – and, presumably, those that best reflect the mission's achievements. While we are unaware of any evidence demonstrating such a bias, some analysts have suggested that progress reports are especially likely to undercount rule-of-law-related activities (Sannerholm et al., 2012). Furthermore, while progress reports are more thorough than any other potential data source that we know of, they may nonetheless exclude relevant activities. And while progress reports allow us to code the intensity of peacekeeper engagement in various activities – distinguishing monitoring from the provision of material assistance,

---

[8] Coders were randomly assigned to progress reports in order to avoid the problem of "coder fixed effects." The alternative would have been to assign each coder particular missions or years to code, but this approach would have conflated systematic differences between coders with systematic differences between missions or years.

[9] In some cases the period covered by a progress report begins in one year and ends in the next. These cases are the minority: the start of the reporting period matches the year the progress report was published 75 per cent of the time; the end of the reporting period matches the year the progress report was published 95 per cent of the time; and both match 73 per cent of the time. To avoid reverse causality, I code activities as occurring in the first year covered by each progress report.

[10] For example, if one coder records police reform but not military reform for a given paragraph, and the other records military reform but not police reform, the first version of the dataset would record both activities as occurring, while the second would record neither. For the roughly 60 per cent of progress reports that were single-coded, these two versions of the dataset are identical. We randomly selected which progress reports would be single-coded and which would be double- or triple-coded.

for example – they invariably omit some potentially relevant details (for example, the amount of material assistance provided). Variation along these dimensions may be important, but we cannot observe it.

In this chapter I focus on four activity categories in particular, aggregated from the report level to the country-year level: police reform, justice sector reform, prison reform, and legal reform. UN missions engaged in at least one of these four activities in roughly 11 per cent of all countries and years included in the dataset. Police reform was most common (11 per cent), legal reform least so (7 per cent). Importantly for my analysis, the four categories of reform were typically implemented in tandem, and the correlation between them is very high.[11] UN missions engaged in rule-of-law-related monitoring (9 per cent), advocacy (6 per cent), or provision of assistance to the government (10 per cent) in roughly one-tenth of all country-years. Implementation of reforms without host government involvement occurred less frequently (5 per cent of country-years). Rule-of-law reform was pursued most consistently in South Sudan (100 per cent of country-years), followed by DRC (57 per cent), Liberia (50 per cent) and Côte d'Ivoire (46 per cent).[12] It was least common in Somalia and Rwanda (7 per cent each), which is unsurprising given these missions' more traditional mandates.

The fact that these four categories of rule-of-law reform are so highly correlated is important in and of itself. As discussed in Chapters 1 and 2, the UN has faced criticism in the past for focusing on police reform at the expense of justice sector, prison, and legal reform (Carlson 2006, 2; UN Security Council 2000, 7). Since the early 2000s, however, the UN has made a more concerted effort to integrate these various dimensions of rule-of-law promotion. The effects of this shift are evident in my data, to the point that the impact of police reform cannot be meaningfully disentangled from other rule-of-law-related activities. While this is unfortunate for my analysis – ideally I could estimate the marginal effect of each type of activity conditional on the others – it is likely advantageous for host countries, which benefit from the more "holistic" strategy that both the UN and its critics believe is most effective in catalyzing change (Carlson 2006, 2).

MEASURING THE RULE OF LAW

To operationalize the rule of law I rely primarily on two widely used cross-national indices: the first created by the World Bank as one of its six *Worldwide*

---

[11] The pairwise correlations between police, justice sector, and prison reform are all roughly 0.9. The correlations between legal reform and police, justice sector, and prison reform are roughly 0.75, 0.81, and 0.74, respectively.

[12] The disproportionately high percentage of country-years in South Sudan may reflect the fact that the country only became independent in 2011. As a result, there are fewer country-years of data available.

Governance Indicators,[13] the second by Freedom House as part of its *Freedom in the World* project.[14] Freedom House's index is based on reports from country and subject matter experts. The World Bank's index aggregates data from thirty-two different sources, including Freedom House, which together encompass a variety of viewpoints from the public, private, and non-profit spheres. The World Bank's rule-of-law indicator is available for most countries in the world beginning in 1996. The Freedom House index is available for most countries beginning in 2003.

The World Bank defines the rule of law as "the extent to which agents have confidence in and abide by the rules of society, and in particular the quality of contract enforcement, property rights, the police, and the courts, as well as the likelihood of crime and violence."[15] This definition is both broader and narrower than my own, encompassing dimensions of the rule of law that I consider secondary (the incidence of crime, for example) while ignoring others that I view as primary (such as the extent to which laws are public, prospective, and comprehensible). Still, it captures several key components of the rule of law, including the quality of state security and justice provision, and the extent to which government officials and other "agents" abide by constitutional constraints. Among the variables included in the World Bank's index are sixteen proxies for the fairness, efficacy, and reputation of the courts; five indicators for the reliability of the police; and four measures of the independence of the judiciary. The World Bank's definition of the rule of law also echoes the UN's, which similarly focuses on compliance with the "rules of society," and similarly encompasses the behavior of both public and private actors.

Freedom House's definition of the rule of law comprises four components: (1) independence of the judiciary; (2) respect for due process; (3) protection from the "illegitimate use of physical force and freedom from war and insurgencies"; (4) and equality of access to justice for all segments of the population.[16] While also broader than my own, this definition nonetheless encompasses the necessary conditions for the rule of law at the macro level that I posit in Chapter 3.

---

[13] The others are "Voice and Accountability," "Political Stability and Absence of Violence," "Government Effectiveness," "Regulatory Quality," and "Control of Corruption." See https://info.worldbank.org/governance/wgi/. Consistent with the minimalist definition proposed in Chapter 3, I do not consider these other indicators to be central to the rule of law.

[14] The rule of law is one of four indicators nested within Freedom House's "Civil Liberties" index. The other three indicators are "Freedom of Expression and Belief," "Associational and Organizational Rights," and "Personal Autonomy and Individual Rights." See https://freedomhouse.org/reports/freedom-world/freedom-world-research-methodology. Again, I do not view these other indicators as central to the rule of law.

[15] See http://info.worldbank.org/governance/wgi/#doc.

[16] See https://freedomhouse.org/reports/freedom-world/freedom-world-research-methodology.

Moreover, each component of Freedom House's index is constructed using responses to a battery of questions that correspond closely to the conceptualization of the rule of law that I adopt in this book. For example:

"Is the judiciary subject to interference from the executive branch of government or from other political, economic, or religious influences?"

"Do judges rule fairly and impartially, or do they commonly render verdicts that favor the government or particular interests, whether in return for bribes or for other reasons?"

"Do executive, legislative, and other governmental authorities comply with judicial decisions, and are these decisions effectively enforced?"

"Do law enforcement officials make arbitrary arrests and detentions without warrants, or fabricate or plant evidence on suspects?"

Freedom House's definition of the rule of law echoes the UN's as well.

The World Bank's rule-of-law index is scaled to have a mean of zero across all countries in the world, including those outside of Africa. The first row in the top panel of Table 5.1 reports the average rule-of-law score for all conflict and post-conflict African countries. Unsurprisingly, this score (−0.96) is well below the global average (0). Among the countries with scores equal to or lower than −0.96 in the post-Cold War period are Afghanistan; Belarus; Cambodia; Guatemala; Haiti; Iraq; Myanmar; Tajikistan; Yemen; Venezuela after the failed coup d'état of 2002; Bolivia after a wave of violence precipitated by demands for regional autonomy in 2008; Ecuador after the election of President Rafael Correa in 2006; and Georgia until the Rose Revolution of 2003.

TABLE 5.1 *Trends in the rule of law across Africa, 1996–2016*

	Mean	S.D.	N
World Bank			
All African countries during and after conflict	−0.96	0.57	546
African countries during conflict	−1.15	0.57	195
Post-conflict African countries at peace for ...			
≥1 year	−0.85	0.55	328
≥2 years	−0.81	0.55	282
≥3 years	−0.78	0.53	250
Freedom House			
All African countries during and after conflict	4.81	3.14	416
African countries during conflict	3.30	2.57	141
Post-conflict African countries at peace for ...			
≥1 year	5.68	3.06	270
≥2 years	5.97	3.03	237
≥3 years	6.20	2.99	210

Note: Descriptive statistics for the World Bank (top panel) and Freedom House (bottom panel) rule-of-law indices in Africa.

The remaining rows in the top panel of Table 5.1 report average scores on the World Bank's rule-of-law index for African countries experiencing an ongoing civil war as defined by the Uppsala Conflict Data Program (second row), and for those that have been at peace for at least one, two, or three years (third, fourth, and fifth rows, respectively). Scores improve steadily with each year of peace, but always remain well below the global average. African countries that have enjoyed at least three years of post-conflict peace have an average score of −0.78, which is comparable to Argentina during its "great depression" of the early 2000s – a period characterized by riots, the fall of the government, and a default on the country's foreign debt – and the Russian Federation after Dmitry Medvedev was elected president in 2008. The USA has never scored below 1.4 on the index; Denmark, Finland, Norway, Sweden, and New Zealand have on numerous occasions scored above 2. These are important benchmarks to keep in mind when interpreting my results. While the UN may succeed in catalyzing state reform in post-conflict African countries, we cannot reasonably expect it to transform them into paragons of the rule of law, even years after the fighting stops.[17]

Freedom House's index is scaled from 0 to 16, with larger values indicating a more robust rule of law. The first row in the bottom panel of Table 5.1 reports the average for all countries in my sample. Worldwide, the average score on Freedom House's index for these years is 8.33; among the countries in my sample, the average is just over half that. This again confirms that by global standards, the rule of law is weak in African countries suffering or recovering from civil war. Indeed, of the sixty-five countries whose scores fell below 4.81 in at least one year since 2003, nearly half (thirty-one) are in Africa. Even after three years of peace, the average score in my sample (6.21) remains well below the global average. Among the countries with scores of 6 in the Freedom House dataset are Ecuador after the ratification of the 2008 constitution; Ukraine after the revolution of 2014 that removed then-president Viktor Yanukovych from power; and East Timor after the crisis of 2006, in which violent protests and a failed coup d'état elicited armed intervention by multiple third parties, ultimately resulting in the resignation of the prime minister.

The rule of law is a multidimensional concept, and the World Bank and Freedom House indices are broad enough to encompass multiple dimensions simultaneously. As a robustness check, I complement these indices with three narrower alternatives that reflect more specific elements of the rule of law. First, I use the Polity IV project's *executive constraints* index to capture "the extent of institutionalized constraints on the decision-making powers of chief executives."[18] Second and related, I use the Varieties of Democracy (V-Dem)

---

[17] Doyle and Sambanis make a similar point. They operationalize "participatory peace" as a score of 3 out of 20 on the Polity index, which represents only a "minimum level of political openness" (Doyle and Sambanis, 2006, 73). They concede that this is a lenient standard, but note that a stricter definition would leave them with almost no cases of participatory peacebuilding success.

[18] See www.systemicpeace.org/inscr/p4manualv2016.pdf.

project's *judicial constraints on the executive* index to capture the extent to which the executive respects the constitution and complies with the courts. Finally, I use data collected by Drew Linzer and Jeffrey Staton to capture the independence of the judiciary (Linzer and Staton, 2015). The Polity and V-Dem indices relate to the macro-level requirement that government officials in general, and executives in particular, must act within their legally circumscribed jurisdictions, as discussed in Chapter 3. The Linzer and Staton index relates to the macro-level requirement that the courts must enjoy some degree of independence from the other branches of government. These indices are all positively correlated, but not so highly correlated as to suggest they are simply substitutes for each other.[19]

ESTABLISHING CAUSE AND EFFECT

The UN does not randomly decide how many or what types of personnel to assign to each of its peacekeeping operations, nor when or how to initiate rule-of-law-related reforms. Changes in the composition of UN missions and the activities they pursue inevitably reflect evolving conditions on the ground, which, in turn, may be correlated with trends in the rule of law. This raises the prospect of selection bias. For example, if UN missions only decide to undertake rule-of-law-related activities in countries where the peace process is relatively advanced and the rule of law has already begun to improve, then I may overestimate the importance of the UN's role in causing that improvement.

While I cannot rule out this possibility entirely, there are reasons to believe the magnitude of selection bias in my case is likely to be small, and that it may in fact attenuate my estimates of the UN's effectiveness towards zero. The rule of law is integral to the mandates of UN missions deployed to some of the most volatile settings, including Mali, CAR, and DRC. Moreover, with the partial exception of legal reform (which sometimes begins later), the UN generally views the four categories of rule-of-law promotion that I study here as necessary for preventing a recurrence of civil war. As a consequence, almost all UN mandates include rule-of-law reform from the outset, and almost all UN missions are expected to begin pursuing rule-of-law promotion immediately upon deployment, even where civil wars are ongoing or only recently terminated (Sannerholm et al., 2012).

Nor does it appear to be the case that UN missions wait to deploy civilian personnel until conditions on the ground stabilize. As Figures 5.1 and 5.2

---

[19] The correlation between the Polity and V-Dem indices is 0.55. The correlation between the Polity and Linzer and Staton indices is 0.76. The correlation between the V-Dem and Linzer and Staton indices is 0.63. The correlations between each of these indices and the World Bank and Freedom House indices ranges from a low of 0.24 (the correlation between the World Bank and Polity indices) to a high of 0.78 (the correlation between the Freedom House and Linzer and Staton indices).

show, the countries with the largest civilian deployments in both absolute and relative terms – DRC, Sudan, South Sudan – are also some of the most conflicted. Nor does it seem that civilian staff were withheld until violence abated in these countries, or that they were withdrawn after violence intensified. In DRC, for example, the number of civilian personnel rose dramatically shortly after the Second Congo War began in 1998. Similarly, in South Sudan, the number of civilians has remained more or less constant since the country gained independence and UNMISS was established, despite persistent violence. In Mali, Liberia, and Côte d'Ivoire as well, the number of civilian staff surged at moments when each country was especially fragile, and, in the latter two cases, receded as each country stabilized.[20]

More generally, as discussed in Chapter 2, previous studies have found that UN missions tend to deploy to the "hardest" cases both within and across countries (Doyle and Sambanis, 2006; Fortna, 2008a; Gilligan and Stedman, 2003; Ruggeri, Dorussen, and Gizelis, 2018). This is especially true in Africa, where twenty-eight of the thirty-six UN missions established between 1989 and 2012 were deployed to countries with "intense" civil wars that caused at least 1,000 battle-related deaths in at least one calendar year (Sannerholm et al., 2012). While there may be more complex selection effects at work here, if the UN follows a similar logic when deciding when and how to engage in rule-of-law reform, then if anything I may *underestimate* the UN's efficacy.

Nonetheless, the threat of bias remains. Bias would be especially likely if I tried to compare different African countries with different UN missions to one another. African countries vary along an almost infinite number of dimensions, many of which may be correlated with the rule of law. Some of these dimensions change over time – for example, the amount of foreign aid that each country receives, or the speed at which each country's economy is growing. Others are fixed: for example, whether the features of each country's topography – mountains, jungles, rivers, deserts – make it easier or harder for the state to establish a physical presence nationwide (Herbst, 2000). Some of these factors may be correlated with peacekeeper presence as well, for example if "rough terrain" necessitates the deployment of additional UN personnel to keep the peace. Unless I control for these variables in my analysis, selection bias may confound my results.

I address this problem in two ways. To eliminate bias from time-invariant confounders, I include fixed effects for each of the countries in my sample. A fixed effects approach has several crucial advantages over the "pooled"

---

[20] Liberia was arguably most fragile after the signing of the Comprehensive Peace Agreement in 2003, and again after a series of riots in Lofa County killed four and wounded dozens more in 2010. Côte d'Ivoire was arguably most fragile in the wake of the violently contested presidential election of 2010, which sparked a civil war. Mali was arguably most fragile after the National Movement for the Liberation of Azawad seized control of the north in 2012. In each of these cases, the number of civilian personnel increased even as the security situation deteriorated, or shortly thereafter.

analyses that are more typical of cross-national peacekeeping research. Most important, by using fixed effects I avoid making dubious assumptions about the comparability of disparate settings. Rather than compare different countries to one another, I instead compare the same countries to themselves over time, since countries tend to be much more comparable to themselves from one year to the next than they are to any other country at any given time. Pooled models require that we assume away any unobserved, time-invariant country characteristics that might confound the relationship between peacekeeping and the rule of law. This assumption is very rarely plausible (Green, Kim, and Yoon, 2001). Fixed effects models eliminate *all* time-invariant confounders, regardless of whether or not we can measure them, and regardless of their source – demographic, historical, geographical, etc.

But fixed effects cannot eliminate bias from time-*varying* confounders. To mitigate this threat, I control for some of the most obvious factors that are likely to correlate with both UN presence and the rule of law. The rule of law should manifest not just in declining levels of violence, but also in a growing economy, a healthier population, and a more stable regime. It should also manifest in higher quality political representation more generally, with governments becoming more open as civil war recedes. As the country stabilizes and democratizes, foreign donors may also become more generous in the amount of aid they offer.

Any one of these variables may be correlated with peacekeeping as well. For example, the presence of a UN mission may reduce violence and attract additional foreign largess. While I cannot assume away these confounders, I can at least control for them. My analysis includes six time-varying controls for GDP per capita, foreign aid, infant mortality, democratic openness, violence against the regime, and population.[21] Controlling for population also allows me to account for the fact that larger countries generally require larger deployments of UN personnel. These controls at least partially capture the political and socioeconomic trajectory of post-conflict countries, allowing me to more credibly isolate the impact of UN presence and minimize the risk of bias.

I also address the possibility that any positive correlation I observe between UN presence and the rule of law is merely an artifact of "trending" – i.e. improvements in the rule of law that occur endogenously, even inevitably, as peace consolidates, or, worse, deterioration that occurs endogenously as UN missions draw down. The fact that the UN generally deploys more rather than fewer personnel (including civilians) at moments of instability suggests that trending is unlikely to explain my results. Trending is also generally not consistent with the patterns in my data. In Liberia, for example, the years between 2008 and 2014 witnessed a steady improvement in the rule of law, culminating in the country's highest-ever score on the World Bank index in

---

[21] Data on population, GDP, and foreign aid is gleaned from the World Bank's Worldwide Development Indicators. Data on infant mortality is from the US Census Bureau's International Data Base. Data on the quality of democracy is from the Polity IV project. Data on violence against the regime is from the Political Instability Task Force.

2014. But UN presence actually declined during these years, from over 13,000 uniformed personnel in 2008 to just 6,500 in 2014, and from nearly 1,700 civilian personnel in 2008 to just over 1,500 in 2014.

Similarly, Côte d'Ivoire's score on the World Bank index increased dramatically between 2011 and 2016, while the size of its UN mission first expanded slightly – from just over 10,000 uniformed personnel in 2011 to just under 11,000 in 2012 – then contracted precipitously, to approximately 4,000 by 2016. The size of the civilian component followed a similar trajectory. Admittedly, these patterns vary across countries. In DRC, for example, the rule of law has fluctuated more idiosyncratically, improving then deteriorating as MONUSCO grew in the early 2000s, then alternating between periods of progression, stagnation, and reversal. Nonetheless, a positive correlation between peacekeeping and the rule of law appears to be far from certain or mechanical, at least in the countries I study here.

Finally, a note on timing. Ideally I could assess the correlation between UN presence and the rule of law both while peacekeepers are on the ground and after they withdraw. Unfortunately, this is not possible. Today's UN mandates are very long: the average peacekeeping operation lasts twenty-eight years, with a median length of nineteen (Howard, 2019, 23). This, combined with the fact that many UN missions (like UNMIL) retain a residual force even after the end of their mandates, makes it impossible to test whether the UN's effects on the rule of law persist even after the last peacekeeper withdraws. Instead, I estimate the correlation between UN presence and the rule of law both during civil war and one, two, and three years after the fighting stops.

Importantly, in some countries, these models do in fact encompass the period after the UN draws down. For example, the Burundian civil war ended in 2005 – one year after the UN deployed, and one year before it withdrew. Similarly, the most recent Chadian civil war ended in 2010, the same year the UN drew down. In these cases my analysis captures the full trajectory from deployment to implementation to withdrawal. Other missions did not complete the process of withdrawal until more than three years after civil war termination, but still began the process sooner, as in Liberia, Sierra Leone, and Côte d'Ivoire. While I do not have enough data to test the relationship between UN presence and the rule of law in these subsets of countries specifically, their presence in the dataset implies that my estimates are not unique to the years when missions are at their most robust. In any event, understanding the impact of long, complex peacekeeping operations while they are still on the ground is important in and of itself. As Howard rightly notes, "researchers, peacekeepers, and the victims of civil war do not have the luxury to wait" (Howard, 2019, 23).

STRONGER UN PRESENCE, STRONGER RULE OF LAW

Table 5.2 reports the relationship between peacekeeper presence and the rule of law using the World Bank (columns 1–4) and Freedom House indices

TABLE 5.2 *Correlation between the rule of law and UN personnel and activities in Africa*

	Rule of law (World Bank)					Rule of law (Freedom House)			
# of uniformed personnel	0.00 [0.00]	0.01 [0.00]***	0.01 [0.00]***	0.01 [0.01]***	0.01 [0.02]	0.20 [0.03]***	0.19 [0.03]***	0.18 [0.04]***
Observations	191	314	271	240	137	260	228	202
# of civilian personnel	0.01 [0.02]	0.09 [0.03]***	0.14 [0.04]***	0.19 [0.06]***	0.03 [0.08]	0.99 [0.25]***	1.16 [0.30]***	1.59 [0.48]***
Observations	191	314	271	240	137	260	228	202
# of personnel assigned to rule of law	−0.09 [0.03]***	0.24 [0.05]***	0.27 [0.06]***	0.28 [0.08]***	−0.30 [0.22]	1.63 [0.36]***	2.04 [0.38]***	1.89 [0.57]***
Observations	123	225	202	183	121	224	201	182
Any rule-of-law-related activities	−0.02 [0.05]	0.20 [0.05]***	0.15 [0.06]**	0.17 [0.07]**	0.04 [0.30]	2.02 [0.41]***	1.57 [0.55]***	1.29 [0.66]*
Observations	191	314	271	240	137	260	228	202
Controls	Y	Y	Y	Y	Y	Y	Y	Y
Country FE	Y	Y	Y	Y	Y	Y	Y	Y
Years of peace	0	≥1	≥2	≥3	0	≥1	≥2	≥3

Note: Coefficients from OLS regressions with controls and country fixed effects. The dependent variables are the World Bank rule-of-law index (columns 1–4) and the Freedom House rule-of-law index (columns 5–8). The independent variables are the number of uniformed personnel deployed to each UN mission in Africa (top panel); the number of civilian personnel deployed to each UN mission in Africa (second panel); the number of personnel assigned specifically to rule-of-law-related tasks (third panel); and a dummy variable for any engagement in rule-of-law-related activities (bottom panel), which takes a 1 if a rule-of-law-related activity was mentioned at least once in a UN Secretary-General progress report in a given year. *** $p < 0.01$, ** $p < 0.05$, * $p < 0.1$.

(columns 5–8). Each panel reports coefficients from a separate ordinary least squares (OLS) regression with country fixed effects and controls for population, GDP, foreign aid, infant mortality, quality of democracy, and violence against the regime.[22] I code the number of UN personnel in units of 1,000. I test the relationship between peacekeeping and the rule of law among countries experiencing an ongoing civil war (columns 1 and 5), and among those that have been at peace for at least one, two, or three years (columns 2, 3, and 4, respectively, and columns 6, 7, and 8, respectively). My independent variables are the number of uniformed personnel deployed to each UN mission in Africa (top panel), the number of civilian personnel deployed to each UN mission in Africa (second panel), the number of personnel assigned specifically to rule-of-law-related tasks (third panel), and a dummy variable for any engagement in rule-of-law-related activities (bottom panel).

My theory of UN missions as catalysts for state reform predicts that peacekeeper presence should increase state authorities' respect for legal limits on their power, enhance the independence of the judiciary, and more generally improve the quality of state security and justice provision. My theory also predicts that these effects should become more pronounced after civil war termination, as peacekeepers shift from preventing violence to rehabilitating state laws and institutions. The results in Table 5.2 are consistent with these predictions. Regardless of the index I use, the correlation between UN presence and the rule of law is weak and sometimes even negative during periods of ongoing conflict. This is not surprising, since UN missions are constrained in their ability to pursue rule-of-law reform during episodes of violence.[23] In the first few years after civil war termination, in contrast, the relationship between UN presence and the rule of law becomes much more pronounced, and much more positive. The relationship is strongest in the subsample of countries that have been at peace for at least one year, though not by much.

Also consistent with my theory, the correlation between peacekeeping and the World Bank's rule-of-law index is stronger for civilian than uniformed personnel, and even stronger for personnel assigned specifically to rule-of-law-related tasks. To put the magnitude of these correlations in perspective,

---

[22] Given that some of my UN personnel counts are coded by fiscal (rather than calendar) year, I lag them by two periods in order to avoid reverse causality, and lag my controls by three periods in order to avoid post-treatment bias.

[23] While my sample is smaller when I subset to countries with ongoing civil wars, sample size alone does not seem to explain these null or negative correlations. In Table 5.2, for example, the correlation between uniformed personnel and the World Bank rule-of-law index is not statistically significantly different from 0 during periods of ongoing civil war (top panel, column 1), nor is the correlation between the World Bank index and actual engagement in rule-of-law-related activities (bottom panel, column 1). The sample size for these two analyses is 191 country-years. While this is a small sample relative to my other specifications, it is not so small as to guarantee nulls. For example, the correlation between the World Bank index and the number of personnel assigned specifically to rule-of-law-related tasks is positive and highly statistically significant after three years of peace (third panel, column 4), despite a sample size of just 183.

recall from Table 5.1 that the average post-conflict African country scores a −0.85 on this index after one year of peace. A score of −0.85 falls in the 22nd percentile worldwide, and the 60th percentile across all conflict and post-conflict African countries in my sample. With the addition of 1,000 personnel assigned specifically to rule-of-law-related tasks, my model predicts that this score should improve by roughly 0.24 points – enough to place these countries in the 31st percentile worldwide, and the 74th percentile of all countries in my sample. This is roughly equivalent to two-thirds the magnitude of the improvement we would expect to observe in an African country that transitions from civil war to at least one year of peace, and is roughly seven times the magnitude of the improvement we would expect from each additional year of peace thereafter. Of course, an increase of 1,000 rule-of-law-related personnel would constitute a dramatic expansion for most peacekeeping operations in Africa. Still, even smaller deployments predict substantively large and highly statistically significant improvements in the rule of law.

My results are similar when I use Freedom House's index to operationalize the rule of law. The correlation between UN presence and Freedom House's index is null or negative during periods of ongoing civil war, but is consistently positive once a peace process has begun. Again, the correlation is much larger for civilian personnel and personnel assigned specifically to rule-of-law-related tasks than for uniformed personnel. The correlation is positive and substantively large for rule-of-law-related activities as well.

Again, to put these correlations in context, the average score on Freedom House's rule of law index among post-conflict African countries is 5.68 after at least one year of peace. My model predicts that this score should improve by 0.20 points with the addition of 1,000 uniformed personnel; by almost one full point with the addition of 1,000 civilian personnel; by 1.63 points with the addition of 1,000 personnel assigned specifically to rule-of-law-related tasks; and by 2.02 points with any actual engagement in rule-of-law-related activities. This latter correlation is between seven and nine times the magnitude of the improvement we would expect to observe from each additional year of peace. It is roughly equivalent to a jump from the 72nd to the 87th percentile among all conflict and post-conflict African countries, and from the 41st to the 55th percentile worldwide.

Tables 5.3 and 5.4 extend these analyses by distinguishing between the different types of rule-of-law-related activities that UN missions pursue – police reform, justice sector reform, prison reform, and legal reform – and the different levels of intensity with which they pursue them: monitoring, advocacy, assistance, and implementation. Because different rule-of-law-related activities are highly correlated with one another, I run a separate regression for each of them in Table 5.3. I run separate regressions for each level of intensity in Table 5.4 as well, but also combine the three levels that involve some degree of coordination with the host government – monitoring, advocacy, and assistance (e.g. training or provision of logistical or material support) – in order

TABLE 5.3 *Correlation between the rule of law and UN activities in Africa, disaggregating by type of activity*

	Rule of law (World Bank)				Rule of law (Freedom House)			
Any police reform	−0.02 [0.05]	0.18 [0.05]***	0.15 [0.06]**	0.17 [0.07]**	0.04 [0.30]	2.02 [0.41]***	1.57 [0.55]***	1.29 [0.66]*
Any justice sector reform	−0.06 [0.05]	0.16 [0.05]***	0.14 [0.05]**	0.09 [0.06]	−0.02 [0.31]	1.59 [0.35]***	1.33 [0.39]***	0.57 [0.51]
Any prison reform	0.03 [0.05]	0.23 [0.05]***	0.20 [0.06]***	0.16 [0.07]**	0.05 [0.30]	2.36 [0.35]***	2.25 [0.39]***	1.79 [0.54]***
Any legal reform	0.01 [0.06]	0.16 [0.05]***	0.13 [0.05]***	0.12 [0.05]**	−0.01 [0.30]	1.23 [0.33]***	1.00 [0.35]***	0.35 [0.39]
Observations	191	314	271	240	137	260	228	202
Controls	Y	Y	Y	Y	Y	Y	Y	Y
Country FE	Y	Y	Y	Y	Y	Y	Y	Y
Years of peace	0	≥1	≥2	≥3	0	≥1	≥2	≥3

Note: Coefficients from OLS regressions with controls and country fixed effects. The dependent variables are the World Bank rule-of-law index (columns 1–4) and the Freedom House rule-of-law index (columns 5–8). The independent variables are dummies for any engagement in police reform (top panel), justice sector reform (second panel), prison reform (third panel), or legal reform (bottom panel). Each dummy takes a 1 if the activity was mentioned at least once in a UN Secretary-General progress report in a given year. *** $p < 0.01$, ** $p < 0.05$, * $p < 0.1$.

TABLE 5.4 *Correlation between the rule of law and UN activities in Africa, disaggregating by intensity of engagement*

	Rule of law (World Bank)				Rule of law (Freedom House)			
Any rule-of-law monitoring, advocacy, or assistance	−0.02 [0.06]	0.25 [0.06]***	0.22 [0.07]***	0.29 [0.07]***	0.33 [0.37]	2.29 [0.46]***	1.92 [0.60]***	1.98 [0.71]***
Any rule-of-law implementation	−0.00 [0.07]	−0.10 [0.06]*	−0.13 [0.06]**	−0.24 [0.07]***	−0.46 [0.36]	−0.44 [0.36]	−0.52 [0.36]	−0.96 [0.40]**
Any rule-of-law monitoring	−0.04 [0.05]	0.17 [0.05]***	0.13 [0.05]**	0.08 [0.06]	−0.08 [0.30]	1.63 [0.34]***	1.39 [0.36]***	0.67 [0.44]
Any rule-of-law advocacy	−0.02 [0.06]	0.14 [0.05]**	0.10 [0.06]*	0.10 [0.06]	−0.09 [0.31]	1.28 [0.33]***	0.75 [0.35]**	0.44 [0.37]
Any rule-of-law assistance	−0.04 [0.05]	0.18 [0.05]***	0.15 [0.06]**	0.17 [0.07]**	−0.02 [0.31]	2.02 [0.41]***	1.57 [0.55]***	1.29 [0.66]*
Any rule-of-law implementation	−0.02 [0.06]	0.01 [0.05]	−0.04 [0.05]	−0.12 [0.06]*	−0.26 [0.29]	0.42 [0.33]	−0.06 [0.34]	−0.52 [0.37]
Observations	191	314	271	240	137	260	228	202
Controls	Y	Y	Y	Y	Y	Y	Y	Y
Country FE	Y	Y	Y	Y	Y	Y	Y	Y
Years of peace	0	≥1	≥2	≥3	0	≥1	≥2	≥3

Note: Coefficients from OLS regressions with controls and country fixed effects. The dependent variables are the World Bank rule-of-law index (columns 1–4) and the Freedom House rule-of-law index (columns 5–8). The independent variables in the top panel are a dummy for any engagement in rule-of-law-related monitoring, advocacy, or assistance and another dummy for any engagement in rule-of-law-related implementation. The independent variables in the remaining panels are dummies for any engagement in rule-of-law-related monitoring (second panel), any engagement in rule-of-law-related advocacy (third panel), any engagement in rule-of-law-related assistance (fourth panel), and any engagement in rule-of-law-related implementation (bottom panel). Each dummy takes a 1 if the type of engagement was mentioned at least once in a UN Secretary-General progress report in a given year. *** $p < 0.01$, ** $p < 0.05$, * $p < 0.1$.

to compare them more directly to the one that does not (implementation). The top panel of Table 5.4 reports my results when I aggregate monitoring, advocacy, and assistance into a single category; the bottom panels report disaggregated results.

As Table 5.3 shows, the correlation between the rule of law and rule-of-law-related activities remains positive and statistically significant when I separate these activities into their component parts. Again, the relationship is strongest in the subsample of African countries that have enjoyed at least one year of peace, and becomes weaker as the conflict becomes more distant. The magnitude of the association is largest for prison reform, though again, the correlation between this and the other three categories of reform suggests that statistical differences may not reflect practical differences on the ground.

Table 5.4 shows that the relationship also generally holds when I distinguish between the different levels of intensity with which UN missions pursue rule-of-law reform. With one important exception, the patterns are essentially the same as before: a substantively small and statistically insignificant relationship between peacekeeping and the rule of law during periods of conflict becomes larger, more positive, and highly statistically significant among countries that have experienced at least one year of peace, before tapering off slightly (and, in general, not statistically significantly) as the peace process progresses.

As predicted, the exception is the implementation of rule-of-law reforms without host state involvement. The relationship between implementation and the World Bank's rule-of-law index is either null or statistically significantly *negative* across all of my models. The correlation is also null across models when I use Freedom House's index instead. Critics of peacekeeping have long argued that international intervention "crowds out" domestic institutions, crippling them in the long term (Beauvais, 2001; Call, 2008b; Lake, 2010; Rubin, 2008; Veit, 2011). My results lend some credence to these concerns, but suggest they are most relevant when UN missions bypass host governments altogether, rather than engaging them in the process of reform. It is in these situations that a "tight embrace" may indeed risk smothering a still-nascent state (Suhrke, 2009).

UNPACKING THE RULE OF LAW

In my analyses thus far I have used World Bank and Freedom House indices to operationalize the rule of law. These indices are advantageous because they are broad, capturing multiple dimensions of the rule of law simultaneously. But by combining multiple dimensions into a single summary index, they also risk conceptual overstretching. As a narrower alternative, columns 1–4 of Table 5.5 report the correlation between peacekeeping and Polity's *executive constraints* index, which captures the extent to which the legislative and judicial branches are capable of constraining the actions of potentially abusive executives.[24]

---

[24] See www.systemicpeace.org/inscr/p4manualv2016.pdf.

TABLE 5.5 *Correlation between executive constraints and UN personnel and activities in Africa*

	Executive constraints (Polity IV)				Judicial constraints (V-Dem)			
# of uniformed personnel	0.01 [0.02]	0.09 [0.02]***	0.09 [0.03]***	0.10 [0.03]***	0.00 [0.00]	0.01 [0.00]***	0.01 [0.00]***	0.01 [0.00]***
Observations	221	353	306	274	278	389	333	293
# of civilian personnel	0.02 [0.05]	0.77 [0.27]***	0.90 [0.29]***	0.90 [0.28]***	0.00 [0.01]	0.01 [0.01]	0.05 [0.01]***	0.11 [0.02]***
Observations	198	331	288	258	242	360	309	272
# of personnel assigned to rule of law	−0.00 [0.08]	0.32 [0.43]	0.39 [0.51]	0.24 [0.53]	−0.03 [0.02]**	−0.01 [0.02]	−0.02 [0.02]	−0.00 [0.03]
Observations	107	212	192	177	123	225	202	183
Any rule-of-law-related activities	0.52 [0.23]**	1.26 [0.27]***	1.34 [0.29]***	1.29 [0.30]***	−0.01 [0.02]	0.10 [0.02]***	0.13 [0.02]***	0.14 [0.02]***
Observations	230	360	312	278	290	398	339	297
Controls	Y	Y	Y	Y	Y	Y	Y	Y
Country FE	Y	Y	Y	Y	Y	Y	Y	Y
Years of peace	0	≥1	≥2	≥3	0	≥1	≥2	≥3

Note: Coefficients from OLS regressions with controls and country fixed effects. The dependent variables are the Policy IV executive constraints index (columns 1–4) and the V-Dem judicial constraints index (columns 5–8). The independent variables are the number of uniformed personnel deployed to each UN mission in Africa (top panel); the number of civilian personnel deployed to each UN mission in Africa (second panel); the number of personnel assigned specifically to rule-of-law-related tasks (third panel); and a dummy variable for any engagement in rule-of-law-related activities (bottom panel), which takes a 1 if a rule-of-law-related activity was mentioned at least once in a UN Secretary-General progress report in a given year. *** $p < 0.01$, ** $p < 0.05$, * $p < 0.1$.

TABLE 5.6 *Correlation between judicial independence and UN personnel and activities in Africa*

	Judicial independence (Linzer & Staton)			
# of uniformed personnel	0.00 [0.00]	0.00 [0.00]***	0.01 [0.00]***	0.01 [0.00]***
Observations	226	314	265	232
# of civilian personnel	0.01 [0.00]***	0.03 [0.01]**	0.04 [0.01]***	0.07 [0.02]***
Observations	190	285	241	211
# of personnel assigned to rule of law	0.01 [0.01]	0.01 [0.01]	0.03 [0.02]*	0.00 [0.03]
Observations	71	150	134	122
Any rule-of-law-related activities	0.03 [0.01]**	0.04 [0.02]**	0.05 [0.02]***	0.05 [0.02]**
Observations	238	323	271	236
Controls	Y	Y	Y	Y
Country FE	Y	Y	Y	Y
Years of peace	0	≥ 1	≥ 2	≥ 3

Note: Coefficients from OLS regressions with controls and country fixed effects. The dependent variable is the Linzer and Staton (2015) judicial independence index. The independent variables are the number of uniformed personnel deployed to each UN mission in Africa (top panel); the number of civilian personnel deployed to each UN mission in Africa (second panel); the number of personnel assigned specifically to rule-of-law-related tasks (third panel); and a dummy variable for any engagement in rule-of-law-related activities (bottom panel), which takes a 1 if a rule-of-law-related activity was mentioned at least once in a UN Secretary-General progress report in a given year. *** $p < 0.01$, ** $p < 0.05$, * $p < 0.1$.

Columns 5–8 operationalize this dimension of the rule of law using V-Dem's *judicial constraints* index instead, which captures the extent to which the executive respects the constitution and complies with the courts, and the extent to which the judiciary is "able to act in an independent fashion."[25] Finally and relatedly, Table 5.6 reports the correlation between peacekeeping and Linzer and Staton's index of *judicial independence*, which combines eight indicators (including the Polity index) into a single score ranging from 0 to 1 (Linzer and Staton, 2015).[26]

---

[25] See www.v-dem.net/en/.
[26] For simplicity, I do not disaggregate rule-of-law-related activities by type or intensity for these analyses, though my results are similar regardless.

In general, my results are similar when I use these narrower proxies for the rule of law. There are, however, some exceptions. Engagement in rule-of-law-related activities is positively and statistically significantly associated with the Polity index even during periods of ongoing conflict, though the relationship is more than twice as strong in the post-conflict period. Civilian personnel and engagement in rule-of-law-related activities are both positively and statistically significantly correlated with the Linzer and Staton index during conflict as well, though again, the relationship is stronger after the fighting stops. Most notably, the number of UN personnel assigned specifically to rule-of-law-related tasks is, in general, not statistically significantly correlated with any of these narrower proxies for the rule of law.

But this latter disparity may not be as stark as it seems. In some cases the correlation with UN personnel assigned specifically to rule-of-law-related tasks is positive but imprecisely estimated. For example, comparing the first and third rows of Table 5.5, the correlation with the Polity index appears to be weaker for uniformed personnel than for personnel assigned specifically to rule-of-law-related tasks in countries that have enjoyed one or more years of peace, but the former correlations are much more precisely estimated than the latter.

Similarly, comparing the first and third rows of Table 5.6, the correlation with the Linzer and Staton index is larger for personnel assigned specifically to rule-of-law-related tasks than for uniformed personnel in countries that have experienced at least one or two years of peace. But again, the latter correlations are much more precisely estimated than the former. These discrepancies notwithstanding, my results in Tables 5.5 and 5.6 suggest that, in general, UN presence is consistently positively correlated with the independence of the judiciary and the robustness of executive constraints. In other words, UN presence is associated not just with general indicators for the rule of law, but with these more specific aspects as well.

ISOLATING RULE-OF-LAW REFORM FROM OTHER UN ACTIVITIES

Or course, rule-of-law reform is just one dimension of the increasingly multidimensional mandates that peacekeeping operations are expected to fulfill. How important is it for the UN to engage in rule-of-law-related activities in the field – rewriting laws, restructuring police forces, or reforming courts and prisons? My analyses thus far suggest that the mere presence of uniformed and civilian personnel may be sufficient to strengthen the rule of law. Does it matter whether or not these personnel perform functions that are actually related to the rule of law? For example, must the UN engage in police reform in order to reduce arbitrary arrests and extrajudicial punishments? Must it engage in justice sector reform in order to enhance the independence of the judiciary? Might we expect

Isolating Rule-of-Law Reform from Other UN Activities

to observe similar correlations between the rule of law and more "traditional" peacekeeping activities?

Answering these questions is challenging for at least two reasons, one theoretical and one empirical. First, theoretically, even activities that fall outside the scope of rule-of-law reform might nonetheless have rule-of-law-enhancing effects, if only indirectly. For example, efforts to stimulate economic growth may involve legal and institutional reforms, which may, in turn, increase the fairness and transparency of state laws and improve the performance of state institutions. Second, empirically, most UN missions that are mandated to promote the rule of law are also mandated to protect civilians, deliver humanitarian relief, educate voters, and facilitate the return of refugees, among myriad other tasks. Even if these activities do not themselves affect the rule of law, the fact that they are implemented simultaneously with rule-of-law-related activities makes it all but impossible to disentangle their effects.

Isolating the impact of rule-of-law reform requires data on an activity that is not likely to affect the rule of law, and that is only weakly correlated with activities that are. In PACT, the activities that best meet these requirements are related to monitoring and enforcement of arms embargoes. The UN has imposed arms embargoes on twenty-three countries,[27] often (but not always) in conjunction with the deployment of a peacekeeping operation. Some UN arms embargoes target specific actors: UNITA in Angola, for example, or the Taliban in Afghanistan. Others target "non-governmental forces" more generally, as in Liberia, Sierra Leone, and DRC. Importantly, however, even more comprehensive embargoes may permit arms transfers to state security forces, as in Côte d'Ivoire and Somalia (since 2007). This suggests that while arms embargoes may disrupt the activities of militias and rebel groups – many of which purchase their weapons through black markets anyway – in most cases they are unlikely to affect host country police forces. They are similarly unlikely to affect host country laws, courts, or prisons, or other dimensions of the rule of law.[28] The correlation between the rule of law and UN arms embargoes thus serves as a sort of "placebo test" for my theory.

Arms embargoes are typical of more traditional peacekeeping operations, which usually do not include rule-of-law promotion in their mandates. Embargoes may be included in the mandates of multidimensional missions as well, though this varies. Intuitively then, we should expect the correlation between arms embargoes and rule-of-law-related activities to be relatively weak – which,

---

[27] This number increases to 24 if I include non-mandatory arms embargoes as well. See https://www.sipri.org/databases/embargoes. The UN also sometimes attempts to enforce arms embargoes imposed by other international organizations.

[28] Of course, even arms embargoes could conceivably affect the rule of law through some other mechanism. I focus on arms embargoes because they are *relatively* unlikely to affect the rule of law, not because they are *certain* not to.

indeed, it is. In PACT, the correlation between embargo-related activities and rule-of-law-related activities is 0.39. While still positive, this is much smaller than the correlation between rule-of-law-related activities and almost all other activities in the dataset, such as the provision of humanitarian relief (0.86), promotion of public health (0.79), or support for economic development (0.64). The weakness of this correlation allows me to include indicators for both embargo-related activities and rule-of-law-related activities in the same model. This, in turn, allows me to test whether the latter are more robustly correlated with the rule of law than the former, as my theory predicts.

My results are consistent with this prediction. Table 5.7 reports the correlation between embargo-related activities and the World Bank and Freedom House rule-of-law indices. (For compactness I do not report results using the Polity, V-Dem, or Linzer and Staton indices, but they are similar to my findings here.) Columns 1–4 report the correlation between each index and engagement in embargo-related activities alone; columns 5–8 report correlations conditional on engaging in rule-of-law-related activities as well. The correlation between the World Bank index and embargo-related activities is null or negative across models. The correlation between the Freedom House index and embargo-related activities is positive and statistically significant after one year of peace, but smaller and no longer statistically significant when I condition on rule-of-law-related activities. With one exception (during an ongoing civil war when using the World Bank index), the correlation with the rule of law is consistently much larger for rule-of-law-related activities than for embargo-related activities. These results confirm the rather intuitive proposition that promoting the rule of law requires actual attempts at rule-of-law promotion.

My findings in this chapter provide empirical evidence to support the theoretical predictions outlined in Chapter 4. The association between UN presence and the rule of law is robustly positive in African countries recovering from civil war, regardless of how I measure UN presence, and regardless of how I measure the rule of law. The correlation is generally (though not always) strongest for civilian personnel and personnel assigned specifically to rule-of-law-related tasks, and is consistent across four different categories of rule-of-law-related activities. The correlation is also strongest when UN missions engage state authorities and institutions in the process of reform, rather than bypassing them altogether. Finally, the correlation is generally null or even negative during ongoing civil war, and is most robust during the "windows of opportunity for institutional reforms" that emerge in the early days of the peace process (Call, 2007b, 11). My results are inconsistent with rival theories suggesting that UN missions are too predatory (Beber et al., 2017), too intrusive (Lake, 2010), or too resource-constrained to improve the rule of law (Jones and Cherif, 2004). While I cannot rule out the possibility of selection bias entirely,

TABLE 5.7 *Placebo test correlation between the rule of law and UN arms embargoes*

	Rule of law (World Bank)							
Any arms-embargo-related activities	−0.19 [0.10]*	0.12 [0.07]	0.05 [0.09]	−0.05 [0.11]	−0.19 [0.10]*	0.06 [0.08]	0.03 [0.09]	−0.05 [0.11]
Any rule-of-law-related activities					0.01 [0.05]	0.19 [0.06]***	0.14 [0.06]**	0.17 [0.07]**
Observations	191	314	271	240	191	314	271	240
Controls	Y	Y	Y	Y	Y	Y	Y	Y
Country FE	Y	Y	Y	Y	Y	Y	Y	Y
Years of peace	0	≥1	≥2	≥3	0	≥1	≥2	≥3

Note: Coefficients from OLS regressions with controls and country fixed effects. The dependent variable is the World Bank rule-of-law index. The independent variable in columns 1–4 is a dummy for any engagement in arms-embargo-related activities, which takes a 1 if an arms-embargo-related activity was mentioned at least once in a UN Secretary-General progress report in a given year. The independent variables in columns 5–6 are a dummy for any engagement in arms-embargo-related activities and another dummy for any engagement in rule-of-law-related activities. *** $p < 0.01$, ** $p < 0.05$, * $p < 0.1$.

TABLE 5.7 *Placebo test correlation between the rule of law and UN arms embargoes (cont.)*

	Rule of law (Freedom House)					
Any arms-embargo-related activities	0.40 [0.55]	1.00 [0.46]**	0.32 [0.54]	−0.10 [0.62]	0.40 [0.55]	0.35 [0.46]	0.09 [0.54]	−0.08 [0.62]
Any rule-of-law-related activities					0.02 [0.30]	1.92 [0.43]***	1.55 [0.56]***	1.28 [0.66]*
Observations	137	260	228	202	137	260	228	202
Controls	Y	Y	Y	Y	Y	Y	Y	Y
Country FE	Y	Y	Y	Y	Y	Y	Y	Y
Years of peace	0	≥1	≥2	≥3	0	≥1	≥2	≥3

Note: Coefficients from OLS regressions with controls and country fixed effects. The dependent variable is the Freedom House rule-of-law index. The independent variable in columns 1–4 is a dummy for any engagement in arms-embargo-related activities, which takes a 1 if an arms-embargo-related activity was mentioned at least once in a UN Secretary-General progress report in a given year. The independent variables in columns 5–6 are a dummy for any engagement in arms-embargo-related activities and another dummy for any engagement in rule-of-law-related activities. *** $p < 0.01$, ** $p < 0.05$, * $p < 0.1$.

I mitigate some of the most problematic time-varying confounders through my use of controls, and I eliminate all time-invariant confounders through my use of fixed effects. Taken together, my results suggest that UN missions have an important role to play in establishing the macro-conditions for the rule of law after civil war. I turn to the micro-foundations of this relationship in the chapters that follow.

6

Sub-national Evidence I

The Rule of Law and Its Discontents in Liberia

In Chapter 5 I used cross-national data spanning thirty-three post-conflict African countries to show that UN presence is robustly positively correlated with the rule of law after civil war. The correlation is stronger for civilian staff than for uniformed personnel, and stronger when the UN engages host states in the process of reform rather than bypassing them altogether. Unsurprisingly, the correlation is null or even negative during periods of ongoing conflict, but becomes consistently positive after a peace process has begun. My findings in Chapter 5 focus on the UN's impact on the rule of law at the macro level – i.e. the quality of state laws and institutions and the behavior of state officials. In the next three chapters, I explore the micro- and meso-level effects of UN intervention through a detailed, mixed methods case study of Liberia. This chapter introduces the Liberian case, providing context and motivation for the analyses that follow in Chapters 7 and 8.

I begin by arguing that Liberia is both a hard and a crucial case for testing the impact of UN intervention on the rule of law. I then trace the trajectory of the rule of law in Liberia from the country's founding to the present, focusing in particular on the ongoing contest between statutory (formal, state) institutions at the macro level and customary (informal, non-state) ones at the meso level. I describe how this contest evolved during fourteen years of civil war, which culminated in the deployment of the UN Mission in Liberia (UNMIL) in 2003. I then discuss the challenges to the rule of law that UNMIL faced at the start of its mandate, and the strategies it adopted to confront them.

While I will focus on estimating UNMIL's impact on the rule of law at the micro and meso levels, for completeness, and because the mission's macro-, micro-, and meso-level efforts were interrelated, I discuss all three dimensions here. My account draws on secondary sources and original primary interviews conducted with dozens of Liberian citizens, local leaders, and civil society representatives, as well as with government and UN personnel.[1]

LIBERIA AS A HARD BUT CRUCIAL CASE

Liberia is a small West African nation still struggling to overcome long legacies of internal colonialism, autocracy, and civil war. It is also in many respects a hard case for testing the impact of international intervention on the rule of law. By the end of the civil wars that ravaged the country from 1989 to 2003, Liberia was a "broken state whose key infrastructure, physical and social, [had] been destroyed by years of fighting and self-interested political leadership and turmoil" (International Crisis Group, 2003a, i). One account went so far as to describe Liberia as the "most glaring world example of a 'failed state' supported by international donors and a large United Nations peacekeeping force" (Sisk and Risley, 2005, 34).

When UNMIL deployed in 2003, the prospects for establishing the rule of law in Liberia must have seemed almost hopelessly dim. The police and courts were broken, tasked with enforcing laws that were outdated and incoherent. State authorities routinely ignored legal limits on their power. Citizens (rightly) feared aggression at the hands of formal security and justice institutions, and typically opted to rely on informal alternatives. The boundaries separating the formal and informal sectors were (and are) ambiguous, and jurisdictional conflicts were (and remain) endemic. While UNMIL had the advantage of being large relative to the population of the country,[2] size alone is unlikely to produce the transformations necessary to cultivate the rule of law in a setting where it had never taken root before (Whalan, 2014).

Liberia is also a crucial case from the perspective of the UN and the international community writ large. In 2003, Liberia was viewed as the "eye of the regional storm" in West Africa (International Crisis Group, 2003b). Stabilizing Liberia was seen as key to building peace in the tumultuous Mano River Basin region, which comprises Liberia, Guinea, Sierra Leone, and Côte d'Ivoire. The UN responded by mobilizing what was, at the time, the largest peacekeeping operation in the institution's history, with 15,000 troops, over 1,100 police officers, and hundreds of civilian personnel. UNMIL was also the first mission to adopt the more holistic approach to rule-of-law promotion advocated by the 2000 Brahimi Report, combining security sector, justice sector, prison, and legal reform. After its high-profile failures in Somalia and Rwanda, and amid the perennial challenges of peacekeeping in DRC and elsewhere,

---

[1] I describe my sampling frame for these interviews in more detail in Chapter 7.
[2] Liberia has a land mass of approximately 43,000 square miles, slightly smaller than the state of Pennsylvania. The 2008 census estimated the population at just under 3.5 million, though this number was likely smaller when the UN first deployed.

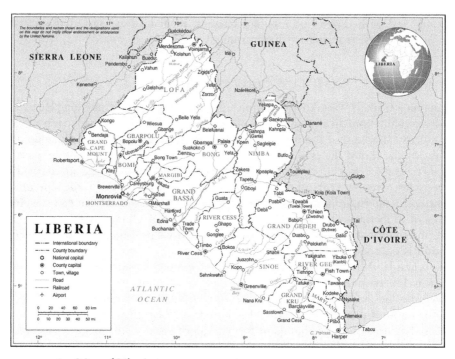

FIGURE 6.1 Map of Liberia
Source: UN Cartographic Section. Map No. 3775 Rev. 9, September 2014.

the UN was desperate for a success story in Africa. Liberia was to be that success story.

The Liberian case is also advantageous from an analytical perspective, given the many similarities between UNMIL and other missions in the region (Mvukiyehe and Samii, 2017). UNMIL's mandate was "quite standard" for missions of its kind (Howard, 2008, 312). While it was deployed under a robust Chapter VII mandate, so too were many recent UN missions in Africa, including MONUC in DRC, UNAMSIL in Sierra Leone, UNOSOM II in Somalia, and UNOCI in Côte d'Ivoire. Moreover, like most peacekeeping operations, UNMIL rarely resorted to the use of physical force in pursuit of its mandate (Howard, 2019). Like other UN missions, UNMIL also operated under budget constraints, especially in the area of rule-of-law reform. While UNMIL was generally perceived to be effective and legitimate (Krasno, 2006; Mvukiyehe and Samii, 2010), its efforts to promote the rule of law were not uncontroversial, and its personnel were dogged by accusations of bias, negligence, and abuse – accusations that have plagued other peacekeeping operations in Africa and beyond.

Liberia itself also shares some important similarities with other cases. In particular, the challenges to establishing the rule of law in Liberia, while severe, are endemic to many post-conflict countries. These parallels to other UN missions and other African settings suggest that lessons learned from Liberia may travel to other cases. Finally, the severity of state collapse in Liberia meant that UNMIL was, for many years, the "only credible security provider for large swathes of the country" (Mvukiyehe and Samii, 2018, 9). From an analytical perspective, this simplifies the task of attributing improvements in the rule of law to UNMIL, rather than to other actors.

THE RULE OF LAW AND ITS DISCONTENTS IN LIBERIA, 1822–1979

The Republic of Liberia was founded by free African Americans and emancipated slaves from the USA, organized under the auspices of the abolitionist American Colonization Society (ACS). The colonists established a small coastal settlement at Cape Mesurado, later renamed Monrovia, in 1822. Known as "Congos" or "Americo-Liberians,"[3] the settlers believed they were conduits of a "Divine Plan" to erect a "model of African self-rule" at a time when most African countries were administered by colonial powers. Liberia, they believed, would serve as a "beacon for Africa and even a light to people of African descent in America" (Ellis 2006, 150; see also Martin 1969, 37).

The new nation would be modeled on the USA, from which it drew inspiration and prestige: both the 1820 Constitution and the 1847 Declaration of Independence[4] were based on their American counterparts, and Monrovia is the only capital city outside the USA named for an American president. The Americo-Liberians embraced American common law principles, including due process and the right to a trial by jury. Meanwhile, they so thoroughly monopolized political power that from the country's founding until 1980, every single Liberian president claimed Americo-Liberian ancestry.

In the early decades of their rule, the Americo-Liberians mostly ignored the hinterlands, rarely venturing more than a short distance inland from their coastal settlements. At the end of the nineteenth century, however, with British and French colonial ambitions in West Africa threatening to impinge on Liberia's poorly defined borders, the settlers found themselves suddenly obliged to exercise "real control" over the territories they claimed (Ellis, 2006, 41, 184).[5] In 1869 they established a Department of the Interior with authority

---

[3] The term "Americo-Liberian" was originally reserved for settlers who arrived with the ACS, while "Congo" referred to freed slaves from ships interdicted by Great Britain or the USA. The latter group assimilated into the former, and the two terms have been used largely interchangeably ever since (Lubkemann, Isser, and Banks III, 2011, 196).

[4] While Liberia was technically independent from its founding, the settlers adopted a Declaration of Independence to reaffirm their sovereignty against encroaching European colonial powers.

[5] As it happened, the colony was almost certainly too weak to defend itself from British or French encroachment, but its affiliation with the USA gave it a plausible claim to American diplomatic protection, which proved helpful in deterring the European powers.

over the hinterlands, and a repressive, colonial-style system of indirect rule whereby centrally appointed district commissioners oversaw a network of local paramount chiefs responsible for collecting taxes and organizing public works, often through forced labor. Indirect rule became the basis for a dual legal system, with the hinterlands subject to customary (informal) law and the settlers subject to its statutory (formal) counterpart, enacted and enforced by secular, publicly designated officials (Ellis, 2006, 207).

The customary sector was defined by a hierarchy with paramount chiefs at the top, followed by a succession of clan chiefs, town chiefs, and quarter chiefs. This hierarchy operated in parallel to a powerful network of sodalities known as "secret societies," which constituted the "most important political institution" in many rural communities (Ellis, 1995, 188), and the "dominant social force" among rural residents (Little, 1965, 349).[6] Secret societies are generally considered more powerful than chiefs, who operate as "purely civic authorities" subject to the "real control" of the societies (Ellis, 1995, 188). The structure of the customary sector was further developed and solidified over time, and the 1948 *Rules and Regulations Governing the Hinterland of Liberia* remain in force today, having been revised but substantively unchanged in 2000. (Secret societies, however, were never explicitly recognized by Liberian law, or by the Liberian state.)

While the Hinterland Regulations preserved some autonomy for customary institutions,[7] taxes and regulations brought the state into more direct conflict with its non-state competitors, and the rule of law in Liberia has been a contest between the two ever since. From the settlers' perspective, the interior was a redoubt of heathenism, where "satanic, superstitious, and backward practices" were deeply entrenched (Ellis, 2006, 238).[8] But it also and more importantly

---

[6] The term "secret society" is in some respects a misnomer. All adults know about the existence and purpose of secret societies, and most know who is and is not a member (Little, 1965, 349). As Stephen Ellis explains, secrecy is "less an attempt to keep knowledge restricted than to transmit certain messages to members in an esoteric form" – e.g. through rituals and symbols from which non-members are excluded (Ellis, 1995, 188).

[7] In instructions transmitted to its agents in 1819, the ACS was explicit in its desire to preserve the autonomy of Liberia's indigenous peoples, demanding "a particular and constant regard to the natives of Africa .... Your rules for the government of the Colony should particularly guard against injury of the natives, or collision with them" (Huberich, 1947, 80). The Hinterland Regulations similarly required that the settlers show "due regard to native customary law and native institutions" (*An Act of Legislature*, January 23, 1869, as cited in Lubkemann, Isser, and Banks III 2011, 196).

[8] In a letter to the ACS in 1873, former Commissioner of Education H. W. Dennis argued that "we have kept ourselves too much aloof from the natives, and have allowed them to follow their old heathenish customs and habits .... They need to be brought under some proper rule and order." In another letter dated 1876, A. F. Russell – a Protestant Episcopal minister who would later serve as both president and vice president of the Republic – enumerated the "sins" of tribalism: "living in unregulated hordes," trial by "magicians," "death by saucywood tests" (trial by ordeal), polygamy, "non-possession of real estate or permanent property," and "slavery in its darkest and most bloody forms" (Martin, 1969, 18, 21, 26).

posed a threat to the survival of the state itself. The government's error, as President Arthur Barclay described in his 1904 inaugural address, was that it "succeeded in grasping an enormous mass of territory," but "neglected to conciliate and attach the resident populations to our interest" (Ellis, 2006, 196). Attempts to project state power nationwide were thus motivated in part by a European-style *mission civilisatrice*, and in part by an existential fear that indigenous peoples, "unreconciled to Liberia," would literally "drive the Americo-Liberians into the sea" – a commonly used expression at the time (Martin, 1969, 23).[9]

The government's strategy for penetrating the hinterlands involved a combination of coercion and persuasion. Recognizing that indigenous peoples' attitudes towards "amalgamation" constituted the "most important key to success or failure" of state consolidation (Martin, 1969, 38), the settlers sought to project an image of the state as a legitimate purveyor of order and the rule of law. In 1879, for example, after the country's southeastern chiefs declared themselves "free of the Liberian government," the State Department responded that

... the Government of Liberia whose citizens you are, and to whom your Fathers with remarkable foresight, of their own free will and accord, ceded these districts, [is] striving to build up an African Nationality here, one that will command the respect of the world, and which will confer upon you, your children, and future generations, the inestimable boon of civil and religious institutions .... Liberia is a country owned and controlled by Africans, your Brethren, your kinsmen; not foreigners .... These are the people, with their descendants returned from exile and oppression, who make up the population of this commonwealth. Our interests then are one, and united should be our objects and aims in seeking to advance the general welfare of the whole body politic. (Martin, 1969, 21–2)

It was through appeals like these, reinforced by the threat of violence, that the Americo-Liberians hoped to create a "uniform system of administration" whose authority would, for the first time, radiate from Monrovia out into the rest of the republic (Ellis, 2006, 42).

For most of the nineteenth century, however, customary institutions at the meso level continued to offer more than viable alternatives to their statutory, macro-level counterparts, though neither provided anything approximating the rule of law. Liberia's indigenous peoples interacted in "loose confederacies" characterized by perennial instability, conflict, and "shifting centers of power"

---

[9] Some historians have argued that despite these fears, the Americo-Liberians never aspired to a "transformational" state, capable of dominating tribal and religious institutions. George Dalton, for example, claims that "when Americo-Liberians speak of the 'nation,' they mean themselves. There is no nationalist mystique in Liberia. The Americo-Liberians do not yearn to transform tribal society" (Dalton, 1965, 584). This, however, does not appear to represent the consensus among historians, and is in any event belied by ambitious Americo-Liberian rhetoric about state formation and penetration.

(d'Azevedo, 1969, 5). Justice was meted out in unpredictable and often brutal ways. Trial by ordeal, for example, was routinely used as a mechanism for divining the identity and guilt of accused criminals. The nature and uses of trial by ordeal vary, but often include ingestion of poison, application of a heated cutlass to the suspect's skin, or immersion of the suspect's hand in a pot of boiling water. In each case, it was (and is) believed that the innocent will be protected from harm, while the guilty will not. Known colloquially as "sassywood," these practices are "physically harmful *prima facie*" – that is, they would be "expected to cause physical harm if applied in any normal situation outside the ritual context" (Lubkemann, Isser, and Banks III, 2011, 224). Trial by ordeal was nonetheless central to adjudication and dispute resolution in the hinterlands, and in some places remains so today.

The government, meanwhile, was basically insolvent and thus obliged to strike bargains with "local potentates," further strengthening their often capricious rule in return for recognition of Monrovia's sovereignty (Ellis, 2006, 208–9). Stephen Ellis aptly summarizes the situation: "as in so many conquest states, the apparent uniformity of the formal system of government which had its centre in Monrovia was in reality a patchwork structure in which local communities and their leaders reached a variety of accommodations with the centre" (Ellis, 2006, 207). Within the formal sector as well, while some government officials adhered to legal limits on their authority, the weakness of the state afforded ample opportunity to skirt them.

This problem afflicted all government institutions. Most political power was concentrated in the hands of the executive, who behaved as though he was above the law. The justice sector was dysfunctional and favored the wealthy, who largely went unpunished while poor people languished in jail without trial or due process (Lubkemann, Isser, and Banks III, 2011, 196). The security sector was equally defective. A Liberian Frontier Force (predecessor to the Armed Forces of Liberia, or AFL) was founded in 1908 to attempt to project state power nationwide, but it quickly developed a reputation for rapacity, applying a "heavy hand" in the hope of coercing indigenous peoples to submit to rule by Monrovia (Ellis, 2006, 46, 209). Repression provoked protests and in some cases insurrection, especially in the country's restive southeastern districts.

It was only after William Tubman assumed the presidency in 1944 that the pace of state penetration began to pick up speed. Arguably the most powerful of Liberia's presidents, Tubman was the first to travel frequently into the interior, usually accompanied by an entourage of ministers and aides. During these visits he would hear complaints against district commissioners, mediate conflicts between paramount chiefs, and intervene in family and marital disputes. He aspired to be a champion of national unification, and the "crowning event" of his administration was the abolition of the Hinterland Jurisdiction in 1963, effectively ending the administrative separation between the coast and the interior and creating a legally unified republic under a single system of governance (Ellis, 2006, 47–8). He also presided over a period of rapid infrastructural expansion, building roads, schools, and hospitals, though the locations of these projects continued to favor coastal towns and cities. This proved to be the apex of state consolidation in Liberia, during which the government finally succeeded in penetrating almost "every corner of the country" (Ellis, 2006, 212).

But while Tubman's policies were ostensibly designed to promote the integration and enfranchisement of indigenous peoples, the Americo-Liberians continued to monopolize political power, and Tubman, like his predecessors, frequently ignored constitutional constraints on his authority (Lubkemann, Isser, and Banks III, 2011, 196). In the 1970s, a new "counter-elite" of indigenous youths, many of them educated in the USA, began to contest Americo-Liberian claims to power.[10] As other West African nations achieved independence, internal colonialism in Liberia came to seem increasingly aberrant. As Ellis puts it, "Liberia could no longer be convincingly described as the beacon of hope to black people the world over, the only independent negro republic, but was looking more like a corrupt and ramshackle neo-colony" (Ellis, 2006, 50). Analogs to the anti-colonial movements proliferating across the continent began to emerge in Liberia as well,[11] agitating for increased representation and an end to the Americo-Liberian oligarchy.

By the time of Tubman's death in 1971, that oligarchy was already showing signs of fracture. In an effort to satisfy mounting demands for representation, Tubman's successor William Tolbert reformed the bureaucracy and widened the pool of recruits for the Liberian armed forces, which had traditionally been dominated by Americo-Liberians (and, in its early years, by African Americans seconded from the USA). But Tolbert's concessions only isolated him from conservatives within his own party. In 1979, the government raised the price of rice in order to stimulate domestic production. Riots ensued, and Tolbert's regime was brought to the brink of collapse. The USA refused to intervene, and began actively searching for a replacement in the event of a coup. And indeed, on the night of April 12, 1980, a group of seventeen soldiers led by Master Sergeant Samuel K. Doe found Tolbert asleep in his office and executed him on the spot. Doe announced the fall of the regime on the radio the next morning, thus ending a century and a half of internal colonialism under the Americo-Liberian elite.

By the time the oligarchy finally collapsed, the rule of law in Liberia was an almost hopelessly distant aspiration. At the macro level, state laws failed to

---

[10] Ironically, it was Tubman's own policies – in particular, his foreign scholarship program, which provided opportunities for Liberians to study abroad – that acted as the "real catalyst for political change," producing a new generation of educated citizens who would return to Liberia and demand representation (Alao, MacKinlay, and Olonisakin, 2000, 17).

[11] These included the Movement for Justice in Africa and the Progressive Alliance of Liberia, which espoused a "quasi-Marxist political ideology of military African nationalism" not unlike those adopted by independence movements in other African countries at the time (Ellis, 2006, 50).

constrain the actions of state officials, and the state institutions responsible for enforcing those laws were predatory and capricious. Non-state authorities at the meso level were nominally subject to the writ of state law, but most ignored it or reached idiosyncratic accommodations with whichever government was in power. And at the micro level, indigenous peoples outside the capital city continued to resist state rule. The division of labor within the hybrid legal system, first codified in the Hinterland Regulations, became increasingly muddled as the state expanded. Multiple sources of law coexisted and competed with one another in a poorly regulated and inconsistently enforced patchwork. Then, in 1980, any semblance of the rule of law collapsed once and for all under the weight of Doe's coup d'état.

DICTATORSHIP AND CIVIL WAR, 1980–2003

Doe began consolidating power immediately, executing rivals and purging state institutions of non-coethnics. Doe was a member of the Krahn tribe, which historically has been concentrated in the country's southeastern counties. Favoritism towards the Krahns was a staple of Doe's regime. He suspended the constitution, vacated the judiciary, and placed all judges and justices under indefinite suspension. The chief justice of the Supreme Court was executed, and the rest of the bench was forced to resign. Once the police and courts had been purged, Doe began using them to silence dissent and neutralize political opponents. From abroad, he enjoyed the support of the USA, which viewed his regime as a bulwark against instability in the region – an impression that Doe actively cultivated. And while he lacked a "legitimate or moral basis" of support at home, Doe exploited ethnic rivalries to manufacture approval for his regime among his co-ethnics and their allies (Alao, MacKinlay, and Olonisakin, 2000, 18–19).

At the behest of the USA, Doe also began a transition to something approximating civilian rule. He drafted a new constitution to be ratified by referendum (which it was), and called for presidential elections to be held in 1985. He won, and despite the polls having been "blatantly rigged," the mere appearance of democracy was sufficient to appease Doe's American backers (Ellis, 2006, 58). At the same time, Doe continued to marginalize real and perceived opponents within his regime, including, most importantly, Charles Taylor and Thomas Quiwonkpa. Taylor, who has mixed Gola and Americo-Liberian ancestry, had benefited from Doe's policies of ethnic favoritism, becoming *de facto* director of the General Services Agency (GSA). Quiwonkpa was a leader of the coup that brought Doe to power in the first place. But Doe viewed them as rival centers of power, and ousted them from the regime.

Taylor fled to the USA, while Quiwonkpa began launching anti-government raids from Côte d'Ivoire and Sierra Leone. The most audacious of these involved an attack on Monrovia in 1985. Quiwonkpa and his men seized the national radio station and announced the formation of a new government, but Doe – who was warned of the impending invasion by American embassy officials – rallied loyalists within the military and responded with a "shocking display of public brutality" (Ellis, 2006, 60). Quiwonkpa was captured and killed, his mutilated body paraded through the streets of Monrovia. Doe's supporters then embarked on a campaign of ethnic cleansing, exacting "terrible retribution" on Quiwonkpa's alleged civilian collaborators, including women and children (Alao, MacKinlay, and Olonisakin, 2000, 20).

Meanwhile, Taylor began organizing dissidents in Côte d'Ivoire under the banner of the National Patriotic Front of Liberia (NPFL). While Doe had eliminated virtually all internal opposition to his regime, his administration proved to be an "economic catastrophe" for Liberia, due in part to a severe recession that had gripped the region, and in part to Doe's own mismanagement (Ellis, 2006, 72). Outside of Liberia, agitation against Doe had spread to multiple countries, notably Côte d'Ivoire, Burkina Faso, and, crucially, Libya, where Colonel Muammar Gaddafi provided Taylor with arms, training, and asylum as he plotted insurrection. Taylor also received support from Americo-Liberians living abroad, many of whom had fled after the 1980 coup d'état. On Christmas Eve, 1989, Taylor and 100 Libyan-trained NPFL fighters crossed the border into Nimba County. The rebels penetrated from Nimba towards the coast and, by July 1990, into Monrovia itself. The military responded with characteristic ferocity, but the NPFL's momentum proved impossible to stop. The Americans refused to come to Doe's rescue, eager to distance themselves from their "expensive and embarrassing ally" (Ellis, 2006, 159). On September 10, the NPFL's assault on Monrovia was complete, and Doe was captured and killed.

With support from ECOWAS, an Interim Government of National Unity (IGNU) was installed in 1990. While the IGNU was mandated to govern the entire country, Taylor refused to cooperate, and in reality, its "writ and presence" never extended beyond Monrovia (Alao, MacKinlay, and Olonisakin, 2000, 35). Other rebel groups, notably the United Liberation Movement of Liberia for Democracy (ULIMO), continued to operate unabated. Taylor, meanwhile, erected a parallel government to preside over the territories he controlled, which he dubbed "Greater Liberia," and which covered virtually all of the country outside of Monrovia, as well as parts of Sierra Leone.

In these territories, chiefs and other local leaders were encouraged to administer justice and oversee civic affairs, as they had before the hostilities began (Ellis, 2006, 143). In some cases customary authorities also helped discipline the rebels (Sawyer, 2005b, 5). Unlike many other conflicts, few Liberian rebel groups established clear rules regulating their behavior or that of the civilians under their control (Arjona, 2016, 32), further elevating the role of informal institutions as purveyors of local order amidst national upheaval. Liberians increasingly took recourse in these informal institutions, many of which either survived the conflict or were quickly restored thereafter (Sawyer, 2005a, 59). Even in places where the customary sector atrophied as a result of the violence, the principles underlying it persisted without being "fundamentally altered" (Isser, Lubkemann, and N'Tow, 2009, 4).

Taylor easily won a presidential election held in 1997 as part of the Abuja Accords – the thirteenth attempt to reach a negotiated end to the conflict – and set about erecting a personalistic, kleptocratic regime that retained many of the same structures and strategies of the NPFL. Wary of the risk of a coup from within, Taylor saturated the police and military with loyalists, further debasing whatever neutrality and professionalism remained among their ranks (Aboagye and Bah, 2004, 2, 10). He withheld salaries from judges, prosecutors, and police and corrections officers, and designated virtually all of the country's natural resources as "essential commodities" under his personal control (Sawyer, 2004, 448). Before long, however, Taylor's support for rebels in Sierra Leone, combined with his antagonism towards particular ethnic and religious groups in Liberia (especially the Mandingo), provoked counter-mobilizations. Several new foreign-backed rebel groups formed, most importantly Liberians United for Reconciliation and Democracy (LURD, supported by Guinea) and later the Movement for Democracy in Liberia (MODEL, supported by Côte d'Ivoire).

Taylor's regime was rapidly losing territorial control, to the point that state authority barely extended beyond the capital city: "vast territories in the interior ... were either under the control of one of the warring factions or waiting to be overrun by one of the feuding armed groups" (Aboagye and Bah, 2004, 14–15). Rural Liberia had already become a "mosaic of militia zones of control" in which civilians faced threats of violence from all sides as they attempted to navigate the "constantly shifting frontier zones" (Ellis, 1995, 185). Simultaneous unrest in Liberia, Guinea, and Sierra Leone soon morphed into a single system of conflict perpetuated by ethnic entrepreneurship, with violence spilling across borders and each country's government aggressively intervening in the affairs of the others (Sawyer, 2004, 439). Multiple insurgencies encircled Taylor, disrupting the timber and diamond trades and threatening the financial underpinnings of his regime. The conflict continued to escalate until 2003, when Taylor could no longer resist the mounting pressure. Under the specter of imminent siege, he fled into exile, and a Comprehensive Peace Agreement (CPA) was signed on August 18, 2003, finally ushering in a period of peace.

The succession of civil wars that wracked Liberia from 1989 to 2003 claimed the lives of some 150,000 people, most of them civilians, injured many thousands more, and displaced most of the population. In a 2009 survey, 86 per cent of respondents reported losing contact with a close family member during the war, and 69 per cent reported that a close family member had died as a result of the fighting. A total of 45 per cent said they had been tortured by one of the armed groups, and 51 per cent said that someone close to them was a victim of sexual violence (Paczynska, 2010, 28). By 2003, the life expectancy of the average Liberian was just 41 years (International Legal Assistance Consortium, 2003).

The effects on the already fragile Liberian government were equally profound. More than a decade of fighting reduced the state to little more than "a shell in which Liberians [continued] to live" (Ellis, 2006, 188). The country's roads, railroads, ports, and other infrastructure were looted or destroyed – a collapse so thorough that even the once-impressive national power grid was sold for scrap metal. By 2003, with an average annual per capita income of just US $140, Liberia was among the poorest countries in the world – so poor that it could not even produce the statistics necessary to be ranked on the UN's annual Human Development Index (Sisk and Risley, 2005, 34).

THE UN ENTERS

The international community's attempts to stabilize Liberia began with a regional peacekeeping operation led by ECOMOG, the first mission of its kind to be deployed by the Economic Community of West African States (ECOWAS). ECOMOG intervened in 1990 with a force of roughly 3,000 troops, which eventually grew to over 10,000. Five countries contributed soldiers to ECOMOG – Gambia, Ghana, Guinea, Nigeria, and Sierra Leone, later joined by Mali – with the bulk of the force composed of Nigerians. ECOMOG was mandated to impose a ceasefire, form an interim government, and hold elections within twelve months.

With the ongoing NPFL onslaught, however, there was no peace to keep, and the mission quickly became embroiled in the conflict. The motives behind ECOMOG's intense involvement in the Liberian civil war have long been a source of speculation and intrigue. Some accused the mission's Nigerian leadership of intervening to support Doe, an ally of Nigerian President Ibrahim Babangida, by, for example, funneling weapons to ULIMO, a Doe-allied rebel group formed by Krahn and Mandingo dissidents from the Liberian army (Alao, MacKinlay, and Olonisakin, 2000, 32). Others, including Taylor, suspected Nigeria of conspiring to expand its sphere of influence in West Africa. Some simply believed that Nigeria and the other ECOWAS countries rightly feared the consequences of allowing an increasingly regional conflict to metastasize further (Human Rights Watch, 1993).

Whatever the explanation, while ECOMOG managed to secure a temporary ceasefire and oversee the creation of the IGNU, peace proved fleeting. In an attempt to neutralize the NPFL, ECOMOG allied with other factions, most notably ULIMO and the remnants of the AFL, both of which were already implicated in numerous atrocities against the civilian population. ECOMOG's collaboration with ULIMO and the AFL altered the dynamic of the conflict and raised further questions about ECOMOG's already dubious commitment to human rights, exemplified by incidents of looting, harassment, and arbitrary detention of civilians (Human Rights Watch, 1993).

It was in this environment that the UN first entered Liberia with an observer mission (UNOMIL) in 1993, deployed shortly after the signing of the

Cotonou Agreement between the NPFL, ULIMO, and the IGNU. UNOMIL was mandated to assist with the implementation of the accord, monitor the accompanying ceasefire, and complement ongoing mediation efforts led by ECOWAS. After overseeing elections that elevated Taylor to the presidency in 1997, UNOMIL was supplanted by the UN Peace-building Support Office in Liberia (UNOL), the first office of its kind. UNOL was tasked with promoting national reconciliation and good governance in the wake of Taylor's electoral victory, but the mission's ability to fulfill its mandate was hamstrung from the outset by widespread human rights abuses committed by Taylor's regime.

Finally, at the request of the signatories to the CPA, UNOL was replaced with UNMIL. UNMIL was given a robust, multidimensional Chapter VII mandate, with an array of units devoted not just to peacekeeping and protection of civilians, but also to criminal justice, civil affairs, human rights, gender, child protection, public health, public information, and disarmament, demobilization, and reintegration (DDR). This diversity of components reflected the scope and ambitiousness of UNMIL's mandate, which included monitoring the ceasefire; providing security at ports and airfields; ensuring the safe return of refugees and internally displaced persons; protecting civilians; advising and training law enforcement and criminal justice personnel; assisting with DDR; organizing elections; monitoring human rights abuses; supporting the establishment of a Truth and Reconciliation Commission; and extending state authority from Monrovia into the hinterlands.

UNMIL was also the first multidimensional mission authorized in the wake of the 2000 Brahimi Report, which chastised UN member states for refusing to provide peacekeeping operations with adequate resources and personnel, including and especially in the rule-of-law sector. The Brahimi Report served as the backdrop for the mission's mandate, which embraced a number of the report's recommendations. UNMIL was the first peacekeeping operation to adhere to the "integrated mission model," designed to improve coordination among the UN's civilian and military components and to facilitate a "system-wide" UN response to crises (McCandless, 2008). This model later became standard for peacekeeping operations around the world. Most important for my purposes, the Brahimi Report also advocated a new approach to rule-of-law promotion structured around rule-of-law "teams," which would combine UN police officers with experts on legal, judicial, and correctional reform (UN Security Council, 2000, 7). UNMIL was the first mission to operationalize this approach in the field.

While technically not a transitional administration, UNMIL shared a number of similarities with the UN missions in Kosovo and East Timor, especially in the breadth of its mandate and the variety of political, economic, and humanitarian functions over which it assumed control. So extensive was UNMIL's mandate that some observers described Liberia as a "UN Protectorate" (Smith-Höhn, 2010), and the mission itself as a "tacit trusteeship" (Neumann and

Schia, 2012, 14). At the height of its deployment, UNMIL was arguably more of a state than the Liberian state itself.

Indeed, beyond small, closely monitored subunits within the Liberian National Police (LNP), UNMIL was the only purveyor of armed force in the country until 2012, when the restructured Liberian military – confined until then to a barracks outside Monrovia – was finally deployed. UNMIL also provided a variety of services, building roads and bridges, repairing schools, clinics, and hospitals, and refurbishing courthouses and police stations. The notion of state surrogacy was explicit in the way UNMIL personnel understood their role in the country. As one Head of Field Office explained to me, in the first years after the CPA was signed, "the government was so feeble that UNMIL appeared as a proxy."[12]

THREATS TO THE RULE OF LAW IN LIBERIA, 2003–PRESENT

The feebleness of the Liberian state was just one of many challenges confronting UNMIL in the early days of its mandate. Obstacles to the rule of law emerged along all three of the dimensions described in Chapter 3, each compounding the others. At the macro level, the Liberian security and justice sectors were hobbled by rampant miconduct and profound institutional decay. Beginning with the Doe regime and continuing through the civil war, the LNP was purged of non-coethnics and deployed to brutalize the population and intimidate political rivals, both real and imagined. By the time the fighting stopped, Liberia had fifteen different security agencies with overlapping functions; many police stations had been abandoned, looted, or seized by armed groups; and many police officers had simply fled the country. Those that remained almost invariably lacked the requisite training and equipment to do their jobs effectively (Friedman and MacAulay, 2014).

The courts and prisons fared no better. Liberia's corrections officers had not received any formal training since 1979, and the civil war destroyed all but one small detention center (UN Department of Peacekeeping Operations, 2011a). By 2007, the rate of pre-trial detention in Liberian prisons had reached a staggering 90 per cent (UN Department of Peacekeeping Operations, 2018). Only two circuit courts were operational in 2003, both of them in Monrovia (UN Department of Peacekeeping Operations, 2018). The government has only recently begun recording, compiling, and publicizing Supreme Court case law, and whatever may have been available before the civil war began was largely lost because of it. Gaps, contradictions, and ambiguities created a "legal free-for-all," with poorly educated lawyers and judges exercising almost limitless discretion and extorting complainants for an "endless and expensive stream of bribes." In some cases, it was difficult or impossible to determine which laws remained in effect, let alone to find authoritative (or any) copies

[12] GRB, Voinjama, November 24, 2012.

of the laws themselves. The weakness of the judiciary extended all the way to the Supreme Court, whose decisions were "blatantly ignored by powerful individuals" (Lubkemann, Isser, and Banks III, 2011, 205–6, 216).

At the micro level, low trust in the courts was matched by even lower trust in the police. A 2008 Afrobarometer survey found that 52 per cent of all Liberians believe corruption is widespread within the LNP, compared to 41 per cent for the legislature and 37 per cent for the judiciary (Topka and Saryee, 2009). Some Liberians view state law itself as "alien," and many believe that "decisions by traditional leaders should take precedent over the formal law" (Siddiqi and Sandefur, 2009, 97).[13] This may not imply a rejection of the "ultimate authority of the state," but many Liberians nonetheless act in ways that undermine state authority (Isser, Lubkemann, and N'Tow, 2009, 6). For example, a 2009 Oxford University survey found that of a total of 3,181 civil cases, only 3 per cent were reported to a formal forum, compared to 38 per cent that were reported to an informal one. Similarly, of 1,877 criminal cases, only 2 per cent were reported to a formal forum, compared to 45 per cent reported to an informal one. More striking still is the proportion of disputants who failed to report at all: 59 per cent and 53 per cent in civil and criminal cases, respectively (Isser, Lubkemann, and N'Tow, 2009). Perhaps unsurprisingly, lynchings and mob violence were (and are) common, and are sometimes believed to be "the only alternative to dealing with criminal threats" (Smith-Höhn 2010, 99–100; see also Lubkemann, Isser, and Banks III 2011, 207).

At the meso level, while customary authorities can be effective at resolving non-violent domestic disputes, they typically struggle to manage more serious crimes, especially those involving multiple ethnic groups (Isser, Lubkemann, and N'Tow, 2009). This was a recurring theme in my interviews with Liberian chiefs and other local leaders. For example, the chairman of one Nimba County community described a violent land dispute between members of the Mano and Mandingo tribes, which he and his colleagues had tried and failed to resolve. When asked why, he explained that because the leaders of the community are mostly Mano, the Mandingos refuse to recognize their authority: "talking with us, it will not solve this problem."[14]

A similar situation arose in a case involving a land dispute between Lorma and Mandingo residents of a Lofa County community. As the town chief explained, "we went through the case but the Mandingo people say we cannot

---

[13] Nowhere is this discrepancy more pronounced than in cases that disproportionately affect women and children – in particular, rape and domestic violence. Liberian law defines rape as any type of intercourse without the victim's consent, a definition that coincides with laws in most Western countries. In contrast, most Liberians reserve the term "rape" for only a subset of these acts – rejecting, for example, the notion that non-consensual sex by a spouse should be considered rape. Many Liberians also reject the concept of statutory rape (Lubkemann, Isser, and Banks III, 2011, 223).

[14] AJD and ZD, Sanniquellie, October 20, 2011.

accept it, because I am a Lorma man .... The Mandingo people were behind one another, and we the Lorma people too. Nothing else we could do."[15] The chief of another ethnically heterogeneous community made a similar admission: "sometimes the devil pass between us, you know we can quarrel. [If we have] confusion [conflict] in town here, the government will have to step in."[16] Another put the point more bluntly: "if it [the conflict] was between only two persons, we able to resolve it. But once it expands to ethnic conflict, it was above us."[17]

Some non-state authorities are cautious about exceeding the legal and practical limits of their power. But many attempt to adjudicate serious cases in contravention of state law. According to the 1986 constitution, customary institutions are authorized to resolve petty claims and non-violent disputes, while magistrate and circuit courts retain jurisdiction over most other civil and criminal cases. But customary authorities often circumvent these restrictions, especially in cases of rape and domestic abuse, where local rules and norms often conflict with national laws.

Customary authorities also sometimes insist that court cases be referred back to them – a demand that extends even to crimes that lie unambiguously within the state's purview. In one community in Lofa County, for example, a man beat his girlfriend for neglecting to cook dinner in time for a guest's arrival. The girlfriend's son confronted the man, threatening to kill him with a shotgun. The chief transferred the case to the court, but the community elders insisted on withdrawing it to "resolve it at home." This only exacerbated the situation: "tension started building. It came to be an ethnic conflict now, not between two persons." The conflict only subsided after the county superintendent intervened, accompanied by the Carter Center (a USA-based NGO) and a delegation of clan and paramount chiefs.[18]

Even in cases that fall under their own jurisdiction, some customary authorities rely on modes of adjudication that undermine due process and are forbidden under state law – most notably, trial by ordeal. Trial by ordeal is illegal in Liberia, and eradicating it has long been a priority for the government and its international patrons. But prohibition has not altogether discredited the practice, nor weakened its "epistemological hold" on many rural communities (Isser, Lubkemann, and N'Tow, 2009, 5), and my qualitative data is replete with examples of trial by ordeal (or "sassywood") being used to ascertain the guilt or innocence of suspected criminals.

In one community, for example,

... a little girl passed away and everybody was surprised of that particular death, so the parents of that little girl decided to go for sassywood, because they started accusing some old ladies and some elders. The sassywood man came and put cutlass on the fire.

---

[15] JLM, Salayea, November 3, 2011.   [16] DH, Zorzor, November 5, 2011.
[17] SK, Zigida, November 6, 2011.   [18] SK, Zigida, November 6, 2011.

If you ain't part of it [the crime], it will be just like water on your skin. They started to do it, going around all the people in the neighborhood, touching them, and the cutlass was able to grab one person. She [the accused] said no, they were lying. The woman's family too said no, "you can't accuse our mother, you not see her doing anything like that." The man who made the sassywood cook another soup, so when she drink it the medicine will catch her to die. But up to this time the woman still living.[19]

Trial by ordeal is also used for less serious incidents. In one Nimba County community, for example, an elder used trial by ordeal to prove that her daughter had stolen some of her lappas – a colorful garment worn as a dress by many West African women.[20]

The use of illegal or extrajudicial mechanisms of adjudication such as trial by ordeal often coincides with mob justice. In another interview, the youth leader of a Lofa County community described a situation in which a series of mysterious deaths provoked accusations of witchcraft, which quickly escalated into mob violence:

We call the witch doctor, we told him that he should look around, because the children are dying, and some are accused as witch. They deny, so we called the witch doctor. The witch doctor started scratching around, but some of them refuse to come out. We collected them, we sent them out, those that refused to come, we started beating them, but we did not beat them to the point of death. We said that if you are caught you will pay 700,000 [Liberian] dollars,[21] that will be the charge for you. Each and every one of them that were caught, they will pay this amount.[22]

Accounts of this sort are not uncommon, especially in rural areas.

Even when traditional leaders adhere to legal limits on their authority, customary institutions are typically dominated by "local influential individuals" (Siddiqi and Sandefur, 2009, 97). Many women, youths, and ethnic or religious minorities believe these institutions are "inherently biased against them," and thus incapable of administering justice (Lubkemann, Isser, and Banks III, 2011, 219). This helps explain why chiefs and other local leaders often fail to resolve conflicts involving members of different tribes. Many minority group members also object to the role that ceremonial figures like the "devil" (described in the anecdote at the start of Chapter 1) play in dispute resolution. As one respondent explained,

Respondent: That [the town devil] is the most powerful. Way back, it was the first government. That is the only way. That is the only way the respect can exist. There

---

[19] Camp Four, March 19, 2013.
[20] Gbedin, March 10, 2013. Trial by ordeal is not always deadly, and the accused may even request it in order to prove their innocence. The latter cases are generally described as "taking an oath." "Sassywood" typically refers to the more dangerous use of a poison or heated cutlass to divine guilt or innocence, and is the focus of this book.
[21] This is roughly equivalent to US $10,000, well beyond the means of all but the wealthiest Liberians to pay. The respondent may have been exaggerating, or the threat of the fine may have been intended only to elicit a confession.
[22] Wolidou, April 28, 2013.

are certain things [rules] that when you violate, they call the town devil. That is town business.

Interviewer: So that one has nothing to do with law business.

Respondent: No.

Interviewer: They will handle it right here.

Respondent: That is what traditional law is for.[23]

The devil is associated with secret societies, from which Muslims and Pentecostal Christians are generally excluded, along with "strangers" who migrate from other communities as adults. Unsurprisingly, these groups tend to be wary of the justice that devils and other religious authorities promise to deliver.

In the first few years after the civil war ended, these meso-level challenges were further compounded by illegal armed groups that remobilized in order to seize control of the country's lucrative diamond mines and rubber plantations. In Bomi and Cape Mount counties, for example, an estimated 3,000–4,000 LURD ex-combatants overran the Guthrie rubber plantation, creating a "High Power Ruling Council" (HPRC) administered by LURD senior commanders to manage the illicit extraction and sale of rubber. Profits were divided between the plantation's private sector sponsors, the HPRC, the Camp Commanders, rubber tappers themselves (most of them ex-combatants, but many of them civilians), and, importantly, the government officials who colluded with LURD, lining their own pockets in the process (Archibald, 2006).

For the ex-combatants who worked the plantation, Guthrie provided "the best of the few employment options available" (Archibald et al., 2006, 10). But for the civilians caught in the middle, the situation was much more tenuous. In a 2006 report, UNMIL described the plantations as "lawless," characterized by an "absence of state authority and respect for the rule of law" that "places the fundamental rights of plantation residents at risk" (IRIN, 2006). As if to underscore the point, the ex-LURD general in charge of one of these operations described himself not just as "police and judge," but as "God" of the plantation (UN Mission in Liberia, 2006, 62).

Liberia thus faced three interrelated sets of challenges to the rule of law at the end of the civil war. At the macro level, the security and justice sectors were under-staffed, under-equipped, and under-funded, their independence and effectiveness compromised by ambiguities in Liberian law and misconduct by Liberian elites. Even Supreme Court decisions were routinely ignored. Aware of these problems, citizens at the micro level refused to report crimes to the police or refer cases to the courts. Many opted to avoid statutory institutions and seek redress for grievances through customary ones instead. At the meso-level, while these customary institutions provided a semblance of stability amidst the turmoil of civil war, they regularly transgressed the legal limits of their authority, or applied mechanisms of dispute resolution that violate state law in and of themselves. The challenge for UNMIL was to preserve the role that

[23] Borkeza, November 5, 2011.

customary institutions played in maintaining order while enforcing a stricter division of labor between them and their statutory counterparts. Meanwhile, the remnants of illegal armed groups had seized control of areas rich in natural resources, erecting new modes of rebel governance to oversee the illicit flow of raw materials onto international markets.

UNMIL was not the only entity concerned with these problems. When the Liberian Truth and Reconciliation Commission (TRC) released its final report in 2009, it identified the absence of the rule of law (and the weakness of the judiciary in particular) as among the most important causes of the civil war, second only to poverty. In the TRC's estimation, Liberia lacked any "permanent or appropriate mechanism for the settlement of disputes." The TRC recognized that Liberia's hybrid legal system was both a cause and symptom of tensions inherent in the country's struggle to reconcile "two opposing ideas – the civilizing mission [of the Americo-Liberians] and the building of an African nationality." This tension created an "unresolved historical problem of political identity and legitimacy," and was one of the "historical root causes" of the civil war (Republic of Liberia Truth and Reconciliation Commission, 2009, 16, 300).

The severity of these problems was evident to other international observers as well. In a report issued shortly after the CPA was signed, the International Legal Assistance Consortium starkly summarized the threats to the rule of law in Liberia:

There is almost unanimous distrust of Liberia's courts and a corresponding collapse of the rule of law. Liberia's Constitution provides for an Anglo-American legal system, but in reality, there is no effective separation of powers, a limited understanding of the principles of transparency and accountability, little knowledge of contemporary notions of human rights, limited access to legal advice and defense council, and unconscionable delays …. Training in judicial and professional independence is a priority, criminal procedure requires a radical overhaul, prosecutors must be recruited, defence counsel must be made available to indigent defendants, and a detention centre must be built. Police and prison officers require comprehensive training in all aspects of their duties, and transparency and accountability must be integrated into all areas of government. (International Legal Assistance Consortium, 2003, Executive Summary)

In other words, if ever there was a "least likely" case for establishing the rule of law after civil war, Liberia was it.[24]

---

[24] One might object that because the rule of law in Liberia was so feeble to begin with, the efforts of international interveners could not help but improve it. This does not strike me as an especially persuasive objection, and a similar line of reasoning is seldom applied to other contexts or outcomes. For example, I am unaware of any analyst who argues that statebuilding in Somalia is made easier by the fact that Somalia never had a state to begin with, or that democracy promotion in Iraq is made easier by the fact that Iraq has never been democratic, or that promotion of women's rights in Yemen is made easier by the fact that Yemeni women have been subjugated to men for as long as the country has existed. If anything, analysts tend to expect the opposite.

RULE-OF-LAW PROMOTION UNDER UNMIL

Addressing these challenges was among UNMIL's highest priorities from the early days of its mandate.[25] In 2003, as part of the CPA, a Governance Reform Commission was established and charged with creating a "national integrity framework ... to promote transparency, accountability, and the rule of law" (Legislature of Liberia, 2007, 1). UNMIL then formed a Rule of Law Implementation Committee tasked with devising and overseeing a "holistic approach" to legal, judicial, and security sector reform (UN Secretary-General, 2004e, 7). The Committee was the first in a long line of commissions and working groups involved in this process, the importance of which was repeatedly reaffirmed in updates to UNMIL's mandate. Restoring the rule of law would subsequently become one of the "top-priority (though underfunded)" elements of the Liberian government's Poverty Reduction Strategy as well (Lubkemann, Isser, and Banks III, 2011, 194). Despite lingering threats to stability, both security and justice sector reform are mentioned as priorities in the UN Secretary-General's very first progress report on the mission (UN Secretary-General, 2003), and in virtually every progress report thereafter.

UNMIL's approach to rule-of-law promotion involved a combination of all of the strategies described in Chapter 4. As a catalyst for state reform at the macro level, UNMIL began by focusing on the police. In an attempt to purge the LNP of war criminals, UNMIL established an "integrity bank" with background information on new recruits, and required that existing officers reapply for enlistment under more rigorous eligibility criteria (UN Secretary-General 2004b, 10, 2004e, 7). Recruits were required to complete three and six months of academy and on-the-job training, respectively, which involved a combination of "hard" tactical skills – forensics, interrogation, crowd control, etc. – and "softer" skills, including techniques for handling crimes committed against women, children, and other vulnerable populations (UN Secretary-General 2004d,e, 2005b). To monitor compliance with these new standards, UNMIL's police contingent (UNPOL) co-located with LNP officers at depots throughout the country. UNPOL also accompanied the LNP on joint patrols beginning as early as 2003.

UNMIL prioritized gender and ethnicity in recruitment, establishing an initial 15 per cent quota for women on the force, then raising that threshold until it reached 20 per cent by 2012 (UN Secretary-General 2004b, 2012d). UNMIL also launched a three-month "educational support" initiative designed to strengthen the qualifications of potential female recruits, which culminated in the conferral of a high-school equivalency diploma (UN Secretary-General, 2007b, 5). In 2007 the mission began offering all-female classes at the police academy in Monrovia (UN Secretary-General, 2007a). Also in 2007, UNMIL

---

[25] This section relies primarily on the UN Secretary-General's progress reports on UNMIL. I discussed the advantages and disadvantages of relying on progress reports to operationalize peacekeeping activities in Chapter 5.

began integrating all-female Formed Police Units (FPUs) into its police contingent, partly in the hope of encouraging Liberian women to enlist in the LNP. FPU officers accompanied their LNP counterparts on patrols in order to overcome the "lingering suspicions of citizens whose trust in the uniform had been eroded by civil war" (The World Bank, 2011, 152). While the mission never set specific ethnic quotas, it nonetheless attempted to maximize "ethnogeographic balance" as well (Aboagye and Bah, 2004, 11), with mixed results (Blair et al. 2018).[26]

Justice sector reform was also a priority (International Legal Assistance Consortium, 2003). While UNMIL never dedicated the same resources to justice sector reform as it did to police reform, mission leadership was apparently aware that "failing to give due consideration to the issue of judicial reform early in the peace process" could have "negative ramifications for efforts to strengthen the rule of law" (UN Secretary-General, 2004b, 6). In this spirit, UNMIL recruited new judges, reconstituted the country's civil, criminal, and specialized courts, many of which had been abandoned during the civil war, and pressured the Liberian National Bar Association to strengthen the selection and vetting procedures for new judicial appointees (UN Secretary-General (2004e, 2005a).

UNMIL also recruited prosecutorial and public defense consultants to attempt to address the acute shortage of qualified justice sector officials in rural areas (UN Secretary-General, 2006a, 9). The mission developed training programs for Liberian magistrates, judges, magisterial court clerks, lawyers, justices of the peace, and corrections officers (UN Secretary-General 2004b, 2005b, c, 2006a, d). As it did with the LNP, UNMIL monitored the activities of newly retrained justice sector personnel by co-locating legal and judicial officers in all "relevant rule-of-law institutions" (UN Secretary-General 2004e, 7; see also UN Secretary-General 2004a). UNMIL also documented infringements on the independence of the judiciary in periodic reports to the government and international community (UN Secretary-General, 2006d).

Alongside efforts to reform and restructure the courts, UNMIL helped rewrite Liberia's legal code through an iterative process of "revision, harmonization, and codification" (UN Secretary-General, 2004a, 7). This began relatively unobtrusively, with mission leadership advocating broad statements of principle to which government institutions and personnel would be expected to adhere. UNMIL also pressured the government to ratify core statutes and protocols of international humanitarian law, including the International Covenant on Economic, Social, and Cultural Rights, the International Covenant on Civil and Political Rights, and the Rome Statute of the International Criminal Court (UN Secretary-General 2003, 2004e). UNMIL then hired consultants to audit

---

[26] For a more extensive discussion of gender balancing in the LNP, see Karim et al. (2018). For a more detailed analysis of ethnic balancing, see Blair et al. (2018).

Liberia's laws and assess their adherence to these newly adopted standards (UN Secretary-General, 2006c).

As UNMIL's legal reform agenda expanded, it launched initiatives targeting an array of issues, including human trafficking, sexual and gender-based violence, narcotics, freedom of the press, bail, jury selection, pre-trial detention, and exploitation of natural resources (Sannerholm et al. 2012, 31; UN Secretary-General 2005a, c). Most ambitiously, in 2010 the UN Human Rights Council conducted a comprehensive review of Liberian law, which generated 113 recommendations addressing some of the most culturally delicate topics in the country, including female genital mutilation and trial by ordeal (UN Secretary-General, 2011c). UNMIL later dispatched technical experts to help Liberia's Constitutional Review Committee navigate the tumultuous process of reforming the 1986 constitution, adopted during the dictatorship of Samuel K. Doe (UN Secretary-General, 2014c).

At the macro level, UNMIL thus combined all of the strategies for catalyzing state reform described in Chapter 4: revising state laws, redesigning state institutions, rehabilitating state infrastructure, and retraining state officials. UNMIL also established a "Task Force for the Restoration of State Authority" within the Ministry of Internal Affairs, which would oversee a "phased and gradual deployment" of government officials to posts throughout the country (UN Secretary-General, 2004e, 9). By March 2006, UNMIL's Civil Affairs component had facilitated the return of over 2,200 government personnel to rural regions, including police officers, superintendents, and customs and immigration officials (UN Secretary-General, 2005b). UNMIL also helped repair the country's dilapidated roads and bridges, which had rendered much of the hinterlands all but inaccessible, thus helping the state broadcast power and facilitating contact between citizens and state agents.

As it sought to catalyze state reform at the macro level, UNMIL also acted as a surrogate for the reformed Liberian state at the micro level, and as a liaison between Liberian citizens and both state and non-state authorities. My qualitative data illustrates how UNMIL intervened to neutralize potentially explosive situations, substituting for Liberian security forces when they proved unable or unwilling to act on their own. In Borkeza, Lofa County, for example, a 9th grade boy stabbed his friend to death after accusing him of stealing a squirrel from a trap he had laid in the forest. The community's neighborhood watch team detained the boy and held him in a cell in a nearby immigration check point, but the cell came under attack from a group of youths. As the chief explained,

> We took the boy there [to the check point] and called the police. They came in, but the boys that was in this town, they say the boy can't go, we have to kill him here. The police say well since you people say we should not carry the boy, we will leave the boy here.[27]

[27] GK, Borkeza, November 4, 2011.

The police officers' decision only aggravated the mob that had gathered around the check point: "the tension was high, they wanted to kill the boy."[28] According to local leaders, it was only after UNMIL's intervention that the situation stabilized: "when they [UNMIL] came these boys really wanted to kill him, but they [UNMIL] said no, we can't allow this. We have seen the man, we will deal with him, so let him be arrested and be carried to the law."[29] UNMIL personnel took the boy to a local hospital to receive medical attention for injuries sustained during the brawl, then to jail. They detained several members of the mob as well.

Importantly, even when UNMIL substituted for the state by operating independently of state security forces, mission personnel often involved their Liberian counterparts in the process of adjudication after order had been restored. In the town of Salayea, for example, violence erupted when the minority Mandingo community refused to retreat indoors upon the appearance of the town devil, as customary law requires them to do. Shortly thereafter, a group of youths gathered to throw stones at the town's Mandingo residents and the local mosque. In response, "UNMIL came, they call us under the town hall. We sit there and they said they wanted to send somebody to come and judge the case." UNMIL diffused the conflict on its own, but then referred the case to the Ministry of Internal Affairs, which is responsible for mediating most conflicts arising from traditional practices. This decision reinforced the Ministry's role as an arbiter of disputes in the eyes of citizens.[30]

UNMIL also sought to legitimize the authority of the LNP and other state institutions by conducting nationwide "community policing awareness campaigns" to encourage civilian cooperation with the police. These campaigns included a school outreach program, spots on local and UN radio, and town hall meetings with citizens expounding on "the importance of good relationships and cooperation between the community and the police," and urging residents to "help the police combat crime in their communities" (UN Secretary-General, 2010b, 13).[31] These themes were reinforced through informal interactions with citizens during patrols and interventions to resolve disputes, and through public service announcements posted on billboards throughout the country, as in Figure 6.2 ("the police is your friend"; "stop mob violence"; "trust the police to keep the peace"). UNMIL also disseminated information about ongoing police reforms by conducting public awareness campaigns and, once those reforms had begun to bear fruit, by touting the LNP's "improved crime-fighting ability" (UN Secretary-General 2004d, 2010a, 12–13).

---

[28] KS, Borkeza, November 4, 2011.   [29] FD, Borkeza, November 5, 2011.
[30] JLM, Salayea, November 3, 2011.
[31] Town hall meeting themes are excerpted from weekly situation reports provided to me by UNMIL's police contingent.

FIGURE 6.2 UN-sponsored billboards in Liberia
Source: Author. The phrase "cold water" is a Liberian euphemism for "bribe."

The mission adopted similar strategies to instill confidence in the courts. UNMIL and the Liberian Ministry of Justice organized workshops and public education seminars to "sensitize" Liberians to the "new and enhanced role of the judiciary in nation-building and on the importance of the rule of law" (UN Secretary-General, 2004b, 7). Much of UNMIL Radio's programming was devoted to similar topics. In 2006, for example, UNMIL launched a radio program called *Community Court* to educate citizens about the functions and activities of the judiciary, and to promote internationally accepted norms around domestic violence and trial by ordeal (UN Secretary-General, 2006c). The mission devised a similar campaign around Liberia's controversial rape law (UN Secretary-General, 2006a), and around new forestry laws designed to stimulate commercial logging (UN Secretary-General, 2007b). UNMIL also convened public consultations and civic education workshops in advance of a constitutional conference in 2015, and mass-produced the text of the existing constitution for dissemination throughout the country (UN Secretary-General 2014b, c).

My qualitative data further illustrates the ways that UNMIL helped mobilize Liberian security forces to respond to criminal complaints, interceding when necessary to ensure that suspects would be arrested and their cases transferred to the courts. UNMIL helped the LNP investigate and make arrests following a murder in the town of Ganta;[32] another murder in the village of Solomba;[33] an abduction and rape in the village of Kailahun;[34] and another rape in the town of Kpaiyea.[35] Interviews with local leaders suggest that these interventions helped avert further escalation, but also and equally importantly helped illustrate the advantages of relying on third parties with coercive capacity when crimes are committed or violence occurs. In one community, for example, a bar fight escalated into an armed confrontation between two brothers that "scared the town chief, the elders." UNMIL mobilized the LNP and forced the brothers to stand down, drawing their weapons "so they [the brothers] can know the heat."[36] Indeed, in some cases, local leaders themselves relied on UNMIL, the government, or both to enforce their own potentially unpopular decisions.[37]

UNMIL also worked with the police to prevent criminal cases from being informally "compromised." This was especially important in cases of sexual violence. In one community, for example, a girl reported that a local boy had sexually assaulted her:

We [the local leaders] transferred this case to the police, and the police was able to take the case to UNMIL. UNMIL send this woman to the hospital, and the doctor check the

---

[32] Ganta, March 6, 2013. [33] Solomba, May 3, 2013. [34] Kailahun, April 20, 2013.
[35] Kpaiyea, March 10, 2013. [36] Lutisu, March 21, 2013.
[37] Salayea, November 3, 2011; Zigida, November 6, 2011.

woman and said it was true. So the government made a decision to send this man to prison, and up to now he is still there. The man's family said they should forget about this, but the police said rape case cannot be compromised, so we as community leaders we said you know we cannot compromise rape case, only government. What so ever that happens in our community today, we transfer it straight to the police, and police can invite UNMIL.[38]

In this case, as in others,[39] UNMIL acted as a state surrogate at the behest of the state itself.

But UNMIL also allowed the Liberian government to claim credit for achievements that would have been more accurately attributed to mission personnel. Even in its earliest progress reports, UNMIL emphasized the "collaborative" efforts of UNPOL officers and their Liberian counterparts (UN Secretary-General, 2004e, 3). As the security situation improved, UNMIL described the change as "due primarily to the efforts of the Liberian National Police, *supported by* UNMIL police" (UN Secretary-General, 2010a, 3, my emphasis). This almost certainly understated UNMIL's role: while the mission's police contingent lacked the authority to effect arrests, it nonetheless assumed primary responsibility for responding to victim and witness reports of crime and violence, conducting criminal investigations, preventing felony offenses from being informally "compromised," and protecting detainees from mob justice (UN Secretary-General, 2004d) – sometimes endangering its own personnel in the process (Lubkemann, Isser, and Banks III, 2011, 207). But in their interactions with civilians during patrols, investigations, and interventions to resolve disputes, UNMIL repeatedly emphasized that they were acting "in support of the new LNP, and not as an independent law enforcement agency" (Malan, 2008, 49).

UNMIL also served as a liaison between citizens and the Liberian state. The mission disseminated information about ongoing security and justice sector reforms through public education campaigns and UN radio programs, and increased access to state institutions by rebuilding courthouses, jails, police stations, and other infrastructure, especially in rural areas. UNMIL also sought to improve coordination and depolarize relations between civilians and the state, especially the LNP. Beginning as early as 2004, the mission established hundreds of Community Police Forums to educate citizens about the role of the police, "empower" them to monitor police activity more closely, discourage the use of vigilantism, and "sensitize" police officers to the needs of civilians. Communities elected members to represent them on the forums, and each police station designated specially trained "community policing representatives" as well (Friedman and MacAulay, 2014, 9–10). UNMIL also encouraged communities to organize neighborhood watch teams that would serve as conduits between citizens and the state in rural regions.

---

[38] Camp Four, March 19, 2013.   [39] Lutisu, March 21, 2013; Solomba, May 3, 2013.

At the meso level, UNMIL first prioritized removing the remnants of illegal armed groups and restoring state control over areas rich in natural resources – especially diamonds, rubber, and timber. UNMIL deployed troops to timber-producing regions in Grand Bassa, Grand Gedeh, and Sinoe counties in 2004 (UN Secretary-General, 2004e), and in 2005 began conducting ground and aerial surveillance operations in illegal diamond mining hot spots, further supported by joint patrols with officials from the Liberian Ministry of Lands, Mines, and Energy (UN Secretary-General, 2005c). Over the following months, UNMIL registered hundreds of ex-combatants at the illegally occupied Guthrie rubber plantation in Bomi and Grand Cape Mount counties; seized dozens of single-barrel shotguns from squatters on the Cocopa rubber plantation in Nimba; and, with assistance from the Ministry of Internal Affairs, evacuated 1,000 illegal miners and hunters from Sapo National Park (UN Secretary-General 2005a, 2007a). Guthrie was returned to state control in August 2006, Cocopa in April 2007, and Cavalla – a rubber plantation in Maryland County – in December of that same year (UN Secretary-General 2007a, 2008e).

Alongside efforts to neutralize remobilized rebel groups and expand state authority nationwide, UNMIL worked to harmonize the relationship between Liberia's statutory and customary sectors and elevate the role of the state as the ultimate arbiter of disputes within a constitutionally hybrid legal system (UN Secretary-General, 2012e). Some observers have criticized UNMIL for attempting to enshrine a "principle of uniformity" in Liberia – to create a "singular legal system and framework that works the same way everywhere for everybody" (Isser, Lubkemann, and N'Tow 2009, 9; see also Lubkemann, Isser, and Banks III 2011, 220). While critics are right that UNMIL engaged more with state authorities than with their non-state counterparts, there is little evidence to suggest that the mission aspired to erase the plurality inherent in Liberian law. Instead, UNMIL sought to improve coordination, repair strained relations, and develop a coherent division of labor between the statutory and customary sectors, with clearly delineated roles for each, but with the latter subordinate to the ultimate jurisdiction of the former.

UNMIL personnel enlisted Liberia's traditional leaders for a variety of purposes: to help resolve disputes over land use, tenure, and inheritance; to encourage reconciliation between ethnic groups riven by wartime rivalries; and to prevent the escalation of small-scale disputes into large-scale crises (UN Secretary-General 2004e, 2005a). UNMIL also trained traditional leaders in constitutional laws and protections, international human rights norms, and strategies for preventing and reporting sexual and gender-based violence – crimes that are often adjudicated informally or dismissed out of hand (UN Department of Peacekeeping Operations 2012a; UN Secretary-General 2006a, 2014c). And through mechanisms like the "consultative forum on traditional justice" described in Chapter 4, UNMIL convened representatives of the statutory and customary sectors in an attempt to stimulate dialogue and mitigate coordination problems between them (UN Department of Peacekeeping Operations, 2010b).

At the same time, UNMIL used a combination of naming and shaming, persuasion, and coercion to enforce legal limits on the jurisdiction of customary institutions, and to prevent customary authorities from applying mechanisms of dispute resolution that violate state laws and due process protections. UNMIL audited the Tribal Governor Court system (UN Department of Peacekeeping Operations, 2011b, 13), tracked the progress of cases adjudicated under customary law (UN Department of Peacekeeping Operations, 2012a), monitored and publicly denounced human rights violations committed in the context of "harmful traditional practices" (UN Secretary-General, 2006d, 8), and pressured the Liberian government to formulate more concrete measures to regulate the customary sector (UN Secretary-General, 2014c).

Trial by ordeal was the target of especially sustained condemnation. As Steven Lubkemann and co-authors explain, "in its most extreme form, trial by ordeal violates the most basic standards of human rights and fairness" (Lubkemann, Isser, and Banks III, 2011, 220). Under pressure from UNMIL and other international organizations, Liberia's solicitor general spearheaded a campaign to eliminate trial by ordeal through "exemplary prosecutions" of individuals implicated in its use (IRIN, 2007).[40] The police reinforced these messages as well, insisting that trial by ordeal is illegal and immoral; that customary authorities must "know their limits";[41] and that chiefs and other traditional leaders must recognize that they have "no authority to investigate criminal cases," only "petty disputes."[42]

UNMIL thus served as a surrogate for the Liberian state and a liaison between citizens and state and non-state authorities, adopting many of the same repertoires of micro- and meso-level rule-of-law promotion described in Chapter 4. Much of UNMIL's engagement with Liberia's civilian population occurred in the context of relatively mundane activities that mimicked the functions of a state – patrols, public works, interventions to resolve impending or ongoing disputes. UNMIL also communicated with civilians through UN radio, and through more occasional workshops and public information campaigns, many of them focused on rule-of-law-related topics. Through these mechanisms, UNMIL sought to sensitive Liberians to increased third-party presence in and

---

[40] This preoccupation with trial by ordeal is not new. The 1876 letter from A. F. Russell cited earlier in this chapter listed trial by ordeal as one of the "sins" of tribalism that the state should seek to eradicate (Martin, 1969, 21). The government has attempted to regulate the practice since at least 1948, when the Hinterland Regulations banned the use of poison as a mechanism for divining guilt, but authorized other forms of trial by ordeal that posed no risk to the life of the accused. The Regulations even created a certification system for those responsible for overseeing these trials, administered by the Department of the Interior (Lubkemann, Isser, and Banks III, 2011, 201). Trial by ordeal has since been banned altogether.
[41] JB, Ganta, October 11, 2010.   [42] IG, Gbarnga, October 12, 2010.

around their communities; demonstrate the relative merits of formal over informal approaches to dispute resolution; create opportunities for the Liberian government to claim credit for the mission's own accomplishments; and more generally legitimize the role of the state as a purveyor of security and justice.

UNMIL also disseminated information about changes to Liberian law, and about the trajectory of ongoing reforms within the Liberian police, courts, and prisons. Through Community Police Forums and other venues, the mission helped sustain contact between citizens and state authorities in the hope of improving coordination and depolarizing previously hostile relations. Finally, UNMIL sought to induce greater adherence to state laws within Liberia's customary sector, training non-state authorities in the use of state-sanctioned mechanisms for resolving petty, non-violent disputes, and encouraging them to defer to the ultimate jurisdiction of the state in more serious criminal cases.

Rule-of-Law Promotion beyond UNMIL

For reasons discussed in the introduction, this book focuses on the UN's role in promoting the rule of law in Liberia and elsewhere. But UNMIL was not, of course, the only actor involved in this arena. International NGOs like the Carter Center, the Norwegian Refugee Council, and Search for Common Ground all contributed to UNMIL's efforts, both independently and in coordination with the mission, as did a variety of foreign donors and local NGOs and civil society organizations. The USA also retained a small military presence in the country, though given the Americans' reluctance to encourage political reform or intervene to curtail violence (Witt, 1990; Woollacott, 2003), it is unlikely that Liberians considered this to be much of a deterrent. While the scope of UNMIL's rule-of-law agenda far exceeded that of any other actor operating in the country, the latter were nonetheless influential in propelling UNMIL's agenda forward.

Equally important, while threats to the rule of law remained ominous in the early years of UNMIL's mandate, the mission's prospects for addressing them improved dramatically following the election of Ellen Johnson Sirleaf as Liberia's 24th president in 2005. The first elected female head of state in Africa, Sirleaf was committed to UNMIL's project from the outset, and brought substantial government and private sector experience to her position as she shepherded Liberia through the fraught transitional period.[43] Sirleaf's reputation was far from spotless: during the civil war she had supported Taylor's NPFL both politically and financially, and she was subsequently included on a list of fifty people that the TRC recommended should be "specifically barred from holding public offices; elected or appointed for a period of thirty years"

---

[43] Sirleaf served as Deputy Minister of Finance under William Tolbert from 1971 to 1974, and as Minister of Finance from 1979 to 1980. In the interim, she worked for the World Bank in the Caribbean and Latin America.

(Republic of Liberia Truth and Reconciliation Commission, 2009, 271). Sirleaf argued that implementation of the ban would violate the Liberian constitution's due process guarantees, and in a case brought by another individual on the TRC's list, the Supreme Court agreed.

Sirleaf was also embroiled in multiple nepotism and corruption scandals over her two terms as president. In her first term alone, more than twenty government ministers were accused of corruption by the General Auditing Commission, but not one of them was prosecuted. Sirleaf also appointed three of her sons and one of her sisters to plum posts in the administration, further fueling suspicions that her government was a vehicle for enriching the already wealthy and powerful (Clarke and Azango, 2017). Still, her commitment to the principles underlying UNMIL's rule-of-law mandate far exceeded what the mission could have expected from other Liberian leaders at the time. It is impossible to say how UNMIL's efforts might have evolved had Sirleaf lost the 2005 election to her opponent, soccer star turned politician George Weah (though clues may emerge in the way Weah governs in the future, having won the 2017 election held at the end of Sirleaf's second term). But there is little doubt that UNMIL benefited significantly from the political will that Sirleaf brought to bear on rule-of-law reform.

EVALUATING UNMIL

UNMIL has received mixed but generally positive reviews for its efforts to build peace and establish the rule of law in Liberia. At the most fundamental level, the mission is widely credited with preventing a recurrence of civil war. In a 2006 survey, Jean Krasno found that 94 per cent of Liberian respondents believed security had improved under UNMIL, 91 per cent believed UNMIL had done a "good or very good job" at making them feel safe, and 91 per cent described the conduct of UNMIL personnel as "good or very good" (Krasno, 2006, 5). In another survey conducted three years later, Eric Mvukiyehe and Cyrus Samii similarly found that a majority of respondents attributed the success of the peace process to UNMIL, and expressed confidence in UNMIL's efforts to demobilize ex-combatants, protect civilians, and curb violence between armed actors (Mvukiyehe and Samii, 2010, 3).

The parties to the conflict have voiced similar sentiments. In a 2012 interview, LURD's senior surviving military officer suggested that the power-sharing arrangement prescribed by the CPA "would not have worked" without UNMIL's presence. MODEL's commanding general similarly applauded UNMIL's efforts to mediate disputes that arose during the implementation of the accords. And MODEL's senior military planner described the mission's work as "essential" for preventing armed factions from fighting over "who was in charge" (Kuperman, 2015, 163).

UNMIL has similarly been credited with catalyzing state reform at the macro level. As one Liberian government official put it, UNMIL conveyed "an idea of how to run a government" (Neumann and Schia, 2012, 29). At the micro level as well, while peacekeepers are often criticized for cloistering in walled, heavily guarded compounds in the capital cities of host countries (Autesserre, 2010; Pouligny, 2006), UNMIL personnel are generally believed to have demonstrated relatively high "sensitivity to local needs" (Neumann and Schia, 2012, 10). Respondents in Krasno's survey praised UNMIL's staff for "going beyond their regular duties":

> Liberians described how UN peacekeepers built roads and bridges, road networks, shelters, health centers, schools, renovated buildings, and built market structures. They gave out free medical care and medicine, food, and clothing. All of these efforts seem to have built good will and trust among the local population. (Krasno, 2006, 5)

Mvukiyehe and Samii similarly found that UNMIL enjoys "high legitimacy as a security provider" in Liberia (Mvukiyehe and Samii, 2010, 3).

These points are contested, however, and some analysts are considerably less rosy in their interpretations of UNMIL's legacy. Writing for the Geneva Centre for the Democratic Control of Armed Forces, for example, Judy Smith-Höhn disputes the notion that UNMIL was particularly sensitive to local needs: while UNMIL's staff were "ever-present," they "attach[ed] little overall significance to local conditions and actors" (Smith-Höhn, 2010, 99). Some have further questioned whether UNMIL was actually "ever-present," especially in rural areas. As Paul Higate and Marsha Henry put it, "it was entirely possible to travel for considerable periods of time in Liberia without ever seeing peacekeepers, even where roads were serviceable" (Higate and Henry, 2009, 76).

Some have gone further, arguing that UNMIL adhered to an excessively narrow interpretation of its mandate to use force in order to prevent or defuse attacks on civilian populations (Aboagye and Bah, 2004, 16) – an all too common critique of UN peacekeeping, even in Chapter VII missions (Matanock, 2017). Even when UNMIL *did* intervene, its efforts were sometimes marred by accusations of bias towards particular ethnic or religious groups. The Liberian civil war pitted the country's Mandingo community, which is largely Muslim, against several predominately Christian tribes – notably the Lorma and Krahn. UNMIL troops have been accused on occasion of favoring the former over the latter (Higate and Henry, 2009, 132). For example, when riots erupted between Lorma and Mandingo residents of the city of Voinjama, Lofa County in 2010, UNMIL's Jordanian and Pakistani personnel were accused of protecting the city's mosques while sitting idly by as Mandingo rioters burned its churches to the ground (Paczynska, 2010, 20).

While incidents of this sort are rare, and while UNMIL is generally perceived as impartial (as we will see in the next chapter), accusations of bias have nonetheless tainted the mission's reputation among some Liberians. Even more problematic were the sexual exploitation and abuse scandals in which UNMIL personnel occasionally found themselves embroiled. Scandals of this sort are tragically common among peacekeepers in African countries, and UNMIL was no exception. In a representative survey of Monrovia residents conducted in 2012, Bernd Beber and colleagues found that more than half of female respondents had engaged in transactional sex, most (over three-quarters) of them with UNMIL personnel, typically in exchange for money. They estimate that for each additional battalion of 1,000 UNMIL peacekeepers, the probability that a Liberian woman would engage in her first act of transactional sex in a given year increased by roughly 3 per cent. Beber and co-authors write that sexual exploitation and abuse "[undermined] the UN's broader peace-building goals in Liberia," leaving behind a "distorted economy" in which selling sex became the norm for many young Liberian women (Beber et al., 2017, 4).

UNMIL's attempts to consolidate state authority nationwide have proven controversial among those who believe the mission did not do enough to "build confidence among the local population in the capacities" of state institutions (Neumann and Schia, 2012, 46), and even more controversial among critics who accuse the mission of alienating and marginalizing customary alternatives to the state. In a report for the Norwegian Institute of International Affairs, Hannah Neumann and Niels Schia describe UNMIL as "largely ignorant" of the nuances of Liberia's customary sector, which has been "widely ignored or used only sporadically when needed for traditional reconciliation" (Neumann and Schia, 2012, 33). Stephen Lubkemann and co-authors argue that UNMIL's attempts to restrict the jurisdiction of customary institutions provoked "helplessness and frustration" among Liberians, and undermined the customary sector's effectiveness in resolving "issues of grave concern to the population." Lubkemann et al. similarly describe UNMIL's campaign to eradicate trial by ordeal as a "frontal attack" on social and cultural practices that had long been responsible for sustaining order at the local level (Lubkemann, Isser, and Banks III, 2011, 195, 221, 231).

How to reconcile these sharply divergent perspectives? Each of the skeptical accounts described above corresponds to one of the rival theories summarized in Chapter 4. Like many multidimensional peacekeeping operations, I argue that UNMIL served as a catalyst for state reform in Liberia, a surrogate for the reformed Liberian state, and a liaison between citizens and state and non-state authorities. According to some critics, however, UNMIL was too time- and resource-constrained to reform state institutions at the macro level, much less to restore the authority of those institutions at the micro and meso levels. To other critics, UNMIL was biased, negligent, and abusive; to others, it "crowded out" both the state and its non-state competitors, provoking a backlash from those most invested in the status quo. If these critics are right, then we should expect exposure to peacekeeping in Liberia to have null or even adverse effects on citizens' willingness to rely on state institutions when crimes are committed or violence occurs. Likewise, we should expect exposure to UNMIL to have null or adverse effects on informal authorities' use of illegal or extrajudicial mechanisms of dispute resolution, and null or adverse effects on their willingness to defer to the ultimate jurisdiction of the state.

Competing perspectives on UNMIL's record thus yield competing empirical predictions for me to test. But with few exceptions (Mvukiyehe and Samii 2010, 2018; Mvukiyehe 2018), assessments of UNMIL's efficacy typically hinge on broad descriptions of the quality of peace, security, and the rule of law in Liberia today. Rarely do analysts consider whether the rule of law in Liberia might have followed a different trajectory over the past decade and a half had UNMIL never deployed, and rarely do they provide evidence that would allow us to adjudicate whether the quality of the rule of law in Liberia today is attributable to UNMIL. Regardless, UNMIL is not an unambiguous success story, and many questions remain. Did UNMIL's presence help repair the ruptured social contract between Liberian citizens and the Liberian state? Did it help rationalize Liberia's hybrid legal system, and inculcate respect for the rule of law? Or did it further estrange Liberians from their own government, provoking a backlash and empowering local competitors to national rule? These are empirical questions to which the next two chapters will provide empirical answers.

7

Sub-national Evidence II

Evaluating the UN from the Bottom-Up

In Chapter 6, I traced the trajectory of the rule of law in Liberia through periods of internal colonialism, dictatorship, civil war, and international intervention. I characterized Liberia as both a hard and a crucial case for testing the impact of UN peacekeeping on the rule of law, and described the myriad challenges to the rule of law that UNMIL encountered when it deployed in 2003. In the next two chapters, I use original qualitative interviews and quantitative survey data collected over fifteen months of fieldwork in Liberia to test the effects of UNMIL's operations on the rule of law at the micro and meso levels. This chapter describes my data and research design, focusing in particular on measurement and causal inference. The next chapter presents my results.

My analysis extends previous assessments of UNMIL in at least six ways. First, I provide rich, highly granular data on exposure to UNMIL at both the individual and community levels over multiple years and multiple Liberian counties. With the exception of recent research by Cyrus Samii and Eric Mvukiyehe (Mvukiyehe and Samii 2010, 2018; Mvukiyehe 2018), studies of UNMIL's efficacy typically rely on qualitative or purely anecdotal accounts of the mission's activities on the ground. My surveys allow me to capture these activities in more nuanced and systematic ways.

Second, my analysis leverages multiple proxies for the rule of law at the micro and meso levels, grounded in the theoretical framework developed in Chapters 3 and 4 and tailored to the Liberian context. In addition to direct questions about Liberians' trust and reliance on both state and non-state security and justice providers, the survey incorporates innovative indirect surveying techniques designed to elicit honest responses to potentially sensitive topics. As discussed in previous chapters, one of the most insidious threats to the rule of law in post-conflict settings is the proliferation of illegal or extrajudicial punishment – mob violence, lynching, trial by ordeal. Testing whether UN intervention mitigates these threats requires measuring behaviors that are, by definition, illegal. Indirect surveying techniques allow me to minimize the risk of under-reporting due to social desirability bias – i.e. "cheap talk" – generating more reliable estimates for the prevalence of these illegal behaviors and thus more credible estimates of UNMIL's impact on them.

Third, the richness of my data allows me to disentangle the effects of different types of exposure to UNMIL at different levels of analysis. I distinguish between patrols, public works projects, and interventions to resolve impending or ongoing disputes, and between UNMIL's community-level operations and citizens' individual-level interactions with UNMIL personnel. These disparate forms of exposure may have equally disparate effects on citizens' attitudes and behaviors, which my analysis is able to capture. Fourth, I combine multiple identification strategies to support a causal interpretation of my results, using interviews with UNMIL personnel to better understand the selection process underlying the geographical distribution of patrols, public works, and interventions, and taking advantage of two different sources of as-if random variation in the intensity of UNMIL's operations to more cleanly estimate their causal effects. Each of these identification strategies has limitations. My goal is to triangulate between them.

Fifth, with multiple waves of survey data to work with, I am able to estimate the impact of UNMIL's presence in both the short and medium term. This is especially important given that UNMIL was already beginning to draw down at the time of my survey. Some critics worry that host states will simply revert more or less quickly and messily to the *status quo ante* after peacekeepers withdraw. While the medium-term effects I estimate only cover a period of two years, they nonetheless provide important insights into the durability of UNMIL's impact on the rule of law in Liberia. Finally, by combining surveys with semi-structured in-depth interviews, I am able to substantiate and contextualize my quantitative findings with qualitative insights gleaned from Liberian citizens, local leaders, and government officials, as well as from UNMIL personnel.

QUANTITATIVE DATA

Selecting Counties

At the core of my research design is an original three-wave panel survey covering 243 rural Liberian towns and villages. All 243 communities are located in one of three border counties – Lofa, Nimba, and Grand Gedeh. (Lofa borders Guinea and Sierra Leone, Nimba borders Côte d'Ivoire and Guinea, and Grand Gedeh borders Côte d'Ivoire.) Nimba is the largest and most densely populated of the three, with a population of 462,000 residents, according to the 2008 census. Grand Gedeh is the smallest and most sparsely inhabited, with a population of just 125,000. Lofa, with a population of 276,000, falls in between. Figure 7.1 maps the 243 communities in the sample.

I focus on these three counties because they were among the most severely affected by the Liberian civil war (Sisk and Risley, 2005, 34); because they

Quantitative Data

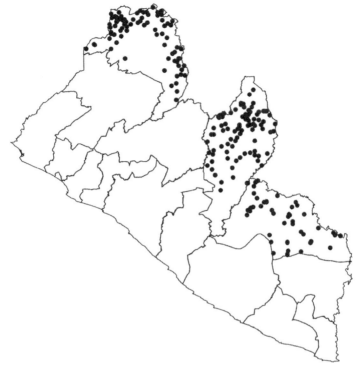

FIGURE 7.1 Distribution of communities in Liberia survey sample
Note: Map showing the distribution of communities in my survey sample in Liberia.

have been repeatedly threatened by spillover from instability in neighboring countries, even after the civil war ended; and, relatedly, because they have become high priorities for both peacekeeping and state consolidation in the post-conflict period (Caparini, 2014). The three counties also occupy a sort of middle ground between statutory and customary law in Liberia. In Monrovia, formal institutions dominate informal ones; in the more distant hinterlands, the opposite is true. In Lofa, Nimba, and Grand Gedeh, in contrast, statutory and customary institutions coexist and compete with one another, and jurisdictional conflicts are rife. These three counties thus constitute an important test case for my theory in Liberia. Lofa, Nimba, and Grand Gedeh also have different ethnic compositions, and suffered disparate forms and levels of violence during the civil war, thus capturing some of Liberia's diversity while remaining demographically similar and physically proximate enough to allow for credible causal inference.

Nimba was the "epicenter of opposition" to the dictatorship of Samuel K. Doe, and was the site of frequent unrest throughout his nine years in power. After Doe's former army commander Thomas Quiwonkpa was ousted from the regime in 1983, his supporters – many of them dissidents from the Gio and Mano tribes – began organizing militias in neighboring Côte d'Ivoire, launching raids into Quiwonkpa's home county of Nimba from across the border. Doe responded with characteristic brutality, singling out young Gio and Mano men for detention, interrogation, and execution. Nimba is also where the civil war began on Christmas Eve, 1989, when Charles Taylor's NPFL crossed from Côte d'Ivoire into the border town of Butuo. Taylor's decision to enter through Nimba was strategic, and the county's Gio and Mano residents subsequently became some of his most loyal recruits (Ellis, 2006, 58, 78, 143, 312).

If Nimba was the epicenter of opposition to Doe, then Grand Gedeh was the epicenter of loyalty. The county is the ancestral homeland of the Krahn tribe, of which Doe was a member, and from which he drew much of his support. Taylor considered Grand Gedeh to be enemy territory, and never managed to incorporate it into his plans for a "Greater Liberia." The county was relatively peaceful during Doe's regime, but was the site of frequent fighting thereafter, as the NPFL struggled to quell a stubborn local resistance. The same was true of Lofa, which suffered virtually uninterrupted violence throughout the conflict as rival factions jockeyed for power. When the NPFL entered the county, one of its first acts was to slaughter some 500 residents of the predominately Mandingo town of Bakedu. The massacre helped catalyze the formation of ULIMO, an armed group organized by Krahn and Mandingo exiles in Guinea and Sierra Leone.

A majority-Mandingo faction of ULIMO known as ULIMO-K eventually seized control of Lofa from the NPFL, establishing its *de facto* capital in the city of Voinjama. Taylor responded by channeling financial and logistical support to the Lofa Defense Force, a militia composed primarily of Lorma and Kpelle refugees who returned to Lofa to fight ULIMO-K. The consequences of this "ethnic contest" between the county's Lorma, Kpelle, and Mandingo inhabitants would reverberate throughout the conflict and post-conflict years (Ellis, 2006, 114, 129). Indeed, Lofa was the site of arguably the single most destabilizing incident of collective violence in the post-conflict period, when four days of riots between Lorma and Mandingo residents of Voinjama resulted in four deaths, dozens of injuries, and the destruction of much of the city's infrastructure.

Finally, Lofa, Nimba, and Grand Gedeh also capture much of the variation in the geographical distribution of UNMIL personnel from different contingents and nationalities. Until 2009, UNMIL divided Liberia into four numbered "sectors," roughly encompassing the northwestern, south central, north central, and southeastern regions of the country. Lofa was assigned to Sector 2, Nimba to Sector 3, and Grand Gedeh to Sector 4.[1] Nationwide, Pakistan and Bangladesh supplied UNMIL with more troops and Military Observers than any other country. Ethiopia was also a significant contributor in the first

---

[1] The only sector not represented in my survey is Sector 1, which encompassed Monrovia and its four surrounding counties – Montserrado, Margibi, Grand Bassa, and River Cess. This scheme was later simplified, and UNMIL's four sectors were collapsed into two: southern (A) and northern (B). All three counties in my survey lie in the northern sector.

half of the mission's mandate, as were China and Ghana in the second half. Nigeria provided a substantial number of troops as well, though these were largely based in Monrovia and its environs. The counties in my sample reflect this distribution, with multiple large contingents of Pakistani troops stationed in Lofa and Grand Gedeh and Bangladeshi troops in Nimba, and smaller contingents of Ethiopian, Chinese, and Nigerian troops rotating in and out, especially in Grand Gedeh. UNMIL police officers hailed from an even wider variety of countries, including India, Jordan, and Nepal, and were dispersed throughout the country, including the three counties in my sample.

Selecting Communities

The survey was conducted in three waves: between March and April 2009, November 2010 and January 2011, and February and April 2013. The 243 communities in the sample constitute the smallest administrative unit in Liberia, with populations ranging from a few hundred to a few thousand residents.[2] Importantly, these communities are not representative of Liberia, nor of the counties from which they were sampled. I designed the survey in collaboration with Christopher Blattman and Alexandra Hartman for purposes of a randomized controlled trial evaluating an alternative dispute resolution program administered by the Catholic Justice and Peace Commission, an NGO (Blattman, Hartman, and Blair, 2014; Hartman, Blair, and Blattman, 2020). Government officials and other stakeholders identified communities they believed were at high risk of violence, and thus especially likely to benefit from the training. While this is an important scope condition, comparison to a nationally representative survey suggests that by 2011, the 243 communities in my sample were not much more conflicted than the average Liberian town or village, either in these three counties or nationwide.[3] These parallels suggest

---

[2] Most communities are villages or small towns. Fifty are neighborhoods (or "quarters") within larger towns, with their own quarter chiefs. The largest town has sixteen quarters, but most have fewer, with a median of five. Due to budget and time constraints, only local leaders were surveyed in 40 of the 243 communities in the third wave. These forty communities do not appear to differ from the others in any systematic way.

[3] Patrick Vinck and co-authors' nationally representative survey was implemented at the same time as our second wave of data collection (Vinck, Pham, and Kreutzer, 2011). The parallels between our samples are striking. A total of 4 per cent of Lofa respondents in Vinck et al.'s survey reported being victims of armed violence in the previous year, compared to 5 per cent in Nimba, 4 per cent in Grand Gedeh, and 7 per cent nationwide. In our survey, 1 per cent of respondents reported being victims of armed violence in Lofa, 3 per cent in Nimba, and 3 per cent in Grand Gedeh. Rates of robbery and burglary were similar as well: in Vinck et al., 12 per cent of Lofa respondents reported a robbery or burglary in the past year, compared to 11 per cent in Nimba, 18 per cent in Grand Gedeh, and 15 per cent nationwide. In our survey, 14 per cent of respondents reported a robbery or burglary in Lofa, 25 per cent in Nimba, and 13 per cent in Grand Gedeh. With the exception of Nimba, these rates are quite comparable. Complaints of witchcraft were similar across surveys as well – indeed, if anything they were less common in our sample than in Vinck et al.'s. While the communities in our sample could be more conflicted along other dimensions, it is not obvious why this would be the case.

that the results of my analysis are likely to generalize to other parts of Liberia. I discuss generalizability to other countries in Chapter 9.

Selecting Respondents

In each community we surveyed a representative sample of twenty randomly elected residents and four purposively selected local leaders – typically a town chief, women's group leader, youth group leader, and minority ethnic group leader. These positions exist in almost all Liberian communities, and represent important and distinct cross-sections of the Liberian populace. In each wave, we collected data from the same four local leaders[4] and a new random sample of twenty residents, with residents and local leaders surveyed independently of one another. The survey covered a wide variety of topics, from demographics, employment, and education to experiences of violence during the civil war. The survey also yielded a wealth of data on respondents' attitudes towards both statutory and customary institutions, their compliance with state laws, their reliance on the police and courts to adjudicate the most serious incidents of crime and violence, and their prior exposure to and perceptions of UNMIL. All surveys were conducted in private to ensure anonymity, usually in or near the respondent's home. Non-response was typically less than 5–10 per cent per community.

QUALITATIVE DATA

I draw on three sources of qualitative data to complement and contextualize my quantitative results. First, I used the UN Secretary-General's progress reports on UNMIL to better understand the nature and intensity of the mission's rule-of-law-related activities in Liberia. Second, I conducted in-depth semi-structured interviews with over a dozen UN civilian and military personnel. I also interviewed Liberian citizens, police and corrections officers, court clerks, magistrates, elected officials, and bureaucrats, as well as the staff of several Liberian NGOs. I conducted forty-two interviews in total: nineteen with UNMIL personnel; six with representatives of local and international NGOs;

The communities in our sample are demographically similar to those in Vinck et al. as well. A total of 48 per cent of respondents in our sample were men, compared to 50 per cent in Vinck et al. The average respondent in our sample was 41 years old, compared to 37 years in Vinck et al. 42 per cent of our sample had no education, compared to 35 per cent in Vinck et al. – a difference attributable to the much higher rate of educational attainment among Monrovia residents in Vinck et al.'s sample. (83 per cent of Monrovia residents had at least some primary education.) 13 per cent of our sample was Muslim, compared to 10 per cent in Vinck et al. Along all of these dimensions, the respondents in my analysis are typical of rural Liberians more generally.

[4] In communities where one or more local leaders died, moved, or left office between waves of data collection, we tracked the position rather than the individual.

six with government officials; and eleven with citizens.⁵ I randomly sampled my citizen respondents, and selected the other respondents non-randomly through referral (i.e. snowball sampling). The goal throughout was to interview individuals who could speak knowledgeably about UNMIL and its role in Liberia. I use these interviews to document the selection process underlying UNMIL's operations, and to motivate my measurement and identification strategies.

Third, I draw on qualitative interviews conducted with dozens of local leaders from the second and third waves of survey data collection. As part of the survey, Liberian enumerators asked local leaders to report on the incidence of various types of crime and violence in their communities. Several months after the second wave of data collection was complete, we hired a Liberian research assistant with extensive experience conducting qualitative research to return to all communities in which at least two local leaders reported an incident of collective violence in the past year, defined for our purposes as violent strikes, violent protests, and violent confrontations between members of different ethnic groups. The research assistant conducted long-form open-ended interviews with multiple local leaders in each of these communities – twenty-six interviews in total – to document why the incidents began, how they escalated, and whether and how they were resolved.

As part of the third wave of survey data collection, enumerators elicited short narrative accounts from local leaders who reported *any* incident of crime or violence in their community in the past year – not just collective violence, but also murder, rape, and trial by ordeal. The enumerators conducted seventy-five interviews in total, giving local leaders an opportunity to describe these potentially destabilizing incidents in much richer detail than is possible in the context of a survey. I use transcriptions of these interviews to better understand how conflicts are resolved in rural Liberia, and how different security and justice providers (including UNMIL and the LNP) contribute.

MEASURING EXPOSURE TO UNMIL

While peacekeepers may engage with communities using a variety of different mechanisms, most of their interactions with citizens and local leaders occur in the context of one of three activities: patrols, public works projects, and interventions to resolve impending or ongoing disputes. Because these three activities are both frequent and universal, their effects in Lofa, Nimba, and Grand Gedeh are likely to generalize to other parts of Liberia, and potentially to other countries as well.

---

⁵ All but two of these interviews were conducted in person between June 2010 and November 2012; the remaining two were conducted via phone and email in October 2013. In-person interviews were conducted in Bong, Lofa, Nimba, and Grand Gedeh counties, as well as in Monrovia.

Ideally I could use UNMIL's own records to operationalize these activities. Unfortunately, this was not possible, as the quality of these records is highly inconsistent, and in some years they are incomplete or missing altogether.[6] Instead, I rely on my survey of local leaders to record the nature and intensity of UNMIL's operations at the community level. As discussed in Chapter 4, local leaders often act as liaisons between peacekeepers and citizens, providing information and lowering cultural and logistical barriers to entry (Autesserre, 2010; Veit, 2011). As such, they can generally offer accurate accounts of the UN's activities in their communities. Indeed, as we will see, local leaders' accounts are highly correlated with residents' own reports of interactions with UNMIL personnel.

I use the survey of local leaders to construct three sets of independent variables:

1. Four binary (or "dummy") variables indicating whether UNMIL patrolled each community weekly, monthly, occasionally, or not at all in the preceding year (i.e. the year prior to data collection).
2. A dummy indicating whether UNMIL built or repaired public works (roads, bridges, clinics, schools, etc.) in the community in the preceding year.
3. A dummy indicating whether UNMIL intervened to resolve impending or ongoing disputes in the community in the preceding year.

To minimize recall bias, each dummy captures the modal response across the four local leaders in each community.[7]

---

[6] Consider, for example, the weekly situation reports (or "sitreps") that UNMIL's police contingent (UNPOL) was required to submit as documentation of its activities in Liberia. I compiled all UNPOL sitreps from 2006 to 2012, then searched them for any mention of UNPOL patrols. Unfortunately, some months have only one or two sitreps, and many have none at all, especially early in the mission. And even the more complete sitreps seem to capture only a fraction of UNMIL's operations in the country. Relying on the sitreps alone, it would appear that only 3 of the 243 communities in my sample were ever patrolled over this six-year period. These three communities happen to be the capital cities of their respective counties. Based on my own survey data and interviews with UNPOL personnel, this is a very incomplete account of UNPOL's presence in these counties. In principle, it might be possible to glean additional information on the locations of patrols from interviews with UNMIL staff, though this approach would likely prove noisy and error-prone at such a low level of disaggregation.

[7] For example, if two of four local leaders reported weekly patrols over the past year, I code weekly patrols in that community, even if the third local leader reported monthly patrols and the fourth reported only occasional patrols. Since not all local leaders were present for all of UNMIL's visits, in communities with multiple modes I take the maximum. For example, if two local leaders reported weekly patrols and two reported monthly patrols, I code weekly patrols. In a handful of communities (less than 6 per cent of the sample), all four local leaders disagreed about the frequency of patrols. I exclude these communities from my analysis, but my results are substantively unchanged if I include them. I discuss recall bias in further detail later in the chapter.

TABLE 7.1 *Exposure to UNMIL in Liberia survey sample*

	2010		2012	
	Mean	N	Mean	N
Community-level exposure				
Weekly patrols	0.14	228	0.14	243
Monthly patrols	0.27	228	0.15	243
Occasional patrols	0.38	228	0.53	243
Interventions	0.28	243	0.21	243
Public works	0.19	243	0.23	243
Individual-level exposure				
Spent time with UNMIL	0.61	4,687	0.60	3,957

Note: Descriptive statistics on exposure to UNMIL in 2010 and 2012. Measures of community-level exposure are from the local leaders survey. For each type of exposure, I report the modal response across the four local leaders surveyed in each community. Measures of individual-level exposure are from the residents survey.

These dummies do not distinguish between activities undertaken by different contingents (e.g. UN troops or police officers). While ideally I could test the effects of different mission contingents relative to one another, in pre-testing I found that it was nearly impossible to elicit these distinctions from local leaders. Respondents do distinguish between military and civilian personnel, though even here the line is sometimes blurred. As an individual-level complement to these community-level measures, I also asked residents whether they had interacted (or "spent time") with any UNMIL personnel in the past. "Spending time" is a Liberian colloquialism that connotes a deeper level of engagement than mere "passing by." Indeed, in my qualitative interviews it was not uncommon to hear Liberians criticize UNMIL for "passing by" their communities without "spending time."

As Table 7.1 shows, even among these rural communities, UNMIL managed to establish a pervasive presence.[8] In both 2010 and 2012, local leaders reported weekly UNMIL patrols in about 14 per cent of communities. Monthly patrols were more common (27 per cent and 15 per cent of communities in 2010 and 2012, respectively), and occasional patrols even more so (38 per cent and 53 per cent in 2010 and 2012, respectively). Less than one-quarter of communities reported no patrols at all – a remarkable figure, given that the average community in the sample was located roughly an hour away from the nearest usable road. UNMIL intervened to resolve disputes in just over one-quarter (28 per cent) of communities in 2010, and just over one-fifth (21 per cent) in 2012. Roughly one-quarter (23 per cent) of communities reported UNMIL public works in 2012, up from roughly one-fifth (19 per cent)

---

[8] Table 7.1 reports exposure to UNMIL in the second (2010) and third (2012) waves of data collection only. Unfortunately, we did not measure exposure in the first (2008) wave.

in 2010. In both waves of the survey, a majority of residents reported having spent time with UNMIL personnel (61 per cent and 60 per cent in 2010 and 2012, respectively).

MEASURING THE RULE OF LAW

UNMIL sought to rationalize Liberia's hybrid legal system and "bring it into compliance with international standards of rule of law" (Lubkemann, Isser, and Banks III, 2011, 220). As discussed in Chapter 6, UNMIL focused on two priorities at the micro and meso levels: inducing citizens and informal authorities to respect the constitutionally mandated division of labor between the statutory and customary sectors – with the latter responsible for petty claims and non-violent disputes, and the former responsible for more serious criminal cases – and eradicating the use of trial by ordeal. UNMIL also sought to improve Liberians' perceptions of the police and courts, while encouraging them to recognize and report acts of corruption. UNMIL's first priority corresponds to the rule-of-law requirement that both citizens and non-state authorities respect the state's claim to original and ultimate jurisdiction over the most severe incidents of crime and violence. The second priority corresponds to the requirement that non-state authorities eschew mechanisms of adjudication that violate state law.

To operationalize the first requirement, enumerators read respondents three hypothetical scenarios of crime and violence, then asked them to select which type of authority they would prefer to respond in each case.[9] The three scenarios involved incidents of increasing severity, all of which fall unambiguously under state jurisdiction: (1) mob violence, (2) murder, and (3) ethnic riots resulting in fatalities.[10] The menu of responses included three categories of authority: statutory (police and other "government people"), customary (chiefs and other "traditional leaders"), and UNMIL. I use these questions to construct three categorical variables indicating respondents' preferences

---

[9] Ideally I could measure citizens' willingness to rely on state authorities in *actual* criminal cases. But since UNMIL sometimes intervened in response to victims' complaints, it is difficult to tell whether more exposure to UNMIL caused more reporting to state authorities, or more reporting to state authorities caused more exposure to UNMIL. For this reason I rely on hypothetical scenarios instead.

[10] Specifically, respondents were asked (in Liberian English):

1) *If there's a big group of people making noise to fight in your community [mob violence], who would you most like to resolve the situation?*
2) *If there's a murder in your community, who would you most like to resolve the situation?*
3) *If there's a hala hala [riot] between two tribes or religions in your community and someone dies, who would you most like to resolve the situation?*

in each scenario, and a fourth indicating their modal preference across the three scenarios.[11] Enumerators also asked respondents whether they believe state institutions are corrupt or "eating money," and whether they believe state institutions treat members of all ethnic and religious groups equally. For purposes of comparison, enumerators asked the same questions about customary authorities and UNMIL. I code dummies indicating whether the respondent agreed or strongly agreed with statements describing each category of authority as biased or corrupt.

Operationalizing the second requirement – that non-state authorities reject modes of adjudication that violate state law – requires quantifying behaviors that are, by definition, illegal. I focus in particular on trial by ordeal, as "no other practice has received as much attention from the United Nations and human rights community" in Liberia in recent years (Lubkemann, Isser, and Banks III, 2011, 220). Because trial by ordeal is illegal, reporting on its use is tantamount to implicating oneself or one's community in a crime. Respondents may be reluctant to do this, even in the context of an anonymous survey.

Due to some combination of fear, social desirability bias, and non-random refusal to respond, direct survey questions would likely underestimate the prevalence of trial by ordeal, and thus overestimate compliance with state law. More problematic, the sensitivity of direct questions would likely correlate with UNMIL's presence. UNMIL was intimately involved in efforts to eliminate trial by ordeal; Liberians who are aware of these efforts are likely to view questions about trial by ordeal as especially sensitive. As a result, they are likely to be less truthful in their responses, or less willing to respond in the first place. In either case, my results will be biased, and will likely overestimate the impact of UNMIL's operations on the rule of law.

In order to mitigate this problem, I included a list experiment in my third wave of data collection. List experiments are designed to increase the credibility of survey self-reports by allowing respondents to answer sensitive questions indirectly (Tourangeau and Yan, 2007). In the conventional setup, respondents are randomly assigned to one of two groups, treatment or control. They are then read a list of items and asked to count the number of items on the list that apply to them – for example, beliefs they hold or policies they support. The list contains a sensitive item for the treatment group – a controversial policy or an unpopular belief – but not for the control group. We can then use the difference between the mean number of items selected in each group to generate an estimate for the prevalence of the sensitive item.

---

[11] For example, if a respondent preferred that the state respond to murders and ethnic riots but that customary authorities respond to mob violence, then I code the state as the respondent's modal preference. For respondents who selected a different authority in each scenario, I code all three as the modal preference. This occurred for approximately 4 per cent of respondents in both the second and third waves of the survey.

If no treatment group respondent selects the sensitive item, then the difference in means should be zero. If *all* treatment group respondents select the sensitive item, then the difference should be one. Advances in the analysis of list experiments have made them increasingly popular in recent years, and they have been used to study a wide variety of sensitive topics, from hate crimes (Rayburn, Earleywine, and Davison, 2003) to vote buying (Gonzalez-Ocantos et al., 2012) to support for illegal armed groups during civil war (Blair, Imai, and Lyall, 2014).

I used a list experiment to measure the prevalence of trial by ordeal as reported by local leaders. I chose to focus on local leaders rather than residents for several reasons. First, trial by ordeal is often conducted in secret, which is part of the reason it has proven so difficult to eradicate (Neumann and Schia, 2012, 33). As a result, "plaintiffs," "defendants," and local leaders may be the only ones who know that a trial has occurred. Since the probability that a plaintiff or defendant will be among the twenty randomly selected residents in any given community is very small, logistically, it made more sense to rely on the reports of local leaders. Moreover, responding to list experiments requires at least a basic level of numeracy. In rural Liberia, local leaders are more likely to be numerate than randomly selected citizens. Relying on local leaders thus allowed me to minimize measurement error and ensure comprehension while still mitigating social desirability bias and non-random non-response.

The list experiment began with a vignette describing a hypothetical burglary in the respondent's community. Burglaries are criminal offenses, and by law should be reported to the police. As I learned in pre-testing, however, chiefs and other informal authorities sometimes refuse to call the police in these cases, instead using trial by ordeal to divine the burglar's identity. Trial by ordeal is less common in more serious cases (like murder), or in cases where the perpetrator is known (like assault). Focusing on burglaries thus allowed me to estimate reliance on the police and the use of trial by ordeal simultaneously.

After the vignette, I randomly assigned respondents to hear one of two lists of options for "handling" the hypothetical burglary. The treatment group list included three control items and one sensitive one (trial by ordeal). Treatment group respondents heard the following script (in Liberian English):

Let say someone bust into your house and took something, and nobody knows who did it. I'm going to tell you some different ways that people can handle that matter. I want you to tell me how many ways can happen in this community. Don't tell me which ones. Just tell me how many.

1. *Call the police*
2. *Just leave it alone and do nothing about it*
3. *Take it to the UNMIL people*
4. *Call for sassywood or hot cutlass [trial by ordeal]*

Control group respondents heard the same scenario and the three control items, without the sensitive one.[12]

ESTABLISHING CAUSALITY

UNMIL does not randomly decide where to patrol, intervene, or build public works. Likewise, residents do not randomly decide whether or not to interact with UNMIL personnel. This raises the risk of selection bias. If individuals and communities that reported exposure to UNMIL differ systematically from those that did not, then my results will be biased. In particular, if individuals and communities that reported exposure to UNMIL were also more receptive to state laws and institutions to begin with, then my analysis will overestimate UNMIL's impact on the rule of law. I use three different identification strategies to mitigate this concern and isolate the effect of UNMIL's operations from potential unobserved confounders.

Identification Strategy 1: Modeling UNMIL's Selection Process

To begin, I combine UN Secretary-General progress reports, the secondary literature on peacekeeping in Liberia and elsewhere, and my own qualitative interviews with UNMIL personnel to generate a principled, contextually grounded set of control variables to include in my analysis. These controls help me model the selection process underlying UNMIL patrols, interventions, and public works. While there is undoubtedly some slippage between the selection process described in these sources and the one implemented on the ground, UNMIL's selection criteria are, for the most part, knowable and quantifiable,

---

[12] I included a semi-sensitive option ("just leave it alone and do nothing") among the control items in order to minimize the risk of floor and ceiling effects (Blair and Imai, 2012). As I discuss in the next chapter, this strategy appears to have worked. Following an innovation introduced by Daniel Corstange, enumerators asked control group respondents direct (yes or no) questions about each control item on the list (Corstange, 2009). This approach has two advantages for my purposes. First, it increases statistical precision (Blair and Imai, 2012; Corstange, 2009). Second and more important, it allows me to assess the impact of UNMIL's activities not just on the sensitive item, but on each of the control items as well.

In most list experiments, the control items are used only to facilitate measurement of the sensitive one(s). But this approach discards data. In my case, the control items are theoretically important in and of themselves. I expect exposure to UNMIL to increase reliance on the police (the first requirement for the rule of law) while simultaneously reducing reliance on trial by ordeal (the second requirement). Using Corstange's modified design, both of these effects can be identified.

Following a recommendation by Graeme Blair and Kosuke Imai, enumerators first read control group respondents all three of the control items together, then asked them to respond to each individually. This maximizes the degree of similarity between the structure of the treatment and control group lists in Corstange's modified design (Blair and Imai, 2012).

facilitating causal inference. Since UNMIL typically did not decide where to patrol, intervene, or implement public works based on the characteristics of particular individuals, and since the selection process underlying individuals' decisions to interact with UNMIL is likely more idiosyncratic, I focus on measuring potential confounders at the community level, though my analysis includes controls for potential individual-level confounders as well, as I discuss later in this section.

I include controls for six sets of community-level confounders in particular.

CRIME AND VIOLENCE: UNMIL was more likely to patrol in places with high rates of crime and violence.[13] The same is true, axiomatically, of interventions to resolve disputes. Much of peacekeepers' "day-to-day work" involves preventing the escalation of small-scale conflicts into large-scale crises (Fortna, 2008a, 96–7). UNMIL was no exception, and the mission's progress reports are replete with examples of peacekeeping personnel engaged in precisely these sorts of activities. To model this aspect of the selection process, I include a dummy indicating whether there was any major destabilizing incident of crime or violence in each community in the past year (e.g. a murder or riot), based on local leaders' reports.

ACCESSIBILITY: While in theory UNMIL's operations could target even "the most remote areas,"[14] in practice they were constrained by accessibility. Roads were an especially important constraint. As one UNMIL volunteer explains, "if your area can't be reached by car, you won't be visited" (Higate and Henry, 2009, 77). Inaccessibility also hindered the construction of public works. As the UN Secretary-General's 20th and 21st progress reports discuss, heavy rains "seriously restrict implementation of infrastructural projects and other development activities" (UN Secretary-General, 2010b, 10), washing away roads, ruining repairs, and limiting construction to the dry season in many far-flung communities (UN Secretary-General, 2010a, 9).

As proxies for accessibility, I include a dummy for cell phone reception and an estimate for the amount of time it takes to walk from each community to the nearest road that remains passable in the rainy season. Because the most accessible communities also tend to be the most urban and the most densely populated, and because, cross-nationally, peacekeepers tend to deploy to cities (Kathman et al., 2017), I include an estimate for the population of each community as well. These variables are from the local leaders survey.

POVERTY AND AVAILABILITY OF SOCIAL SERVICES: UNMIL public works were designed to improve the quality of infrastructure and social service provision, typically by targeting poor, under-served communities.[15] As proxies for poverty and social services, I include an index of twelve household assets (including cell phones, radios, generators, and livestock), aggregated from the household to the

---

[13] MS, Gbarnga, October 11, 2010. [14] KY, Gbarnga, October 11, 2010.
[15] AD, Monrovia, March 20, 2014.

Establishing Causality

community level,[16] and an index of fourteen different social services available in each community (including clinics, schools, wells, and latrines). The assets index is from the residents survey, while the social services index is from the local leaders survey. Because the most accessible communities also tend to be the largest, most urbanized, and most developed, these measures serve as proxies for accessibility as well.

NATURAL RESOURCES: As discussed in Chapter 6, UNMIL prioritized restoring the government's access to, and control over, areas rich in natural resources – especially rubber, but also gold, iron, diamonds, and timber.[17] To operationalize proximity to natural resources, I include a dummy indicating the presence of any rubber or timber plantation, or any diamond, gold, or iron mine, within an hour's walk of each community, based on reports from the local leaders survey.

POLICE AND NGO PRESENCE: While UNMIL personnel often patrolled on their own, they also frequently conducted joint patrols with LNP officers. The LNP's presence may have had an independent effect on Liberians' perceptions of state institutions, for better or worse (Blair, Karim, and Morse, 2019). UNMIL also frequently hosted workshops and other "sensitization" activities with local or international NGOs. To disentangle the impact of UNMIL's operations from police and NGO presence, I include proxies for the frequency of LNP patrols and NGO visits to each community in the year prior to data collection, again based on the local leaders survey.

EXPOSURE TO WARTIME VIOLENCE: Finally, UNMIL prioritized communities that were most severely affected by the Liberian civil war (Mvukiyehe and Samii, 2018). The same is true of UN missions worldwide: peacekeepers tend to deploy to the most conflicted areas both across countries (Fortna, 2004; Gilligan and Stedman, 2003) and within them (Ruggeri, Dorussen, and Gizelis, 2018). To measure exposure to wartime violence, I construct an additive index of thirteen different forms of victimization and participation in the Liberian civil war (including beatings, shootings, and forced labor), aggregated from the individual to the community level. This index is from the residents survey. I also include estimates for the number of ex-combatants and the proportion of returned refugees or internally displaced persons (IDPs) in each community. These estimates are from the local leaders survey.

Table 7.2 provides descriptive statistics for each of these control variables in 2008 and 2010.[18] Liberia experienced rapid demographic, economic, and infrastructural growth during these years, and that growth is evident in the survey. The average community in my sample had a population of approximately 2,000 residents in 2008; by 2010, the average population had grown to over

---

[16] In other words, I first construct an additive index of household assets for each respondent in the community, then take the community-level mean of that index.
[17] CC, Monrovia, October 27, 2011. See also Archibald 2006; Archibald et al. 2006; IRIN 2006.
[18] Community-level controls were not measured in the third (2012) wave of the survey. Since I lag all of my controls by one period, 2012 controls are not needed for my analysis.

TABLE 7.2 *Community characteristics in Liberia survey sample*

	2008			2010		
	Mean	S.D.	N	Mean	S.D.	N
Population	2,033	1,332	242	3,115	1,689	243
Hours to nearest road	1.05	1.57	242	0.92	0.95	243
Cell coverage	0.58	0.49	242	0.74	0.44	243
Social services index (0–14)	5.76	2.67	242	6.81	2.76	243
Any natural resources nearby	0.64	0.48	242	0.71	0.45	243
Frequent visits by police	0.55	0.50	242	0.45	0.50	243
Frequent visits by NGOs	0.71	0.45	242	0.73	0.45	243
Wealth index (PCF)	−0.02	0.57	243	−0.03	0.43	243
Wartime violence index (0–13)	4.29	1.64	243	5.07	1.26	243
% displaced	0.80	0.23	243	0.84	0.17	243
# of ex-combatants	25.67	32.09	242	51.48	54.34	243
Any major incident of violence	0.29	0.45	242	0.16	0.36	243

Note: Descriptive statistics for community characteristics in 2008 and 2010. The wealth index, wartime violence index, and estimate for per cent displaced are from the citizens survey. All other variables are from the local leaders survey. For dummy variables, I report the modal response across the four local leaders surveyed in each community. For continuous variables, I report the mean response. The wealth index is created using principal components analysis.

3,000. Between 2008 and 2010, the proportion of communities with cell phone coverage increased from just over half to nearly three-quarters; the distance to the nearest usable road decreased by approximately 13 per cent; and the average number of social services available increased from around six to around seven. Liberia became more secure during this period as well: the proportion of communities reporting a major destabilizing incident of crime or violence in my sample decreased from 29 per cent in 2008 to 16 per cent in 2010. Police patrols were common in both periods, and NGO visits even more so. Yet while most communities became safer, legacies of the conflict still loomed large. On my additive index of exposure to wartime violence, the average score was over four in both 2008 and 2010, with minimum scores of one and two, respectively. In other words, every single community in the sample was affected in some way by the conflict.

To test the effects of individual-level exposure to UNMIL, I also code a dummy for residents' interpersonal interactions with UNMIL personnel. Again, these interactions were not random, and may have been endogenous to respondents' demographic (and other) characteristics, some of which may also correlate with their attitudes towards state laws and institutions. To mitigate the threat of selection bias, I include individual-level controls for age, gender, years of education, ethnicity (a dummy for ethnic minorities), occupation (a dummy for farmers), and wartime displacement (a dummy for returned refugees and IDPs).

Establishing Causality

TABLE 7.3 *Citizen characteristics in Liberia survey sample*

	2008			2010			2012		
	Mean	S.D.	N	Mean	S.D.	N	Mean	S.D.	N
Age	40.65	12.73	4,669	41.39	16.34	4,801	40.25	14.58	4,064
Male	0.56	0.50	4,669	0.48	0.50	4,801	0.48	0.50	4,063
Education	5.21	5.12	4,669	5.55	5.31	4,801	6.21	5.32	4,063
Minority	0.13	0.33	4,669	0.13	0.33	4,798	0.13	0.33	4,063
Farmer	0.68	0.47	4,669	0.55	0.50	4,801	0.64	0.48	4,063
Refugee or IDP	0.79	0.40	4,669	0.84	0.37	4,801	0.80	0.40	4,056

Note: Descriptive statistics for resident characteristics in 2008, 2010, and 2012.

Table 7.3 summarizes these variables. The average 2008 respondent was a 41-year-old farmer with just over five years of primary school education. The proportion of farmers dropped between the first and second waves of the survey, as did the proportion of men, though the former increased again by the third wave. Average educational attainment increased by about a year between 2008 and 2012. Around 13 per cent of residents were ethnic or religious minorities in all three periods, and about 80 per cent reported being displaced at some point during the Liberian civil war.

Identification Strategy 2: Exploiting Variation Generated by UNMIL's Initial Deployment Decisions

My first identification strategy mitigates the threat of selection bias by controlling for as many confounders as possible at both the individual and community levels. But of course, not all confounders can be measured or even observed. My second and third identification strategies alleviate selection effects using instrumental variables instead. Instrumental variables are exogenous (i.e. random or as-if random) variables that are assumed to be uncorrelated with potential confounders, and to have no impact on the dependent variable except through their "first stage relationship" with the endogenous regressor – in my case, exposure to UNMIL. These two assumptions are known as "independence" and "excludability," respectively, and the validity of any given instrument depends crucially on the plausibility of these assumptions. I use two different instrumental variables strategies to more cleanly estimate the causal impact of UNMIL's presence in Liberia.

First, drawing on research by Eric Mvukiyehe and Cyrus Samii (Mvukiyehe, 2018; Mvukiyehe and Samii, 2018), I use the locations of UNMIL bases established early in the mission's mandate as a source of as-if random variation in the intensity of exposure to UNMIL at the individual level later on.[19] As UN

---

[19] My approach draws on but departs from Mvukiyehe and Samii, who compare Liberian "clans" (one administrative unit above the community level) that did and did not host bases, using coarsened exact matching to create samples of broadly similar "treatment" and "control" units.

missions prepare to deploy, they must make costly decisions about where to site their bases using highly incomplete information on the characteristics of potential host communities. The quality of this information is likely to be especially poor in rural regions, where data is scarce and obstacles to communication and transportation limit intelligence gathering.

Initial siting decisions also depend on the preferences of troop-contributing countries at the Department of Peacekeeping Operations in New York, which may or may not correspond to the preferences of mission leadership, and which may reflect external considerations as much as they reflect factors internal to the host state itself (Higate and Henry, 2009). This helps explain why peacekeepers tend to deploy to the most conflicted areas within host countries, but only after a delay (Ruggeri, Dorussen, and Gizelis, 2018). In other words, while the locations of bases may become more endogenous to community characteristics over time, initial siting decisions are likely to be as-if random.

I use UNMIL's deployment maps to calculate the proximity of each community in my sample to the nearest UNMIL base. I focus on bases that were established by the end of the first full year of UNMIL's mandate (2004), after which new and better information should have become available. Figure 7.2 shows the distribution of these bases. Because establishing a base requires substantial fixed costs, initial siting decisions tend to be "sticky": while new bases were added over the lifespan of UNMIL's mandate, existing ones were almost never removed until the mission began drawing down, even as new and better information arose. I then use proximity to the nearest base as an instrument for individual-level exposure to UNMIL in 2010.[20] To further reduce the risk of bias, I follow Mvukiyehe and Samii in constructing additional control variables using the same data that UNMIL consulted when making its initial siting decisions, including a "rapid needs assessment" conducted by the UN Office for the Coordination of Humanitarian Affairs (OCHA) in early 2004.[21]

The validity of this identification strategy hinges on two assumptions. First, I assume that conditional on covariates, UNMIL's initial siting decisions were as-if random, such that any other community could have just as easily been chosen to host a base. Second, I assume that conditional on the same covariates, the only mechanism through which proximity to a base might have affected

---

[20] Because my analysis is "just-identified" for one endogenous regressor, I can only instrument for individual-level exposure. In principle, I could use proximity to the nearest base as an instrument in 2012 as well, but the first stage relationship is weak. This is likely because UNMIL began dismantling some of its bases between 2010 and 2012, limiting opportunities for engagement with civilians living in the vicinity. Weak instruments can cause severe bias.

[21] Specifically, I control for the number of households in the community; dummies for whether there were any schools or health clinics in the community; a dummy for whether the community was accessible in the rainy season; and an estimate for the number of incidents of violence that each community witnessed between 1997 (the first year data is available) and 2003 (the end of the civil war). All but the last of these controls are gleaned from the OCHA rapid needs assessment. The last is from the Armed Conflict Location and Event Data (ACLED) project.

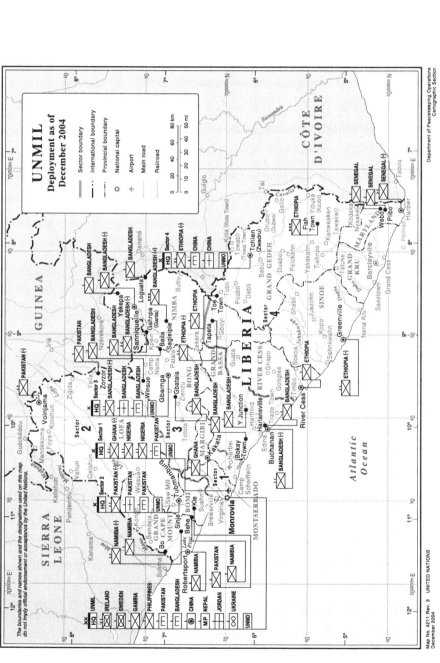

FIGURE 7.2 Distribution of UNMIL bases as of December 2004

Source: UN Cartographic Section. Map No. 4211 Rev. December 3, 2004. Extracted from UN Secretary-General 2004a, 19.

Liberians' attitudes was the more intense exposure to peacekeeping they subsequently received. These are the independence and excludability assumptions, respectively. Based on UNMIL's deployment maps, the most obvious threat to both of these assumptions is the mission's clear preference for establishing bases in county capitals and other relatively large cities and towns. Proximity to cities may affect citizens' attitudes through a variety of mechanisms unrelated to peacekeeping per se, threatening the validity of my identifying assumptions.

Controlling for population and accessibility should help allay this threat, but to mitigate it further, I restrict this component of my analysis to communities located within 5 km of *either* an UNMIL base *or* a city that did *not* host a base in 2004, using UNMIL's own deployment maps to identify locations that the mission might have considered as viable alternatives to the host sites that it ultimately selected. These maps are sparse, and I assume that if a city is listed, it is because it was considered large and strategically important enough to warrant the mission's attention. I choose a 5 km bandwidth because it is wide enough to ensure sufficient statistical power even in a reduced sample, but narrow enough to exclude communities that are obviously outside the range of UNMIL's initial siting decisions. These communities also share similar demographic, economic, and political profiles, lending further credence to the assumptions needed for clean causal inference. My results are robust to wider (6 km) and narrower (4 km) bandwidths as well.

Table 7.4 reports the first stage relationship between citizens' interactions with UNMIL in 2010 and proximity to the nearest UNMIL base that was

TABLE 7.4 *First stage relationship between exposure to UNMIL and proximity to the nearest UNMIL base*

	Spent time with UNMIL		
Proximity to nearest UNMIL base	0.01 [0.00]***	0.01 [0.00]***	0.01 [0.00]***
Observations	948	1,250	1,699
F	13.40	12.20	19.77
Community-level controls	Y	Y	Y
Individual-level controls	Y	Y	Y
Proximity to nearest city	4 km	5 km	6 km

Note: Coefficients from OLS regressions. The dependent variable is a dummy for individual-level exposure to UNMIL from the 2010 residents survey. The independent variable is an estimate for proximity to the nearest UNMIL base that had already been established by the end of 2004. Proximity is measured in km units. To mitigate potential exclusion violations, I restrict my sample to communities located within 4 km, 5 km, and 6 km of a city in columns 1, 2, and 3, respectively. Estimates are weighted by the inverse probability of sampling. Standard errors, clustered by community, are in brackets. *** $p < 0.01$, ** $p < 0.05$, * $p < 0.1$.

Establishing Causality 175

already established by the end of 2004. In column 1, I restrict my sample to communities located within 4 km of either an UNMIL base or a city. In columns 2 and 3 I expand this bandwidth to 5 km and 6 km, respectively. Each column reports coefficients from a separate ordinary least squares (OLS) regression.[22] Regardless of the bandwidth I use, my first stage results suggest that proximity to the nearest UNMIL base is a statistically and substantively significant predictor of citizens' interactions with UNMIL personnel. Citizens were, on average, one percentage point more likely to report spending time with UNMIL for every 1 km closer they lived to an UNMIL base. A rule of thumb is that strong instruments must have a first stage F-statistic of at least ten (Sovey and Green, 2011). My instrument exceeds this threshold at all three bandwidths.

Identification Strategy 3: Using Changes Caused by the Deaths of Seven Peacekeepers in Côte d'Ivoire

My third identification strategy uses a tragedy in neighboring Côte d'Ivoire to generate as-if random variation in the intensity of exposure to UNMIL during the third wave of survey data collection. As discussed in Chapter 4, the violently contested 2010 presidential election in Côte d'Ivoire ignited a civil war between loyalists of incumbent Laurent Gbagbo and supporters of Alassane Ouattara, the challenger and internationallyrecognized victor. With help from the French military and the UN Operation in Côte d'Ivoire (UNOCI), Ouattara's forces eventually assumed control of most of the country. Gbagbo was arrested in April 2011, and Ouattara was inaugurated as president shortly thereafter.

While violence subsided after Gbagbo's capture, militias continued to wreak havoc in the country's volatile western departments, several of which share a border with Liberia. In June 2012, seven UNOCI peacekeepers were killed in an ambush near the small Ivorian border town of Para. The killing shocked the UN missions in both countries. While UNMIL and UNOCI had already intensified patrolling and other joint operations along the border, the ambush focused attention much more specifically on the area surrounding Para, and catalyzed more aggressive efforts to support the "development and strengthening of State authority in border areas" (UN Secretary-General, 2012e).

I use proximity to Para as an instrument for individual-level exposure to UNMIL in 2012. This identification strategy again rests on two assumptions. First, I assume that the area surrounding Para is not especially strategically

---

[22] I measure proximity in kilometer (km) units, multiplied by -1 such that larger values indicate closer proximity. All models include individual- and community-level controls and inverse probability weights. Since I sampled the same number of respondents per community regardless of population, the probability of being selected varied from one community to the next. Inverse probability weights adjust for this feature of the design. Standard errors are clustered at the community level. The dependent variable in Table 7.4 is a dummy. My results are substantively unchanged if I use a logit or probit estimator instead of OLS.

important, and therefore that the 2012 ambush, and UNMIL's reaction to it, could have just as easily occurred elsewhere along the border. Given that violence both during and after the Ivorian civil war occurred throughout the country's southwestern districts, and that the district in which Para is located did not witness any other incidents of violence in the first half of 2012 (and only two more in the second half),[23] this seems like a reasonable assumption to make.

Second, I assume that conditional on covariates, the only mechanism through which proximity to Para might have affected Liberians' attitudes was the greater intensity of peacekeeper presence to which they were subsequently exposed. The most obvious threat to this assumption is the fact that communities located near Para are, by definition, also located near the Ivorian border. Border communities are different from other towns and villages in many respects, and these differences may be especially pronounced during periods of conflict. To minimize the risk of confounding, for this part of my analysis I restrict my sample to communities located within 20 km of the Ivorian border. Again, this bandwidth is wide enough to ensure statistical power but narrow enough to include only communities that share similar demographic, economic, and political characteristics due to their proximity to Côte d'Ivoire. (My results are robust to 15 km and 25 km bandwidths as well.)

Table 7.5 reports the first stage relationship between proximity to Para and citizens' reports of individual-level exposure to UNMIL in 2012. Each column again reports coefficients from a separate OLS regression. I restrict my sample to communities located within 15 km, 20 km, and 25 km of the Ivorian border in columns 1, 2, and 3, respectively.[24] UNMIL's heightened focus on the region surrounding the site of the ambush is evident in my survey data, and regardless of bandwidth, proximity to Para strongly predicts interactions with UNMIL personnel. Even in this subset of border communities, respondents were three percentage points more likely to interact with UNMIL for every 1 km closer to Para that they lived in 2012. My first stage F-statistics again exceed the rule of thumb threshold of ten at all three bandwidths.

But might the ambush near Para have affected Liberians' attitudes through some mechanism other than UNMIL's increased presence? While excludability

---

[23] Para is located in the northwestern-most corner of the Bas-Sassandra district, just south of Montagnes. Based on data from ACLED, Bas-Sassandra witnessed four incidents of violence in the first half of 2011, but none in the second half, and only one – the attack near Para – in the first half of 2012. Montagnes witnessed five incidents in the first half of 2012, down from seven in the second half of 2011. Incidents in Bas-Sassandra and Montagnes constituted just 2.7 per cent and 6.8 per cent, respectively, of the nationwide total in 2012, with 50 per cent of all incidents occurring in Abidjan, 18.9 per cent in the district surrounding Abidjan, and 13.5 per cent in Comoé, a southeastern district on the opposite side of the country from Liberia.

[24] Proximity is again measured in km. All models include the same individual- and community-level controls as before, and the same inverse probability weights. Standard errors are again clustered at the community level.

TABLE 7.5 *First stage relationship between exposure to UNMIL and proximity to Para*

	Spent time with UNMIL		
Proximity to Para	0.03	0.03	0.03
	[0.01]***	[0.01]***	[0.01]***
Observations	943	1,384	1,556
F	28.30	34.79	31.90
Community-level controls	Y	Y	Y
Individual-level controls	Y	Y	Y
Proximity to Ivorian border	15 km	20 km	25 km

Note: Coefficients from OLS regressions. The dependent variable is a dummy for individual-level exposure to UNMIL from the 2012 residents survey. The independent variable is an estimate for proximity to the town of Para. Proximity is measured in 10 km units. To mitigate potential exclusion violations, I restrict my sample to communities located within 15 km, 20 km, and 25 km of the Ivorian border in columns 1, 2, and 3, respectively. Estimates are weighted by the inverse probability of sampling. Standard errors, clustered by community, are in brackets.
*** $p < 0.01$, ** $p < 0.05$, * $p < 0.1$.

is ultimately an untestable assumption, I can explore three of the most obvious potential violations empirically: (1) that the ambush precipitated a flood of Ivorian refugees fleeing to Liberia for (relative) safety; (2) that it catalyzed an increase in LNP as well as UNMIL presence; and (3) that it generated renewed waves of violence in proximate Liberian communities. Any one of these dynamics might have shaped Liberians' attitudes towards the Liberian government, irrespective of UNMIL's presence.

Fortunately for my analysis (and probably for Liberians as well), the Liberian government closed the border with Côte d'Ivoire on June 12, just four days after the attack, and did not reopen it until November of that year. This, combined with UNOCI's increased military and police presence in Côte d'Ivoire's southwestern districts, should have mitigated any consequences of the attack for communities on the Liberian side of the border. While thousands of refugees *did* cross into Liberia during the Ivorian civil war, I am unaware of any evidence that they congregated in the region surrounding Para. Moreover, while Liberia's security forces did increase their activities along the border in response to the ambush, their capacity remained severely constrained and their presence extremely limited. Indeed, in a special report issued just two months before the killing, the UN Secretary-General warned that "Liberian security agencies are still not able to maintain stability without the support of UNMIL" (UN Secretary-General, 2012c, 9). This problem would have been especially acute at the time of the ambush, which occurred in the middle of Liberia's rainy season, during which many rural roads become impassable.

I confirm these intuitions in Tables 7.6–7.8. While I do not have data on the population of Ivorian refugees living in the communities in my sample, I do have

TABLE 7.6 *Correlation between birthplace and proximity to Para*

	Born in community		
Proximity to Para	−0.01	−0.01	−0.01
	[0.01]	[0.01]	[0.01]
Observations	966	1,418	1,597
Community-level controls	Y	Y	Y
Individual-level controls	Y	Y	Y
Proximity to Ivorian border	15 km	20 km	25 km

Note: Coefficients from OLS regressions. The dependent variable is an individual-level dummy indicating whether 2012 residents survey respondents were born in the same community where they were surveyed. The independent variable is an estimate for proximity to the town of Para. Proximity is measured in 10 km units. To mitigate potential exclusion violations, I restrict my sample to communities located within 15 km, 20 km, and 25 km of the Ivorian border in columns 1, 2, and 3, respectively. Estimates are weighted by the inverse probability of sampling. Standard errors, clustered by community, are in brackets. *** $p < 0.01$, ** $p < 0.05$, * $p < 0.1$.

TABLE 7.7 *Correlation between police presence and proximity to Para*

	Frequent police patrols		
Proximity to Para	−0.02	0.00	0.00
	[0.02]	[0.02]	[0.02]
Observations	59	88	97
Community-level controls	Y	Y	Y
Individual-level controls	N	N	N
Proximity to Ivorian border	15 km	20 km	25 km

Note: Coefficients from OLS regressions. The dependent variable is a community-level dummy for communities that reported at least monthly exposure to the police in the 2012 local leaders survey. The independent variable is an estimate for proximity to the town of Para. Proximity is measured in 10 km units. Since the dependent variable is operationalized at the community level, I exclude individual-level controls. To mitigate potential exclusion violations, I restrict my sample to communities located within 15 km, 20km, and 25 km of the Ivorian border in columns 1, 2, and 3, respectively. Estimates are weighted by the inverse probability of sampling. Standard errors, clustered by community, are in brackets. *** $p < 0.01$, ** $p < 0.05$, * $p < 0.1$.

data on the proportion of migrants (i.e. respondents who were not born in the same community where they were surveyed). Since refugees are by definition migrants, this is an imperfect but still informative proxy.[25] Table 7.6 shows that

---

[25] This proxy will only be misleading if communities near Para hosted more Ivorian refugees but fewer migrants from other locations, and if the latter difference offsets the former. In this case, there will appear to be a zero or negative correlation between migration and proximity to Para, despite a positive (but unobserved) correlation between displacement and proximity to Para. I see no reason to suspect this is the case.

TABLE 7.8 *Correlation between violence and proximity to Para*

	Interpersonal violence	Collective violence	Interpersonal violence	Collective violence	Interpersonal violence	Collective violence
Proximity to Para	0.00 [0.01]	−0.00 [0.01]	−0.00 [0.01]	−0.00 [0.01]	−0.00 [0.01]	0.00 [0.00]
Observations	966	966	1,418	1,418	1,597	1,597
Community-level controls	Y	Y	Y	Y	Y	Y
Individual-level controls	Y	Y	Y	Y	Y	Y
Proximity to Ivorian border	15 km	15 km	20 km	20 km	25 km	25 km

Note: Coefficients from OLS regressions. The dependent variables are individual-level dummies for any capital crimes or incidents of collective violence in the past year in the 2012 residents survey. The independent variable is an estimate for proximity to the town of Para. Proximity is measured in 10 km units. To mitigate potential exclusion violations, I restrict my sample to communities located within 15 km, 20 km, and 25 km of the Ivorian border in columns 1, 2, and 3, respectively. Estimates are weighted by the inverse probability of sampling. Standard errors, clustered by community, are in brackets.
*** $p < 0.01$, ** $p < 0.05$, * $p < 0.1$.

residents living near Para were no more or less likely to be migrants than those living further away. Table 7.7 further shows that local leaders of communities near Para were no more or less likely to report frequent (weekly or monthly) police patrols than local leaders in communities located further away.[26] And Table 7.8 shows that residents living near Para were no more or less likely to report incidents of interpersonal (rape or murder) or collective (ethnic riots or violent strikes or protests) violence than those living further away. These nulls provide evidence against the most obvious exclusion restriction violations, and in favor of my identifying assumptions.

Triangulating between Methods to Establish Causality

Of course, none of these identification strategies is flawless. All depend on untestable assumptions, and while I take multiple precautions to minimize potential violations, I cannot eliminate them entirely. Rather than rely on any one identification strategy, my goal is to triangulate between them. Triangulation is especially fruitful in my case, since each identification strategy is susceptible to biases of a different sort. For example, communities located near UNMIL bases tend to be larger, more urban, and more accessible than the average Liberian town or village, while those located near Para tend to be smaller, more rural, and less accessible. Intuitively, we should expect any resulting exclusion restriction violations to bias my estimates in different directions. Similarly, while UNMIL's decision to patrol, construct public works, or intervene to resolve disputes in particular communities may be driven by unobservable selection dynamics, these dynamics are likely different from those that explain why some Liberians interact with UNMIL personnel while others do not. There is no reason to expect these biases to have the same size, or even the same direction. If my results are consistent across all of these identification strategies, then we can be more confident they are not artifacts of selection bias or exclusion restriction violations alone.

ADDRESSING OTHER POTENTIAL SOURCES OF BIAS

In addition to selection bias, there are three more empirical challenges that my analysis needs to overcome: recall bias, social desirability bias, and reverse causality.

---

[26] To estimate the frequency of police patrols, I take the modal response across the four local leaders in each community, following the same procedure used to estimate the frequency of UNMIL patrols. Unfortunately, I do not have data on military patrols, but given that all of Liberia's security forces were involved in the response to the ambush in some way, the correlation with police patrols should be equally informative.

Recall Bias

I use surveys of residents and local leaders to measure exposure to UNMIL at the individual and community levels, respectively. But what if respondents misremembered the nature or intensity of UNMIL's activities in their communities? Might this bias my results? While recall bias is always a concern in surveys, there are several reasons to believe it is a relatively minor one in my case. First, in the vast majority of communities, local leaders agreed on the extent of UNMIL's presence over the preceding year.[27] Second, in several of my analyses, I use different samples to measure my independent and dependent variables. To confound my results, recall bias in one sample (composed of local leaders) would have to correlate with attitudes in the other (composed of residents). This seems unlikely.[28]

Third, as I show in Table 7.9, residents' reports of exposure to UNMIL are very highly correlated with local leaders' reports, despite being measured independently of one another. Residents were much more likely to report interacting with UNMIL personnel in communities where local leaders reported UNMIL patrols or interventions. The correlation is smaller for less frequent patrols, smaller than that for interventions, and smaller still (and statistically indistinguishable from zero) for public works. These discrepancies make sense. For many civilians, patrols are the most visible reminder of the UN's presence (Pouligny, 2006, 28). As a Military Observer explained to me, during patrols, "we sit with them [civilians], eat with them, interact with them, and spend most of the time with them just mingling." These interactions are indispensable in that they allow peacekeepers to "guarantee the local population that the UN is on the ground."[29] Interventions are less common, and involve contact with fewer individuals (e.g. the parties to the dispute). Construction sites for public works provide opportunities for interaction, but fewer than patrols or interventions.

Fourth and related, as we saw in Table 7.4, residents' reports of exposure to UNMIL are very highly correlated with the locations of UNMIL bases. UNMIL was constrained by the long distances and rough roads that characterize much of rural Liberia. Given these constraints, we should expect opportunities for engaging with UNMIL to be greater in communities located near UNMIL bases than those located further away. Table 7.4 demonstrates that this is indeed the

---

[27] Ninety-four per cent of local leaders agreed on whether or not UNMIL had built public works in the past year, and 87 per cent agreed on whether or not it had intervened to resolve disputes. A majority of leaders agreed on the frequency of patrols in 94 per cent of communities as well.

[28] The rate of disagreement among local leaders about the nature and frequency of UNMIL's activities is not correlated with any of the outcomes I measure. Most importantly, the correlation between disagreements among local leaders and my key dependent variable – citizens' willingness to rely on state institutions – is minuscule (just 0.0084).

[29] MS, Gbarnga, October 11, 2010.

TABLE 7.9 *Correlation between individual- and community-level exposure to UNMIL*

	Spent time with UNMIL
Weekly patrols	0.26
	[0.05]***
Monthly patrols	0.24
	[0.04]***
Occasional patrols	0.16
	[0.03]***
Interventions	0.10
	[0.02]***
Public works	0.02
	[0.04]
Observations	4,369
District FE	Y
Community controls	Y
Individual controls	Y

Note: Coefficients from OLS regressions. The dependent variable is a dummy for individual-level exposure to UNMIL from the 2010 residents survey. The independent variables are dummies for weekly, monthly, and occasional UNMIL patrols, interventions to resolve disputes, and public works projects from the 2010 local leaders survey. Estimates are weighted by the inverse probability of sampling. Standard errors, clustered by community, are in brackets.
*** $p < 0.01$, ** $p < 0.05$, * $p < 0.1$.

case: the closer the community is to an UNMIL base, the more likely residents of that community were to report interacting with UNMIL personnel. Finally, my results are unchanged if I "weight" my analyses by the amount of disagreement in local leaders' reports.[30]

Social Desirability Bias

Beyond recall bias in my independent variables, my reliance on survey data raises the possibility of social desirability bias in my dependent variables as well. If peacekeepers succeed only in teaching respondents to say what they

---

[30] To do this, I code the proportion of local leaders in each community that reported each type of exposure, then use those proportions (rather than dummies) as independent variables. For example, if three local leaders in a given community reported weekly patrols and one reported monthly patrols, then for that community, weekly patrols will be coded as 0.75, monthly patrols will be coded as 0.25, and occasional patrols will be coded as 0.

think enumerators want to hear – that the police and courts should adjudicate the most serious incidents of crime and violence, for example, or that trial by ordeal is never used in their communities – then I will overestimate UNMIL's impact on the rule of law. This problem afflicts any study that uses survey data to measure outcomes, and mine is no exception.

Still, there are several reasons to believe the problem is minor in my case. First, all surveys were conducted in private by trained Liberian enumerators who were affiliated with a local research NGO, not with the government or the UN. These enumerators repeatedly reassured respondents of their anonymity and the confidentiality of their answers. Second, there is no social norm against expressing one's views about the government in Liberia, and it is not clear why respondents would have felt inhibited in the context of an anonymous, confidential survey. Indeed, as I show in the next chapter, many respondents were very critical of the government in their responses, suggesting they were willing to express even potentially controversial views. Finally, my use of a list experiment to measure the prevalence of trial by ordeal should further mitigate social desirability concerns. While no method can eliminate social desirability bias altogether, list experiments have proven effective at minimizing it (Blair and Imai, 2012).

Reverse Causality

Finally, is it possible that respondents who preferred relying on the state were more likely to interact with UNMIL in the first place? If so, then any positive correlation I detect between UNMIL and the rule of law may turn out to be an artifact of reverse causality. Since UNMIL typically did not decide where to patrol, intervene, or construct public works on the basis of residents' individual-level attitudes, reverse causality is only really a concern for the components of my analysis that use local leaders' community-level reports of exposure to UNMIL as independent variables. Yet, as I show in the next chapter, reverse causality cannot easily explain the results of these analyses.

Intuitively, if reverse causality were a problem, we would expect to find a positive correlation between exposure to UNMIL and citizens' preferences for UNMIL as a security and justice provider. (It would be strange if citizens who preferred relying on the state were more likely to interact with UNMIL, while those who preferred relying on UNMIL were not.) But the evidence I find for such a correlation is limited and inconsistent. This further supports a causal interpretation of my results, which I present in the next chapter.

8

Sub-national Evidence III

UN Intervention and the Rule of Law in Liberia

In Chapter 7, I summarized my empirical strategy for testing UNMIL's impact on the rule of law at the micro and meso levels in Liberia. My research design is both quantitative and qualitative, combining a survey and list experiment with interviews conducted with dozens of UN personnel, Liberian citizens, local leaders, government officials, and civil society representatives. The survey spans a period of four years, covers a wide range of topics, and captures the views of over 10,000 rural Liberians across three waves of data collection. With such rich data, I am able to isolate the causal effect of UNMIL's activities from multiple analytical angles. Each component of my research design complements the others, helping to support a causal interpretation of my results. With multiple rounds of data to draw on, I am also able to test the impact of UNMIL's operations in both the short and medium terms – something that previous sub-national studies of peacekeeping have been unable to do.

This chapter presents my findings. I begin by documenting a paradox in Liberians' attitudes towards the Liberian state. On the one hand, most of my survey respondents preferred to rely on formal institutions to adjudicate the most serious incidents of crime and violence. On the other hand, most also perceived formal institutions as corrupt and biased, especially relative to informal (e.g. chiefs) and international (UNMIL) alternatives. This combination of attitudes is inconsistent with research in criminology suggesting that citizens' willingness to rely on the police and courts depends on their perceptions of those institutions as transparent and fair (Tyler and Huo 2002; Tyler 2004, 2006). But it resonates with several recent studies from Liberia and elsewhere (Blair, Karim, and Morse, 2019; Gottlieb, 2016; Smith-Höhn, 2010), suggesting that the paradox is not specific to the communities or respondents in my sample.

I then use my survey to test three empirical propositions that follow immediately from the theoretical framework developed in Chapter 4. My theory predicts that UNMIL's presence should increase citizens' willingness to rely on formal over informal authorities to resolve the most serious incidents of crime and violence; should increase informal authorities' willingness to defer to their formal counterparts in criminal cases that fall unambiguously under state jurisdiction; and should decrease informal authorities' reliance on illegal mechanisms of dispute resolution – especially, in the Liberian case, trial by ordeal. My results provide strong, consistent evidence in support of these hypotheses.

Somewhat surprisingly, I also find that UNMIL's presence did not mitigate and may in fact have exacerbated Liberians' perceptions of state corruption, at least in the short term. Importantly, however, I show that while UNMIL's beneficial effects on citizens' willingness to rely on state institutions persisted even after two years, and even in communities that reported no further exposure to UNMIL personnel, its apparently adverse effects on perceptions of state corruption dissipated over time. While I cannot say for certain whether these effects will endure even after UNMIL's withdrawal, taken together, my results suggest the possibility of a lasting and overall positive change in the rule of law at both the micro and meso levels in Liberia, induced in part by UNMIL's presence. I conclude the chapter by considering UNMIL's impact on the rule of law at the macro level, drawing on secondary sources and the mission's own annual budget performance reports.

PARADOXES IN CITIZENS' PERCEPTIONS OF THE LIBERIAN STATE

As discussed in Chapter 3, the rule of law at the micro level requires that citizens defer to state over non-state institutions to adjudicate criminal cases that fall unambiguously under state jurisdiction. I operationalize this requirement in Liberia using my survey, which gauged respondents' willingness to rely on state institutions in three hypothetical scenarios of crime and violence: a murder, an incident of mob violence, and an ethnic riot resulting in fatalities. Under Liberian law, these incidents fall under the purview of the state, though, as we saw in Chapter 6, non-state authorities routinely claim jurisdiction over incidents of this severity. The survey also asked respondents whether they perceive the police and other state institutions as corrupt or biased. For purposes of comparison, they were asked the same questions about non-state security and justice providers, and about UNMIL as well.

Table 8.1 summarizes respondents' answers to these questions in the second (2010) and third (2012) waves of data collection.[1] As the communities in my sample grew and developed, residents became increasingly reliant on the state as a purveyor of security and justice. A majority of respondents in both the second and third waves of the survey preferred relying on the state to resolve the most destabilizing incidents of crime and violence. The size of the majority

---

[1] Unfortunately, these questions were not asked in the first (2008) wave of data collection.

TABLE 8.1 *Citizens' preferences over potential security and justice providers in Liberia*

	2010		2012	
	Mean	N	Mean	N
Rely on formal overall	0.56	4,799	0.68	4,063
Rely on formal for murder	0.64	4,799	0.70	4,063
Rely on formal for mob violence	0.35	4,799	0.48	4,063
Rely on formal for ethnic riots	0.58	4,799	0.66	4,063
Rely on informal overall	0.32	4,799	0.14	4,063
Rely on informal for murder	0.25	4,799	0.10	4,063
Rely on informal for mob violence	0.59	4,799	0.42	4,063
Rely on informal for ethnic riots	0.30	4,799	0.14	4,063
Rely on UNMIL overall	0.12	4,799	0.18	4,063
Rely on UNMIL for murder	0.11	4,799	0.18	4,063
Rely on UNMIL for mob violence	0.6	4,799	0.8	4,063
Rely on UNMIL for ethnic riots	0.11	4,799	0.18	4,063

Note: Descriptive statistics on preferences over potential security and justice providers from the 2010 and 2012 residents surveys.

grew between 2010 and 2012, from 58 to 66 per cent for ethnic riots; 64 per cent to 70 per cent for murder; and 35 to 48 per cent for mob violence.[2] 68 per cent of respondents preferred relying on the state in at least two of these three scenarios in 2012, up from 56 per cent in 2010.

Liberians' increasing deference to state authorities came at the expense of non-state alternatives. The proportion of respondents that preferred relying on informal institutions as security and justice providers fell by more than half between 2010 and 2012, from 32 to just 14 per cent. The drop was most precipitous for murder (25 to 10 per cent) and ethnic riots (30 to 14 per cent), but was marked for mob violence as well (59 to 42 per cent). Overall, respondents preferred formal to informal authorities by a twenty-four percentage point margin in 2010. By 2012, that margin had more than doubled. The analyses in this chapter will show that these changes can be attributed at least in part to UNMIL's presence.

Interestingly, relatively few respondents preferred relying on UNMIL, despite the fact that UNMIL was often responsible for diffusing precisely the sorts of incidents captured in these hypothetical scenarios. While the proportion of respondents that expressed a preference for UNMIL grew between the second and third waves of the survey – from 11 to 18 per cent for both

---

[2] Preferences for the state may have been less pronounced in this third hypothetical scenario because mob violence is itself an informal mechanism of adjudication, and thus falls naturally, if still illegally, under the purview of informal authorities. Alternatively, respondents may have perceived mob violence as less severe than the other scenarios, perhaps because it was the only one of the three that did not explicitly mention fatalities.

murder and ethnic riots, and from 6 to 8 per cent for mob violence – it never exceeded one in five, regardless of the severity of the incident. This growth in respondents' (still weak) preferences for UNMIL came at the expense of informal authorities rather than formal ones. In 2010, respondents preferred informal authorities to UNMIL by a ratio of more than two to one for murder, nearly three to one for ethnic riots, and nearly ten to one for mob violence – differences of fourteen percentage points, nineteen percentage points, and fifty-three percentage points, respectively. By 2012, however, respondents preferred relying on UNMIL for both murder and ethnic riots by margins of eight percentage points and four percentage points, respectively. Respondents continued to prefer informal authorities over UNMIL for mob violence, but by a smaller thirty-four percentage point margin. In contrast, preferences for UNMIL and preferences for the state grew roughly in parallel over time.

These patterns are instructive in and of themselves. Between the second and third waves of the survey, rural Liberians' attitudes changed in ways that reflect a consolidation of the rule of law at the micro level, with more and more respondents becoming more and more reliant on formal institutions to resolve capital crimes and collective violence, and less and less reliant on informal alternatives. While respondents became increasingly reliant on peacekeepers as well, they nonetheless continued to prefer the state to UNMIL by a ratio of nearly four to one overall. The rule of law requires that citizens respect the state's claim to original and ultimate jurisdiction over the most serious criminal cases, and that they adhere to the constitutionally delineated division of labor between formal and informal institutions. The trends in Table 8.1 suggest that, over time, this requirement was increasingly being met.[3]

Yet while large and growing majorities expressed a *preference* for state institutions as providers of security and justice, their *perceptions* of those same institutions remained virtually unchanged between the second and third waves of the survey. A number of studies have documented deep distrust of government among Liberian citizens (Blair, Morse, and Tsai, 2017; Human Rights Watch, 2013; Isser, Lubkemann, and N'Tow, 2009), and mine is no exception. As Table 8.2 shows, in both 2010 and 2012, a majority of respondents described state institutions as corrupt (61 and 58 per cent, respectively). In contrast, approximately one-third described non-state institutions as corrupt (33 and 32 per cent in 2010 and 2012, respectively), and less than one-sixth described UNMIL as corrupt (15 and 16 per cent in 2010 and 2012, respectively). Moreover, while a relatively small minority described formal institutions as biased against particular ethnic or religious groups (33 and 32 per cent in 2010 and 2012, respectively), even smaller minorities said the same of informal institutions (11 and 13 per cent) or UNMIL (9 and 11 per cent).

---

[3] Respondents likely would have expressed stronger preferences for informal authorities in less severe incidents (e.g. land disputes), but these are less relevant for my purposes, since informal authorities are legally authorized to adjudicate them.

TABLE 8.2 *Citizens' perceptions of potential security and justice providers in Liberia*

	2010		2012	
	Mean	N	Mean	N
Believes formal is corrupt	0.61	4,368	0.58	3,777
Believes formal is biased	0.33	4,615	0.32	3,944
Believes informal is corrupt	0.30	4,419	0.32	3,829
Believes informal is biased	0.11	4,721	0.13	4,033
Believes UNMIL is corrupt	0.15	3,642	0.16	3,306
Believes UNMIL is biased	0.9	4,343	0.11	3,718

Note: Descriptive statistics on perceptions of potential security and justice providers from the 2010 and 2012 residents surveys.

These numbers reveal what appears to be a persistent tension in rural Liberians' attitudes towards the Liberian state. On the one hand, most respondents preferred relying on formal authorities to adjudicate the most serious incidents of crime and violence; on the other, most also described those same authorities as corrupt, and as *more* corrupt, and more biased, than informal or international alternatives. This tension only became more marked over time, as Liberians became increasingly reliant on state institutions without updating their perceptions of those institutions in any noticeable way. The tension is evident both within and across respondents. Respondents who expressed a preference for the state were no less likely to describe it as corrupt or biased than those who did not. Indeed, in many cases, respondents who preferred the state and those who described it as corrupt and biased were one and the same.

This tension is apparent in my qualitative data as well. Most of the Liberians I interviewed expressed distrust of the police and courts, but most also perceived these institutions as the most appropriate purveyors of security and justice in serious criminal cases. One respondent complained that "if you report to the police, before they search and get the criminal it will be hard. So I just forget about it." But when serious crimes are committed, "we can't withdraw it from the police. We all live by the government."[4] Another respondent expressed similar misgivings: "when there's palava [conflict], don't even call them [the LNP] because the first thing they will talk about is money to buy gas in their police car." This respondent explicitly endorsed vigilantism as an alternative to the police: "we have big big [powerful] people in our area. Anything happens, we tell them and they will call us to talk [adjudicate] the case. Anybody found guilty, they punish you. Sometimes beat you." But serious crimes were again the exception: "if anybody kills, we will call the police to come and catch the person."[5]

---

[4] DG, Gbarnga, October 25, 2010. [5] WY, Gbarnga, October 13, 2010.

While surprising, I am not the first to detect this tension in Liberians' attitudes towards the state, and towards security sector institutions in particular. In a 2010 survey, for example, Judy Smith-Höhn found that most Liberians gave state security forces "remarkably positive ratings," despite "obvious shortcomings in terms of equipment and training as well as their general history of violence and oppression." She describes this combination of results as one of her "more remarkable findings." Nor does she attribute optimism merely to naiveté: her respondents were "well aware of the all-too-blatant shortcomings of this set of actors," but they nonetheless expressed a "pronounced preference for state agencies to provide for security." She posits a number of possible explanations for this mismatch, including "wishful thinking," "high expectations," and adoption of a Westernized "notion of a modern state" – the very notion that UNMIL in many ways sought to inculcate (Smith-Höhn, 2010, 95, 135, 145).

I have found evidence of this tension in my other research in Liberia as well. In a randomized controlled trial, my co-authors and I found that exposure to newly retrained, better-equipped police officers increased rural Liberians' willingness to report crimes to the LNP, but had no effect on their perceptions of the LNP as corrupt or biased. We attributed these results in part to the mixed messages that LNP officers delivered to civilians, exhorting them to report crimes to the police while simultaneously emphasizing the capacity constraints under which the LNP continued to operate – constraints that incentivized (and in some cases arguably necessitated) petty bribe-seeking (Blair, Karim, and Morse, 2019). As we saw in Figure 6.2 in Chapter 6, UNMIL's messaging on these points was not altogether consistent either. Even as the mission urged citizens to obey state laws and trust state institutions, it also encouraged them to recognize and report acts of state misconduct. I will return to these mixed messages later in the chapter.

MORE EXPOSURE TO UNMIL, MORE RELIANCE ON STATE OVER NON-STATE AUTHORITIES

How did UNMIL's presence shape Liberians' attitudes towards the Liberian state? My theory of UN missions as state surrogates predicts that exposure to UNMIL should increase citizens' reliance on the state when crimes are committed or violence occurs. But this is an optimistic prediction. If peacekeepers engage in predatory or exclusionary behavior, then exposure may have the perverse effect of estranging citizens from state institutions (Beber et al., 2017; Pouligny, 2006). Alternatively, if peacekeepers pander to informal authorities in order to lower barriers to entry into rural communities, then UN presence may only entrench these authorities' role as purveyors of security and justice, potentially in opposition to state law (Barnett, Fang, and Zürcher, 2014; Veit, 2011). Peacekeepers may also prove so effective and legitimate that they induce dependence on their own presence (Lake, 2010), or so time- and resource-constrained that they do not affect citizens' attitudes at all (Kahler, 2009). These rival perspectives, summarized in Chapter 4, yield competing empirical predictions for me to test.

Using Control Variables to Model UNMIL's Selection Process

My first set of results relies on the selection on observables identification strategy described in Chapter 7. I leverage secondary sources and my own qualitative interviews to identify variables that might confound the relationship between UNMIL's operations and micro-level indicators for the rule of law, then measure and control for as many of those confounders as possible. My dependent variable captures respondents' preferences over potential security and justice providers at the individual level. My independent variables are dummies for five forms of community-level exposure to UNMIL from my survey of local leaders: public works, interventions to resolve disputes, and weekly, monthly, or occasional patrols.

Figure 8.1 displays the effect of these activities on respondents' preferences.[6] The symbols denote changes in the predicted probability of relying on each of the three potential security and justice providers: negative values indicate that residents became less likely to rely on formal authorities, informal authorities, or UNMIL as a result of UNMIL's presence, while positive values indicate the opposite. The lines represent 90 and 95 per cent confidence intervals. The figure presents the short-term effects of UNMIL's presence, with both the dependent and independent variables measured in the same year (2010). I explore the medium-term effects of exposure to UNMIL later in the chapter.

Consistent with my theory, Figure 8.1 shows that exposure to UNMIL increased rural Liberians' reliance on the police and other state institutions to respond to serious criminal cases, while decreasing their reliance on chiefs and other non-state alternatives. The effects are consistent across all types of exposure, but are substantively and statistically most significant for patrols. Residents of communities that reported weekly patrols were fifteen percentage points more likely to prefer relying on formal institutions, and sixteen percentage points *less* likely to prefer relying on informal ones. These countervailing effects are highly statistically significant both in absolute terms

---

[6] More specifically, Figure 8.1 reports the marginal effects of UNMIL patrols, public works projects, and interventions to resolve disputes from a multinomial logit regression with district fixed effects and all individual- and community-level controls held at their means. To avoid post-treatment bias, all community-level controls are measured in the period prior to exposure to UNMIL. I avoid post-treatment bias in my individual-level controls by including only variables that either cannot (e.g. age) or are extremely unlikely (e.g. years of education) to be affected by UNMIL's presence over the course of a single year.

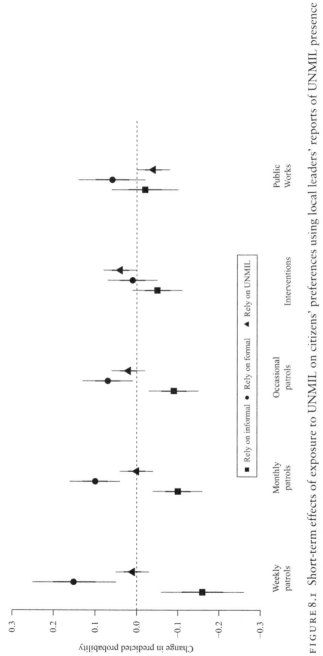

FIGURE 8.1 Short-term effects of exposure to UNMIL on citizens' preferences using local leaders' reports of UNMIL presence

Note: Marginal effects and 90 and 95 per cent confidence intervals from multinomial logit regressions holding all controls at their means. The dependent variable is an individual-level categorical variable indicating each respondent's modal preference over potential security and justice providers in the 2010 residents survey. The independent variables are community-level dummies for weekly, monthly, and occasional UNMIL patrols, interventions to resolve disputes, and public works projects from the 2010 local leaders survey. Estimates are weighted by the inverse probability of sampling. Standard errors are clustered by community. A version of this figure first appeared in Blair (2019), and is reprinted with permission. © The IO Foundation 2019, published by Cambridge University Press.

and relative to one another. Given that about 56 per cent of all respondents preferred relying on formal authorities in 2010, a change of fifteen percentage points is also substantively a very large effect. The effects are smaller for monthly and occasional patrols, though not by much, and not statistically significantly so.

The effects of interventions and public works are more mixed. Both appear to have reduced reliance on informal institutions, but only the former effect is statistically significant, and only marginally so. Both also appear to have increased reliance on formal over informal institutions, though the difference between these effects is only weakly significant. A possible explanation for the disparity with patrols lies in the distinct opportunities for interpersonal interaction with UNMIL personnel that arise during these different types of activities. As I showed in Table 7.9 in the last chapter, respondents were more likely to have spent time with UNMIL in communities that reported patrols than in communities that reported public works or interventions. This makes sense, as patrols arguably provide more opportunity to connect with a wider cross-section of the population than interventions or public works. If peacekeepers encourage respect for state laws and institutions in part through day-to-day, face-to-face interactions, then it is not surprising that patrols have a more pronounced effect than these other activities.

Equally important, Figure 8.1 shows that exposure to UNMIL generally did not induce dependence on the mission itself, belying concerns that peacekeeper presence "crowds out" and delegitimizes the state in the eyes of citizens (Lake, 2016). UNMIL patrols did not affect citizens' reliance on UNMIL one way or the other. UNMIL interventions do appear to have strengthened preferences for UNMIL over non-state authorities, but the effects on preferences for the mission and preferences for the state are statistically indistinguishable from one another. In other words, to the extent that UNMIL interventions increased reliance on UNMIL, it did so at the expense of informal rather than formal authorities.

In contrast, public works appear to have weakened preferences for UNMIL, both in absolute terms and relative to formal authorities. While perhaps surprising, this is consistent with Beatrice Pouligny's observation that in many cases, "far from the mission being thanked for its efforts" to provide social services, public works are viewed as evidence that peacekeepers "could have done more" (Pouligny, 2006, 116). Whatever the explanation, these results are inconsistent with skeptics' concerns about crowding out at the micro level.

Figure 8.1 tests UNMIL's impact on the rule of law by exploiting variation in peacekeeper presence across communities – e.g. by comparing communities where UNMIL patrolled weekly to communities where it patrolled monthly, occasionally, or not at all. Figure 8.2 exploits variation across *individuals* instead, drawing on residents' reports of spending time with UNMIL personnel

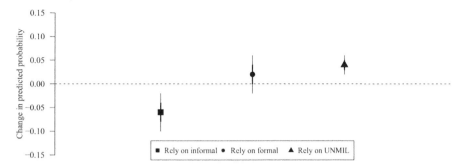

FIGURE 8.2 Short-term effects of exposure to UNMIL on citizens' preferences using citizens' reports of UNMIL presence

Note: Marginal effects and 90 and 95 per cent confidence intervals from multinomial logit regressions holding all controls at their means. The dependent variable is an individual-level categorical variable indicating each respondent's modal preference over potential security and justice providers in the 2010 residents survey. The independent variable is a dummy for individual-level exposure to UNMIL from the 2010 residents survey. Estimates are weighted by the inverse probability of sampling. Standard errors are clustered by community. A version of this figure first appeared in Blair (2019), and is reprinted with permission. © The IO Foundation 2019, published by Cambridge University Press.

in the past.[7] The selection process underlying UNMIL's decisions about where to patrol, intervene, or build public works at the community level is likely quite different from the selection process driving citizens' decisions to engage with UNMIL personnel at the individual level, meaning that the sources of bias in Figure 8.1 are likely quite different from those in Figure 8.2. But my conclusions are substantively similar regardless.

Residents who interacted with UNMIL were six percentage points less likely to prefer relying on non-state authorities, and two percentage points more likely to prefer relying on state authorities instead. While the latter effect on preferences for state authorities is not statistically significant on its own, it *is* significantly different from the former effect on preferences for non-state alternatives. Residents who interacted with UNMIL were also four percentage points more likely to prefer relying on the mission itself. This effect is statistically significant on its own, and is statistically different from the effect on preferences for informal authorities. It is not, however, statistically different from the effect on preferences for the state. This again suggests that to the extent

---

[7] My survey question about spending time with UNMIL did not specify a particular time frame. While most respondents likely reported recent interactions, to eliminate the possibility of post-treatment bias I only include community-level controls that were measured before the mission deployed. These are the same controls that I use in my instrumental variables analysis later in the chapter.

that UNMIL induced reliance on its own personnel, it did so at the expense of informal authorities rather than formal ones.

Using Instrumental Variables

Thus far I have attempted to isolate the causal effect of UNMIL's operations by controlling for as many potential confounding factors as possible. Ultimately, however, I can only control for factors I can measure, and I am still at risk of bias from unobservable confounders. As discussed in Chapter 7, I use two instrumental variables strategies to reduce this risk. The first leverages as-if random variation in the geographical distribution of UNMIL personnel generated by the mission's initial deployment decisions. UN missions make these decisions on the basis of highly incomplete information about conditions on the ground, and in response to the idiosyncratic preferences of troop-contributing countries. To exploit this randomness I first calculate the distance from each community in my sample to the nearest UNMIL base that was already established by the end of the mission's first full year (2004), then use that distance as an instrument for residents' interactions with UNMIL personnel in 2010.

Table 8.3 summarizes my results. Each column reports estimates from a separate two-stage least squares regression.[8] The dependent variables are dummies indicating the respondent's modal preference over potential security and justice providers across the same three hypothetical scenarios of crime and violence as before – a murder, an incident of mob violence, and an ethnic riot.[9] To avoid potential independence and exclusion restriction violations, I restrict my sample to communities located within 5 km of *either* an UNMIL base *or* a city that did not host an UNMIL base in 2004. My results are robust to wider (6 km) and narrower (4 km) bandwidths.

Consistent with my results in Figure 8.2, I find that exposure to UNMIL increased reliance on formal authorities and decreased reliance on informal ones. Within this sub-sample of more urban communities, residents who interacted with UNMIL were thirty-three percentage points more likely to prefer relying on state security and justice providers, and thirty-four percentage points *less* likely to prefer relying on non-state alternatives. Unlike in Figure 8.2, residents who reported interacting with UNMIL as a function of proximity to a base were no more or less likely to prefer relying on UNMIL itself, again belying concerns about crowding out – and, importantly, belying concerns

---

[8] In the first stage, I regress my endogenous independent variable (spending time with UNMIL) on my exogenous instrument (proximity to the nearest UNMIL base). I reported these first stage results in Chapter 7. In the second stage, I regress my dependent variable (citizens' preferences over potential security and justice providers) on the predicted values from the first stage.

[9] Because distance to the nearest UNMIL base is highly correlated with district, I omit district fixed effects from these models.

TABLE 8.3 *Short-term effects of exposure to UNMIL on citizens' preferences using proximity to nearest UNMIL base as instrument*

	Rely on informal	Rely on formal	Rely on UNMIL
Spent time with UNMIL	−0.34 [0.16]**	0.33 [0.18]*	0.01 [0.10]
Observations	1,249	1,249	1,249
Individual-level controls	Y	Y	Y
Community-level controls	Y	Y	Y
Proximity to nearest city	5 km	5 km	5 km

Note: Coefficients from two-stage least squares regressions using proximity to the nearest UNMIL base as an instrument for individual-level exposure to UNMIL in 2010. The dependent variables are individual-level dummies indicating each respondent's modal preference over potential security and justice providers in the 2010 residents survey. The endogenous independent variable is a dummy for individual-level exposure to UNMIL from the 2010 residents survey. The instrument is an estimate for proximity to the nearest UNMIL base that had already been established by the end of 2004. Proximity is measured in km units. To mitigate potential exclusion violations, I restrict my sample to communities located within 5 km of a city. All results are robust to 4 km and 6 km bandwidths as well. Estimates are weighted by the inverse probability of sampling. Standard errors, clustered by community, are in brackets.
*** $p < 0.01$, ** $p < 0.05$, * $p < 0.1$.

about reverse causality as well.[10] These results are unchanged if I tighten or loosen the bandwidth used to restrict my sample.

My second instrumental variables strategy uses as-if random variation in the intensity of exposure to UNMIL generated by the killing of seven UNOCI peacekeepers near the Ivorian border town of Para in June of 2012. As discussed in Chapter 7, I can use randomness in the location of the ambush to reduce the risk of confounding. I reduce this risk further by restricting my sample to communities located within 20 km of the Ivorian border. Table 8.4 reports my results, using distance to Para as an instrument for residents' interactions with UNMIL in 2012.

Consistent with the results in Table 8.3, I find that residents who interacted with UNMIL as a function of the mission's activities around Para were forty-two percentage points more likely to prefer relying on state institutions to resolve criminal cases that fall unambiguously under state jurisdiction. They were also eleven percentage points more likely to prefer relying on non-state institutions, though this effect is not statistically significant at conventional levels, and is much smaller than the effect on preferences for the state. My results are virtually identical at wider (25 km) and narrower (15 km) bandwidths.

[10] As discussed in Chapter 7, if reverse causality were a concern, we should expect to observe a positive correlation between exposure to UNMIL and preferences for relying on UNMIL. I find no evidence of such a correlation here.

TABLE 8.4 *Short-term effects of exposure to UNMIL on citizens' preferences using proximity to Para as instrument*

	Rely on informal	Rely on formal	Rely on UNMIL
Spent time with UNMIL	0.11	0.42	−0.53
	[0.14]	[0.14]***	[0.13]***
Observations	1,384	1,384	1,384
Individual-level controls	Y	Y	Y
Community-level controls	Y	Y	Y
Proximity to Ivorian border	20 km	20 km	20 km

Note: Coefficients from two-stage least squares regressions using proximity to Para as an instrument for individual-level exposure to UNMIL in 2012. The dependent variables are individual-level dummies indicating each respondent's modal preference over potential security and justice providers in the 2012 residents survey. The endogenous independent variable is a dummy for individual-level exposure to UNMIL from the 2012 residents survey. The instrument is an estimate for proximity to the town of Para. Proximity is measured in 10 km units. To mitigate potential exclusion violations, I restrict my sample to communities located within 20 km of the Ivorian border. All results are robust to 15 km and 25 km bandwidths as well. Estimates are weighted by the inverse probability of sampling. Standard errors, clustered by community, are in brackets. *** $p < 0.01$, ** $p < 0.05$, * $p < 0.1$. A version of this table first appeared in Blair (2019), and is reprinted with permission. © The IO Foundation 2019, published by Cambridge University Press.

Interestingly, these residents were also fifty-three percentage points *less* likely to prefer relying on UNMIL – a substantively large and highly statistically significant effect. One possible explanation for this result is that Liberians interpreted UNMIL's increased presence after the ambush as a signal of its prior inability or unwillingness to adequately protect civilians along the volatile border with Côte d'Ivoire. Alternatively, it is possible that UNMIL's highly militarized response to the ambush alienated citizens in ways that more typical peacekeeping activities do not. Pouligny and others have raised concerns about over-reliance on military (rather than civilian) personnel as the "face" of peacekeeping operations (Pouligny, 2006); my results seem to resonate with these concerns. Whatever the explanation, the net effect on citizens' reliance on formal authorities is clear, and is consistent with the results of my selection on observables strategy presented earlier.

MORE EXPOSURE TO UNMIL, MORE RELIANCE ON LEGAL OVER ILLEGAL MECHANISMS OF DISPUTE RESOLUTION

At the meso level, the rule of law requires that informal authorities defer to their formal counterparts in serious criminal cases, and that they renounce mechanisms of dispute resolution that violate state law in and of themselves. The third wave of my survey included a list experiment designed to operationalize this requirement in Liberia. The list experiment focused in particular on measuring the prevalence of trial by ordeal, which is illegal but still widely practiced in rural regions of the country.

As discussed in Chapter 7, enumerators first read local leaders a hypothetical scenario describing an unsolved burglary in their community, then gave them a list of options for "handling" the situation. The control group list contained two non-sensitive items – "call the police" and "call UNMIL" – and a semi-sensitive one ("just leave it alone and do nothing"), which I included to minimize the risk of ceiling and floor effects. The treatment group list included a sensitive item as well (trial by ordeal). I used Daniel Corstange's modified design, asking control group respondents direct questions about the control items (Corstange, 2009). Corstange's modification allows me to estimate the impact of UNMIL's presence on local leaders' responses to the non-sensitive items. These items are theoretically relevant in and of themselves, since they capture the extent to which local leaders were willing to rely on the police to respond to crimes that fall under police jurisdiction.

Table 8.5 summarizes the distribution of local leaders' responses to the list experiment in the treatment and control groups. The top panel displays the average number of ways that local leaders believed their communities might handle a hypothetical unsolved burglary, ranging from 0 to 3 in the control group and 0 to 4 in the treatment group. The bottom panel provides local leaders' responses to direct questions in the control group alone. A plurality of local leaders (41 per cent) believed the police would be called to investigate an unsolved burglary. More striking, they were almost twice as likely to believe nothing would be done (26 per cent) as they were to believe UNMIL would be

TABLE 8.5 *Local leaders' responses to list experiment in Liberia*

	Control	Treatment
Item count		
0	0.36	0.12
1	0.47	0.37
2	0.15	0.36
3	0.01	0.13
4		0.02
Direct questions (control group only)		
Call the police	0.41	
Do nothing	0.26	
Call UNMIL	0.14	

Note: Descriptive statistics from the list experiment in the 2012 local leaders survey. Control items include "call the police," "just leave it alone and do nothing about it," and "take it to the UNMIL people." The sensitive item is "call for sassywood or sand cutter," a Liberian colloquialism for trial by ordeal. Following Corstange (2009), control group respondents were asked the control items directly.

called (14 per cent) – a disparity that echoes the results in Table 8.1. Notably, the item count in the treatment group is much larger than in the control group, suggesting that reliance on trial by ordeal was common in these communities.[11]

Figure 8.3 displays the impact of exposure to UNMIL on local leaders' responses to the list experiment.[12] My theory predicts that UN presence should increase informal authorities' deference to their formal counterparts in criminal cases that fall unambiguously under state jurisdiction (like burglary), while simultaneously diminishing their reliance on illegal mechanisms of dispute resolution (like trial by ordeal). My results in Figure 8.3 are generally consistent with these predictions. Exposure to UNMIL appears to have increased the probability that the police would be called to respond to burglary, though the magnitude of the effect varies by type of exposure. In communities that reported weekly patrols, local leaders were approximately twenty-five percentage points more likely to believe the police would be called, and twenty-five percentage points *less* likely to believe trial by ordeal would be used. These effects are each statistically significant on their own, and are also statistically different from one another. Local leaders were more likely to believe the police would be called in communities that reported interventions and public works as well. While they were no more or less likely to believe trial by ordeal would be used, the positive effect on calling the police is significantly larger than the null effect on using trial by ordeal in communities that reported interventions, and is also larger in communities that reported public works, albeit only marginally so.

The effects of less frequent patrols are mixed. Occasional patrols had no effect. More surprisingly, monthly patrols appear to have increased the probability that trial by ordeal would be used while *decreasing* the probability that the police would be called, though the latter effect is not statistically significant, and the former only weakly so. These two effects are also only weakly statistically different from each other. Exposure to UNMIL increased the likelihood that peacekeepers would be called as well, though the magnitude of the effect again varies: local leaders were more likely to believe UNMIL would be called in communities that reported weekly patrols, interventions, and public works, *less* likely to believe UNMIL would be called in communities that reported monthly patrols, and no more or less likely to believe UNMIL

---

[11] The distribution of responses in the top panel also suggests that my strategy of including a semi-sensitive item was successful in mitigating design effects. I confirm this using a diagnostic test proposed by Blair and Imai, which estimates the probability that inclusion of the sensitive item affected respondents' answers to the control items. The null hypothesis is no design effect. I fail to reject the null with a Bonferroni-corrected p-value of 0.27 (Blair and Imai, 2012).

[12] Given the need to estimate multiple conditional probabilities for relatively rare events, multivariate list experiment analyses can generally only accommodate a small number of regressors. For tractability, this analysis includes community-level controls only. Marginal effects and 90 and 95 per cent confidence intervals are derived from Monte Carlo simulations, following Blair and Imai (2012). For consistency with my other specifications, I measure the frequency of UNMIL patrols, interventions, and public works in the year prior to data collection (2012), and measure controls in 2010 to avoid post-treatment bias.

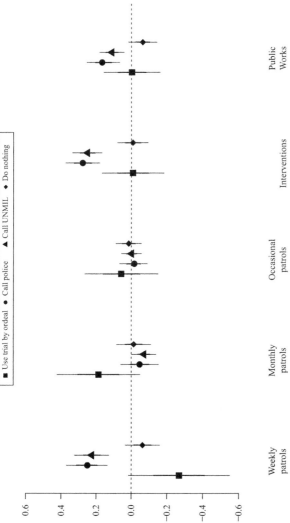

FIGURE 8.3 Short-term effects of exposure to UNMIL on local leaders' responses to list experiment

Note: Marginal effects and 90 and 95 per cent confidence intervals from the LISTIT maximum likelihood estimator proposed in Corstange (2009) holding all controls at their means. Confidence intervals are derived from Monte Carlo simulations as in Blair and Imai (2012). The dependent variable is an individual-level categorical variable indicating responses to the list experiment in the 2012 local leaders survey. The independent variables are community-level dummies for weekly, monthly, and occasional UNMIL patrols, interventions to resolve disputes, and public works projects from the 2012 local leaders survey. A version of this figure first appeared in Blair (2019), and is reprinted with permission. © The IO Foundation 2019, published by Cambridge University Press.

would be called in communities that reported occasional patrols. Importantly, the effect on calling UNMIL is statistically identical to the effect on calling the police. This again suggests that insofar as UNMIL induced dependence on peacekeeper presence, it did so at the expense of informal authorities rather than formal ones.

My qualitative interviews yield further insights into the mechanisms underlying this increased reliance on the police and UNMIL that I observe among local leaders in the quantitative data. Especially in communities that reported more frequent exposure to UNMIL, local leaders often expressed respect for the division of legal labor between Liberia's customary and statutory sectors. As the community chairman of Sanniquellie's Dokie Quarter explained, "I can compromise violation [of town laws] but not crime. If you commit a crime, I take you to police because I am only here to compromise minor problem .... We were told to relay any crime to the police. We don't go against the law, we don't have our own laws different from the government."[13] Perhaps not coincidentally, Dokie Quarter reported the most intense possible exposure to UNMIL in 2010: interventions, public works, and weekly patrols.

In the town of Borkeza, which reported monthly UNMIL patrols in 2010, local leaders typically rely on the community police to resolve petty complaints and non-violent domestic disputes: "if somebody steals and he admits the fact that he did the stealing, we can allow them [the community police] to go through it, and let the owner of the property receive it [compensation]. Then that one will be finished." But when the perpetrator is unknown, or when an arrest must be made, "UNMIL will come for the person and carry them. Those are the people who can investigate them."[14] Local leaders were less likely to draw distinctions of this sort in communities that reported less frequent exposure to UNMIL personnel.

Other local leaders expressed willingness to abide by even controversial decisions issued by the police and courts, in some cases citing the state's claim to ultimate jurisdiction to justify their own reluctance to intervene. This was especially common in conflicts involving multiple ethnic groups. In Dokie Quarter, the police ordered a woman from the Mano tribe to evacuate the home in which she was squatting after its Mandingo owners produced documentation proving that the property was theirs. When she refused, she was forcibly evicted:

> The old ma was angry, crying, coming to me as the community chairman. She said "you sitting down, people taking my house from me." I told the old ma that I am not above the law. Now the law has decided this case, that you must leave the house, and police people came and put your things out. I am not above the law, so I got nothing to do." She had no document to show. The [Mandingos] was having document. Land dispute can bring violence in this community.[15]

---

[13] AJD and ZD, Dokie Quarter, Sanniquellie, October 20, 2011.
[14] FD, Suman Quarter, Borkeza, November 5, 2011.
[15] AJD and ZD, Dokie Quarter, Sanniquellie, October 20, 2011.

Again, accounts of this sort were less common in communities that reported less frequent exposure to UNMIL.

Some local leaders were explicit in their approval of the LNP's increased presence in their communities, and in their desire for even greater LNP presence in the future. In the town of Salayea, which, like Dokie Quarter, reported the most intense possible exposure to UNMIL in 2010, the chief praised UNMIL's decision to construct a police station in the community, and described the community's relationship with the police as constructive and symbiotic: "we thank God that the police barrack has been built here. Sometimes if we encounter problem we can rush to them and they can come to us and help, and they too if they are in problem they can come to us. We also help them, because the police are not enough." The chief explained that the community was lobbying the government to deploy more police officers to the area. "Sometimes we can write and say we want more police to come. We need manpower. When the police in the town, it can make our job easy."[16]

In Bozoe Quarter in the town of Borkeza, local leaders solicited the LNP's help to organize a community watch team that would patrol the town and coordinate with the police: "we ask the government to help us with training, because the security is not enough. That is why we ask the National Police to help us with community police, and they did."[17] Bozoe Quarter reported both interventions and occasional UNMIL patrols in 2010. Of course, the fact that efforts of this sort were less common in communities that reported less frequent exposure to UNMIL does not prove that UNMIL's presence *caused* local leaders to engage with the LNP. But these qualitative accounts are nonetheless consistent with my quantitative results, lending them additional credibility and illuminating local leaders' reactions to UNMIL's efforts in greater detail than is possible through a survey alone.

MORE UNMIL PRESENCE, MORE PERCEIVED STATE CORRUPTION, BUT ONLY IN THE SHORT TERM

My results thus far are consistent with the predictions of my theory. In the short term at least, I find that exposure to UNMIL increased citizens' willingness to rely on the state to resolve the most serious incidents of crime and violence – incidents over which the state claims both original and ultimate jurisdiction. Following the conceptual framework developed in Chapter 3, this is a necessary condition for the rule of law at the micro level. Exposure to UNMIL also reduced informal authorities' reliance on illegal mechanisms of dispute resolution, and increased their deference to formal authorities in criminal cases that fall unambiguously under formal jurisdiction – necessary conditions for the rule of law at the meso level.

---

[16] JLM, Salayea, November 3, 2011.   [17] GK, Bozoe Quarter, Borkeza, November 4, 2011.

These effects were more pronounced for patrols than for interventions or public works, perhaps because patrols provided more opportunities for contact between peacekeepers and civilians. While I find some evidence that exposure to UNMIL increased reliance on the mission itself, these effects do not seem to have come at the expense of the state. My results belie concerns that peacekeepers are too abusive to increase reliance on formal authorities, too "compromised" to reduce reliance on informal ones, or too time- and resource-constrained to affect state/society relations at all. My results also belie the concern that UN missions induce dependence on their own personnel, crowding out and delegitimizing the state.

Taken together, my results thus lend support for the predictions of my theory against the three rival alternatives summarized in Chapter 4. But of course, the fact that citizens respect the constitutionally defined division of labor between state and non-state authorities does not necessarily imply that they trust state institutions to resolve disputes fairly or transparently. As we saw in Table 8.2, my survey respondents were more likely to perceive formal authorities as corrupt and biased, especially relative to informal (chiefs) and international (UNMIL) alternatives. Criminologists have long argued that citizens will only cooperate with the police and courts if they view those institutions as procedurally fair (Tyler and Huo 2002; Tyler 2004, 2006). But as Tables 8.1 and 8.2 illustrate, it seems that many Liberians were willing to rely on state security and justice providers despite their relative shortcomings as purveyors of security and justice.

What might explain this paradoxical combination of results? One possibility is that by encouraging citizens to rely on a corrupt and biased state, UNMIL exacerbated perceptions of state corruption and bias, especially in places where formal institutions proved to be imperfect substitutes for informal ones. Moreover, by demonstrating how security and justice provision "should" be done, it is possible that UNMIL heightened Liberians' awareness (and, potentially, disapproval) of misconduct on the part of state security and justice actors. Tables 8.6 and 8.7 explore this possibility using local leaders' reports of UNMIL patrols, interventions, and public works and residents' reports of interpersonal interactions with UNMIL personnel, respectively. The dependent variables are dummies indicating whether residents perceive formal authorities, informal authorities, and UNMIL as corrupt and biased. Each column reports coefficients from a separate OLS regression with the same control variables as before.[18] Since the dependent and independent variables are both measured in the same year (2010), I again characterize these as short-term effects.

The results are striking, especially when juxtaposed against my findings earlier in the chapter. I find that exposure to UNMIL actually *exacerbated* citizens' perceptions of state corruption, at least in the short term. This effect

---

[18] For ease of interpretation I use OLS for these regressions, even though the dependent variables are binary. The results are substantively unchanged if I use logit or probit instead.

TABLE 8.6 Short-term effects of exposure to UNMIL on citizens' perceptions using local leaders' reports of UNMIL presence

	Believes formal is corrupt	Believes formal is biased	Believest informal is corrupt	Believes informal is biased	Believes UNMIL is corrupt	Believes UNMIL is biased
Weekly patrols	0.10 [0.04]**	−0.00 [0.04]	0.00 [0.04]	0.01 [0.03]	0.06 [0.04]	0.02 [0.03]
Monthly patrols	0.11 [0.04]***	−0.01 [0.03]	0.02 [0.04]	−0.01 [0.02]	−0.00 [0.03]	0.02 [0.02]
Occasional patrols	0.08 [0.03]***	0.03 [0.03]	0.03 [0.03]	0.01 [0.02]	0.04 [0.03]	0.02 [0.02]
Interventions	0.05 [0.02]*	0.00 [0.02]	0.07 [0.02]***	0.03 [0.02]*	−0.01 [0.02]	−0.01 [0.02]
Public works	−0.01 [0.03]	−0.04 [0.03]	0.02 [0.04]	−0.01 [0.02]	0.01 [0.03]	0.03 [0.02]
Observations	4,078	4,304	4,123	4,404	3,402	4,049
District FE	Y	Y	Y	Y	Y	Y
Community-level controls	Y	Y	Y	Y	Y	Y
Individual-level controls	Y	Y	Y	Y	Y	Y

Note: Coefficients from OLS regressions. The dependent variables are individual-level dummies indicating each respondent's perceptions of potential security and justice providers in the 2010 residents survey. The independent variables are dummies for weekly, monthly, and occasional UNMIL patrols, interventions to resolve disputes, and public works projects from the 2010 local leaders survey. Estimates are weighted by the inverse probability of sampling. Standard errors, clustered by community, are in brackets. *** $p < 0.01$, ** $p < 0.05$, * $p < 0.1$. A version of this table first appeared in Blair (2019), and is reprinted with permission. © The IO Foundation 2019, published by Cambridge University Press.

TABLE 8.7 *Short-term effects of exposure to UNMIL on citizens' perceptions using citizens' reports of UNMIL presence*

	Believes formal is corrupt	Believes formal is biased	Believest informal is corrupt	Believes informal is biased	Believes UNMIL is corrupt	Believes UNMIL is biased
Spent time with UNMIL	0.05 [0.02]**	−0.02 [0.02]	0.03 [0.02]	−0.01 [0.01]	−0.04 [0.02]**	−0.04 [0.01]***
Observations	4,022	4,235	4,073	4,324	3,387	4,001
District FE	Y	Y	Y	Y	Y	Y
Community-level controls	Y	Y	Y	Y	Y	Y
Individual-level controls	Y	Y	Y	Y	Y	Y

Note: Coefficients from OLS regressions. The dependent variables are individual-level dummies indicating each respondent's perceptions of potential security and justice providers in the 2010 residents survey. The independent variable is a dummy for individual-level exposure to UNMIL from the 2010 residents survey. Estimates are weighted by the inverse probability of sampling. Standard errors, clustered by community, are in brackets. *** $p < 0.01$, ** $p < 0.05$, * $p < 0.1$. A version of this table first appeared in Blair (2019), and is reprinted with permission. © The IO Foundation 2019, published by Cambridge University Press.

is consistent across all types of exposure except public works. Residents of communities that reported weekly, monthly, or occasional patrols were, respectively, ten, eleven, and eight percentage points more likely to describe the state as corrupt. Residents of communities that reported interventions were five percentage points more likely to describe the state as corrupt as well, though this effect is only marginally statistically significant.

Similarly, residents who reported spending time with UNMIL were five percentage points more likely to describe the state as corrupt. Interestingly, residents who reported interacting with UNMIL were four percentage points less likely to describe UNMIL as corrupt, and four percentage points less likely to describe UNMIL as biased. Exposure to UNMIL does not appear to have changed perceptions of state impartiality. Exposure does not appear to have changed perceptions of non-state authorities either: residents of communities that reported UNMIL interventions were seven percentage points more likely to describe informal authorities as corrupt and three percentage points more likely to describe them as biased, but otherwise these effects are null across the board.

Together my results suggest that, if anything, exposure to UNMIL heightened the tension between Liberians' preferences for state institutions on the one hand and their perceptions of those same institutions on the other. I find that exposure to UNMIL induced Liberians to rely on state over non-state authorities, and induced non-state authorities to rely on legal over illegal mechanisms of dispute resolution. But I also find that UNMIL did not mitigate citizens' perceptions of state bias, and, if anything, *exacerbated* their perceptions of state corruption. In other words, interactions with UNMIL reinforced Liberians' preference for the state, but also magnified their perception of the state as corrupt.

One possible explanation for these findings lies in the somewhat mixed messages that UNMIL delivered to Liberian citizens, encouraging them to obey state laws, reject vigilantism, and defer to the police and courts while simultaneously instructing them to recognize and report acts of misconduct. (For examples of UNMIL's mixed messages, see the billboards pictured in Chapter 6.) It is possible that Liberians simply internalized these somewhat conflicting messages simultaneously, at least in the short term. Mixed messages may have compounded one another if citizens increasingly opted to rely on state institutions that they increasingly recognized as corrupt. Meanwhile, demonstration effects may have also brought the deficiencies of Liberia's state security and justice sectors into sharper relief as citizens contrasted the treatment they received from UNMIL with the treatment they received from the Liberian police and courts.

These short-term results thus have ambiguous medium- and long-term implications. Heightened awareness of state corruption may improve the quality of state security and justice provision if it motivates citizens to demand greater transparency and fair play (Gottlieb, 2016). If citizens are more attuned to state corruption, they may be more willing to apply pressure of this sort. Increased citizen cooperation may also alleviate corruption if it helps the police and courts investigate crimes and resolve disputes more fairly and efficiently (Tyler and Huo, 2002). Alternatively, deference to the state in the short term may dissipate over the medium and long term if state institutions fail to meet citizens' elevated expectations. Andrea Talentino, for example, argues that international intervention in Liberia "encouraged Liberians to expect more and better, but it is unlikely that those desires can be met." The result, she argues, is a "crisis of expectations" that will erode the rule of law over time (Talentino, 2007, 165–6).

The availability of multiple rounds of survey data gives me some leverage to adjudicate between these competing possibilities. In Figure 8.4, I test the persistence of UNMIL's impact after two years. To do this, I simply replicate my analysis in Figure 8.1, matching residents' preferences in 2012 to local leaders' reports of UNMIL presence in 2010. My medium-term analysis is thus identical to my short-term analysis, except that my dependent variable and individual-level controls are measured in 2012, while my independent variables are measured in 2010. But my results are broadly the same regardless. In communities that reported weekly, monthly, or occasional patrols in 2010, citizens continued to express a pronounced preference for formal over informal institutions even two years later. Unsurprisingly, these effects are weaker in the medium term than in the short term, with one exception: while weekly patrols had no effect on citizens' preference for UNMIL in the short term, they appear to have strengthened that preference in the medium term – though, as before, this effect is not statistically different from the effect on preferences for the state. Also unsurprisingly, the effects of public works, which were only weakly statistically significant in the short term, are no longer statistically distinguishable from zero in the medium term.

Nor do my results appear to depend on the continued physical presence of UNMIL personnel. Figure 8.5 replicates the analysis in Figure 8.4, this time focusing on the subset of communities that reported no further exposure to UNMIL of any kind in 2012 – no patrols, no interventions, and no public works. Because this model requires stretching my data rather thin, I exclude public works and combine weekly and monthly patrols into a single dummy. But the results are again broadly consistent with those in Figure 8.1, and are in some cases even stronger. Residents of communities that reported weekly or monthly patrols in 2010 but no further exposure in 2012 were still twenty-five percentage points more likely to prefer relying on state institutions to resolve criminal cases, and sixteen percentage points less likely to prefer non-state alternatives. These countervailing effects are highly statistically significant on their own, and the difference between them is highly statistically significant as well.

This degree of persistence is even more remarkable given that I estimate the short- and medium-term effects of UNMIL's presence on different samples of

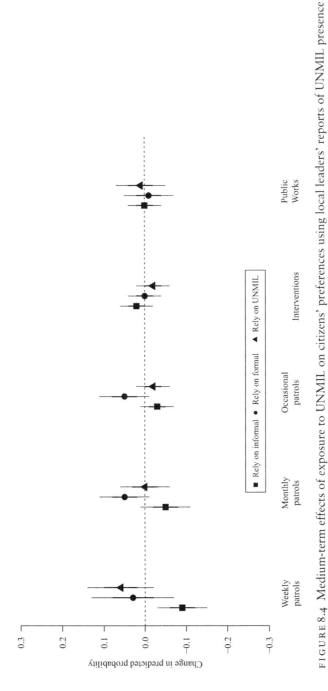

FIGURE 8.4 Medium-term effects of exposure to UNMIL on citizens' preferences using local leaders' reports of UNMIL presence

Note: Marginal effects and 90 and 95 per cent confidence intervals from multinomial logit regressions holding all controls at their means. The dependent variable is an individual-level categorical variable indicating each respondent's modal preference over potential security and justice providers in the 2012 residents survey. The independent variables are dummies for weekly, monthly, and occasional UNMIL patrols, interventions to resolve disputes, and public works projects from the 2010 local leaders survey. Estimates are weighted by the inverse probability of sampling. Standard errors are clustered by community. A version of this figure first appeared in Blair (2019), and is reprinted with permission. © The IO Foundation 2019, published by Cambridge University Press.

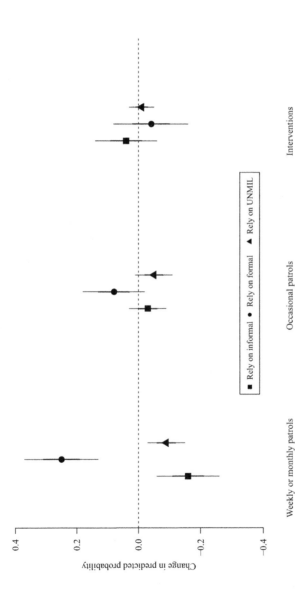

FIGURE 8.5 Medium-term effects of exposure to UNMIL on citizens' preferences using local leaders' reports of UNMIL presence, subsetting to communities exposed in 2010 only

Note: Marginal effects and 90 and 95 per cent confidence intervals from multinomial logit regressions holding all controls at their means. The dependent variable is an individual-level categorical variable indicating each respondent's modal preference over potential security and justice providers in the 2012 residents survey. The independent variables are community-level dummies for weekly, monthly, and occasional UNMIL patrols, interventions to resolve disputes, and public works projects from the 2010 local leaders survey. I restrict my sample to communities that reported no exposure to UNMIL in 2012. Estimates are weighted by the inverse probability of sampling. Standard errors are clustered by community.

residents,[19] suggesting that my results are neither temporary nor specific to a particular set of individuals. Interestingly, in this subset of communities, patrols actually *reduced* citizens' reliance on UNMIL over time, both in absolute terms and relative to the state. This provides further evidence that UNMIL did not induce dependence on its own personnel.

Tables 8.8 and 8.9 extend this analysis by testing UNMIL's impact on citizens' perceptions of state corruption and bias in 2012, both in the full sample (Table 8.8) and in the subset of communities that reported no further exposure to UNMIL after 2010 (Table 8.9). In the short term, exposure to UNMIL exacerbated citizens' perceptions of state corruption. Over time, however, this effect appears to have decayed to a null. Regardless of the type or frequency of exposure, two years later, residents were no more or less likely to view the state as corrupt or biased.

Table 8.9 provides some suggestive evidence that UNMIL interventions aggravated perceptions of state bias in the medium term, but this effect is only weakly statistically significant, and is only detectable in the subset of communities that reported no further exposure to UNMIL after 2010. Interestingly, Table 8.8 also provides some suggestive evidence that interventions mitigated perceptions of UNMIL corruption and (weakly) bias, while public works exacerbated perceptions of UNMIL bias. But again, these results are sensitive to specification, and are only detectable in the full sample. Most important, regardless of specification, the medium-term effects on perceptions of the state are almost uniformly null.

These last results should be interpreted with some caution, since UNMIL may have decided to discontinue patrols, interventions, and public works in particular communities for reasons that are correlated with citizens' perceptions. For example, once the mission detected that a particular community was open to renewed state security and justice provision, it may have moved on to other locations. Nonetheless, my results indicate that the potential adverse effects of UNMIL's presence on citizens' perceptions dissipated over time, while the beneficial effects on citizens' preferences persisted for at least two years, even if their magnitude decayed. Taken together, these results suggest that UNMIL induced a marked and potentially lasting change in norms of dispute resolution in Liberia; that UNMIL's impact did not depend on the continued physical presence of UNMIL personnel; and that Liberians' increased perceptions of state corruption in the short term did not last, and did not deter them from relying on state institutions in the longer run. I cannot say for certain whether these effects will persist beyond two years, much less after the mission's withdrawal. (UNMIL's mandate did not conclude until 2018.) But my results suggest the possibility of a durable and overall positive change in citizens' attitudes towards state authority in Liberia, strengthening the rule of law at both the micro and meso levels.

---

[19] Recall from Chapter 7 that a different group of 20 residents per community was sampled in each wave of the survey.

TABLE 8.8 *Medium-term effects of exposure to UNMIL on citizens' perceptions using local leaders' reports of UNMIL presence*

	Believes formal is corrupt	Believes formal is biased	Believest informal is corrupt	Believes informal is biased	Believes UNMIL is corrupt	Believes UNMIL is biased
Weekly patrols	0.00	-0.01	-0.02	-0.02	-0.07	-0.01
	[0.04]	[0.03]	[0.04]	[0.03]	[0.03]**	[0.03]
Monthly patrols	0.02	-0.01	-0.01	-0.01	-0.01	-0.02
	[0.03]	[0.03]	[0.04]	[0.02]	[0.02]	[0.02]
Occasional patrols	0.04	0.01	-0.02	-0.03	-0.00	-0.01
	[0.03]	[0.03]	[0.03]	[0.02]*	[0.02]	[0.02]
Interventions	-0.02	-0.01	0.01	-0.00	-0.05	-0.03
	[0.03]	[0.02]	[0.02]	[0.02]	[0.02]***	[0.01]*
Public works	0.03	0.04	0.08	0.02	0.01	0.05
	[0.03]	[0.02]*	[0.04]**	[0.02]	[0.02]	[0.02]***
Observations	3,543	3,705	3,600	3,788	3,114	3,501
District FE	Y	Y	Y	Y	Y	Y
Community-level controls	Y	Y	Y	Y	Y	Y
Individual-level controls	Y	Y	Y	Y	Y	Y

Note: Coefficients from OLS regressions. The dependent variables are individual-level dummies indicating each respondent's perceptions of potential security and justice providers in the 2012 residents survey. The independent variables are dummies for weekly, monthly, and occasional UNMIL patrols, interventions to resolve disputes, and public works projects from the 2010 local leaders survey. Estimates are weighted by the inverse probability of sampling. Standard errors, clustered by community, are in brackets. *** $p < 0.01$, ** $p < 0.05$, * $p < 0.1$. A version of this table first appeared in Blair (2019), and is reprinted with permission. © The IO Foundation 2019, published by Cambridge University Press.

TABLE 8.9 *Medium-term effects of exposure to UNMIL on citizens' perceptions using local leaders' reports of UNMIL presence, subsetting to communities exposed in 2010 only*

	Believes formal is corrupt	Believes formal is biased	Believes informal is corrupt	Believes informal is biased	Believes UNMIL is corrupt	Believes UNMIL is biased
Weekly or monthly patrols	0.08	−0.05	−0.14	0.02	−0.00	−0.02
	[0.05]	[0.06]	[0.10]	[0.04]	[0.05]	[0.07]
Occasional patrols	0.04	−0.04	−0.03	0.08	−0.06	−0.02
	[0.05]	[0.05]	[0.07]	[0.03]**	[0.05]	[0.05]
Interventions	−0.03	0.07	−0.06	−0.00	−0.01	−0.02
	[0.05]	[0.04]*	[0.04]	[0.04]	[0.03]	[0.04]
Observations	909	944	933	974	790	872
District FE	Y	Y	Y	Y	Y	Y
Community-level controls	Y	Y	Y	Y	Y	Y
Individual-level controls	Y	Y	Y	Y	Y	Y

Note: Coefficients from OLS regressions. The dependent variables are individual-level dummies indicating each respondent's perceptions of potential security and justice providers in the 2012 residents survey. The independent variables are dummies for weekly, monthly, and occasional UNMIL patrols, interventions to resolve disputes, and public works projects from the 2010 local leaders survey. I restrict my sample to communities that reported no exposure to UNMIL in 2012. Estimates are weighted by the inverse probability of sampling. Standard errors, clustered by community, are in brackets. *** $p < 0.01$, ** $p < 0.05$, * $p < 0.1$.

UNMIL'S IMPACT AT THE MACRO LEVEL

My quantitative analysis focuses on UNMIL's impact at the micro and meso levels. This is by design and necessity, since my survey and list experiment focus on these two levels of analysis only. But my conceptual framework in Chapter 3 posits that all three dimensions of the rule of law are closely interconnected, and that progress along one dimension depends in part on progress along the others. Was UNMIL as successful in promoting the rule of law at the macro level as it was at the micro and meso levels? The rest of this chapter will offer some suggestive answers to this question.

Proving causality at the macro level is much more difficult than at the micro and meso levels. While I can document trends in the rule of law in Liberia over time, I cannot attribute any changes I find to UNMIL's presence specifically, at least not in a definitive way – though, as we saw in Chapter 5, UN presence is positively correlated with the rule of law across post-conflict African countries more generally, including Liberia. These limitations notwithstanding, macro-level trends are informative, and allow me to speculate as to the likely trajectory of the rule of law in Liberia had UNMIL never intervened.

The phrasing of this last point is intentional and important. Skeptics of UN missions often frame their critiques in terms of absolutes rather than counterfactuals. This approach is misguided, and encourages more pessimism than is warranted by the UN's record. By absolute standards, UNMIL's efforts at macro-level rule-of-law promotion must be judged a failure. The Liberian police remain corrupt and ineffective. The Liberian judiciary is still susceptible to encroachment by the executive and legislative branches, and government officials continue to ignore court rulings when it benefits them to do so. Liberian prisons remain overcrowded, with alarmingly high rates of pre-trial detention. Liberian laws are still convoluted and in some cases contradictory. None of this is in doubt. But none of it is quite to the point either. The relevant question is not whether the rule of law in Liberia is strong in some absolute sense – it is not. The relevant question is whether the rule of law *would have been weaker* had UNMIL never intervened. By this more appropriate standard, I argue that UNMIL was a success.

Following the conceptual framework developed in Chapter 3, the rule of law at the macro level requires that state authorities abide by legal limits on their power, and that they defer to a constitutionally designated arbiter (typically a Supreme Court) when disagreements about those limits arise. This, in turn, requires that laws themselves be clear and consistent. Macro-level rule of law also requires that the courts enjoy some degree of independence, and that the police and prisons refrain from arbitrary arrests, indefinite detentions, and extralegal punishments, all of which constitute exercises of power outside the bounds of the law. This section explores the extent to which UNMIL helped establish these conditions on the ground, however imperfectly, drawing on secondary sources and UNMIL's own budget performance reports, which document the mission's successes and shortcomings over time.

UNMIL's Impact at the Macro Level

As I discussed in Chapter 6, one of UNMIL's most urgent priorities from the outset was to overhaul the LNP. The mission was tasked with building or repairing police stations that had been damaged or destroyed during the civil war; vetting, recruiting, and training police officers; and ensuring adherence to professional codes of conduct and respect for the rights of citizens under Liberian law. When UNMIL first deployed in 2003, Liberia's security forces operated with impunity. The early days of the peace process were marred by riots and other incidents of civil unrest, to which the LNP responded with characteristic brutality. UNMIL was instrumental in curbing these abuses. As a 2013 Human Rights Watch report notes, UNMIL "played a critical role in the oversight and logistical support of the LNP, conducting joint patrols, ... providing vehicle and other transportation and logistics support, and helping to mediate protests and major clashes with the police" (Human Rights Watch, 2013, 14).

Anecdotal evidence suggests that these efforts bore fruit. As early as 2005, Freedom House observed that violations of due process protections and other rule-of-law principles by the police were becoming "less frequent ... than in previous years" (Freedom House, 2005). Demonstrations persisted throughout the volatile transitional period, but the police increasingly "refrained from using force in response" (Freedom House, 2008). In 2007, for example, ex-combatants rioted in Monrovia to protest unpaid salaries and delayed disarmament, demobilization, and reintegration (DDR) packages. The LNP "quickly dispersed the crowd and arrested five protesters, and only a handful of people were injured, none seriously" (Freedom House, 2008).

The LNP's capacity to respond to criminal complaints and civil unrest gradually improved during this period, including outside of Monrovia. This was thanks in no small part to UNMIL's efforts. By January 2006, UNMIL had recommissioned sixty-two police stations in all of Liberia's fifteen counties. The number of police officers trained, equipped, and redeployed rose from 866 in mid-2005 to 5,571 in 2014, before dipping again during the deadly Ebola epidemic of 2014–15 (UN Secretary-General, 2015a). Beginning in 2011, UNMIL began tracking the number of "public disorder incidents" that proved "beyond the capacity of Government institutions to successfully address" without assistance from UNMIL personnel. This number fell from twenty-five in 2012 to eighteen in 2013, seven in 2014, three in 2015, and just two in 2016 (UN Secretary-General, 2016, 11). Around this time UNMIL also began to note "increased reporting of national security agencies to relevant legislative committees," suggesting that the LNP and other state security institutions were increasingly being subjected to more stringent civilian oversight (UN Secretary-General, 2015a, 21).

Most internal and external observers credit UNMIL with improving the LNP's performance. In Jean Krasno's 2006 survey of Liberian citizens, 92 per cent described UNMIL's efforts to retrain the LNP as "good or very good," despite their lack of confidence in the LNP overall (Krasno, 2006, 5).

Jonathan Friedman, in an assessment for Princeton University's *Innovations for Successful Societies* initiative, describes police reform under UNMIL as "relatively successful ... from a global viewpoint" (Friedman and MacAulay, 2014, 14). LNP officers themselves routinely cite the training they received from UNMIL as evidence of their improved performance, and as a reason for civilians to trust them (Blair, Karim, and Morse, 2019). And while government officials in Liberia are quick to assert their independence, many nonetheless praise the transformative role that UNMIL played in reconstituting the collapsed state (Neumann and Schia, 2012, 29).

UNMIL was similarly instrumental in reducing pre-trial detention. UNMIL's Legal and Judicial System Support Division tracked the records of pre-trial detainees through the criminal justice system, reviewing case files and compiling data on proceedings initiated in the courts. In line with the mission's objectives, the rate of pre-trial detention dropped from a staggering 80 per cent in 2013 to 75 per cent in 2014, and 70 per cent in 2015. When UNMIL failed to meet its 60 per cent target the following year – pre-trial detention continued to fall, but only to 65 per cent – it introduced several additional initiatives related to plea bargaining and alternative dispute resolution in an attempt to clear the case backlog more quickly (UN Secretary-General, 2016). UNMIL's police contingent (UNPOL) was also central in pursuing these goals. As the 2013 Human Rights Watch report observes, "UNPOL monitoring can be credited with reducing the number of arbitrary arrests and detentions. UNPOL has done this through frequent visits to police depots and detention cells, where UNPOL staff check record keeping and speak with detainees" (Human Rights Watch, 2013, 13–14).

The numbers bear this out. As of mid-2005, only half of Liberia's circuit, specialized, and magisterial courts were open and functional; by mid-2007, all of them were (UN Secretary-General, 2008c). As of January 2006, UNMIL had overseen the appointment of twenty judges for circuit courts, fifty for specialized courts, and magistrates for all 145 magisterial courts, in accordance with the terms of the 2003 Comprehensive Peace Agreement (UN Secretary-General, 2006b). By mid-2008, public defenders had also been assigned to all of Liberia's fifteen counties (UN Secretary-General, 2008d). As the human and infrastructural capacity of the judiciary expanded, so too did the number of indictable offenses prosecuted and cleared by the courts, which increased from just ten in mid-2005 to seventy in 2006, 100 in 2007, and 160 in 2008 (UN Secretary-General, 2008c). The circuit courts, in particular, became increasingly active during this period, clearing over five times as many cases in 2011 as they had just three years earlier (UN Secretary-General, 2012a). UNMIL attributed this rising clearance rate to "improvement in the preparation of cases and improved coordination between the prosecution, defense, and courts" (UN Secretary-General, 2011a, 34).

The judiciary's ability to constrain the actions of government officials increased during this period as well. Beginning in 2010, Freedom House observed that the executive branch "interfered less in the judicial system" than it had in previous years (Freedom House, 2011). As judicial independence improved, so too did the judiciary's willingness to "intervene to protect people's rights" (Freedom House, 2016). This became especially relevant during the Ebola epidemic, when the government adopted several measures of questionable legality in an attempt to contain the spread of the virus. In December 2014, the Supreme Court ruled that the president's ban on political rallies was unconstitutional. And in August of the following year, it ordered the government to lift a ban on the *National Chronicle* newspaper, imposed in 2014 after reporters began publishing conspiracy theories about the origins of the epidemic.

The Sirleaf administration argued that the ban was necessary for public health, but the Court disagreed. It held that the newspaper's continued closure "long after the state of emergency is a violation of the [journalists'] rights not supported by the laws." Nor were these types of decisions specific to the executive branch. In December 2015, the Court issued a stay to prevent the mayor of Monrovia from demolishing residents' private property as part of her controversial "Beautification Taskforce." It also adjudicated allegations of fraud in the 2014 Senatorial elections without political interference (Freedom House, 2016).

There is evidence that other state authorities became increasingly deferential to the rulings of legislative and judicial oversight bodies during UNMIL's tenure. An audit of all government ministries in 2006 resulted in the dismissal of five mid-level Ministry of Finance employees, as well as three high-level officials from the Ministries of Health and Commerce and the Civil Aviation Authority (Freedom House, 2007). The General Auditing Commission conducted another series of audits in 2010, and while the process was politicized – generating resistance to several of the resulting recommendations – it did precipitate the resignation of the Minister of Information on allegations of fraud and embezzlement (Butty, 2011; Freedom House, 2011). The National Elections Commission (NEC) successfully oversaw a referendum on four proposed constitutional amendments in 2011, and when the results were challenged in the Supreme Court, the NEC implemented the Court's decision without obstruction (Freedom House, 2013; Global Legal Monitor, 2011).

Perhaps most important, when Sirleaf's second term as president expired, she voluntarily complied with the two-term limit imposed under the Liberian constitution. Extending term limits is one of the most common ways that executives in Africa and other parts of the developing (and, indeed, developed) world skirt the rule of law in order to retain power (Carter, 2016; Corrales and Penfold, 2014). Sirleaf's willingness to step down without force or violence marked an important milestone for the rule of law in Liberia.

The election to pick Sirleaf's successor was a milestone as well. The first round of the 2017 Liberian general election was held on October 10, and while the NEC certified the results, a coalition of political parties led by opposition candidate Charles Brumskine, whose third-place finish would have disqualified him from the runoff, challenged the NEC's finding, citing various irregularities (Al Jazeera News, 2017). Had the Supreme Court ruled in Brumskine's favor, it would have forced a redo of the first round. Wary of a potential constitutional crisis, the US Embassy in Monrovia issued a strong statement urging the NEC to proceed with the runoff despite the pending court case (US Embassy in Liberia, 2017). A former US Ambassador to Liberia and Assistant Secretary of State for African Affairs similarly rebuked Brumskine for "failing" Liberia's citizens by contesting the results of the poll (Dodoo, 2017).

But as two Liberian analysts rightly argued in a co-authored op-ed, the US Embassy's recommendation would have privileged "political expediency" over the rule of law: "by using the rule of law to resolve electoral disputes, Liberia is taking pages out of the ... US playbook. The US would do well to refrain from making alarmist political statements and allow Liberia's current litigation process to reach its logical conclusion" (Pailey and Dillon, 2017). To its credit, the NEC postponed the runoff to allow Brumskine's case to proceed. He lost, and the runoff was held on December 26. When Sirleaf's preferred candidate was defeated by former soccer star George Weah, she accepted the result, and Weah was inaugurated in the country's first peaceful transfer of power from one democratically elected president to another in over half a century.

These developments are reflected in Liberia's scores on the Freedom House and World Bank rule-of-law indices that I use in my cross-national analysis in Chapter 5. In 2004, Liberia scored a two out of sixteen on Freedom House's rule-of-law index. Only five other countries in the world received an equal or lower score that year: Cameroon (0), Sudan (0), the DRC (1), Equatorial Guinea (1), and Zimbabwe (2). Liberia's score of −1.56 on the World Bank's 2004 Worldwide Governance Indicator for the rule of law placed it 10th from the bottom of the list, slightly outperforming the Central African Republic and slightly underperforming Sudan. But this pattern did not last. Liberia's Freedom House rating rose to four in 2005 and seven in 2006, where it held steady for all but one of the following years.[20] Scores on the World Bank's rule-of-law index fluctuated more widely, rising as high as −0.81 in 2014 – in the same range as Mozambique, Bangladesh, and Ukraine – before falling again in 2015 with the onset of the Ebola crisis. Even with that dip, however, Liberia's score has not dropped below −1 since 2009.

This is not to suggest that UNMIL was solely responsible for orchestrating improvements in the rule of law in Liberia, or that Liberia has become an exemplar of the rule of law under UNMIL's tutelage. It has not. As discussed in Chapter 6, a variety of foreign donors and domestic and international NGOs contributed to strengthening the rule of law in Liberia, and UNMIL undoubtedly benefited from the political will that Sirleaf and her allies

---

[20] Liberia's rating dropped to six at the height of the Ebola epidemic, but returned to seven thereafter.

(generally) brought to the process of rule-of-law reform. That process is far from complete. Allegations of corruption, incompetence, and abuse continue to dog the LNP; the courts remain slow, and are susceptible to bribery and political interference; the prisons are dangerously overcrowded; arbitrary and politically motivated arrests still occur, albeit less frequently;[21] and government officials, especially members of the executive branch, continue to breach jurisdictional boundaries.[22]

Nonetheless, there is compelling (if not exactly causal) evidence that the rule of law in Liberia is stronger today than it would have been had UNMIL never deployed. UNMIL is generally believed to have been a success – perhaps even "one of the UN's most successful peacekeeping missions to date" (Roby, 2018). As two members of the US House Foreign Affairs Committee wrote in a 2018 op-ed, the "powerful transitions" that Liberia has witnessed over the last decade and a half were "made possible by the presence of United Nations peacekeepers and the scores of UN agencies that helped stabilize and rebuild a failed state." Those efforts have "allowed Liberia to flourish into a country that can stand on its own and, hopefully with time, help other embattled nations follow its example" (Kinzinger and Cicilline, 2018).

While it is impossible to say whether Liberia will indeed "stand on its own" after the last UN staffer departs – a moment that is still years away, as the Security Council has pledged to maintain "a robust United Nations country team comprised of 16 agencies, funds, and programmes" even after UNMIL's withdrawal (UN Meetings Coverage, 2018) – early indications are encouraging. On June 30, 2016, UNMIL officially ceded "full security responsibility" to Liberia's police, military, and Bureau of Immigration and Naturalization (BIN), including responsibility for prison security, VIP security, airfield security, maritime patrolling, and explosive ordinance disposal, among other tasks (UN Secretary-General, 2016, 6). These agencies then successfully and independently oversaw the 2017 general election, with minimal assistance from UNMIL.

In its final budget performance report before the mission's withdrawal in 2018, UNMIL met or exceeded its training targets for the LNP, BIN, judiciary, and Bureau of Corrections and Rehabilitation. These targets were ambitious, designed to ensure that Liberia would have a corps of LNP and BIN officers with the experience necessary to draft regulations "supporting the implementation of the police and immigration service acts"; commanders able to diffuse crises "in compliance with human rights and protection of civilians principles"; judges and clerks capable of disposing cases "within

---

[21] To cite just one example, Mulbah Morlu, former chairman of the Forum for the Establishment of a War Crimes Court for Liberia and current chairman of Weah's Coalition for Democratic Change party, was arrested multiple times between 2008 and 2013, always on dubious charges related to his work for the political opposition (Butty, 2011; Cassell, 2007; Weedee, 2013).

[22] In one high profile case from 2014, Minister of Justice Christiana Tah resigned her post after accusing Sirleaf of impeding the ministry's investigation into allegations of fraud at the National Security Agency, which was led at the time by one of the president's sons (Giahyue, 2014).

constitutional and legislative requirements"; and prison guards and wardens with the knowledge and skills needed for managing prisons "in line with international standards and application of accountability measures for violations" (UN Secretary-General, 2017, 13, 21). Of course, meeting numerical targets is not the same as ensuring compliance with the underlying standards of conduct. But the fact that UNMIL was willing to withdraw at all, after fifteen years and multiple delays, is reason for some confidence in and of itself.

In her last speech as president before the UN General Assembly in 2017, Sirleaf surveyed the progress Liberia made towards peace, democracy, economic development, and the rule of law since the end of the civil war in 2003. "Liberia has come a long way," she said. She went on to frame Liberia's progress in terms of the key counterfactual that I posed before:

We could not have accomplished all of this without the world body, its political leadership, the generosity of its economic development support, humanitarian contributions, and, most importantly, the stabilization and security provided to our country through the United Nations Mission in Liberia (UNMIL) .... Liberia's transformation was powered by a world community that made a shared commitment to deliver peace to a country, and a subregion, beset by civil conflict and cross border destabilization. The UN and its partner nations were of one mind, and from that global unity, a new Liberian democratic state was born. Liberia is a post conflict success story. It is your post conflict success story. (*Statement by Her Excellency Mrs. Ellen Johnson Sirleaf, President of Liberia*, 2017, 6)

Sirleaf's perspective may be rosier than the empirical record warrants. Still, the prospects for a more robust rule of law in Liberia – and, in turn, for a deeper and more lasting peace – are almost certainly more promising today than they were in 2003. And they are almost certainly more promising than they would have been had UNMIL never intervened.

9

Implications for Africa and beyond

The second time the police visited the small rural Liberian village of Zowienta was very different from the first. On their first visit, described in the opening paragraphs of Chapter 1, the "devil" came out to protest the officers' presence in the village, and a group of young men threatened them with machetes and emptied the air from the tires on their truck. As a Liberian research assistant hired to accompany the officers during the visit explained, "the citizens did not have trust and confidence in them. They believed that the officers may have some hidden agenda against the community." Residents of Zowienta had been brutalized by Liberia's security forces during the civil war, and remained understandably "unfriendly" and "unreceptive," wary of the new role the police hoped to play as purveyors of security and justice in the post-conflict period.[1]

By the second visit six months later, however, the tenor had changed. The commander leading the patrol explained that he and his colleagues had come to "reach out to the citizens to interact with them, so as to regain their trust and confidence," which had been lost over fourteen years of civil strife – years characterized by cruelty and predation at the hands of the police. "As a result of these actions and behaviors," the commander explained, "the citizens had fear in the officers, and when they see the officers coming, they run away." But the police had since undergone over a decade of reform under UNMIL's tutelage. The process was intensive and transformational: UNMIL had vetted, recruited, and trained over 4,000 police officers; monitored their performance through joint patrols and co-location at police stations around the country, many of which the mission itself had built or rehabilitated; and hosted Community Police Forums to "sensitize" officers to the needs of civilians (Friedman and MacAulay, 2014).

The commander appealed to the citizens' trust in UNMIL as a reason for them to trust his officers as well: "UNMIL trained the officers that they may

[1] Zowienta, August 9, 2014.

serve the citizens by protecting their lives and properties. UNMIL transformed them that they may be friends of the citizens again." Many of UNMIL's efforts were aimed at repairing Liberians' deeply damaged relations with the police and other state security and justice institutions. Most Liberians approved of UNMIL's performance, and many credited UNMIL with catalyzing security and justice sector reforms (Krasno, 2006). The commander's appeal in Zowienta appears to have resonated, and the youths who had threatened the officers before were now "interacting and making friends with them." The town's leaders also requested that the police open a depot in the community, focused in particular on curtailing domestic violence – a request that would have seemed unimaginable six months before.[2]

As discussed in Chapter 3, rule-of-law trajectories diverge widely in countries recovering from civil war. In some countries, constitutions constrain the actions of potentially overzealous executives, while in others, government officials routinely ignore legal limits on their power. In some countries, the police abide by some minimal standards of fairness, competence, and professionalism; in others they indulge in excessive force and extrajudicial punishment. In some countries, the judiciary enjoys at least a modicum of independence from the executive and legislative branches, while in others the courts are subjected to relentless political meddling.

Variation occurs at the local level as well, especially in "hybrid" legal systems like those found in most post-conflict settings, where state security and justice institutions compete for citizens' loyalties with ever-evolving constellations of non-state alternatives – chiefs, elders, warlords, gangs, rebel groups themselves. Some citizens trust state institutions as competent and fair; others perceive them as corrupt and biased. Some rely on formal authorities to intervene when crimes are committed or violence occurs, while others depend on informal authorities instead. Some of these informal authorities respect the state and defer to the police and courts to adjudicate cases that fall unambiguously under state jurisdiction. Others usurp the state by claiming the right to adjudicate even the most serious incidents of crime and violence, or by resolving disputes in ways that flout state law, for example through mob justice or trial by ordeal.

This book argues that third-party intervention by the UN and other international intermediaries can help explain this variation both across countries and over time. The book's core theoretical claim, developed in Chapter 4, is that UN missions promote the rule of law by acting as catalysts for state reform at the macro level, surrogates for reformed states at the micro and meso levels, and liaisons between citizens and both state and non-state authorities across the three levels of my analysis. At the macro level, UN missions assume responsibility for rewriting laws and constitutions, recruit and retrain judges and police officers, monitor prisons for arbitrary arrests and indefinite

---

[2] Zowienta, February 4, 2015.

detentions, and more generally ensure that state agencies and officials abide by constitutional constraints on their power.

As these reforms progress at the macro level, UN missions "act out" the state at the micro level, demonstrating, by example, the relative merits of formal over informal dispute resolution; sensitizing citizens to an increased third-party presence in their communities; creating opportunities for host states to claim credit for the benefits the UN provides; ensuring that criminal cases are adjudicated within the bounds of state law; and cultivating norms that legitimize the state's role as a provider of security, justice, and other public goods. At the same time, UN missions devise mechanisms to improve communication and coordination between citizens, the state, and non-state authorities at the meso level, integrating the often-disjointed appendages of hybrid legal systems into a more unified whole.

My theoretical framework generates multiple empirical predictions for me to test. I test them by combining new cross-national administrative data on UN personnel and activities in Africa with original sub-national survey data from Liberia, one of the world's weakest and most war-torn states. My cross-country analyses in Chapter 5 show that peacekeeping is only weakly correlated with the rule of law during periods of ongoing conflict, but strongly positively correlated after the fighting stops. The relationship is stronger for civilian than for uniformed personnel, and is consistent across four different approaches to rule-of-law promotion – police reform, justice sector reform, prison reform, and legal reform. UN missions appear to be most effective at promoting the rule of law in the one-to-two year period after civil war termination, and they seem to be most successful when they engage the state in the process of reform, rather than bypassing it entirely.

The within-country analyses in Chapters 6–8 explore the micro-foundations of these cross-country results through an in-depth, multi-methods case study of Liberia. I show that UNMIL's presence in Liberia increased citizens' reliance on state over non-state authorities to resolve the most severe cases of crime and violence, and increased non-state authorities' reliance on legal over illegal mechanisms of dispute resolution. Exposure to UNMIL also exacerbated citizens' perceptions of state corruption, but only in the short term: after two years the mission's beneficial effects persisted, while its adverse effects decayed. I use multiple identification strategies to support a causal interpretation of these results, and further substantiate my quantitative findings with qualitative insights gleaned from both primary and secondary sources, including UN progress reports and interviews conducted with dozens of UN and government personnel, NGOs, local leaders, and civilians over the course of fifteen months of fieldwork on the ground.

Taken together, the theory and empirics in this book show that UN peacekeeping can serve as an effective mechanism for promoting the rule of law by rehabilitating state institutions and repairing their relationship with citizens long accustomed to state absence or abuse. These conclusions stand in stark contrast to the pessimism that pervades much of the recent academic literature on international intervention. Many scholars believe that building peace after civil war requires consolidating and legitimizing state authority and mending the ruptured social contract that binds citizens to states (Call 2008a; Doyle and Sambanis 2006; Lake 2010, 2016; Paris and Sisk 2009b). The difficulty of achieving this transformation, however, has led some to conclude that failure is all but inevitable.

Skeptics worry that UN missions may be too predatory (Beber et al., 2017), too heavy-handed (Lake 2010, 2016), or too time- and resource-constrained to promote the rule of law (Jones and Cherif, 2004). They argue that the international community should abandon intervention altogether (Luttwak, 1999; Weinstein, 2005), or focus instead on supporting the multitude of civil society organizations that deliver services in areas beyond the state's reach (Autesserre, 2010; Pouligny, 2006). Yet surprisingly few skeptical accounts include systematic data on the quality of citizens' relationships with post-conflict states, and fewer still grapple with the thorny counterfactual question of how those relationships might have evolved in the absence of third-party intervention. This book provides both theoretical and empirical reasons to believe that international intervention is a more promising mechanism for rule-of-law promotion and state consolidation and legitimation than the prevailing pessimism would suggest.

EXTENDING THE ARGUMENT BEYOND AFRICA

Empirically, this book focuses on UN intervention in Africa since the end of the Cold War. But how generalizable are my results likely to be? Are they applicable to other countries or regions, or other types of international intervention, or other outcomes that may be empirically related to, but conceptually distinct from, the rule of law, such as democracy, economic growth, and human rights? While every country is unique, the macro-, micro-, and meso-level obstacles to the rule of law that afflict many African countries are endemic throughout the developing world. In Afghanistan, for example, the Taliban erected sophisticated mechanisms of dispute resolution that compete with and often exceed the performance of the police and courts, crystallizing civilians' loyalties to Taliban rule (Baczko, 2013; Miller, 2011). In East Timor, "significant gulfs" between state institutions and "local governance values and practices" have long proved an impediment to the penetration of state law (Brown and Gusmao, 2009, 61).

Similarly, in Guatemala, a deep-rooted tradition of Mayan law produced chronic conflict between the state and indigenous communities, who demanded that the promise of a "pluricultural" political system enshrined in the 1996 Accord for a Firm and Lasting Peace be honored through a pluricultural *legal* system as well (Hessbruegge and García, 2011, 77). Nor are these examples especially unique. Tensions between state and non-state authorities are often a source of violence in post-conflict countries (Sisk and Risley, 2005), and have obstructed reconstruction and the rule of law in a wide variety of settings – not just Afghanistan, East Timor, and Guatemala, but also Iraq (Asfura-Heim, 2011), Peru (Desmet, 2011), Indonesia (Clark and Stephens, 2011), and elsewhere (Isser, Lubkemann, and N'Tow, 2009; Ubbink, 2011). My theoretical framework and empirical findings are potentially applicable to all of these settings.

This is true even of my within-country results from Liberia. While UNMIL was large relative to the size of the country, its mandate was typical of other multidimensional missions (Howard 2008, 312; Mvukiyehe 2018), and the three activities whose impact I evaluate – patrols, public works, and interventions to resolve disputes – are common to peacekeeping operations around the world. The two largest troop-contributing countries in my Liberian survey sample (and in Liberia more generally) were Pakistan and Bangladesh, which also happen to be the two largest troop-contributing countries worldwide.[3]

Moreover, some of the potential scope conditions for my within-country results may not be as restrictive as they seem. For example, while UNMIL was perceived as competent and legitimate by most Liberians, it was also embroiled in multiple scandals over the course of its mandate. Indeed, one of the few systematic studies of sexual exploitation and abuse by peacekeepers was conducted in Monrovia, and found astronomical rates of transactional sex between UNMIL personnel and Liberian women and girls (Beber et al., 2017). UNMIL was also occasionally accused of bias and neglect (Higate and Henry, 2009; Paczynska, 2010). Some UN missions may be so despised, and so unprofessional, that they cannot promote the rule of law at all. But consistently virtuous behavior on the part of UN personnel does not appear to be a scope condition for my analysis.

Some might argue that the UN's ability to promote the rule of law depends on some pre-existing level of state capacity. But this does not appear to be a scope condition either. At the time of my study, Liberia was one of the world's weakest, poorest, and most aid-dependent states. According to the World Bank, between 2008 and 2011 – the period covered by my first and second waves of data collection – Liberia was by far the most aid-dependent country in the world, with an aid-to-GDP ratio roughly twice that of the world's second-most aid-dependent country (Afghanistan).[4] And while the performance of the Liberian police and courts improved dramatically between 2003 and 2013 – thanks in no small part to UNMIL's efforts – they remained dysfunctional even at the time of my survey, and were frequently accused of corruption and other forms of malfeasance (Human Rights Watch, 2013). There may be

---

[3] This observation is based on data from the *Providing for Peacekeeping* project, available at www.providingforpeacekeeping.org/.

[4] These calculations are based on data from the World Bank's World Development Indicators project, available at https://data.worldbank.org/products/wdi.

some governments that are so abusive and exclusionary that the UN cannot improve citizens' relationships with them, no matter how hard it may try. But consistently virtuous behavior on the part of state institutions does not appear to be a scope condition for my analysis either.

My within-country results echo findings from several recent micro-level studies of peacekeeping in other parts of Liberia, and other parts of the developing world. In particular, my results mirror Eric Mvukiyehe and Cyrus Samii's finding that UN security committees increased the vote share of national over "parochial" candidates in Liberia (Mvukiyehe and Samii, 2017); Mvukiyehe's finding that exposure to UN personnel increased national but not local political participation in Liberia, and increased Liberians' willingness to contact government officials for assistance, while decreasing their willingness to contact traditional leaders (Mvukiyehe, 2018); William Nomikos' finding that MINUSMA's presence in Mali improved relations between rival ethnic groups (Nomikos, 2016); Hannah Smidt's finding that a UNOCI-sponsored civic education campaign in Côte d'Ivoire reduced fears of electoral violence and increased voters' sense of political efficacy (Smidt, 2020); Grant Gordon and Lauren Young's finding that UN provision of security and humanitarian relief in Haiti improved civilians' perceptions of the mission and increased their willingness to convey information to MINUSTAH personnel (Gordon and Young, 2017); and Jessica di Salvatore's finding that UN policing reduces the risk of criminal violence in post-conflict settings more generally (Salvatore, 2019). These parallels further support the external validity of my results.

In my view, the most likely scope condition for my analysis is some prior degree of peace and stability. Previous studies have shown that UN missions are more effective at consolidating an existing peace than they are at fighting an ongoing civil war (Doyle and Sambanis, 2006; Gilligan and Sergenti, 2008). My own results in Chapter 5 suggest that peacekeeping is weakly or even negatively correlated with the rule of law during periods of conflict. Intervention during these periods also generally necessitates a more militarized approach to peacekeeping, which previous studies have suggested is especially likely to alienate civilians (Pouligny, 2006) – a finding that resonates with my results in Chapter 8. While Liberia has suffered episodes of instability since the end of the civil war, and while some of these have escalated into regional or even national crises (Blair, Blattman, and Hartman, 2017), most have been localized and relatively manageable. Other countries have not been so fortunate. Where there is no peace to keep, establishing the rule of law may be impossible, at least in the short term.

What about generalizability to other types of international intervention – military occupation, for example, or peacekeeping by regional rather than global bodies, such as the African Union? The UN is atypical in the depth and comprehensiveness of its approach to rule-of-law promotion, and in its willingness to intervene in the most challenging settings to reconstruct state security and justice institutions virtually from the ground up

(Trenkov-Wermuth, 2010, 10). A similar level of engagement is likely necessary for international interveners to serve as catalysts for state reform or surrogates for reformed states.

But while the UN's approach to rule-of-law promotion is unusual, it is not altogether unique. In Iraq and Afghanistan, for example, the USA has similarly attempted to resuscitate collapsed states and repair their fraught relationships with local populations. The USA has sometimes pursued these goals in ways that mimic the mechanisms described in Chapter 4. Just as UN missions build public works in order to bolster the legitimacy and capacity of state institutions (UN Department of Peacekeeping Operations Policy and Best Practices Service, 2012, 224–5), the American military has rehabilitated infrastructure in order to "visibly convey" state authority in otherwise inaccessible or contested spaces in Afghanistan. Often these projects are intended not only to legitimize the state, but also to de-legitimize its non-state competitors. In Kandahar, for example, the USA helped the Afghan government finish a mosque begun but never completed by Taliban commander Mullah Mohammad Omar. Omar's blueprint was updated to include a mosque for women – a symbolic revision intended to emphasize the state's (ostensibly) egalitarian policies as an alternative to Omar's fundamentalism (Coll, 2012, 45).

Similarly, just as UN missions use radio and other media to disseminate information about ongoing security and justice sector reforms, in Afghanistan's Helmand Province, the US military posted signs on residents' doors and windows bordered with the colors of the Afghan national flag to announce that "the Afghan National Security Forces are coming" (Mogelson, 2012). The goal was to win civilians' hearts and minds not just for the Americans, but also and more urgently for the Afghan government itself. There is some evidence that these and related efforts paid off, at least in the short term (Beath, Christia, and Enikolopov, 2013; Lyall, Zhou, and Imai, 2020). These parallels offer additional reasons to believe my results may generalize to at least some other forms of international intervention, both in Africa and beyond.

But of course, unlike most UN missions, the USA was responsible for the upheaval that arguably necessitated such intrusive third-party intervention in Afghanistan in the first place. While both Iraq and Afghanistan were governed by brutal dictatorial regimes in the years before the USA invaded, it was the invasions themselves that precipitated civil war and state collapse. My theory characterizes UN missions as temporary and (largely) benevolent state surrogates – a role that occupiers may struggle to play. Occupations and interventions by former colonial powers may lack the "source legitimacy" that UN missions typically enjoy (Whalan, 2014, 65). Staffed by personnel from multiple countries and wielding mandates approved by the UN Security Council, UN missions can plausibly claim to represent the collective will of the international community (UN Criminal Law and Judicial Advisory Service, 2016, 3) – a claim that helps foster deference to UN policy priorities (Barnett and Finnemore 2005; Finnemore and Sikkink 1998; Hurd 1999,

2002; Whalan 2014). The "legitimacy pull" of the Security Council may also distinguish UN peacekeeping operations from their regional counterparts – African Union missions, for example – though these too may derive source legitimacy from their multinational composition and their association with multinational institutions (Hurd, 1999, 402). Whether missions of this sort are equally effective at promoting the rule of law remains an open empirical question and a fruitful avenue for future research to explore.

What of generalizability to outcomes other than the rule of law? While answering this question is beyond the scope of this book, a number of processes that are related to but nonetheless distinct from the rule of law rely crucially on citizens' willingness to comply with state laws and institutions at the micro level: taxation, for example, or collective action in the provision and maintenance of public goods, or adherence to the principles of international human rights law, especially when those principles conflict with local norms and customs. At the macro level as well, dynamics that are integral to establishing the rule of law may prove conducive to related outcomes. Democracy is likely to be more resilient in countries whose executives do not routinely defy legal limits on their power; human rights are likely to be more secure in places where the police do not regularly abuse civilians; economic growth is likely to be more robust in settings where the courts are not exposed to incessant political interference. It is precisely for these reasons that the rule of law is so often perceived as a panacea (Rajagopal, 2008, 1348). While this perception is problematic for reasons described in Chapter 3, promoting the rule of law may nonetheless have beneficial spillover effects on other outcomes. Especially to the extent that these outcomes *depend* on the rule of law, we might expect international intervention to promote them as well. This, too, is a promising angle for future research.

CONNECTIONS TO RELATED BODIES OF RESEARCH

This book provides a corrective to the prevailing pessimism that characterizes much of the large and growing literature on state-building, democratization, and rule-of-law promotion after civil war. But the book is equally relevant to multiple strands of scholarship in comparative politics, international relations, development economics, and criminology. Most directly, the book contributes to research exploring the effects of third-party public goods provision on the legitimacy of recipient states, typically in the context of counterinsurgency (Beath, Christia, and Enikolopov, 2013; Lyall, Zhou, and Imai, 2020) or foreign aid (Blair and Roessler, 2018; Cruz and Schneider, 2017; Dietrich, Mahmud, and Winters, 2017). For many years, the consensus in this literature was bleak. Analysts warned that third-party public goods provision exacerbates corruption (Svensson, 2000), diminishes bureaucratic quality and accountability (Brautigam and Knack, 2004), insulates authoritarian regimes from civil unrest (Ahmed, 2012), fosters a culture of dependency (Moyo, 2010), and alienates citizens from governments that prioritize, or appear to prioritize, donor preferences over constituent needs (Brautigam, 1992).

Other studies suggest, however, that these warnings may be overblown. Scholars have found that foreign donors and other third parties can bolster state capacity, reduce corruption, and enhance transparency (e.g. through "good governance" conditions and other mechanisms), thus improving citizens' perceptions of government performance and cultivating state legitimacy (Blair and Roessler, 2018; Brautigam, 2009; Dietrich, Mahmud, and Winters, 2017; Goldsmith, 2001; Jones and Tarp, 2016; Sacks, 2012). The theory and empirics in this book provide further evidence in support of these findings.

The book is also relevant to research on mechanisms for repairing relationships between civilians and police forces in deeply divided societies. Despite some influential early contributions by political scientists (e.g. Wilson, 1978), for many years the study of policing was dominated by criminologists, psychologists, and, to a lesser extent, economists. Much of this literature has focused on estimating the causal effects of police presence on crime.[5] Even studies that address police/community relations more directly have been mostly confined to the USA, UK, Australia, and other stable, developed democracies (Sunshine and Tyler, 2003; Tyler and Huo, 2002; Tyler, 2004; Tyler and Fagan, 2008). These studies may not generalize to post-conflict settings, where resource constraints are much tighter, and where state security institutions must overcome especially long legacies of negligence and abuse. This book complements a nascent body of research assessing the effects of specific security sector reforms in the developing world, often using experimental or quasi-experimental methods.[6] Many of these reforms were propelled by the UN and other international organizations; some were adopted in the context of peace processes following civil war. While this book extends beyond police/community relations to test the effects of international intervention on the rule of law more broadly defined, my findings are nonetheless applicable to this new and exciting line of research.

Finally, this book contributes to scholarship on the diffusion of international legal and human rights norms, especially at the local level, and especially in places where international and local norms collide (Búzás, 2018; Simmons, Lloyd, and Stewart, 2018). Much of the literature on norm diffusion examines how norms surrounding the use of chemical weapons, universal suffrage, or

---

[5] The literature is voluminous. See, for example, Braga and Bond (2008); Di Tella and Schargrodsky (2004); Levitt (1997); Ratcliffe et al. (2011); Sherman and Weisburd (1995); Weisburd and Green (1995).

[6] See, for example, Banerjee et al. (2014); Blair, Karim, and Morse (2019); Blair et al. (2018); Blattman et al. (2019); Cooper (2019); Curtice (2019); Karim et al. (2018); Magaloni, Franco, and Melo (2015); Nanes (2019, 2020); Samii (2013). An important initiative by the Evidence in Governance and Politics (EGAP) network will experimentally evaluate the effects of community policing across six different countries. See http://egap.org/metaketa/metaketa-iv-community-policing.

Apartheid (to cite just a few examples) are transmitted across borders, typically from the Global North to the Global South, and from more developed to less developed countries. But as Karisa Cloward observes, norm diffusion within countries is arguably just as important, and just as challenging, as norm diffusion between them (Cloward, 2015, 380). This book shows that international interveners can help resolve this problem, legitimizing the "traditional institutional forms of the state" (Higate and Henry, 2009, 11) – police forces, courts, etc. – and instilling a stronger commitment among state authorities, non-state authorities, and citizens alike to "[maintain] social order through prescribed procedures and the rule of law" (Chesterman, Ignatieff, and Thakur, 2005, 2–3).

IMPLICATIONS FOR RESEARCH ON INTERNATIONAL INTERVENTION

Above all, this book contributes to the study and practice of international intervention in the world's weakest and most war-torn states. My findings point to a number of potentially useful questions for future researchers to explore. Ever since the seminal contributions of Michael Doyle, Nicholas Sambanis, and Page Fortna in the early and mid-2000s, the study of UN peacekeeping in political science and international relations has been dominated by large-N, cross-country quantitative analyses. While scholars like Séverine Autesserre have conducted influential sub-national qualitative studies, these remain rare relative to their cross-national quantitative counterparts, which continue to proliferate. These studies inevitably ignore the micro-level dynamics that are increasingly recognized as key to peacekeeping success (Autesserre 2014a; Campbell, Chandler, and Sabaratnam 2011, 2–3; Kathman et al. 2017).

Cross-country studies are valuable in that they can yield generalizable insights into the impact of peacekeeping either regionally or globally. But most also rely on coarse proxies for exposure to UN missions, and on strong and ultimately untestable assumptions about the similarities and differences between countries in which the UN does and does not intervene. While I attempt to mitigate these problems by eliminating or controlling for potential confounders, and by operationalizing the UN's involvement in rule-of-law promotion with a higher level of granularity than was previously possible, my results in Chapter 5 are still susceptible to these concerns. Some cross-national studies also implicitly assume that the benefits of international intervention at the national level will "automatically trickle down to the local spheres" (Autesserre, 2014a, 493). Successes across countries can mask important and understudied failures within them, and vice versa. The intensity of violence, the quality of democracy, the robustness of the rule of law – these outcomes vary within as well as across countries, and peacekeeping's impact on them may vary accordingly. By design, cross-national studies cannot capture this variation.

Sub-national analyses help overcome these limitations. By assessing the impact of peacekeeping within rather than across countries, sub-national studies minimize contextual differences and eliminate many potential sources of bias, thereby improving our ability to make credible causal inferences. Sub-national analyses also focus our attention on what peacekeepers actually do in the field, not just in the capital city, but throughout their area of operations. Understanding the impact of these actions is arguably of greater practical use to peacekeepers themselves, who tend to have little discretion over the broad features of their mandates, but considerably more discretion over the specific activities they pursue on the ground. Sub-national studies also call our attention to the perceptions of citizens, which the UN itself increasingly recognizes as vital to peacekeeping effectiveness (High-Level Independent Panel on United Nations Peace Operations, 2015, 66). While cross-country analyses help illuminate the conditions under which peacekeeping does and does not "work," they necessarily overlook within-country dynamics that may be instrumental in shaping the relationships between citizens and host states.

But of course, micro-level studies have their own limitations, including questions about external validity. This book is unusual in combining the micro with the macro to present a more comprehensive account of the role that international interveners play not just in preventing violence, but also in reshaping the social and political fabric of the societies in which they intervene. Analyses of this sort will only become more urgent as peacekeepers pursue increasingly ambitious mandates aimed at increasingly transformative changes in the performance of state institutions and the attitudes and behaviors of citizens. As Jeni Whalan argues, UN missions are "two faced institutions": they "straddle the international-domestic divide of international relations theory, with goals that depend for their accomplishment on the decisions and actions of actors in the local realm" (Whalan, 2014, 19). Whalan rightly notes that analyses of this local realm are "sorely lacking," but even rarer are analyses that address the UN's two faces simultaneously. More studies of this sort are needed to understand both the micro- and macro-foundations of peacekeeping failure and success.

Relatedly, future research should prioritize assessing the increasingly diverse roles that UN missions are expected to play in host countries. Most studies conceptualize peacekeeping as a mechanism for resolving commitment problems and mitigating information asymmetries between armed actors.[7] These are important roles, but they capture only a fraction of the variation in what UN missions actually do in the field, from monitoring elections to removing land

---

[7] See, among many other examples, Hultman, Kathman, and Shannon (2016); Matanock (2017); Ruggeri, Gizelis, and Dorussen (2012); Walter (1997).

mines, and from protecting the rights of children to regulating the extraction of diamonds and other natural resources.

These activities raise a host of questions for researchers to answer. Do UN-funded public information campaigns promoting gender equality increase the vote share of female candidates in national elections? Do the UN's efforts to control the circulation of small arms and light weapons improve civilians' perceptions of personal safety? Does UN support to political parties and electoral commissions yield democratic dividends – boosting turnout, mitigating fraud, and fostering trust in the democratic process? Do UN-sponsored training programs for local media enhance freedom of the press and increase adherence to international standards of journalistic integrity? These are important questions to which existing studies provide no or only incomplete answers. UN missions have dramatically expanded their operational repertoire since the first peacekeeping operation was deployed over half a century ago – an expansion that has only accelerated since the turn of the millennium. Researchers should try to keep pace.

In so doing, researchers should continue their efforts to more fully disaggregate peacekeeping activities, especially at the micro level. The dataset I introduced in Chapter 5 captures much of the variation in these activities across countries and over time, at least in Africa, and at least since 1989. Variation *within* countries, however, may be equally instrumental in determining peacekeeping failure or success. This variation remains largely undocumented and unexplored. In Chapter 8, I tested the impact of UNMIL patrols, interventions, and public works on Liberians' relationships with the state; I also tested the effect of individual-level interactions with UN personnel. Mvukiyehe similarly differentiates between seeing UN patrols and speaking with UN staff (Mvukiyehe, 2018). Smidt focuses on UN civic education (Smidt, 2020). Gordon and Young distinguish between UN provision of security and humanitarian relief (Gordon and Young, 2017). Bernd Beber and colleagues estimate the incidence of transactional sex with UN personnel (Beber et al., 2017); Gordon and Young measure the prevalence of abuse more broadly defined. But peacekeepers do much more than this. More disaggregated data at low levels of granularity (e.g. the community or individual level) is needed to assess the effects of the multifaceted activities that peacekeepers pursue. Generating and analyzing this data is one of the literature's most promising frontiers.

LESSONS FOR THE PRACTICE OF PEACEKEEPING

Finally, this book has several implications for the practice of peacekeeping in Africa and beyond. First and most obviously, my findings suggest that UN missions can help establish the rule of law even in the world's weakest and most war-torn states, and that their impact manifests both within and across countries, at the micro, macro, and meso levels. Of course, even in my cross-national analysis, I cannot be sure whether the average effects that I estimate will hold when applied to a particular country or peacekeeping operation. But the countries in my sample are the sites of some of the most vexing conflicts in Africa, including Mali, DRC, CAR, and South Sudan. While I cannot run country-specific analyses for all of these cases, the fact that my results are robust to their presence in the data suggests that peacekeeping's efficacy in promoting the rule of law is not limited to the most auspicious settings. The fact that I find such robust effects at the micro level in Liberia – one of the most severe cases of state collapse in Africa – lends further credence to this interpretation of my results. While some degree of peace may be necessary for rule-of-law promotion to succeed, this scope condition is not overly restrictive. The UN should be ambitious in its rule-of-law agenda, and should not limit its efforts to the "easy" cases.

Second, my results suggest that UN missions should invest more heavily in their civilian components, especially as the scope of their mandates continues to expand. While I find that the presence of uniformed personnel is positively correlated with the rule of law in post-conflict settings, the correlation is much stronger for civilian personnel. This is not surprising, as civilian personnel are typically responsible for the activities that contribute most directly to the rule of law – writing statutes, retraining judges, monitoring prisons, etc. (The exception is UNPOL, which is usually responsible for police recruitment and retraining.) UN troops and Military Observers may be indispensable for creating an environment conducive to rule-of-law promotion. But the UN has long under-invested in the civilian components of its missions, especially in the rule-of-law arena. As the 2000 Brahimi Report lamented, in many cases the UN Security Council has authorized the deployment of thousands of uniformed personnel, but has resisted authorizing even a handful of experts on legal, constitutional, justice sector, and prison reform (UN Security Council, 2000, 7).

While this situation has improved in the two decades since the Brahimi Report was published, given the current configuration of most UN missions, the marginal benefit of hiring an additional civilian staff member almost certainly exceeds the marginal benefit of deploying an additional blue helmet – a proposition supported by my results in Chapter 5. This will only become more true as the UN penetrates into ever more facets of the social and political life of host states. Correcting this imbalance will require recruiting more civilian personnel to fill these roles, both at UN headquarters and from among troop-contributing countries themselves (The World Bank, 2011, 199). It will also require continued collaboration with both national and international NGOs, as well as other UN agencies, which are already helping to fill human resource gaps in peacekeeping operations (World Bank Group and United Nations, 2018, 260).

Using increased civilian capacity to more effectively promote the rule of law will require patience, flexibility, and long time horizons. The 2011 World

Development Report argues, somewhat ominously, that third-party assistance must be sustained for at least fifteen years in order for necessary legal and institutional transformations to take root (The World Bank, 2011, 193). The rule of law is not a binary variable; it is a continuum. My cross-national results in Chapter 5 suggest that significant measurable progress along that continuum can be made even early in the peacebuilding process. But as my description of the Liberian case in Chapters 6–8 illustrates, progress in these early years should be viewed as the beginning rather than the end of a potentially lengthy trajectory towards the rule of law, and should be treated as the impetus for a shift in priorities from short-term rehabilitation to long-term prevention of future crises.

Whether UN missions will continue to expand their civilian components remains very much an open question, but the current trend towards ever more militarized missions intervening in ever more complex civil wars is not promising. The UN is increasingly tasked with deploying to active conflict zones like Mali and South Sudan, where there is little peace to keep, and where war-fighting capabilities are paramount. Scholars have long argued that UN missions are more effective at building peace than fighting wars (Doyle and Sambanis, 2006; Fortna, 2004; Gilligan and Sergenti, 2008). While my analysis does not address this question directly, it does suggest that ongoing conflicts are not conducive to state reform, or to rule-of-law promotion more generally,[8] and that the UN's efficacy in catalyzing these processes hinges on some prior degree of stability. This is unsurprising but instructive nonetheless. The UN will likely become less rather than more effective at promoting the rule of law if the trend towards militarization continues.

Third, this book suggests that UN missions should be proactive in their efforts to legitimize state institutions in the eyes of civilians. This departs from the more "institutionalist" approach to state-building that characterizes most academic and policy writing on the subject (Lake, 2016). As discussed in Chapter 3, state-building, by most definitions, is "the creation of new government institutions and the strengthening of existing ones" (Fukuyama, 2004, ix); it is a set of policies "undertaken by international or national actors to establish, reform, or strengthen the institutions of the state" (Call and Cousens, 2008, 4); it is "not limited to 'top-down' approaches of institution-strengthening," but it nonetheless "focuses primarily on public institutions – the machinery of the state, from courts and legislatures to laws and bureaucrats" (Paris and Sisk, 2009a, 14–15). Constitutions are written; elections are held; bureaucrats, soldiers, and police officers are hired and trained. States, eventually, are built.

Yet in focusing so single-mindedly on institutional restructuring and reform, these accounts ignore the arguably more complex question of extending state authority from the capital city to the hinterlands (Manning, 2003, 27). These

---

[8] On this point, see also Rupesinghe (2016).

accounts also typically (if only implicitly) assume that citizens' demand for state institutions will emerge endogenously, even automatically, from renewed supply. This, I argue, is wrong. While some citizens will welcome the reintroduction of state rule, others will not. Some degree of resistance is especially likely in places where alternatives to the state thrive at the meso level, as is common in most post-conflict settings (Isser, 2011). International interveners should anticipate this problem, and address its multiple dimensions simultaneously.

The inevitability of local resistance to national authority poses a delicate normative question that this book has only indirectly addressed. If citizens prefer informal over formal mechanisms for sustaining order, then even if UN missions *can* restore the primary of state law, *should* they? For some analysts, the answer is no. According to these scholars, the state is not and has never been a particularly successful or even benign mode of organizing social, economic, and political life. If this is true of Western Europe, then it is especially true of Africa and other parts of the developing world, where the state has offered citizens "all the violence that accompanied European state formation and few of the corresponding benefits" (Brooks, 2005, 1173–4). In the most extreme cases, there may be compelling normative reasons to devolve political power to non-state authorities, especially when those authorities prove more capable than the state itself, and more legitimate in the eyes of citizens. As I have argued elsewhere, states that forfeit their "right to rule" endow non-state authorities with a corollary right to consolidate power in the territories they control – territories that lie within the state's *de jure* borders but beyond its *de facto* command (Blair and Kalmanovitz, 2016).

But these are limiting cases, and they are quite rare. In most countries, there is no viable alternative to the reconstruction of state institutions and the re-imposition of state laws. This is true even if formal authorities serve as nothing more than enablers of informal ones – a reality that many proponents of "bottom-up" peacebuilding acknowledge, albeit sometimes only obliquely.[9] The UN should not ignore non-state institutions, or attempt to marginalize them altogether. But nor should it romanticize them, or imagine they can substitute for the state in the long term. Except in some unusual cases, they cannot. UN missions should be attentive to points of contention and complementarity between formal and informal authorities. Managing these relationships is often an urgent priority in the wake of civil war, and failure to do so has stymied many post-conflict reconstruction processes in the past (Sisk and Risley, 2005). Future UN missions should not repeat this mistake.

A subtle corollary of this argument is that UN missions should continue their efforts to integrate women into the ranks of both uniformed and civilian personnel. Women are often severely disadvantaged under informal mechanisms for sustaining order and resolving disputes (Isser, 2011). Formal mechanisms may be biased as well, but in many cases they offer the prospect of greater

---

[9] On this point, see the discussion of East Timor, Liberia, and DRC in Chapter 4.

fairness and impartiality than women can expect to find in the informal sector alone. To the extent that UN missions act as surrogates for reformed states, the presence of female peacekeepers may help convince women, in particular, to view state security and justice institutions as a viable exit option from the non-state status quo. Of course, there are many other reasons to incorporate women into peacekeeping operations, both normative and practical (Karim and Beardsley, 2017). The need to legitimize state authority in the eyes of citizens is one more to add to the list.

Lastly, peacekeeping personnel should be aware of the impact that even apparently routine actions can have not just on citizens' support for the mission, but also on their receptiveness to renewed state rule. As Autesserre rightly argues, "mundane elements ... strongly impact the effectiveness of intervention efforts" and "shape overall interventions from the bottom up" (Autesserre, 2014b, 9). Just as the behavior of individual police officers can affect the reputation of the police more generally (Tyler and Huo, 2002), so can the actions of individual peacekeepers shape perceptions of the mission as a whole (Whalan, 2014, 73).

Peacekeeping's academic critics tend to focus on the harmful consequences of these individual actions – on their tendency to produce programs that are inefficient, ineffective, and counterproductive (Autesserre, 2014b, 36–7). In the public imagination as well, peacekeeping as an enterprise is increasingly evaluated on the basis of negligent or even criminal acts committed by specific UN personnel. I do not wish to diminish the importance or severity of these acts, and accountability is of course vital if the UN hopes to address critics and improve its own performance. Indeed, accountability will only become more essential if UN missions begin to incorporate larger numbers of civilian personnel, as I recommend. Civilian personnel are less likely than their uniformed counterparts to be confined to bases, and less likely to be subjected to hierarchies of command and control. This may create additional opportunities for sexual exploitation and abuse and other acts of malfeasance. These transgressions must be punished.

But analysts should resist the temptation to equate peacekeeping as a practice with the misdeeds of individual peacekeepers, noxious as they sometimes are. And observers should also recognize that individual actions can have both harmful and beneficial effects. This book has shown that some of the apparently mundane elements of peacekeeping repertoires – patrols, public works, interventions to resolve disputes, etc. – can reshape state/society relations in positive and potentially lasting ways. I have shown that across Africa, UN presence is associated with stronger constitutional constraints, greater judicial independence, and more effective security and justice provision by state institutions. In Liberia, I have also shown that the UN's presence increased cooperation with the police and courts and reduced reliance on trial by ordeal, and that this effect was transmitted at least in part through localized, everyday interactions between citizens, local leaders, and peacekeeping personnel. I have

Lessons for the Practice of Peacekeeping

also provided reasons to believe these effects may persist even after the UN's withdrawal, and that lessons learned from the Liberian case may generalize to other countries.

In recent years, UN peacekeeping has increasingly come under attack from detractors, including within the US government, who deride it as "unproductive, unsuccessful, and unaccountable."[10] I hope this book has demonstrated that such blanket critiques are misguided, and that they ignore the UN's impressive (and arguably unlikely) record of success. UN missions can help not just to prevent a relapse into violence, but also to repair the ruptured social contract between citizens and war-wracked states. This role is too often overlooked. The UN undoubtedly deserves some of the criticism it has received. But often the most tendentious assessments are grounded in anecdotes alone. A closer look at the empirical evidence reveals remarkable successes belied by a fixation on failure.

---

[10] These are the words of former US National Security Advisor John Bolton; see Babb (2018). Former US Ambassador to the UN Nikki Haley made similar, albeit less pointed, critiques; see Lederer (2018).

Bibliography

Aboagye, Festus B. and Alhaji M. S. Bah. 2004. *Liberia at a Crossroads: A Preliminary Look at the United Nations Mission in Liberia (UNMIL) and the Protection of Civilians*. Pretoria: Institute for Security Studies.

Ahmed, Faisal Z. 2012. "The Perils of Unearned Foreign Income: Aid, Remittances, and Government Survival." *American Political Science Review* 106(1):146–65.

Al Jazeera News. 2017. "Supreme Court delays vote runoff amid fraud allegations." *Al Jazeera*, November 6. www.aljazeera.com/news/2017/11/supreme-court-delays-vote-runoff-fraud-allegations-171106133850539.html

Alao, Abiodun, John MacKinlay, and Funmi Olonisakin. 2000. *Peacekeepers, Politicians, and Warlords: The Liberian Peace Process*. Tokyo: UN University Press.

Aldashev, Gani, Imane Chaara, Jean-Philippe Platteau, and Zaki Wahhaj. 2012. "Formal Law As a Magnet to Reform Custom." *Economic Development and Cultural Change* 60(4):795–828.

Allen, Susan Hannah and Amy T. Yuen. 2014. "The Politics of Peacekeeping: UN Security Council Oversight Across Peacekeeping Missions." *International Studies Quarterly* 58(3):621–32.

Anderson, Lisa. 2004. "Antiquated before They Can Ossify: States That Fail before They Form." *Journal of International Affairs* 58(1):1–16.

Archibald, Steven. 2006. *Feasibility Study into the Rehabilitation & Reintegration of Unregistered Ex-combatants Guthrie Rubber Plantation, Liberia: September–December 2006*. Monrovia: Landmine Action.

Archibald, Steven, Urias Davis, Daniel Johnson, Korlu Kpissay, Sarah Passawe, Boye T. Sartee, and Moses Sumo. 2006. *Rehabilitation and Reintegration of Unregistered Ex-combatants: Guthrie Plantation Feasibility Study, September–November 2006*. Monrovia: CHF International.

Arjona, Ana. 2014. "Wartime Institutions: A Research Agenda." *Journal of Conflict Resolution* 58(8):1360–89.

Arjona, Ana. 2016. *Rebelocracy: Social Order in the Colombian Civil War*. Cambridge, UK: Cambridge University Press.

Asfura-Heim, Patricio. 2011. "Tribal Customary Law and Legal Pluralism in Anbar, Iraq." In *Customary Justice and the Rule of Law in War-Torn Societies*, ed. Deborah Isser. Washington, DC: United States Institute of Peace, pp. 239–84.

Autesserre, Séverine. 2010. *The Trouble with the Congo: Local Violence and the Failure of International Peacebuilding*. Cambridge, UK: Cambridge University Press.

Autesserre, Séverine. 2014a. "Going Micro: Emerging and Future Peacekeeping Research." *International Peacekeeping* 21(4):492–500.

Autesserre, Séverine. 2014b. *Peaceland: Conflict Resolution and the Everyday Politics of International Intervention*. Cambridge, UK: Cambridge University Press.

Babb, Carla. 2018. "US Rethinking Peacekeeping Role in Africa." *Voice of America*, December 13. www.voanews.com/a/us-rethinking-peacekeeping-role-in-africa/4699587.html

Baczko, Adam. 2013. "Judging in the Midst of Civil War: The Taliban Courts in Afghanistan (2001-2013)." *Politix* 4(104):25–46.

Baker, Bruce. 2005. "Who Do People Turn to for Policing in Sierra Leone?" *Journal of Contemporary African Studies* 23(3):371–90.

Baldwin, Kate. 2015. *The Paradox of Traditional Chiefs in Democratic Africa*. Cambridge, UK: Cambridge University Press.

Banerjee, Abhijit V., Raghabendra Chattopadhyay, Esther Duflo, Daniel Keniston, and Nina Singh. 2014. "Improving Police Performance in Rajasthan, India: Experimental Evidence on Incentives, Managerial Autonomy and Training." NBER Working Paper No. 17912. www.nber.org/papers/w17912

Barakat, Sultan. 2009. "The Failed Promise of Multi-donor Trust Funds: Aid Financing As an Impediment to Effective State-Building in Post-conflict Contexts." *Policy Studies* 30(2):107–26.

Barnett, Michael, Songying Fang, and Christoph Zürcher. 2014. "Compromised Peacebuilding." *International Studies Quarterly* 58(3):608–20.

Barnett, Michael and Martha Finnemore. 2005. "The Power of Liberal International Organizations." In *Power in Global Governance*, ed. Michael Barnett and Raymond Duvall. Cambridge, UK: Cambridge University Press, pp. 161–84.

Barnett, Michael N. and Martha Finnemore. 1999. "The Politics, Power, and Pathologies of International Organizations." *International Organization* 53(4):699–732.

Barro, Robert. 2000. "Democracy and the Rule of Law." In *Governing for Prosperity*, ed. Bruce Bueno de Mesquita and Hilton L. Root. New Haven, CT: Yale University Press, pp. 209–31.

Bateson, Regina Anne. 2013. *Order and Violence in Postwar Guatemala*. New Haven, CT: Yale University. PhD dissertation.

Beardsley, Kyle. 2011. "Peacekeeping and the Contagion of Armed Conflict." *The Journal of Politics* 73(04):1051–64.

Beardsley, Kyle and Kristian Skrede Gleditsch. 2015. "Peacekeeping As Conflict Containment." *International Studies Review* 17(1):67–89.

Beath, Andrew, Fotini Christia, and Ruben Enikolopov. 2013. "Winning Hearts and Minds through Development Aid: Evidence from a Field Experiment in Afghanistan." SSRN Scholarly Paper 2303475. https://papers.ssrn.com/sol3/papers.cfm?abstract_id=2303475

Beauvais, Joel C. 2001. "Benevolent Despotism: A Critique of UN State-Building in East Timor." *New York University Journal of International Law and Politics* 33:1101.

Beber, Bernd, Michael J. Gilligan, Jenny Guardado, and Sabrina Karim. 2017. "Peacekeeping, Compliance with International Norms, and Transactional Sex in Monrovia, Liberia." *International Organization* 71(1):1–30.

Bellamy, Alex J., Paul Williams, and Stuart Griffin. 2004. *Understanding Peacekeeping*. 1st ed. Malden, MA: Polity.

Benson, Michelle and Jacob D. Kathman. 2014. "United Nations Bias and Force Commitments in Civil Conflicts." *The Journal of Politics* 76(02):350–363.

Bertram, Eva. 1995. "Reinventing Governments." *Journal of Conflict Resolution* 39(3):387–418.

Biddle, Stephen. 2011. "Running Out of Time for Afghan Governance Reform." *Foreign Affairs*, December. www.foreignaffairs.com/articles/136875/stephen-biddle/leaving-afghanistan-to-the-warlords?cid=rss-rss_xml-leaving_afghanistan_to_the_war-000000

Bingham, Tom. 2011. *The Rule of Law*. London: Penguin.

Blair, Graeme and Kosuke Imai. 2012. "Statistical Analysis of List Experiments." *Political Analysis* 20(1):47–77.

Blair, Graeme, Kosuke Imai, and Jason Lyall. 2014. "Comparing and Combining List and Endorsement Experiments: Evidence from Afghanistan." *American Journal of Political Science* 58(4):1043–63.

Blair, Robert, Christopher Blattman, and Alexandra Hartman. 2011. *Patterns of Conflict and Cooperation in Liberia (Part 1): Results from a Longitudinal Study*. New Haven, CT: Innovations for Poverty Action.

Blair, Robert, Sabrina Karim, Michael J. Gilligan, and Kyle C. Beardsley. 2018. "Policing Ethnicty: Lab-in-the-Field Evidence on Discrimination, Cooperation and Ethnic Balancing in the Liberian National Police." *American Political Science Review* 113(3):641–57.

Blair, Robert A. 2019. "International Intervention and the Rule of Law after Civil War: Evidence from Liberia." *International Organization* 73(2):365–98.

Blair, Robert A., Christopher Blattman, and Alexandra Hartman. 2017. "Predicting Local Violence: Evidence from a Panel Survey in Liberia." *Journal of Peace Research* 54(2):298–312.

Blair, Robert A. and Pablo Kalmanovitz. 2016. "On the Rights of Warlords: Legitimate Authority and Basic Protection in War-Torn Societies." *American Political Science Review* 110(3):428–40.

Blair, Robert A., Sabrina M. Karim, and Benjamin S. Morse. 2019. "Establishing the Rule of Law in Weak and War-Torn States: Evidence from a Field Experiment with the Liberian National Police." *American Political Science Review* 113(3):641–57.

Blair, Robert A., Benjamin S. Morse, and Lily L. Tsai. 2017. "Public Health and Public Trust: Survey Evidence from the Ebola Virus Disease Epidemic in Liberia." *Social Science & Medicine* 172:89–97.

Blair, Robert A. and Philip Roessler. 2018. "The Effects of Chinese Aid on State Legitimacy in Africa: Cross-national and Sub-national Evidence from Surveys, Survey Experiments, and Behavioral Games." AidData Working Paper 59. www.aiddata.org/publications/the-effects-of-chinese-aid-on-state-legitimacy-in-africa-cross-national-and-sub-national-evidence-from-surveys-survey-experiments-and-behavioral-games

Blattman, Christopher, Donald Green, Daniel Ortega, and Santiago Torbon. 2019. "Place-Based Interventions at Scale: The Direct and Spillover Effects of Policing and City Services on Crime." NBER Working Paper No. 23941. www.nber.org/papers/w23941

Blattman, Christopher, Alexandra C. Hartman, and Robert A. Blair. 2014. "How to Promote Order and Property Rights under Weak Rule of Law? An Experiment in Changing Dispute Resolution Behavior through Community Education." *American Political Science Review* 108(01):100–20.

Bliesemann de Guevara, Berit. 2008. "The State in Times of Statebuilding." *Civil Wars* 10(4):348–68.

Boaventura de Sousa, Santos. 2002. *Toward a New Common Sense: Law, Gloablisation, and Emancipation*. London: Butterworth.

Boege, Volker, M. Anne Brown, and Kevin P. Clements. 2009. "Hybrid Political Orders, Not Fragile States." *Peace Review* 21:13–21.

Boone, Catherine. 2014. *Property and Political Order in Africa: Land Rights and the Structure of Politics*. Cambridge, UK: Cambridge University Press.

Bowles, Edith and Tanja Chopra. 2008. "East Timor: Statebuilding Revisited." In *Building States to Build Peace*, ed. Charles T. Call and Vanessa Wyeth. Boulder, CO: Lynne Rienner, pp. 271–302.

Braga, Anthony A. and Brenda J. Bond. 2008. "Policing Crime and Disorder Hot Spots: A Randomized Controlled Trial." *Criminology* 46(3):577–607.

Brautigam, Deborah. 1992. "Governance, Economy, and Foreign Aid." *Studies in Comparative International Development* 27(3):3–25.

Brautigam, Deborah. 2009. *The Dragon's Gift: The Real Story of China in Africa*. Oxford: Oxford University Press.

Brautigam, Deborah A. and Stephen Knack. 2004. "Foreign Aid, Institutions, and Governance in Sub-Saharan Africa." *Economic Development and Cultural Change* 52(2):255–85.

Brooks, Rosa. 2003. "The New Imperialism: Violence, Norms, and the 'Rule of Law.'" *Georgetown Law Faculty Publications and Other Works* 101(7):2275–340.

Brooks, Rosa Ehrenreich. 2005. "Failed States, or the State As Failure?" *The University of Chicago Law Review* 72(4):1159–96.

Brown, M. Anne and Alex Freitas Gusmao. 2009. "Peacebuilding and Political Hybridity in East Timor." *Peace Review* 21(1):61–9.

Brzoska, Michael and David Law. 2013. *Security Sector Reconstruction and Reform in Peace Support Operations*. London: Routledge.

Butty, James. 2011. "Liberian Authorities Arrest Another Opposition Official." *Voice of America*, December 28. www.voanews.com/a/butty-liberia-opposition-arrests-cephus-29december11-136361178/159378.html

Búzás, Zoltán I. 2018. "Is the Good News about Law Compliance Good News about Norm Compliance? The Case of Racial Equality." *International Organization* 72(2):351–85.

Call, Charles T. 2007a. "Introduction: What We Know and Don't Know about Postconflict Justice and Security Reform." In *Constructing Justice and Security after War*, ed. Charles T. Call. Washington, DC: United States Institute of Peace, pp. 3–26.

Call, Charles T. 2008a. "Building States to Build Peace?" In *Building States to Build Peace*, ed. Charles T. Call and Vanessa Wyeth. Boulder, CO: Lynne Rienner, pp. 365–88.

Call, Charles T. 2008b. "Ending Wars, Building States." In *Building States to Build Peace*, ed. Charles T. Call and Vanessa Wyeth. Boulder, CO: Lynne Rienner, pp. 1–24.

Call, Charles T. 2008c. "The Fallacy of the 'Failed State.'" *Third World Quarterly* 29:1491–507.

Call, Charles T., ed. 2007b. *Constructing Justice and Security after War*. Washington, DC: United States Institute of Peace.

Call, Charles T. and Elizabeth M. Cousens. 2008. "Ending Wars and Building Peace: International Responses to War-Torn Societies." *International Studies Perspectives* 9(1):1–21.

Campbell, Susanna, David Chandler, and Meera Sabaratnam, eds. 2011. *A Liberal Peace?: The Problems and Practices of Peacebuilding*. London: Zed Books.

Cao, Lan. 2007. "Culture Change." *Virginia Journal of International Law* 47(2): 357–412.

Caparini, Marina. 2014. *Extending State Authority in Liberia: The Gbarnga Justice and Security Hub*. Oslo: Norwegian Institute of International Affairs. NUPI Report No. 5.

Carlson, Scott N. 2006. *Legal and Judicial Rule of Law Work in Multi-dimensional Peacekeeping Operations: Lessons-Learned Study*. New York: UN Department of Peacekeeping Operations.

Carnegie Corporation of New York. 1997. *Preventing Deadly Conflict: Final Report*. New York: Carnegie Corporation of New York.

Carothers, Thomas. 1998. "The Rule of Law Revival." *Foreign Affairs* 77(2):95–106.

Carothers, Thomas. 2009. "Rule of Law Temptations." *Fletcher Forum of World Affairs* 33:49–61.

Carothers, Thomas, ed. 2006. *Promoting the Rule of Law Abroad: In Search of Knowledge*. Washington, DC: Carnegie Endowment for International Peace.

Carter, Brett L. 2016. "The Struggle over Term Limits in Africa: How International Pressure Can Help." *Journal of Democracy* 27(3):36–50.

Cassell, Webster D. 2007. "'I Was Questioned about War Crimes, Ellen's Issues'– Says Mulbah Morlu." *The Inquirer*, February 16. https://allafrica.com/stories/200702160936.html

Cawthra, Gavin and Robin Luckham, eds. 2003. *Governing Insecurity: Democratic Control of Military and Security Establishments in Transitional Democracies*. London: Zed Books.

Chesterman, Simon. 2001. *East Timor in Transition: From Conflict Prevention to State-building*. New York: International Peace Academy.

Chesterman, Simon. 2002. "Walking Softly in Afghanistan: The Future of UN State-building." *Survival* 44(3):37–45.

Chesterman, Simon. 2005. *You, the People: The United Nations, Transitional Administration, and State-Building*. Oxford: Oxford University Press.

Chesterman, Simon. 2007. "Ownership in Theory and in Practice: Transfer of Authority in UN Statebuilding Operations." *Journal of Intervention and Statebuilding* 1(1): 3–26.

Chesterman, Simon, Michael Ignatieff, and Ramesh Thakur. 2005. "Introduction: Making States Work." In *Making States Work: State Failure and the Crisis of Governance*, ed. Simon Chesterman, Michael Ignatieff, and Ramesh Thakur. Tokyo: United Nations University Press, pp. 1–10.

Cialdini, Robert B. 2008. *Influence: Science and Practice*. 5th ed. Boston: Allyn and Bacon.

Clark, Samuel and Matthew Stephens. 2011. "Reducing Injustice? A Grounded Approach to Strengthening Hybrid Justice Systems: Lessons from Indonesia." In *Customary Justice: Perspectives on Legal Empowerment*, ed. Janine Ubink. Rome: International Development Law Organization, pp. 67–90.

Clarke, Prue and Mae Azango. 2017. "The Tearing Down of Ellen Johnson Sirleaf." *Foreign Policy*, October 9. https://foreignpolicy.com/2017/10/09/the-tearing-down-of-ellen-johnson-sirleaf-liberia-elections/

Cloward, Karisa. 2015. "Elites, Exit Options, and Social Barriers to Norm Change: The Complex Case of Female Genital Mutilation." *Studies in Comparative International Development* 50(3):378–407.

Clunan, Anne and Harold Trinkunas. 2010. "Alternative Governance and Security." In *Ungoverned Spaces: Alternatives to State Authority in an Era of Softened Sovereignty*, ed. Anne Clunan and Harold Trinkunas. Stanford: Stanford University Press, pp. 275–94.

Coll, Steve. 2012. "Looking For Mullah Omar." *The New Yorker* January 23:44–55.

Colvin, Eric. 1978. "The Sociology of Secondary Rules." *The University of Toronto Law Journal* 28(2):195–214.

Cooper, Jasper. 2019. "State Capacity and Gender Inequality: Experimental Evidence from Papua New Guinea." Working Paper.

Corrales, Javier and Michael Penfold. 2014. "Manipulating Term Limits in Latin America." *Journal of Democracy* 25(4):157–68.

Corstange, Daniel. 2009. "Sensitive Questions, Truthful Answers? Modeling the List Experiment with LISTIT." *Political Analysis* 17(1):45–63.

Cruz, Cesi and Christina J. Schneider. 2017. "Foreign Aid and Undeserved Credit Claiming." *American Journal of Political Science* 61(2):396–408.

Curtice, Travis. 2019. "Police and Co-ethnic Bias: Evidence from a Conjoint Experiment in Uganda." Working Paper.

Dalton, George. 1965. "History, Politics, and Economic Development in Liberia." *Journal of Economic History* 25(4):569–91.

Davidson, Basil. 1993. *The Black Man's Burden: Africa and the Curse of the Nation-State*. New York: Times Books.

d'Azevedo, Warren. 1969. "A Tribal Reaction to Nationalism, Part 1." *Liberian Studies Journal* 1(2):1–22.

Debiel, Tobias, Rainer Glassner, Conrad Schetter, and Ulf Terlinden. 2009. "Local State-Building in Afghanistan and Somaliland." *Peace Review* 21:38–44.

Desmet, Ellen. 2011. "Interaction between Customary Legal Systems and the Formal System of Peru." In *Customary Justice: Perspectives on Legal Empowerment*, ed. Janine Ubink. Rome: International Development Law Organization, pp. 151–68.

Di Tella, Rafael and Ernesto Schargrodsky. 2004. "Do Police Reduce Crime? Estimates Using the Allocation of Police Forces after a Terrorist Attack." *The American Economic Review* 94(1):115–33.

Diamond, Michael Jay and W. Charles Lobitz. 1973. "When Familiarity Breeds Respect: The Effects of an Experimental Depolarization Program on Police and Student Attitudes toward Each Other." *Journal of Social Issues* 29(4):95–109.

Diène, Doudou. 2014. *Report of the Independent Expert on the Situation of Human Rights in Côte d'Ivoire*. New York: UN General Assembly Human Rights Council. A/HRC/25/73.
Dietrich, Simone, Minhaj Mahmud, and Matthew S. Winters. 2017. "Foreign Aid, Foreign Policy, and Domestic Government Legitimacy: Experimental Evidence from Bangladesh." *The Journal of Politics* 80(1):133–48.
Dietrich, Simone and Matthew S. Winters. 2015. "Foreign Aid and Government Legitimacy." *Journal of Experimental Political Science* 2(02):164–71.
Dodoo, Lennart. 2017. "Amb. Thomas Greenfield – Liberian Leaders Have Failed Liberians." *Front Page Africa*, November 19. https://allafrica.com/stories/201711200839.html
Dorff, Robert H. 1999. "Responding to the Failed State: The Need for Strategy." *Small Wars & Insurgencies* 10(3):62–81.
Dorussen, Han and Theodora-Ismene Gizelis. 2013. "Into the Lion's Den: Local Responses to UN Peacekeeping." *Journal of Peace Research* 5(6):691–706.
Doyle, Michael W. and Nicholas Sambanis. 2000. "International Peacebuilding: A Theoretical and Quantitative Analysis." *American Political Science Review* 94(4):779–801.
Doyle, Michael W. and Nicholas Sambanis. 2006. *Making War and Building Peace: United Nations Peace Operations*. Princeton: Princeton University Press.
Duncan, Gustavo. 2006. *Los Señores de La Guerra: De Paramilitares, Mafiosos y Autodefensas en Colombia*. Bogotá: Planeta.
Dworkin, Ronald. 1986. *Law's Empire*. Cambridge, MA: Belknap Press of Harvard University Press.
Dworkin, Ronald M. 1967. "The Model of Rules." *The University of Chicago Law Review* 35(1):14–46.
The Economist. 2008. "Economics and the Rule of Law: Order in the Jungle." *The Economist*, March 13. www.economist.com/node/10849115
Ellis, Stephen. 1995. "Liberia 1989–1994: A Study of Ethnic and Spiritual Violence." *African Affairs* 94(375):165–97.
Ellis, Stephen. 2006. *The Mask of Anarchy: The Destruction of Liberia and the Religious Dimension of an African Civil War*. New York: New York University Press.
Englebert, Pierre. 2000. *State Legitimacy and Development in Africa*. Boulder, CO: Lynne Rienner.
Englebert, Pierre and Denis M. Tull. 2008. "Postconflict Reconstruction in Africa: Flawed Ideas about Failed States." *International Security* 32(4):106–39.
Ero, Comfort. 2003. "Sierra Leone: The Legacies of Authoritarianism and Political Violence." In *Governing Insecurity: Democratic Control of Military and Security Establishments in Transitional Democracies*, ed. Gavin Cawthra and Robin Luckham. London: Zed Books, pp. 242–53.
Fearon, James D. and David D. Laitin. 2011. "Neotrusteeship and the Problem of Weak States." *International Security* 28(4):5–43.
Finnemore, Martha. 2004. *The Purpose of Intervention: Changing Beliefs about the Use of Force*. Ithaca: Cornell University Press.
Finnemore, Martha and Kathryn Sikkink. 1998. "International Norm Dynamics and Political Change." *International Organization* 52(4):887–917.
Fortna, Virginia Page. 2003. "Inside and Out: Peacekeeping and the Duration of Peace after Civil and Interstate Wars." *International Studies Review* 5(4):97–114.

Fortna, Virginia Page. 2004. "Does Peacekeeping Keep Peace? International Intervention and the Duration of Peace after Civil War." *International Studies Quarterly* 48(2):269–92.

Fortna, Virginia Page. 2008a. *Does Peacekeeping Work?: Shaping Belligerents' Choices after Civil War*. Princeton: Princeton University Press.

Fortna, Virginia Page. 2008b. "Peacekeeping and Democratization." In *From War to Democracy: Dilemmas of Peacebuilding*, ed. Anna K. Jarstad and Timothy D. Sisk. Cambridge, UK: Cambridge University Press, pp. 39–79.

Freedom House. 2005. *Freedom in the World 2005: Liberia*. New York: Freedom House. https://freedomhouse.org/report/freedom-world/2005/liberia

Freedom House. 2007. *Freedom in the World 2007: Liberia*. New York: Freedom House. https://freedomhouse.org/report/freedom-world/2007/liberia

Freedom House. 2008. *Freedom in the World 2008: Liberia*. New York: Freedom House. https://freedomhouse.org/report/freedom-world/2008/liberia

Freedom House. 2011. *Freedom in the World 2011: Liberia*. New York: Freedom House. https://freedomhouse.org/report/freedom-world/2011/liberia

Freedom House. 2013. *Freedom in the World 2013: Liberia*. New York: Freedom House. https://freedomhouse.org/report/freedom-world/2013/liberia

Freedom House. 2016. *Freedom in the World 2016: Liberia*. New York: Freedom House. https://freedomhouse.org/report/freedom-world/2016/liberia

Friedman, Jonathan and Christine MacAulay. 2014. *Building Civilian Police Capacity: Post-conflict Liberia, 2003–2011*. Monrovia: Innovations for Successful Societies.

Fukuyama, Francis. 2004. *State-Building: Governance and World Order in the 21st Century*. Ithaca: Cornell University Press.

Fukuyama, Francis. 2010. "Transitions to the Rule of Law." *Journal of Democracy* 21(1):33–44.

Fuller, Lon L. 1969. *The Morality of Law*. Revised ed. New Haven, CT: Yale University Press.

Ganzglass, Martin. 1997. "The Restoration of the Somali Justice System." In *Learning from Somalia: The Lessons of Armed Humanitarian Intervention*, ed. Walter Clarke and Jeffrey Herbst. Boulder, CO: Westview Press, pp. 20–41.

Geneva Centre for the Democratic Control of Armed Forces. 2012. "Measuring the Impact of Peacekeeping Missions on Rule of Law and Security Institutions: Report of the Expert Workshop." UN Office of Rule of Law and Security Institutions (OROLSI) and Geneva Centre for the Democratic Control of Armed Forces (DCAF).

Giahyue, James. 2014. "Liberia Justice Minister Quits, Says President Blocked Investigation." *Reuters*, October 7. www.reuters.com/article/us-liberia-politics/liberia-justice-minister-quits-says-president-blocked-investigation-idUSKCN0HW17220141007

Giffen, Alison. 2013. *Community Perceptions As a Priority in Protection and Peacekeeping*. Washington, DC: Stimson Center. Civilians in Conflict Issue Brief No. 2.

Gilley, Bruce. 2009. *The Right to Rule: How States Win and Lose Legitimacy*. New York: Columbia University Press.

Gilligan, Michael and Stephen Stedman. 2003. "Where Do the Peacekeepers Go?" *International Studies Review* 5(4):37–54.

Gilligan, Michael J. and Ernest I. Sergenti. 2008. "Do UN Interventions Cause Peace? Using Matching to Improve Causal Inference." *Quarterly Journal of Political Science* 3(2):89–122.

Global Legal Monitor. 2011. "Liberia: Supreme Court Ratifies a Constitutional Amendment." *The Law Library of Congress*, September 27. www.loc.gov/law/foreign-news/article/liberia-supreme-court-ratifies-a-constitutional-amendment/

Goldsmith, Andrew. 2002. "Policing Weak States: Citizen Safety and State Responsibility." *Policing and Society* 13(1):3–21.

Goldsmith, Arthur A. 2001. "Foreign Aid and Statehood in Africa." *International Organization* 55:123–48.

Golub, Stephen. 2003. "Beyond Rule of Law Orthodoxy: The Legal Empowerment Alternative." Carnegie Endowment Rule of Law Series Working Paper #41. http://carnegieendowment.org/2003/10/14/beyond-rule-of-law-orthodoxy-legal-empowerment-alternative/1ydz

Gonzalez-Ocantos, Ezequiel, Chad Kiewiet de Jonge, Carlos Meléndez, Javier Osorio, and David W. Nickerson. 2012. "Vote Buying and Social Desirability Bias: Experimental Evidence from Nicaragua." *American Journal of Political Science* 56(1):202–17.

Gordon, Grant M. and Lauren E. Young. 2017. "Cooperation, Information, and Keeping the Peace: Civilian Engagement with Peacekeepers in Haiti." *Journal of Peace Research* 54(1):64–79.

Gottlieb, Jessica. 2016. "Greater Expectations: A Field Experiment to Improve Accountability in Mali." *American Journal of Political Science* 60(1):143–57.

Green, Donald P., Soo Yeon Kim, and David H. Yoon. 2001. "Dirty Pool." *International Organization* 55(02):441–68.

Griffiths, John. 1986. "What Is Legal Pluralism?" *The Journal of Legal Pluralism and Unofficial Law* 18(24):1–55.

Grimmer, Justin, Solomon Messing, and Sean J. Westwood. 2012. "How Words and Money Cultivate a Personal Vote: The Effect of Legislator Credit Claiming on Constituent Credit Allocation." *American Political Science Review* 106:703–19.

Grindle, Merilee S. 2002. *Good Enough Governance: Poverty Reduction and Reform in Developing Countries*. Cambridge, MA: Harvard University Kennedy School of Government.

Guiteras, Raymond and Ahmed Mushfiq Mobarak. 2015. "Does Development Aid Undermine Political Accountability? Leader and Constituent Responses to a Large-Scale Intervention." NBER Working Paper No. 21434. www.nber.org/papers/w21434

Hadfield, Gillian K. and Barry R. Weingast. 2014. "Microfoundations of the Rule of Law." *Annual Review of Political Science* 17(1):21–42.

Haggard, Stephan and Lydia Tiede. 2013. "The Rule of Law in Post-conflict Settings: The Empirical Record." *International Studies Quarterly* 58:1–13.

Hampson, Fen Osler. 1997. "Can Peacebuilding Work?" *Cornell International Law Journal* 30:701–16.

Hart, H. L. A. 1965. "Book Review: Lon Fuller, The Morality of Law." *Harvard Law Review* 78:1281–96.

Hart, H. L. A. 2012. *The Concept of Law*. Oxford: Oxford University Press.

Hartman, Alexandra C., Robert A. Blair, and Christopher Blattman. 2020. "Engineering Informal Institutions: Long Run Impacts of Alternative Dispute Resolution on Violence and Property Rights in Liberia." *Journal of Politics* Forthcoming.

Hayek, F. A. 2006. *The Road to Serfdom*. New York: Routledge Classics.

Heldt, Birger. 2012. "Peacekeeping and Transitions to Democracy." In *Building Peace, Creating Conflict?: Conflictual Dimensions of Local and International Peacebuilding*, ed. Hanne Fjelde and Kristine Hoglund. Lund: Nordic Academic Press, pp. 47–72.

Heldt, Birger and Peter Wallensteen. 2011. "Peacekeeping Operations: Global Patterns of Intervention and Success, 1948–2004." SSRN Scholarly Paper 1899505. https://papers.ssrn.com/sol3/papers.cfm?abstract_id=1899505

Hellweg, Joseph. 2011. *Hunting the Ethical State: The Benkadi Movement of Côte d'Ivoire*. Chicago: University of Chicago Press.

Herbst, Jeffrey. 1996. "Responding to State Failure in Africa." *International Security* 21(3):120–44.

Herbst, Jeffrey. 2000. *States and Power in Africa*. Princeton: Princeton University Press.

Hessbruegge, Jan and Carlos Fredy Ochoa García. 2011. "Mayan Law in Post-conflict Guatemala." In *Customary Justice and the Rule of Law in War-Torn Societies*, ed. Deborah Isser. Washington, DC: United States Institute of Peace, pp. 77–118.

Higate, Paul and Marsha Henry. 2009. *Insecure Spaces: Peacekeeping in Liberia, Kosovo and Haiti*. London: Zed Books.

High-Level Independent Panel on United Nations Peace Operations. 2015. *Uniting Our Strength for Peace: Politics, Partnership and People*. New York: United Nations. Report of the High-Level Independent Panel on United Nations Peace Operations (HIPPO Report).

Hohe, Tanja. 2003. "Justice without Judiciary in East Timor." *Conflict, Security and Development* 3(3):335–57.

Holt, Victoria K. and Glyn Taylor. 2009. *Protecting Civilians in the Context of UN Peacekeeping Operations: Successes, Setbacks and Remaining Challenges*. New York: United Nations.

Howard, Lise Morjé. 2008. *UN Peacekeeping in Civil Wars*. Cambridge, UK: Cambridge University Press.

Howard, Lise Morjé. 2019. *Power in Peacekeeping: How the UN Works to End War*. Cambridge, UK: Cambridge University Press.

Huberich, Charles Henry. 1947. *The Political and Legislative History of Liberia*, Volume 2. New York: Central Book Co.

Hultman, Lisa. 2010. "Keeping Peace or Spurring Violence? Unintended Effects of Peace Operations on Violence against Civilians." *Civil Wars* 12(1–2):29–46.

Hultman, Lisa, Jacob Kathman, and Megan Shannon. 2013. "United Nations Peacekeeping and Civilian Protection in Civil War." *American Journal of Political Science* 57(4):875–91.

Hultman, Lisa, Jacob Kathman, and Megan Shannon. 2014. "Beyond Keeping Peace: United Nations Effectiveness in the Midst of Fighting." *American Political Science Review* 108(04):737–53.

Hultman, Lisa, Jacob D. Kathman, and Megan Shannon. 2016. "United Nations Peacekeeping Dynamics and the Duration of Post-Civil Conflict Peace." *Conflict Management and Peace Science* 33(3):231–49.

Human Rights Watch. 1993. "Waging War to Keep the Peace: The ECOMOG Intervention and Human Rights." June 1. www.hrw.org/report/1993/06/01/liberia-waging-war-keep-peace/ecomog-intervention-and-human-rights

Human Rights Watch. 2010. "Côte d'Ivoire: Ensure Security, Protect Expression, Movement." December 4. www.hrw.org/news/2010/12/04/cote-divoire-ensure-security-protect-expression-movement

Human Rights Watch. 2013. *"No Money, No Justice:" Police Corruption and Abuse in Liberia*. New York: Human Rights Watch.

Hurd, Ian. 1999. "Legitimacy and Authority in International Politics." *International Organization* 53(2):379–408.
Hurd, Ian. 2002. "Legitimacy, Power, and the Symbolic Life of the UN Security Council." *Global Governance* 8(1):35–51.
International Crisis Group. 2003a. *Liberia: Security Challenges*. Freetown/Brussels: International Crisis Group. Africa Report No. 71.
International Crisis Group. 2003b. *Tackling Liberia: The Eye of the Regional Storm*. Freetown/Brussels: International Crisis Group. Africa Report No. 62.
International Legal Assistance Consortium. 2003. *Liberia Mission Report*. Stockholm: International Legal Assistance Consortium.
IRIN. 2006. "Rubber Plantations 'Lawless', Says UN." *IRIN*, May 11. www.irinnews.org/news/2006/05/11/rubber-plantations-%E2%80%9Clawless%E2%80%9D-says-un
IRIN. 2007. "Trial by Ordeal Makes the Guilty Burn but 'Undermines Justice.'" *IRIN*, November 1. www.irinnews.org/report.aspx?reportid=75111
IRIN. 2014. "Tackling Liberia's High Rape Rate." *IRIN*, July 18. www.irinnews.org/report/100364/tackling-liberia%E2%80%99s-high-rape-rate
Isser, Deborah, ed. 2011. *Customary Justice and the Rule of Law in War-Torn Societies*. Washington, DC: United States Institute of Peace.
Isser, Deborah H., Stephen C. Lubkemann, and Saah N'Tow. 2009. *Looking for Justice: Liberian Experiences and Perceptions of Local Justice Options*. Washington, DC: United States Institute of Peace.
Janse, Ronald. 2013. "A Turn to Legal Pluralism in Rule of Law Promotion?" *Erasmus Law Review* 3/4:181–90.
Janssens, Jelle. 2015. *State-Building in Kosovo: A Plural Policing Perspective*. Antwerp: Maklu.
Jensen, Erik G. 2008. "Justice and the Rule of Law." In *Building States to Build Peace*, ed. Charles T. Call and Vanessa Wyeth. Boulder, CO: Lynne Rienner, pp. 119–42.
Johns, Robert. 2011. "Credit Where It's Due? Valence Politics, Attributions of Responsibility, and Multi-Level Elections." *Political Behavior* 33(1):53–77.
Jones, Bruce and Feryal Cherif. 2004. *Evolving Models of Peacekeeping: Policy Implications and Responses*. New York: UN Department of Peacekeeping Operations. External Study for the UN DPKO Peacekeeping Best Practices Unit.
Jones, Sam and Finn Tarp. 2016. "Does Foreign Aid Harm Political Institutions?" *Journal of Development Economics* 118:266–81.
Joseph, Gilbert M. and Daniel Nugent. 1994. *Everyday Forms of State Formation: Revolution and the Negotiation of Rule in Modern Mexico*. Durham, NC: Duke University Press.
Kahler, Miles. 2009. "Statebuilding after Iraq and Afghanistan." In *The Dilemmas of Statebuilding: Confronting the Contradictions of Postwar Peace Operations*, ed. Roland Paris and Timothy D. Sisk. London: Routledge, pp. 287–303.
Kalyvas, Stathis N. 2006. *The Logic of Violence in Civil War*. Cambridge, UK: Cambridge University Press.
Karim, Sabrina and Kyle Beardsley. 2017. *Equal Opportunity Peacekeeping: Women, Peace, and Security in Post-conflict States*. Oxford: Oxford University Press.
Karim, Sabrina, Michael J. Gilligan, Robert Blair, and Kyle Beardsley. 2018. "International Gender Balancing Reforms in Postconflict Countries: Lab-in-the-Field Evidence from the Liberian National Police." *International Studies Quarterly* 62(3):618–31.

Kaspersen, Anja T., Espen Barth Eide, and Annika S. Hansen. 2004. "International Policing and the Rule of Law in Transitions from War to Peace." NUPI Challenges to Collective Security Paper No. 4. www.nupi.no/en/Publications/CRIStin-Pub/International-Policing-and-the-Rule-of-Law-in-Transitions-from-War-to-Peace

Kathman, J., K. Beardsley, T.-I. Gizelis, L. Olsson, V. Bove, A. Ruggeri, R. Zwetsloot, J. van der Lijn, T. Smit, L. Hultman, H. Dorussen, A. Ruggeri, P. F. Diehl, L. Bosco, and C. Goodness. 2017. "The Known Knowns and Known Unknowns of Peacekeeping Data." *International Peacekeeping* 24(1):1–62.

Kattel, Rainer, Jan A. Kregel, and Erik S. Reinert, eds. 2011. *Ragnar Nurkse: Trade and Development*. London: Anthem Press.

Kavanagh, Camino and Bruce Jones. 2011. "Shaky Foundations: An Assessment of the UN's Rule of Law Support Agenda." New York: New York University Center on International Cooperation.

Keck, Margaret E. and Kathryn Sikkink. 1998. *Activists beyond Borders: Advocacy Networks in International Politics*. Ithaca: Cornell University Press.

Kinzinger, Adam and David Cicilline. 2018. "Opinion: Liberia the Latest Success Story of UN Peacekeepers." *Roll Call*, May 29. www.rollcall.com/news/opinion/liberia-united-nations-peacekeeping-mission

Krasner, Stephen D. 2004. "Sharing Sovereignty: New Institutions for Collapsed and Failing States." *International Security* 29(2):85–120.

Krasno, Jean. 2005. *Public Opinion Survey of UNAMSIL's Work in Sierra Leone*. New York: UN Peacekeeping Best Practices Section.

Krasno, Jean. 2006. *Public Opinion Survey of UNMIL's Work in Liberia*. New York: UN Peacekeeping Best Practices Section.

Kreps, Sarah and Geoffrey Wallace. 2009. "Just How Humanitarian are Interventions? Peacekeeping and the Prevention of Civilian Killings during and after Civil Wars." SSRN Scholarly Paper 1450574. papers.ssrn.com/sol3/papers.cfm?abstract_id=1450574

Kuperman, Alan J. 2015. "Liberia: How Diplomacy Helped End a 13-Year Civil War." In *Negotiating in Times of Conflict*, ed. Gilead Sher and Anat Kurz. Tel Aviv: Institute for National Security Studies, pp. 155–71.

Lake, David A. 2010. "Building Legitimate States after Civil Wars." In *Strengthening Peace in Post-civil War States: Transforming Spoilers into Stakeholders*, ed. Matthew Hoddie and Caroline A. Hartzell. Chicago: University of Chicago Press.

Lake, David A. 2016. *The Statebuilder's Dilemma: On the Limits of Foreign Intervention*. Ithaca: Cornell University Press.

Last, David M. 1997. *Theory, Doctrine and Practice of Conflict de-Escalation in Peacekeeping Operations*. Clementsport, Nova Scotia: Canadian Peacekeeping Press.

Leander, Anna. 2002. "Wars and the Un-making of States: Taking Tilly Seriously in the Contemporary World." In *Copenhagen Peace Research: Conceptual Innovations and Contemporary Security Analysis*, ed. Stefano Guzzini and Dietrich Jung. London: Routledge, pp. 69–80.

Lederer, Edith M. 2018. "US Seeks Tougher UN Action against Peacekeepers' Failures." *Associated Press*, September 12. www.apnews.com/6179f08f2f23498baafe438e26126bda

Legislature of Liberia. 2007. *An Act of the Legislature to Establish the Governance Commission*. Monrovia: Republic of Liberia.

Lemay-Hébert, Nicolas. 2009. "Statebuilding without Nation-Building? Legitimacy, State Failure and the Limits of the Institutionalist Approach." *Journal of Intervention and Statebuilding* 3(1):21–45.

Leonardsson, Hanna and Gustav Rudd. 2015. "The 'Local Turn' in Peacebuilding: A Literature Review of Effective and Emancipatory Local Peacebuilding." *Third World Quarterly* 36(5):825–39.

Levitt, Steven D. 1997. "Using Electoral Cycles in Police Hiring to Estimate the Effect of Police on Crime." *American Economic Review* 87(3):270–90.

Lewis, David and Tim Cocks. 2010. "Ivory Coast Seals Borders after Opposition Win." *Reuters*, December 2. https://reliefweb.int/report/c%C3%B4te-divoire/ivory-coast-seals-borders-after-opposition-win

Linzer, Drew A. and Jeffrey K. Staton. 2015. "A Global Measure of Judicial Independence, 1948–2012." *Journal of Law and Courts* 3(2):223–56.

Little, Kenneth. 1965. "The Political Function of the Poro. Part I." *Africa* 35(4):349–65.

Lloyd, Garbiella. 2017. *Mandating (In)Security: How UN Missions Endanger the Civilians They Intend to Protect*. Columbus, OH: The Ohio State University. PhD dissertation.

Lubkemann, Stephen C., Deborah H. Isser, and Philip A. Z. Banks III. 2011. "Unintended Consequences: Constraint of Customary Justice in Post-conflict Liberia." In *Customary Justice and the Rule of Law in War-Torn Societies*, ed. Deborah Isser. Washington, DC: United States Institute of Peace, pp. 193–237.

Lubkemann, Stephen C., Helene Maria Kyed, and Jennifer Garvey. 2011. "Dilemmas of Articulation in Mozambique: Customary Justice in Transition." In *Customary Justice and the Rule of Law in War-Torn Societies*, ed. Deborah Isser. Washington, DC: United States Institute of Peace, pp. 13–75.

Luttwak, Edward N. 1999. "Give War a Chance." *Foreign Affairs* 78(4):36–44.

Lyall, Jason, Yang-Yang Zhou, and Kosuke Imai. 2020. "Can Economic Assistance Shape Combatant Support in Wartime? Experimental Evidence from Afghanistan." *American Political Science Review* 114(1):126–43.

Magaloni, Beatriz, Edgar Franco, and Vanessa Melo. 2015. "Killing in the Slums: An Impact Evaluation of Police Reform in Rio de Janeiro." Stanford University Center for Democracy, Development, and the Rule of Law Working Paper. https://cddrl.fsi.stanford.edu/publication/killing-slums-impact-evaluation-police-reform-rio-de-janeiro

Malan, Mark. 2008. *Security Sector Reform in Liberia: Mixed Results from Humble Beginnings*. Carlisle, PA: Strategic Studies Institute.

Mamdani, Mahmood. 1996. *Citizen and Subject: Contemporary Africa and the Legacy of Late Colonialism*. Princeton: Princeton University Press.

Mampilly, Zachariah Cherian. 2011. *Rebel Rulers: Insurgent Governance and Civilian Life during War*. Ithaca: Cornell University Press.

Mani, Rama. 2002. *Beyond Retribution: Seeking Justice in the Shadows of War*. Cambridge, UK: Polity Press.

Manning, Carrie. 2003. "Local Level Challenges to Post-conflict Peacebuilding." *International Peacekeeping* 10(3):25–43.

Marten, Kimberly Zisk. 2004. *Enforcing the Peace: Learning from the Imperial Past*. New York: Columbia University Press.

Martin, Jane J. 1969. "How to Build a Nation: Liberian Ideas about National Integration in the Later Nineteenth Century." *Liberian Studies Journal* 2(1):15–42.

Matanock, Aila M. 2017. *Electing Peace: From Civil Conflict to Political Participation*. Cambridge, UK: Cambridge University Press.

Mayall, James. 2005. "The Legacy of Colonialism." In *Making States Work: State Failure and the Crisis of Governance*, ed. Simon Chesterman, Michael Ignatieff, and Ramesh Thakur. Tokyo: United Nations University Press, pp. 36–58.

Mazerolle, Lorraine, Emma Antrobus, Sarah Bennett, and Tom R. Tyler. 2013. "Shaping Citizen Perceptions of Police Legitimacy: A Randomized Field Trial of Procedural Justice." *Criminology* 51(1):33–63.

McCandless, Erin. 2008. "Lessons from Liberia: Integrated Approaches to Peacebuilding in Transitional Settings." ISS Paper 161. https://issafrica.org/research/papers/lessons-from-liberia-integrated-approaches-to-peacebuilding-in-transitional-settings

McLeod, Allegra M. 2010. "Exporting U.S. Criminal Justice." *Yale Law & Policy Review* 29(1):83–164.

Melander, Erik. 2009. "Selected to Go Where Murderers Lurk? The Preventive Effect of Peacekeeping on Mass Killings of Civilians." *Conflict Management and Peace Science* 26(4):389–406.

Menkhaus, Kenneth. 2008. "Somalia: Governance vs. Statebuilding." In *Building States to Build Peace*, ed. Charles T. Call and Vanessa Wyeth. Boulder, CO: Lynne Rienner, pp. 187–215.

Merry, Sally Engle. 1988. "Legal Pluralism." *Law & Society Review* 22(5):869–96.

Migdal, Joel S. 1994. "The State in Society: An Approach to Struggles for Domination." In *State Power and Social Forces: Domination and Transformation in the Third World*, ed. Joel S. Migdal, Atul Kohli, and Vivienne Shue. Cambridge, UK: Cambridge University Press, pp. 7–36.

Migdal, Joel S. and Klaus Schlichte. 2005. "Rethinking the State." In *The Dynamics of States: The Formation and Crises of State Domination*, ed. Klaus Schlichte. Aldershot, England: Ashgate, pp. 1–40.

Miller, Richard W. 2011. "The Ethics of America's Afghan War." *Ethics & International Affairs* 25:103–31.

Mogelson, Luke. 2012. "The Hard Way Out of Afghanistan." *The New York Times Magazine*, February 1. www.nytimes.com/2012/02/05/magazine/afghanistan.html

Moore, Barrington. 1966. *Social Origins of Dictatorship and Democracy: Lord and Peasant in the Making of the Modern World*. Boston: Beacon Press.

Moore, Sally Falk. 1973. "Law and Social Change: The Semi-autonomous Social Field As an Appropriate Subject of Study." *Law & Society Review* 7(4):719–46.

Moyo, Dambisa. 2010. *Dead Aid: Why Aid Makes Things Worse and How There Is Another Way for Africa*. London: Penguin.

Mudde, Cas. 2007. *Populist Radical Right Parties in Europe*. Cambridge, UK: Cambridge University Press.

Mukhopadhyay, Dipali. 2014. *Warlords, Strongman Governors, and the State in Afghanistan*. Cambridge, UK: Cambridge University Press.

Müller, Jan-Werner. 2016. *What Is Populism?* Philadelphia: University of Pennsylvania Press.

Murtazashvili, Jennifer Brick. 2016. "Afghanistan: A Vicious Cycle of State Failure: Commentary." *Governance* 29(2):163–6.

Mvukiyehe, Eric. 2018. "Promoting Political Participation in War-Torn Countries: Micro-level Evidence from Postwar Liberia." *Journal of Conflict Resolution* 62(8):1686–726.

Mvukiyehe, Eric and Cyrus Samii. 2008. *Laying a Foundation for Peace? A Quantitative Impact Evaluation of the United Nations Operation in Cote d'Ivoire*. New York: Columbia University.

Mvukiyehe, Eric and Cyrus Samii. 2010. *Quantitative Impact Evaluation of the United Nations Mission in Liberia: Final Report*. New York: Columbia University.

Mvukiyehe, Eric and Cyrus Samii. 2017. "Promoting Democracy in Fragile States: Field Experimental Evidence from Liberia." *World Development* 95:254–67.

Mvukiyehe, Eric and Cyrus Samii. 2018. "Peacekeeping and Development in Fragile States: Micro-level Evidence from Liberia." World Bank Policy Research Working Paper No. 8389. https://papers.ssrn.com/sol3/papers.cfm?abstract_id=3152692

Nagin, Daniel S. and Cody W. Telep. 2017. "Procedural Justice and Legal Compliance." *Annual Review of Law and Social Science* 13(1):5–28.

Nanes, Matthew. 2019. "Policing in Divided Societies: Officer Inclusion, Citizen Cooperation, and Crime Prevention." *Conflict Management & Peace Science* Forthcoming.

Nanes, Matthew. 2020. "Police Integration and Support for Anti-Government Violence: Evidence from Iraq." *Journal of Peace Research* 57(2):329–43.

Neumann, Hannah and Niels Nagelhus Schia. 2012. *Contextualizing Peacebuilding Activities to Local Circumstances: Liberian Case-Study Field Report*. Oslo: Norwegian Institute of International Affairs.

Newby, Vanessa F. 2018. *Peacekeeping in South Lebanon: Credibility and Local Cooperation*. Syracuse: Syracuse University Press.

Nomikos, William G. 2016. "Can International Actors Encourage Interethnic Cooperation after Conflict? Evidence from Peacebuilding in Mali." Paper presented at the American Political Science Association Annual Meeting, Philadelphia.

Olken, Benjamin A. 2010. "Direct Democracy and Local Public Goods: Evidence from a Field Experiment in Indonesia." *American Political Science Review* 104(2):243–67.

Paczynska, Agnieszka. 2010. *Liberia ICAF Report*. Monrovia, Liberia: USAID Coordinator for Reconstruction and Stabilization.

Pailey, Robtel Neajai and Edward Emmett Dillon. 2017. "Liberia Needs the Rule of Law, Not Political Expediency." *Al Jazeera*, November 62. www.aljazeera.com/indepth/opinion/liberia-rule-law-political-expediency-171126103342342.html

Palus, Nancy. 2013. "UN Urges Probe into Serious Human Rights Abuses by Traditional Hunters in Côte d'Ivoire." *UN News Centre*, December 6. https://news.un.org/en/story/2013/12/457182-un-urges-probe-serious-human-rights-abuses-traditional-hunters-cote-divoire#.VnhizJMrKi6

Paris, Roland. 1997. "Peacebuilding and the Limits of Liberal Internationalism." *International Security* 22(2):54–89.

Paris, Roland. 2002. "International Peacebuilding and the 'Mission Civilisatrice.'" *Review of International Studies* 28(04):637–56.

Paris, Roland and Timothy D. Sisk. 2009a. "Introduction: Understanding the Contradictions of Postwar Statebuilding." In *The Dilemmas of Statebuilding: Confronting the Contradictions of Postwar Peace Operations*, ed. Roland Paris and Timothy D. Sisk. London: Routledge, pp. 1–20.

Paris, Roland and Timothy D. Sisk, eds. 2009b. *The Dilemmas of Statebuilding: Confronting the Contradictions of Postwar Peace Operations*. London: Routledge.

Pfaff, William. 1995. "A New Colonialism? Europe Must Go Back into Africa." *Foreign Affairs* 74(1):2–6.

Pouligny, Beatrice. 2006. *Peace Operations Seen from Below: UN Missions and Local People*. Bloomfield, CT: Kumarian Press.

Prins, Brandon and Anup Phayal. 2018. "Armed Peacekeepers Really Do Protect Civilians – with One Big Exception." *Monkey Cage*, June 14. www.washingtonpost.com/news/monkey-cage/wp/2018/06/13/yes-armed-peacekeepers-actually-do-protect-civilians-except-when-governments-are-the-source-of-the-attacks/

Pugh, Michael. 2011. "Local Agency and Political Economies of Peacebuilding." *Studies in Ethnicity and Nationalism* 11(2):308–20.

Radin, Margaret Jane. 1989. "Reconsidering the Rule of Law." *Boston University Law Review* 69:781–822.

Rajagopal, Balakrishnan. 2008. "Invoking the Rule of Law in Post-conflict Rebuilding: A Critical Examination." *William & Mary Law Review* 49(4):1347–76.

Ratcliffe, Jerry H., Travis Taniguchi, Elizabeth R. Groff, and Jennifer D. Wood. 2011. "The Philadelphia Foot Patrol Experiment: A Randomized Controlled Trial of Police Patrol Effectiveness in Violent Crime Hotspots." *Criminology* 49(3):795–831.

Rayburn, Nadine Recker, Mitchell Earleywine, and Gerald C. Davison. 2003. "An Investigation of Base Rates of Anti-Gay Hate Crimes Using the Unmatched-Count Technique." *Journal of Aggression, Maltreatment & Trauma* 6(2):137–52.

Raz, Joseph. 1979. *The Authority of Law: Essays on Law and Morality*. 2nd ed. Oxford: Oxford University Press.

Reno, William. 2008. "Bottom-Up Statebuilding?" In *Building States to Build Peace*, ed. Charles T. Call and Vanessa Wyeth. Boulder, CO: Lynne Rienner, pp. 143–62.

Republic of Liberia Truth and Reconciliation Commission. 2009. *Volume II: Consolidated Final Report*. Monrovia: Republic of Liberia Truth and Reconciliation Commission.

Roby, Christin. 2018. "UNMIL Provides Lessons on What Makes a Successful Peacekeeping Mission." *Devex*, April 5. www.devex.com/news/unmil-provides-lessons-on-what-makes-a-successful-peacekeeping-mission-92477

Rodriguez, Daniel B., Matthew D. McCubbins, and Barry R. Weingast. 2009. "The Rule of Law Unplugged." *Emory Law Journal* 59:1455–94.

Rubin, Barnett R. 2008. "The Politics of Security in Postconflict Statebuilding." In *Building States to Build Peace*, ed. Charles T. Call and Vanessa Wyeth. Boulder, CO: Lynne Rienner, pp. 25–47.

Ruggeri, Andrea, Han Dorussen, and Theodora-Ismene Gizelis. 2017. "Winning the Peace Locally: UN Peacekeeping and Local Conflict." *International Organization* 71(1):163–85.

Ruggeri, Andrea, Han Dorussen, and Theodora-Ismene Gizelis. 2018. "On the Frontline Every Day? Subnational Deployment of United Nations Peacekeepers." *British Journal of Political Science* 48(4):1005–25.

Ruggeri, Andrea, Theodora-Ismene Gizelis, and Han Dorussen. 2011. "Events Data As Bismarck's Sausages? Intercoder Reliability, Coders' Selection, and Data Quality." *International Interactions* 37(3):340–61.

Ruggeri, Andrea, Theodora-Ismene Gizelis, and Han Dorussen. 2012. "Managing Mistrust: An Analysis of Cooperation with UN Peacekeeping in Africa." *Journal of Conflict Resolution* 57(3):387–409.

Rupesinghe, Natasja. 2016. "How Can Peacekeepers Strengthen Their Engagement with Local Communities? Opportunities and Challenges in the Field." NUPI Policy Brief No. 30.
Rusinko, William T., Knowlton W. Johnson, and Carlton A. Hornung. 1978. "The Importance of Police Contact in the Formulation of Youths' Attitudes toward Police." *Journal of Criminal Justice* 6(1):53–67.
Sacks, Audrey. 2012. "Can Donors and Nonstate Actors Undermine Citizens' Legitimating Beliefs?" World Bank Poverty Reduction and Economic Management (PREM) Network Working Paper No. 95. http://siteresources.worldbank.org/EXTPREMNET/Resources/EP95.pdf
Sahin, Nusret, Anthony A. Braga, Robert Apel, and Rod K. Brunson. 2017. "The Impact of Procedurally-Just Policing on Citizen Perceptions of Police During Traffic Stops: The Adana Randomized Controlled Trial." *Journal of Quantitative Criminology* 33(4):701–26.
Salvatore, Jessica Di. 2019. "Peacekeepers against Criminal Violence – Unintended Effects of Peacekeeping Operations?" *American Journal of Political Science* 63(4):840–58.
Sambanis, Nicholas. 2008. "Short- and Long-Term Effects of United Nations Peace Operations." *The World Bank Economic Review* 22(1):9–32.
Samii, Cyrus. 2013. "Perils or Promise of Ethnic Integration? Evidence from a Hard Case in Burundi." *American Political Science Review* 107(03):558–73.
Sannerholm, Richard Zajac, Frida Möller, Kristina Simion, and Hanna Hallonsten. 2012. *UN Peace Operations and Rule of Law Assistance in Africa 1989–2010: Data, Patterns and Questions for the Future*. Stockholm: Folke Bernadotte Academy.
Sawyer, Amos. 2004. "Violent Conflicts and Governance Challenges in West Africa: The Case of the Mano River Basin Area." *The Journal of Modern African Studies* 42(03):437–63.
Sawyer, Amos. 2005a. *Beyond Plunder: Toward Democratic Governance in Liberia*. Boulder, CO: Lynne Rienner.
Sawyer, Amos. 2005b. "Social Capital, Survival Strategies, and Their Potential for Post-conflict Governance in Liberia." UNU-Wider Research Paper No. 2005/15. www.wider.unu.edu/publication/social-capital-survival-strategies-and-their-potential-post-conflict-governance-liberia
Scott, James C. 2010. *The Art of Not Being Governed: An Anarchist History of Upland Southeast Asia*. New Haven: Yale University Press.
Shapiro, Scott J. 2009. "What Is the Rule of Recognition (and Does It Exist)?" Yale Law School Public Law & Legal Theory Research Paper No. 181. https://law.yale.edu/sites/default/files/documents/pdf/Faculty/Shapiro_Rule_of_Regulation.pdf
Shapiro, Scott J. 2013. *Legality*. Cambridge, MA: Belknap Press.
Sherman, Lawrence W. and David Weisburd. 1995. "General Deterrent Effects of Police Patrol in Crime 'Hot Spots:' A Randomized, Controlled Trial." *Justice Quarterly* 12(4):625–48.
Shklar, Judith N. 1998. "Political Theory and the Rule of Law." In *Political Thought & Political Thinkers*, ed. Stanley Hoffman. Chicago: University of Chicago Press, pp. 21–38.
Siddiqi, Bilal and Justin Sandefur. 2009. *Appendix: Community-Based Justice and the Rule of Law in Liberia*. Washington, DC: United States Institute of Peace.

Sieder, Rachel. 2001. Rethinking Citizenship: Reforming the Law in Postwar Guatemala. In *States of Imagination: Ethnographic Explorations of the Postcolonial State*, ed. Thomas Blom Hansen and Finn Stepputat. Durham, NC: Duke University Press, pp. 203–21.

Simmons, Beth A., Paulette Lloyd, and Brandon M. Stewart. 2018. "The Global Diffusion of Law: Transnational Crime and the Case of Human Trafficking." *International Organization* 72(2):249–81.

Sisk, Timothy and Paul Risley. 2005. *Democracy and Peacebuilding at the Local Level: Lessons Learned*. Stockholm: International Institute for Democracy and Election Assistance (IDEA) Programme in Democracy and Conflict Management. Working Draft.

Sitaraman, Ganesh. 2012. *The Counterinsurgent's Constitution: Law in the Age of Small Wars*. Oxford: Oxford University Press.

Skogan, Wesley G. 2006. "Asymmetry in the Impact of Encounters with Police." *Policing and Society* 16(2):99–126.

Smidt, Hannah. 2016. "Beyond Deploying Troops: What UN Peacekeeping Operations Do on the Ground during Elections Times." Working Paper.

Smidt, Hannah M. 2020. "United Nations Peacekeeping Locally: Enabling Conflict Resolution, Reducing Communal Violence." *Journal of Conflict Resolution* 64(2–3): 344-72

Smith, David. 2010. "Ivory Coast: Death Squads on the Rise As Civil War Looms." *The Guardian*, December 22. www.theguardian.com/world/2010/dec/22/ivory-coast-death-squads

Smith, David. 2011. "Ivory Coast: UN's Intervention Broke the Impasse." *The Guardian*, April 5. www.theguardian.com/world/2011/apr/05/ivory-coast-un-intervention

Smith-Höhn, Judy. 2010. *Rebuilding the Security Sector in Post-conflict Societies: Perceptions from Urban Liberia and Sierra Leone*. Zurich: Lit Verlag and Geneva Centre for the Democratic Control of Armed Forces (DCAF).

Sovey, Allison J. and Donald P. Green. 2011. "Instrumental Variables Estimation in Political Science: A Readers' Guide." *American Journal of Political Science* 55(1):188–200.

Staniland, Paul. 2012. "States, Insurgents, and Wartime Political Orders." *Perspectives on Politics* 10(2):243–64.

Stanley, William and Robert Loosle. 1998. "El Salvador: The Civilian Police Component of Peace Operations." In *Policing the New World Disorder: Peace Operations and Public Security*, ed. Michael J. Dziedzic, Eliot M. Goldberg, and Robert B. Oakley. Washington, DC: National Defense University Press, pp. 103–42.

Statement by Her Excellency Mrs. Ellen Johnson Sirleaf, President of Liberia. 2017. New York: UN General Assembly. Seventy-Second Regular Session, September 19.

Stedman, Stephen John, Donald Rothchild, and Elizabeth M. Cousens, eds. 2002. *Ending Civil Wars: The Implementation of Peace Agreements*. Boulder, CO: Lynne Rienner.

Steinert, Janina Isabel and Sonja Grimm. 2015. "Too Good to Be True? United Nations Peacebuilding and the Democratization of War-Torn States." *Conflict Management and Peace Science* 32(5):513–35.

Stromseth, Jane, David Wippman, and Rosa Brooks. 2006. *Can Might Make Rights?: Building the Rule of Law after Military Interventions*. Cambridge, UK: Cambridge University Press.

Suhrke, Astri. 2009. "The Dangers of a Tight Embrace: Externally Assisted Statebuilding in Afghanistan." In *The Dilemmas of Statebuilding: Confronting the Contradictions of Postwar Peace Operations*, ed. Roland Paris and Timothy D. Sisk. London: Routledge, pp. 227–51.
Sunshine, Jason and Tom R. Tyler. 2003. "The Role of Procedural Justice and Legitimacy in Shaping Public Support for Policing." *Law & Society Review* 37(3):513–48.
Svensson, Jakob. 2000. "Foreign Aid and Rent-Seeking." *Journal of International Economics* 51(2):437–61.
Szasz, Paul C. 1994. "Creating the Namibian Constitution." *Verfassung und Recht in Übersee / Law and Politics in Africa, Asia and Latin America* 27(3):346–57.
Talentino, Andrea Kathryn. 2007. "Perceptions of Peacebuilding: The Dynamic of Imposer and Imposed Upon." *International Studies Perspectives* 8(2):152–71.
Tamanaha, Brian Z. 2004. *On the Rule of Law: History, Politics, Theory*. Cambridge, UK: Cambridge University Press.
Tamanaha, Brian Z. 2008. "Understanding Legal Pluralism: Past to Present, Local to Global." *Sydney Law Review* 30:375–411.
Tansey, Oisín. 2009. *Regime-Building: Democratization and International Administration*. New York: Oxford University Press.
Tilly, Charles, ed. 1975. *The Formation of National States in Western Europe*. Princeton: Princeton University Press.
Topka, Alaric and Dan Saryee. 2009. "Popular Opinions on Democracy in Liberia, 2008." Afrobarometer Briefing Paper No. 122. https://afrobarometer.org/publications/bp73-popular-opinions-democracy-liberia-2008
Tourangeau, Roger and Ting Yan. 2007. "Sensitive Questions in Surveys." *Psychological Bulletin* 133(5):859–83.
Trenkov-Wermuth, Calin. 2010. *United Nations Justice: Legal and Judicial Reform in Governance Operations*. Tokyo: UN University Press.
Tyler, Tom R. 2004. "Enhancing Police Legitimacy." *The Annals of the American Academy of Political and Social Science* 593(1):84–99.
Tyler, Tom R. 2006. *Why People Obey the Law*. Princeton: Princeton University Press.
Tyler, Tom R. and Jeffrey Fagan. 2008. "Legitimacy and Cooperation: Why Do People Help the Police Fight Crime in Their Communities?" *Ohio State Journal of Criminal Law* 6:231–75.
Tyler, Tom R. and Yuen J. Huo. 2002. *Trust in the Law: Encouraging Public Cooperation with the Police and Courts*. New York: Russell Sage Foundation.
Ubink, Janine, ed. 2011. *Customary Justice: Perspectives on Legal Empowerment*. Rome: International Development Law Organization.
UN Criminal Law and Judicial Advisory Service. 2013. *Report to the Special Committee on Peacekeeping Operations: DPKO Support for Strengthening Legal, Judicial and Prison Systems*. New York: UN Special Committee on Peacekeeping Operations.
UN Criminal Law and Judicial Advisory Service. 2016. *DPKO Support for Strengthening Justice and Corrections Systems*. New York: UN Department of Peacekeeping Operations. Non-paper.
UN Department of Peacekeeping Operations. 2009. *Corrections Update*. New York: United Nations. Volume 1, October.
UN Department of Peacekeeping Operations. 2010a. *Corrections Update*. New York: United Nations. Volume 2, October.

UN Department of Peacekeeping Operations. 2010b. *Justice Update*. New York: United Nations. Volume 1, April.
UN Department of Peacekeeping Operations. 2011a. *Corrections Update*. New York: United Nations. Volume 3, September.
UN Department of Peacekeeping Operations. 2011b. *Justice Update*. New York: United Nations. Volume 2, May.
UN Department of Peacekeeping Operations. 2012a. *Justice Review*. New York: United Nations. Volume 3, June.
UN Department of Peacekeeping Operations. 2012b. *The United Nations SSR Perspective*. New York: United Nations.
UN Department of Peacekeeping Operations. 2013. *UN Police Magazine*. New York: United Nations. 11th ed. July.
UN Department of Peacekeeping Operations. 2014a. *Justice & Corrections Update*. New York: United Nations.
UN Department of Peacekeeping Operations. 2014b. *Justice & Corrections Update*. New York: United Nations. December.
UN Department of Peacekeeping Operations. 2015a. *Justice & Corrections Update*. New York: United Nations. Issue 3, December.
UN Department of Peacekeeping Operations. 2015b. *Justice & Corrections Update*. New York: United Nations. Issue 2, April.
UN Department of Peacekeeping Operations. 2018. *Justice & Corrections Update*. New York: United Nations. Issue 6, June.
UN Department of Peacekeeping Operations and UN Department of Field Support. 2014. *DPKO/DFS Policy on United Nations Police in Peacekeeping Operations and Special Political Missions*. New York: United Nations.
UN Department of Peacekeeping Operations and UN High Commissioner for Human Rights. 2011. *The United Nations Rule of Law Indicators: Implementation Guide and Project Tools*. New York: United Nations.
UN Department of Peacekeeping Operations Policy and Best Practices Service. 2012. *United Nations Department of Peacekeeping Operations and Department of Field Support Civil Affairs Handbook*. New York: United Nations.
UN Meetings Coverage. 2018. "As Mission in Liberia Closes, Security Council Intends to Consider Best Practices in Ongoing Efforts to Enhance Effectiveness of Peacekeeping." *United Nations Meetings Coverage and Press Releases*, April 19. www.un.org/press/en/2018/sc13308.doc.htm
UN Mission in Liberia. 2006. *Human Rights in Liberia's Rubber Plantations: Tapping into the Future*. Monrovia: UN Mission in Liberia.
UN Office of Internal Oversight Services. 2014. *Evaluation of the Implementation and Results of Protection of Civilians Mandates in United Nations Peacekeeping Operations*. New York: UN General Assembly. A/68/787.
UN Peacekeeping Best Practices Section. 2008. *United Nations Peacekeeping Operations: Principles and Guidelines*. New York: United Nations.
UN Secretary-General. 1992. *An Agenda for Peace: Preventive Diplomacy, Peacemaking and Peace-Keeping. Report of the Secretary-General Pursuant to the Statement Adopted by the Summit Meeting of the Security Council on 31 January 1992*. New York: UN Security Council. A/47/277-S/24111.
UN Secretary-General. 2003. *First Progress Report of the Secretary-General on the United Nations Mission in Liberia*. New York: UN Security Council. S/2003/1175.

Bibliography

UN Secretary-General. 2004a. *Fifth Progress Report of the Secretary-General on the United Nations Mission in Liberia.* New York: UN Security Council. S/2004/972.

UN Secretary-General. 2004b. *Fourth Progress Report of the Secretary-General on the United Nations Mission in Liberia.* New York: UN Security Council. S/2004/725.

UN Secretary-General. 2004c. *The Rule of Law and Transitional Justice in Conflict and Post-conflict Societies.* New York: UN Security Council. S/2004/616*.

UN Secretary-General. 2004d. *Second Progress Report of the Secretary-General on the United Nations Mission in Liberia.* New York: UN Security Council. S/2004/229.

UN Secretary-General. 2004e. *Third Progress Report of the Secretary-General on the United Nations Mission in Liberia.* New York: UN Security Council. S/2004/430.

UN Secretary-General. 2005a. *Eighth Progress Report of the Secretary-General on the United Nations Mission in Liberia.* New York: UN Security Council. S/2005/560.

UN Secretary-General. 2005b. *Ninth Progress Report of the Secretary-General on the United Nations Mission in Liberia.* New York: UN Security Council. S/2005/764.

UN Secretary-General. 2005c. *Sixth Progress Report of the Secretary-General on the United Nations Mission in Liberia.* New York: UN Security Council. S/2005/177.

UN Secretary-General. 2006a. *Eleventh Progress Report of the Secretary-General on the United Nations Mission in Liberia.* New York: UN Security Council. S/2006/376.

UN Secretary-General. 2006b. *Performance Report on the Budget of the United Nations Mission in Liberia for the Period from 1 July 2004 to 30 June 2005.* New York: UN General Assembly. A/60/645.

UN Secretary-General. 2006c. *Thirteenth Progress Report of the Secretary-General on the United Nations Mission in Liberia.* New York: UN Security Council. S/2006/958.

UN Secretary-General. 2006d. *Twelfth Progress Report of the Secretary-General on the United Nations Mission in Liberia.* New York: UN Security Council. S/2006/743.

UN Secretary-General. 2007a. *Fifteenth Progress Report of the Secretary-General on the United Nations Mission in Liberia.* New York: UN Security Council. S/2007/479.

UN Secretary-General. 2007b. *Fourteenth Progress Report of the Secretary-General on the United Nations Mission in Liberia.* New York: UN Security Council. S/2007/151.

UN Secretary-General. 2007c. *Fourteenth Progress Report of the Secretary-General on the United Nations Operation in Côte d'Ivoire.* New York: UN Security Council. S/2007/593.

UN Secretary-General. 2008a. *Fifteenth Progress Report of the Secretary-General on the United Nations Operation in Côte d'Ivoire.* New York: UN Security Council. S/2008/1.

UN Secretary-General. 2008b. *Guidance Note of the Secretary-General: UN Approach to Rule of Law Assistance.* New York: UN Secretary General.

UN Secretary-General. 2008c. *Performance Report on the Budget of the United Nations Mission in Liberia for the Period from 1 July 2006 to 30 June 2007.* New York: UN General Assembly. A/62/648.

UN Secretary-General. 2008d. *Performance Report on the Budget of the United Nations Mission in Liberia for the Period from 1 July 2007 to 30 June 2008.* New York: UN General Assembly. A/63/588.

UN Secretary-General. 2008e. *Sixteenth Progress Report of the Secretary-General on the United Nations Mission in Liberia.* New York: UN Security Council. S/2008/183.

UN Secretary-General. 2009. *Report of the Secretary-General on the United Nations Mission in the Central African Republic and Chad.* New York: UN Security Council. S/2009/359.

UN Secretary-General. 2010a. *Twentieth Progress Report of the Secretary-General on the United Nations Mission in Liberia.* New York: UN Security Council. S/2010/88.

UN Secretary-General. 2010b. *Twenty-First Progress Report of the Secretary-General on the United Nations Mission in Liberia.* New York: UN Security Council. S/2010/429.

UN Secretary-General. 2011a. *Budget Performance of the United Nations Mission in Liberia for the Period from 1 July 2010 to 30 June 2011.* New York: UN General Assembly. A/66/602.

UN Secretary-General. 2011b. *Report of the Secretary-General on the African Union United Nations Hybrid Operation in Darfur.* New York: UN Security Council. S/2011/643.

UN Secretary-General. 2011c. *Twenty-Fifth Progress Report of the Secretary-General on the United Nations Mission in Liberia.* New York: UN Security Council. S/2011/72**.

UN Secretary-General. 2012a. *Budget Performance of the United Nations Mission in Liberia for the Period from 1 July 2011 to 30 June 2012.* New York: UN General Assembly. A/67/609.

UN Secretary-General. 2012b. *Report of the Secretary-General on the United Nations Organization Stabilization Mission in the Democratic Republic of the Congo.* New York: UN Security Council. S/2012/65.

UN Secretary-General. 2012c. *Special Report of the Secretary-General on the United Nations Mission in Liberia.* New York: UN Security Council. S/2012/230.

UN Secretary-General. 2012d. *Twenty-Fifth Progress Report of the Secretary-General on the United Nations Mission in Liberia.* New York: UN Security Council. S/2013/124**.

UN Secretary-General. 2012e. *Twenty-Fourth Progress Report of the Secretary-General on the United Nations Mission in Liberia.* New York: UN Security Council. S/2012/641.

UN Secretary-General. 2014a. *Thirty-Fifth Progress Report of the Secretary-General on the United Nations Operation in Côte d'Ivoire.* New York: UN Security Council. S/2014/892.

UN Secretary-General. 2014b. *Twenty-Eighth Progress Report of the Secretary-General on the United Nations Mission in Liberia.* New York: UN Security Council. S/2014/598.

UN Secretary-General. 2014c. *Twenty-Seventh Progress Report of the Secretary-General on the United Nations Mission in Liberia.* New York: UN Security Council. S/2014/123.

UN Secretary-General. 2015a. *Budget Performance of the United Nations Mission in Liberia for the Period from 1 July 2014 to 30 June 2015.* New York: UN General Assembly. A/70/595.

UN Secretary-General. 2015b. *Report of the Secretary-General on South Sudan.* New York: UN Security Council. S/2015/118.

UN Secretary-General. 2016. *Budget Performance of the United Nations Mission in Liberia for the Period from 1 July 2015 to 30 June 2016.* New York: UN General Assembly. A/71/645.

UN Secretary-General. 2017. *Budget Performance of the United Nations Mission in Liberia for the Period from 1 July 2016 to 30 June 2017.* New York: UN General Assembly. A/72/640.

UN Secretary-General's Advisory Group of Experts. 2015. *The Challenge of Sustaining Peace: Report of the Advisory Group of Experts for the 2015 Review of the United Nations Peacebuilding Architecture*. New York: UN Security Council and General Assembly.
UN Security Council. 1996. *Resolution 1040*. New York: United Nations. S/RES/1040.
UN Security Council. 2000. *Report of the Panel on United Nations Peace Operations (Brahimi Report)*. New York: United Nations. A/55/305-S/2000/809.
UN Security Council. 2007a. *Resolution 1739*. New York: United Nations. S/RES/1739.
UN Security Council. 2007b. *Resolution 1778*. New York: United Nations. S/RES/1778.
UN Security Council. 2009. *Resolution 1906*. New York: United Nations. S/RES/1906.
UN Security Council. 2011a. *Resolution 1996*. New York: United Nations. S/RES/1996.
UN Security Council. 2011b. *Resolution 2000*. New York: United Nations. S/RES/2000.
UN Special Committee on Peacekeeping Operations. 2015. *Report of the Special Committee on Peacekeeping Operations*. New York: United Nations. A/69/19.
UNOCI News. 2013. "UNOCI Educates Dozos on the Values of Peace." *UNOCI News*, November 14. https://onuci.unmissions.org/en/unoci-educates-dozos-values-peace
US Embassy in Liberia. 2017. "US Embassy Statement on Liberia's Electoral Process." November 15. https://lr.usembassy.gov/u-s-embassy-statement-liberias-electoral-process/
Veit, Alex. 2011. *Intervention As Indirect Rule: Civil War and Statebuilding in the Democratic Republic of Congo*. Frankfurt: Campus Verlag.
Véron, René, Glyn Williams, Stuart Corbridge, and Manoj Srivastava. 2006. "Decentralized Corruption or Corrupt Decentralization? Community Monitoring of Poverty-Alleviation Schemes in Eastern India." *World Development* 34(11):1922–41.
Vinck, Patrick, Phuong Pham, and Tino Kreutzer. 2011. *Talking Peace: A Population-Based Survey on Attitudes about Security, Dispute Resolution, and Post-conflict Reconstruction in Liberia*. Berkeley: University of California, Berkeley Human Rights Center.
Waldron, Jeremy. 2002. "Is the Rule of Law an Essentially Contested Concept (in Florida)?" *Law and Philosophy* 21(2):137–64.
Waldron, Jeremy. 2008. "The Concept and the Rule of Law." *Georgia Law Review* 43:91–123.
Walter, Barbara F. 1997. "The Critical Barrier to Civil War Settlement." *International Organization* 51(3):335–64.
Weedee, Emmanuel. 2013. "CDC Engages Police Over Mulbah Morlu's Arrest." *Heritage*, October 13. https://allafrica.com/stories/201310100982.html
Weinstein, Jeremy M. 2005. "Autonomous Recovery and International Intervention in Comparative Perspective." Center for Global Development Working Paper Number 57. http://papers.ssrn.com/sol3/papers.cfm?abstract_id=1114117
Weisburd, David and Lorraine Green. 1995. "Policing Drug Hot Spots: The Jersey City Drug Market Analysis Experiment." *Justice Quarterly* 12(4):711–35.
Whalan, Jeni. 2014. *How Peace Operations Work: Power, Legitimacy, and Effectiveness*. Oxford: Oxford University Press.
Wickham-Crowley, Timothy P. 1987. "The Rise (and Sometimes Fall) of Guerrilla Governments in Latin America." *Sociological Forum* 2(3):473–99.
Wilson, James Q. 1978. *Varieties of Police Behavior: The Management of Law and Order in Eight Communities, with a New Preface by the Author*. Cambridge, MA: Harvard University Press.

Witt, Howard. 1990. "American Refusal to Intervene in Liberia Draws Condemnation." *Chicago Tribune*, August 16.

Woollacott, Martin. 2003. "America Helped Ruin Liberia. Now It Must Help Repair It." *The Guardian*, July 31.

The World Bank. 2011. *World Development Report 2011: Conflict, Security, and Development*. Washington, DC: The World Bank.

World Bank Group and United Nations. 2018. *Pathways for Peace: Inclusive Approaches to Preventing Violent Conflict*. Washington, DC: International Bank for Reconstruction and Development and the World Bank.

Zack-Williams, Alfred B. 2002. "Sierra Leone after the End of the Armed Conflict." *Cadernos de Estudos Africanos* 2:57–75.

Zartman, I. William. 1995a. "Introduction: Posing the Problem of State Collapse." In *Collapsed States: The Disintegration and Restoration of Legitimate Authority*, ed. I. William Zartman. Boulder, CO: Lynne Rienner, pp. 1–11.

Zartman, I. William. 1995b. "Putting Things Back Together." In *Collapsed States: The Disintegration and Restoration of Legitimate Authority*, ed. I. William Zartman. Boulder, CO: Lynne Rienner, pp. 267–73.

Index

Abuja Accords, 132
Afghanistan, 7, 66, 67, 102, 117, 223, 225
  non-state authorities in, 40, 44, 222, 223
  UN mission in, *see* UNAMA
  US intervention in, 2, 30
African independence movements, 129
African Union, 81, 224, 226
Agenda for Peace, 17
Americo-Liberians, 127, 129, 131, 140
Angola, 93, 117
Annan, Kofi, 20, 22
Argentina, 103
Autesserre, Séverine, 16, 30, 31, 78, 162, 222, 228, 233
authoritarianism, 56, 57, *see also* military dictatorship

Bangladesh, 158, 216, 223
Barnett, Michael, 8, 68, 78, 81, 82, 190, 225
Belarus, 102
BINUB, 7, 80
BINUCA, 5, 107
  legal training by, 69
Blattman, Christopher, 44, 159, 224
Bolivia, 102
Bosnia and Herzegovina, 19
  UN missions in, *see* UNMIBH
Boutros-Ghali, Boutros, 17
Brahimi Report, 18, 21, 22, 24, 231
Burundi, 7, 26, 93, 94, 97

  civil war in, 107
  UN missions in, *see* ONUB

Cambodia, 19, 20, 71, 77, 102
  UN missions in, *see* UNTAC
  elections in, 79
Cameroon, 216
Carothers, Thomas, 2, 3, 8, 33, 49
ceasefire, 79
  and UN monitoring, 95
Central African Republic (CAR), 5, 23, 26, 66, 69, 93, 94, 97, 104, 107, 231
  UN missions in, *see* BINUCA, MINURCAT, MINURCA
Chad, 23, 75, 93
  civil war in, 104
  UN missions in, *see* MINURCAT
Chesterman, Simon, 4, 6, 8, 49, 62, 87, 228
chiefs, *see* local leaders
China, 159
civil society, 7, 22, 30, 54, 184, 222
Cold War, 9, 11, 13, 14, 18, 90, 92, 102, 222
Colombia
  non-state authorities in, 40
colonialism, 57, 155
constitutions and UN reform
  and civil war, 65
  in Liberia, 74, 75, 215
  in Namibia, 66
constructivism, 8, 83
corruption, 10, 59, 164

261

Côte d'Ivoire, 81, 82, 93, 94, 97, 100, 105, 117
  killing of peacekeepers in, 10, 175, 195, 196
  non-state authorities in, 40, 44, 50
  elections in, 79
coup d'état, 47
  in Côte d'Ivoire, 45
  in Mali, 67
  in Venezuela, 102
  in East Timor, 103
  in Liberia, 130
courts, *see* judiciary
credit claiming, 6, 72, 220
crime reporting, 161
  norms of, 49, 70, 165, 166, 185, 197, 198

Darfur, 7, 26
  non-state authorities in, 69
Democratic Republic of Congo (DRC), 6, 7, 18, 23, 26, 28, 66, 68, 78, 93, 94, 97, 100, 117, 231
  and Mai Mai militias, 75
demonstration effects, 6, 70, 72, 74, 83, 86, 202, 205
Denmark, 103
disarmament, demobilization, and reintegration (DDR), 95
Doe, Samuel K., 157
Dorussen, Han, 11, 25, 63, 98, 105, 169, 172
Doyle, Michael, 25, 27, 53, 63, 92, 105, 222, 224, 228, 232
dozos, 40, 45, 50, 82, 83
due process, 101
  international standards of, 65

East Timor, 6, 11, 18, 66, 71, 87, 103
  legal pluralism in, 45
Eastern Slavonia, 18
Ebola epidemic, 215, 216
Economic Community of West African States (ECOWAS), 81
Economic Community of West African States Monitoring Group (ECOMOG), 11, 133
Ecuador, 102, 103
El Salvador, 5, 6, 19, 67
elections, 215, 216, 224
  UN support for, 66, 229, 232
Equatorial Guinea, 216
Ethiopia, 158
ethnic conflict, 158, 161, 164, 178, 185, 195, 201
European Union, 77

executive constraints, 3, 14, 26, 55, 102, 103, 113–116, 214, 215
extrajudicial punishment, 2, 3, 5, 15, 29, 34, 47, 50, 70, 80, 86, 87, 116, 197, 201, 219, 221
  and mob justice, 156
  and trial by ordeal, 10, 155, 161, 163, 166, 167, 182, 185, 198, 221, 235

Finland, 103
Finnemore, Martha, 8, 65, 68, 69, 78, 81–84, 225
foreign aid, 72, 78, 92, 99, 105, 106, 109, 217, 223, 227
  dependency on, 227
formal authorities, *see* state authorities
Fortna, Page, 25, 27, 28, 31, 65, 71, 92, 105, 168, 169, 228, 232
France, 82, 175
Freedom House, 101–103, 107–109, 111–113, 118, 120, 216
Fuller, Lon, 36, 40, 42, 47, 52

Gaddafi, Muammar 189
Gambia 192
Gbagbo, Laurent, 82, 175
gender-based violence, 75, 220
Georgia, 102
Germany, 77
Ghana, 159
Gio tribe, 158
Gizelis, Theodora-Ismene, 11, 25, 63, 98, 105, 169, 172
good governance, 29
Guatemala, 102
  non-state authorities in, 41, 50, 222
Guinea, 156, 158

Haggard, Stephen, 2, 8, 26, 27, 36
Haiti, 6, 20, 25, 66, 102
  legal pluralism in, 45
Hart, H. L. A, 33, 37–39, 44, 48, 52, 53
Hartman, Alexandra, 44, 159, 224
Howard, Lise Morjé, 5, 18–20, 22, 27, 31, 67, 68, 70, 71, 73, 74, 77, 79, 107, 223
human rights, 4, 13, 19, 32, 53, 55, 68, 72, 77, 95, 97, 213, 222, 226, 227
  in Côte d'Ivoire, 69
  in El Salvador, 67
  in Mozambique, 20
  in Sudan, 69
  in Liberia, 140, 149

Index

India, 159
  non-state authorities in, 44
Indigenous Liberians, 124, 125, 126, 127, 129
Indonesia, 223
  Free Aceh Movement in, 42
infant mortality, 109
informal authorities, *see* non-state authorities
infrastructure, 225
  and civil war, 158
  UN construction of, 63, 68, 70, 72, 76, 77, 86, 155, 161, 163, 167–169, 181–183, 192, 198, 200, 206, 209, 212, 219, 222
International Covenant on Civil and Political Rights, 53
International Covenant on Economic, Social and Cultural Rights, 142
international intervention, 3, 5, 15, 60
  and democracy, 33, 62, 90, 221, 222
  and neglect of local-level reform, 8, 62, 87
  failure of, 3, 13, 27, 30
  success of, 29
international legitimacy, 78, 79, 226
Iraq, 102, 223, 225
  legal pluralism in, 45
  US intervention in, 30

Jordan, 159
judiciary
  equal access to, 101
  in Liberia, 160, 188, 213, 223
  independence of, 2, 3, 5, 14, 29, 34, 47, 52, 53, 60, 64, 67, 91, 104, 115, 116, 219
justice chain, 18–21, 47, 62, 100
justice sector reform, 95
  interdependency of, 18

kamajors, 40, 51
Kosovo, 5, 6, 18, 66, 71, 75
  non-state authorities in, 41
Krahn tribe, 158

Lebanon, 73
legal centralism, 43
legal pluralism, 33, 43, 44, 46, 52, 54
legal positivism, 4, 33, 36, 43, 44, 46, 48, 51, 53–55
legal reform, 95
legal systems
  ambiguities in, 61, 65, 73, 101, 212
  and primary rules, 33, 37, 38, 40
  and secondary rules, 33, 37, 39, 46, 48, 52, 61
  civil law, 46, 55
  common law, 46, 55
  religious law, 55
Liberia, 6, 7, 9, 10, 15, 26, 66, 75, 93, 94, 97, 100, 105, 106, 117, 176, 177, 223, 224
  police-community relations in, 1, 212, 213, *see also* UNMIL: police reform and citizen perceptions of the state
  civil war in, 9, 107, 160, 169, 170
  non-state authorities in, 1, 80, 157, 184–186, 188–190, 192, 197, 205, 219
  public information campaigns in, 74, 225
  colonialism in, 123, 125, 126, 130
  map of, 156, 157, 173
  and Côte d'Ivoire, 156, 158, 175–177, 195
  Interim Government of National Unity (IGNU) in, 131, 133, 134
  elections in, 215
  Truth and Reconciliation Commission (TRC), 134, 140, 150, 151
Liberians United for Reconciliation and Democracy (LURD), 132, 139, 151
Libya, 66
list experiments, 10, 165, 183, 184, 196–201
local leaders, 42, 74, 161, 162, 166, 184, 197, 198, 200, 201
  and chiefs, 2, 40, 220

Mali, 26, 67, 93, 94, 97, 104, 224, 231
Mandingo tribe, 158
Mano River Basin region, 123
Mano tribe, 157, 158
media repression, 214, 229
military
  in El Salvador, 67
  in Democratic Republic of Congo, 82
  in Liberia, 217
military dictatorship, 155, 157, *see also* authoritarianism
MINURCA, 26
MINURCAT, 6
  mandate of, 23
  and prison reform, 68
  legal training by, 75, 76
MINUSCA, 26
  legal training by, 71
MINUSMA, 26, 68, 224
MINUSTAH, 224
  and justice sector reform, 21, 26, 66

Monrovia, 157, 159
  vs. rural Liberia, 126, 127, 131, 132, 135
MONUC, 26
  mandate of, 23
MONUSCO, 6, 7, 26, 68, 82, 107
  and mobile courts, 75
Movement for Democracy in Liberia
    (MODEL), 132, 152
Mozambique, 20, 93, 216
  and UN police, 19
  Mozambican National Resistance in, 42
  legal pluralism in, 45
  non-state authorities in, 51
  elections in, 19
Mvukiyehe, Eric, 25, 62, 74, 155, 169, 171,
    172, 223, 224, 230
Myanmar, 102

Namibia, 18, 20, 66
  elections in, 19
National Patriotic Front of Liberia (NPFL),
    158
National Union for Total Independence of
    Angola (UNITA), 117
natural resources
  government control of, 169
  and rebels, 105
neotrusteeship, 30
Nepal, 159
  non-state authorities in, 40
New Zealand, 103
NGOs, *see* nongovernmental organizations
Nigeria, 159
non-state authorities
  and competition with the state, 1–4, 6, 9,
    15, 29, 34, 43–45, 48, 50, 52, 55, 57,
    61, 80, 157, 185, 187, 220, 221,
    223, 225
  and cooperation with the state, 41, 44, 60,
    75, 196, 200, 221
  and UN training, 63, 74
  and rebel groups, 41, 50, 222, 223
  citizen support for, 48, 54, 86
  and UN legitimization, 78, 88
  biases of, 204
nongovernmental organizations (NGOs), 71,
    73, 98, 159, 160, 169, 216, 231
norm diffusion, 3, 6, 7, 15, 43, 49, 52, 61, 62,
    70, 82, 220, 227, *see also* UN missions:
    norm diffusion
normative resources, 8, 62, 68
Norway, 103

ONUB, 26
ONUMOZ, 19, 20
ONUSAL, 5, 67
  and justice sector reform, 19
  and police reform, 19
Ouattara, Alassane, 45, 82, 175

Pakistan, 158, 223
participatory peacekeeping, 22
peace agreements, 79, 81
  and commitment problems, 24, 62, 229
  and information asymmetries, 24, 229
  and non-state authorities, 52
  in Liberia, 214
Peacekeeping Activities Dataset (PACT),
    98–100, 118
peacekeeping, multidimensional, 1, 2, 11, 13,
    17, 22, 27, 79, 80, 117, 223
peacekeeping, traditional, 11, 17, 117
Peru, 223
  non-state authorities in, 40, 223
police
  abuses by, 82, 212, 213, 219, 227
  and UN training, 6, 68, 71, 212, 220, 221
  arbitrary arrests by, 6, 34, 47, 53, 61, 80,
    102, 117, 214, 221
  corruption, *see* corruption
  in Bosnia and Herzegovina, 19
  in Cambodia, 19, 20
  in Central African Republic, 71
  in El Salvador, 19, 67
  in Liberia, 1, 160, 169, 170, 177, 186, 188,
    192, 198, 200, 201, 213, 214, 217, 219,
    223
  in Mozambique, 19
  in Namibia, 18, 79, 82
  in Sierra Leone, 41
  politicization of, 2, 19
  reform of, 60
  UN training, 17
police-community relations, 1, 7, 15, 227
Pouligny, Beatrice, 6, 25, 30, 45, 181, 190,
    192, 196, 222, 224
prisons
  in Liberia, 212, 214, 217
  and indefinite detentions, 6, 34, 54, 80,
    102, 220
  reform of, *see* UN missions: and
    prison reform
Providing for Peacekeeping (P4P), 92–94

Index 265

Quiwonkpa, Thomas, 157

Raz, Joseph, 35, 36, 40, 42, 44, 52, 54, 55
realism, 8
refugees, 66, 117, 158, 169–171, 176, 177, 180
Rome Statute of the International Criminal Court, 142
Ruggeri, Andrea, 11, 25, 63, 98, 105, 169, 172
rule of law
    macro, micro, and meso dimensions of, 3, 5, 7, 11, 14, 33, 34, 46, 53, 56, 60, 61, 64, 84, 90, 121, 185, 186, 212, 222, 229, 230
    necessary conditions for, 4, 5, 35, 36, 59, 60, 201
    citizens' belief in, 8, 58, 61
    measurement of, 14, 46, 102–104, 216
    academic consensus on, 33
    and democracy, 27, 32, 36, 55, 56, 106, 107, 216, 222, 226, 227
    and economic growth, 32, 91, 106, 107, 117, 118, 218, 222, 226, 227
    moral foundations of, 35, 36, 54, 56
rule of law reform, 48
    UN template for, 3, 4, 60, 61, 84, 90, 121, 185, 186
    political will for, 8
    window of opportunity for, 66, 86, 92, 109, 121, 221
    UN standards for, 23, 45
rule of law, definitions of, 4, 14, 33, 46
    maximalist, 34–36, 55
    positivist, 36, 43, 52, 54, 55
    and the World Bank, 101
    and Freedom House, 101
Russia, 103
Rwanda, 13, 20, 93, 100

Sambanis, Nicholas, 25, 27, 53, 63, 92, 105, 222, 224, 228, 232
Samii, Cyrus, 62, 74, 155, 169, 171, 172, 224
sassywood, *see* extrajudicial punishment: trial by ordeal
separation of powers, 5, 53, 66, 86, 102
Sierra Leone, 5, 26, 66, 93, 94, 97, 117, 156, 158
    non-state authorities in, 41, 51
Sirleaf, Ellen Johnson, 215–218
Smidt, Hannah, 97, 98, 224, 230
social contract, 6, 7, 222, 225
Somalia, 13, 20, 57, 93, 100, 117
source legitimacy, *see* international legitimacy
South Africa, 80
South Sudan, 7, 23, 26, 66, 68, 75, 93, 94, 97, 100, 104, 231
state authorities
    ultimate jurisdiction of, 4, 5, 10, 15, 34, 38, 39, 45, 48, 50, 54, 61, 64, 70, 165, 182, 186, 187, 196, 201, 221, 227
    citizen cooperation with, 38, 43, 48–52, 54, 56, 57, 70
    crowding out of, 29, 86–88, 113, 187, 189, 192–195, 202, 209, 222, 227
    legal limits on, 2, 5, 29, 46, 47, 51, 57, 60, 61, 65, 91, 109, 220
    biases of, 165, 185, 202, 204, 209
state collapse, 57, 58, 231
state legitimacy, 2, 22, 72, 80, 88, 225, 227
state predation, 1, 3, 48, 54, 76, 86, 189
states
    as a failed model, 3, 30
    sovereignty of, 6, 17, 38, 39
    and shared sovereignty, 30
Sudan, 26, 93, 94, 97, 216
    Sudan People's Liberation Movement, 42
Supreme Courts, 46
    in Liberia, 215
Sweden, 103

Tajikistan, 102
Taliban, 117, 222
Taylor, Charles, 158
Tiede, Lydia, 2, 9, 26, 27, 36
Tolbert, William, 129
Tubman, William, 128, 129, 130

Ukraine, 103, 216
UN Advisory Committee on Administrative and Budgetary Questions (ACABQ), 91, 95
UN Department of Peacekeeping Operations, 172
UN Development Programme, 77, 98
UN General Assembly, 91, 95
UN mandates, 6, 9, 11, 92, 229
    and rule of law promotion, 2, 11, 13, 17, 18, 23, 26, 27, 91, 97, 105, 118
    and legal reform, 11, 62, 65
    expansions of, 12, 23, 220, 229, 230
    Chapter VI, 28
    Chapter VII, 28, 81
    for executive policing, 71, 83
    for the use of force, 89

UN missions
  and norm diffusion, 3, 6, 15, 29, 68, 69, 82, 84, 189, 220
  and credit claiming, *see* credit claiming
  and democratization, 27, 28
  and demonstration effects, *see* demonstration effects
  as proxies for the state, 5, 6, 11, 15, 62, 70
  and legal reform, 5, 10, 14, 17, 55, 66, 92, 95, 100, 105, 111, 113, 117, 221
  and constitutional reform, 8, 10, 66, 67, 221
  and police reform, 7, 14, 17, 18, 92, 95, 111, 113, 117, 221
  and conflict intervention, 6, 10, 73, 156, 161–163, 167, 168, 181–183, 192, 198, 209, 223, 235
  and public information campaigns, 7, 73, 75, 86, 99
  and prison reform, 14, 17, 68, 91, 95, 97, 100, 111, 113, 117, 221
  and justice sector reform, 14, 17, 92, 95, 97, 100, 111, 113, 117, 221
  withdrawal of, 15, 17, 107, 109, 212, 218
  abuses by, 16, 29, 30, 86, 222
  as impartial actors, 17
  and resource constraints, 19, 20, 29, 31, 80, 88, 92, 121, 189, 201, 202, 222
  failures of, 20
  coordination between, 22
  and participatory peace, 27
  deployment patterns of, 28, 103–105, 166–169, 171–173, 192
  and patrols, 69–71, 73–75, 86, 155, 161, 167, 175, 180–183, 190, 192, 198, 200, 206, 209, 223
  and material assistance, 9
  and monitoring, 79, 80, 91, 98–100, 110, 112
  crowding out by, *see* state authorities: crowding out
  and public works projects, *see* infrastructure: UN construction of
  and electoral participation, 223, 224, 229
UN Office for the Coordination of Humanitarian Affairs (OCHA), 172
UN personnel
  deployment rates of, 9, 11–13, 92, 93, 95, 107, 109, 116
  Military Observers, 11, 17, 92, 94, 96
  troops, 11, 13, 17, 71, 91, 92, 94, 96, 223, 224
  civilian vs. military, 11, 17, 62, 63, 85, 86, 92, 94, 95, 109, 110, 163, 196, 221, 231
  civilian, 13, 88, 91, 95, 97
  legal experts, 135
  police, *see* UN police
UN police (UNPOL), 11, 13, 17, 18, 72, 84, 91, 92, 95, 97, 159, 163, 224
  patrols by, 7, 18, 71, 169, 220
  in Cambodia, 71
  in Kosovo, 71
  in Liberia, 142, 147
UN radio, 77, 225, *see also* UN missions: public information campaigns
UN sanctions, 82
  and arms embargoes, 117–120
UN Secretary-General, 22, 23
  progress reports of, 9, 90, 95, 98, 160
  budget requests of, 90, 95
UN Security Council, 17, 18
UNAMA, 7, 67
UNAMID
  and legal aid offices, 7
  legal training by, 26, 68, 77
UNAMIR, 13, 20
UNAMSIL, 26, 79
UNIFIL, 73, 77
United Kingdom, 227
United Liberation Movement of Liberia for Democracy (ULIMO), 158
United States
  foreign policy of, 2, 30, 225
  and Liberia, 215, 216
UNMIBH, 19
UNMIK, 5, 6, 18
  mandate of, 71
UNMIL, 6, 7, 10, 15, 26, 74, 107, 155, 156, 163, 177, 183–185, 187–191, 194–198, 200, 201, 205, 206, 216, 223
  and police reform, 1, 212, 219, 220
  and justice sector reform, 214, 215, 220
  and legal reform, 141, 142
  and constitutional reform, 8, 10, 67, 146, 221
  successes of, 9, 15, 212, 217, 218
  failures of, 20, 153
  withdrawal of, 15
  legal training by, 76, 80
  abuses by, 165, 223
  citizen perceptions of, 160, 164, 186, 195, 202, 209, 213, 219, 223
  bases, 171–174, 180, 181, 192, 195

Index

UNMIS, 26
UNMISS, 26
  and mobile courts, 7
  mandate of, 23
  legal training by, 68, 76
UNMIT, 74
UNOCI, 6, 26, 68, 82, 95, 97, 107, 175, 176, 195, 224
  mandate of, 23
  legal training by, 69
UNOL, 134,
UNOMIL, 133, 134
UNOSOM I, 13
UNOSOM II, 20
UNTAC, 19
  and legal reform, 20
  mandate of, 71
  and radio programs, 77
UNTAES, 18

UNTAET, 6, 11, 18, 87
  mandate of, 71
UNTAG, 66, 74
  and police reform, 18, 79
  and legal reform, 20
  and constitutional reform, 66

Venezuela, 102

war crimes, 51, 82
Weah, George, 216
Western ideals, 27, 189
World Bank, 99–102, 107, 108, 110–113, 118, 119, 216

Yemen, 102

Zambia
  non-state authorities in, 40
Zimbabwe, 216